ARISTOTLE'S ETHICS AND POLITICS

ARISTOTLE'S ETHICS AND POLITICS

JOHN GILLIES

Published by

FacsiMile Publisher
12 Pragati Market
Ashok Vihar, Ph-2
Delhi - 110052, India
Phone: 011-47034999
Email: www.facsimilepublishers.com
info@facsimilepublishers.com

Distribution Network
gyanbooks.com
India, USA, Canada, UK, Australia

ISBN: 978-93-6878-656-6 (PB)

First Published, 1797

2nd Impression 2025

Printed at: Gyan Press, Delhi.

ARISTOTLE'S ETHICS AND POLITICS
Author: JOHN GILLIES

ARISTOTLE's
ETHICS AND POLITICS,

COMPRISING HIS

PRACTICAL PHILOSOPHY,

TRANSLATED FROM THE GREEK.

ILLUSTRATED BY INTRODUCTIONS AND NOTES;

THE CRITICAL HISTORY OF HIS LIFE;

AND A NEW ANALYSIS OF HIS SPECULATIVE WORKS;

BY JOHN GILLIES, LL.D.

F. R. S. and S. A. LONDON; F. R. S. EDINBURGH; and Historiographer to his Majesty for SCOTLAND.

Magna animi contentio adhibenda est in explicando Aristotele.

CICERO FRAGMENT. PHILOSOPH.

IN TWO VOLUMES.

VOL. I.

LONDON:

Printed for A. STRAHAN; and T. CADELL Jun. and W. DAVIES, in the Strand.

1797.

PREFACE.

ARISTOTLE is the moſt voluminous, and generally deemed the moſt obſcure, of all the Greek writers of claſſic antiquity. His imperfect yet copious remains, which are now rather admired than read [*], and which were formerly much read and little underſtood, ſtill naturally arrange themſelves in the minds of thoſe capable of digeſting them, under their original form of an encyclopedy of ſcience; in many parts of which, the author's labours are, doubtleſs, excelled by thoſe of modern philoſophers; while in other parts, and thoſe of the moſt important nature, his intellectual exertions remain hitherto unrivalled. It ſeemed high time, therefore, to draw the line between thoſe writings of the Stagirite which

[*] I except the ſmall but incomparable Treatiſe on Poetry, excellently tranſlated and commented in two recent publications in Engliſh; the books on Rhetoric and the Hiſtory of Animals, to which Mr. Caſſandre and Mr. Camus have reſpectively done juſtice in French; and the Organum, or Logic, ſtill ſtudied in ſome Univerſities.

which ſtill merit the moſt ſerious attention of the modern reader, and thoſe of which the peruſal is ſuperſeded by more accurate and more complete information. This line I have preſumed to draw in the preſent work, by endeavouring to the beſt of my abilities to tranſlate the former perſpicuouſly and impreſſively, while I contented myſelf with giving a diſtinct and comprehenſive analyſis of the latter.

The "Ethics to Nicomachus and the Politics" ought never to have been disjoined, ſince they are conſidered by Ariſtotle himſelf as forming eſſential parts of one and the ſame work[b]; which, as it was the laſt and principal object of his ſtudies, is of all his performances the longeſt, the beſt connected, and incomparably the moſt intereſting. The two treatiſes combined, conſtitute what he calls his *practical* philoſophy[c]; an epithet to which, in compariſon with other works of the ſame kind, they will be found peculiarly entitled. In the Ethics, the reader will ſee a full and ſatisfactory delineation of the moral

[b] See vol. i. p. 150, and p. 408, & ſeq.

[c] Compare vol. i. p. 408, & ſeqq. and vol. ii. pp. 338, 369. The Magna Moralia and Ethics to Eudemus are chiefly to be conſidered as the firſt imperfect ſketch of this great work.

[d] See vol. i. p. 176. He elſewhere calls it "His Philoſophy concerning Human Affairs." Ibid. p. 408.

moral nature of man, and of the diſcipline and exerciſe beſt adapted to its improvement. The Philoſopher ſpeaks with commanding authority to the heart and affections, through the irreſiſtible conviction of the underſtanding. His morality is neither on the one hand too indulgent, nor on the other impracticable. His leſſons are not cramped by the narrow, nor perverted by the wild, ſpirit of ſyſtem; they are clear inductions, flowing naturally and ſpontaneouſly from a copious and pure ſource of well-digeſted experience.

According to the Stagirite, men are and always have been not only moral and ſocial, but alſo *political* animals; in a great meaſure dependent for their happineſs and perfection on the public inſtitutions of their reſpective countries. The grand inquiry, therefore, is, what are the different arrangements that have been found under given circumſtances, practically moſt conducive to theſe main and ultimate purpoſes? This queſtion the Author endeavoured to anſwer in his "Politics," by a careful examination of two hundred ſyſtems of legiſlation, many of which are not any where elſe deſcribed; and by proving how uniformly, even in political matters, the reſults of obſervation and experiment

periment conſpire with and confirm the deductions of an accurate and full theory. In this incomparable work, the reader will perceive "the genuine ſpirit of laws" deduced from the ſpecific and unalterable diſtinctions of governments; and with a ſmall effort of attention, may diſcern not only thoſe diſcoveries in ſcience, unjuſtly claimed by the vanity of modern writers[e], but many of thoſe improvements in practice[f], erroneouſly aſcribed to the fortunate events of time and chance in theſe latter and more enlightened ages. The ſame invaluable treatiſe diſcloſes the pure and perennial ſpring of all legitimate authority; for in Ariſtotle's "Politics," and HIS *only*, government is placed on ſuch a natural and ſolid founda-tion,

[e] Compare, for example, the works of the modern œconomiſts, not excepting thoſe of Hume and Smith, with the Fifth Book of the Ethics, p. 270, and the Firſt Book of the Politics, p. 38, & ſeq. Compare Monteſquieu's Spirit of Laws with Books iii, vi, and viii, of the Politics throughout: and judge whether the admirable French work be, as the Author's motto boaſts, "Proles ſine matre creata." Compare likewiſe Machiavel's "Prince," with the laſt chapters of Book vii. of the Politics, p. 374, & ſeqq. from which the Italian treatiſe is entirely copied. Yet none of all thoſe Authors acknowledge their obligations to Ariſtotle.

For the doctrine of repreſentative government, (with which the ancients are ſaid to have been totally unacquainted,) ſee the following tranſlation, vol. ii. pp. 64, & ſeqq. 304, & ſeqq. and 408, & ſeqq. For that of governments of reciprocal controul, ſee p. 293, & ſeqq.

tion, as leaves neither its origin incomprehenſible, nor its ſtability precarious: and his concluſions, had they been well weighed, muſt have ſurmounted or ſuppreſſed thoſe erroneous and abſurd doctrines which long upheld deſpotiſm on the one hand, and thoſe equally erroneous and ſtill wilder ſuppoſitions of conventions and compacts, which have more recently armed popular fury on the other.

But our Author's principles and doctrines will ſpeak convincingly for themſelves. The intention of this Preface is merely to explain the plan and object of the preſent performance; which, beſides giving a tranſlation of Ariſtotle's practical philoſophy, contains a new analyſis of his ſpeculative works. This addition appeared the more neceſſary, becauſe the Stagirite's intellectual ſyſtem is ſo compactly built, and ſo ſolidly united, that its ſeparate parts cannot be completely underſtood, unleſs the whole be clearly comprehended. The writings indeed here tranſlated, ſtand more detached and more independent than almoſt any other; yet, without the aid of the prefixed "Analyſis," even the Ethics and Politics would require frequent, almoſt perpetual elucidation. The reader, I feared, would be ſoon tired with the

 uncon-

unconnected prolixity of notes[a]; he will, I hope, be entertained by the Analysis even of those treatises to which, independently of any substantial utility, his attention may be still allured by a liberal and commendable curiosity.

In my work throughout, I am ambitious of exhibiting fully, yet within a narrow compass, the discoveries and attainments of a man deemed the wisest of antiquity; and to whom, even in modern times, it will be easier to name many superiors in particular branches of knowledge, than to find any one rival in universal science. Considered under this general aspect, my "English Aristotle" is the natural companion and fit counterpart to my "History of Ancient Greece;" since the learning of that country properly terminates in the Stagirite, by whom it was finally embodied into one great work; a work rather impaired than improved by the labours of succeeding ages. My time, I acknowledge, was miserably misspent

[a] I have also avoided to swell my work with historical notes; a thing as easy as it is useless. Aristotle relates with the utmost precision, the particulars necessary for justifying his conclusions; and to introduce other events and circumstances, altogether unconnected with the subject, appears to me to be better calculated for displaying an author's erudition, than for informing the mind of his reader.

ſpent in examining his numerous commentators[h]; Greek, Arabic, and Latin; but the attention with which I have many times peruſed the whole of his invaluable remains, with a view of rendering him a perpetual commentary on himſelf, and thereby expreſſing his genuine ſenſe clearly and forcibly, will not, I hope, prove uſeleſs to thoſe who ſtudy Greek literature on an enlarged and liberal plan; not merely as grammarians and philologiſts, but as philoſophers, moraliſts, and ſtateſmen. To this claſs of readers, many pages of the preſent work are peculiarly addreſſed; but the far greater part of it, bearing an immediate reference to the people at large, will not, it is hoped, by the public, be either unregarded or unapplied; eſpecially in an age when, through the ardent activity of the preſs, ſalutary information, whatever be its *original* form, ſpeedily circulates to all claſſes of the community in *new* and fit channels.

PORTMAN-STREET, J. G.
September 1797.

[h] I am diſpenſed from the neceſſity of ſpeaking of former tranſlations of the Ethics and Politics, becauſe I have not borrowed a ſingle ſentence, nor derived the ſmalleſt aſſiſtance, from any of them. The Ethics, which is incomparably the more difficult work of the two, has never, as far as I know, been tranſlated into any modern language.

CONTENTS.

CHAP. I.

LIFE OF ARISTOTLE.

CHAP. II.

A NEW ANALYSIS OF ARISTOTLE's SPECULATIVE WORKS.

ARISTOTLE's ETHICS.

BOOK I.

BOOK II.

BOOK III.

BOOK IV.

BOOK V.

BOOK VI.

BOOK VII.

BOOK VIII.

BOOK IX.

BOOK X.

ERRATA in VOL. I.

Page 98. line 18. *for* acceſſaries *read* acceſſories
108. — 7 of the note, *for* εναντωσεις *read* εναντιωσεις
109. — 4 of the note, *for* ἑυατον *read* ἑαυτον
127. — 20. *for* a microſcope *read* the microſcope
129. — 15 of the note, *for* gems *read* germs
216. — *antepenult.* *for* Scyonians *read* Sicyonians

THE

WORKS

OF

ARISTOTLE.

CHAP. I.

LIFE OF ARISTOTLE.

ARGUMENT.

Aristotle's birth-place—His education at Atarneus—at Athens—His residence with Hermeias—Singular fortune of that Prince—Aristotle's residence in Lesbos—in Macedon—Plan pursued in the education of Alexander—Aristotle's residence in Athens—Employment there—Calumnies against him—His retreat to Chalcis, and death—His testament—Sayings—Extraordinary fate of his Works—Published at Rome by Andronicus of Rhodes—Their number and magnitude.

CHAP. I. Introduction.

IT is my design in the present work to give a more distinct, and, I flatter myself, a juster view, than has yet been exhibited, of the learning of an age, the most illustrious in history for great events and extraordinary revolutions, yet still more pre-eminent in speculation than it is renowned in action. A century before the reign of Alexander the Great, there sprang up

CHAP. I.

up and flouriſhed in Greece a ſpecies of learning, or ſcience, totally unlike to any thing before known in the world. This ſcience was carried to its higheſt perfection by Ariſtotle: it decayed with the loſs of his writings, and revived with their recovery. But the imperfect and corrupt ſtate of thoſe writings rendered them peculiarly liable to be miſinterpreted by ignorance, and miſrepreſented by envy; his philoſophy, therefore, has been leſs frequently inculcated or explained, than diſguiſed, perverted, and calumniated. It has not certainly, ſince his own time, received any material improvement. To the philoſophical works of Cicero, though that illuſtrious Roman profeſſes to follow other guides, the world at large is more indebted for a familiar notion of ſeveral of Ariſtotle's moſt important doctrines, than to the labours of all his commentators[a] collectively. But how looſe and feeble (and often how

[a] All theſe commentators lived many centuries after Ariſtotle. They are Greek, Arabic, and Latin. The firſt began in the age of the Antonines, in Alexander Aphrodiſienſis at Rome, and Ammonius Sacchus in Alexandria; they continued to flouriſh through the whole ſucceſſion of Roman emperors, under the once revered names of Aſpaſius, Plotinus, Porphyry, Proclus, the ſecond Ammonius, Simplicius, and Philoponus. Ariſtotle was ardently ſtudied, or rather ſuperſtitiouſly adored, by the Saracens, during upwards of four centuries of their proud domination, till the taking of Bagdat by the Tartars in 1258. The names of the Arabian commentators, Alſarabius, Avicenna, and Averroes, long reſounded even in the ſchools of Europe. But the Ariſtotelian philoſophy, or rather logic, had early aſſumed a Latin dreſs in the tranſlation of Boethius Severinus, the laſt illuſtrious conſul of Rome, in the beginning of the ſixth century. After a long interval of more than ſix hundred years, Latin tranſlations and commentaries began to abound, through the induſtry of Albertus Magnus, Thomas Aquinas, and the ſucceeding ſcholaſtics; and multiplied to ſuch a pitch that, towards the cloſe of the ſixteenth century, Patricius reckons twelve thouſand commentators on different works of the Stagirite. (Diſcuſſ. Peripatet.) This vaſt and cold maſs of Gothic and Saracenic dulneſs is now conſigned to juſt oblivion. But even to the beſt of Ariſtotle's commentators there are two unanſwerable objections:

how erroneous?) is the Roman tranſcript, when compared with the energetic preciſion of the Greek original! Yet the works of Cicero are known univerſally to the whole literary world, while thoſe of Ariſtotle (with the exception of a few ſhort and popular treatiſes) are allowed to moulder away in the duſt of our libraries, and condemned to a treatment little leſs ignominious than that which, as we ſhall have occaſion to relate, befel them ſoon after their compoſition, when they were immured in a dungeon, and remained for near two centuries a prey to dampneſs and to worms. It is time once more to releaſe them from their *ſecond* unmerited captivity; to revive, and, if poſſible, to brighten, the well-earned fame of an author, ſometimes as prepoſterouſly admired, as at others unaccountably neglected; and whoſe fate with poſterity is moſt ſingular in this, not that his authority ſhould have been moſt reſpected in the ages leaſt qualified to appreciate his merit, but that philoſophers ſhould have deſpiſed his name almoſt exactly in proportion as they adopted his opinions. The multiplied proofs of this aſſertion, which I ſhall have occaſion to produce in examining his works, will not, it is preſumed, appear unintereſting to men of letters. Thoſe who know ſomething of Ariſtotle, muſt naturally be deſirous of knowing all that can be told; and of ſeeing, compriſed within a narrow compaſs, the life and writings of a man, whoſe intellectual magnitude ought to have preſerved and ſhewn him in his proper ſhape to the impartial eye

tions: firſt, they univerſally confound his ſolid ſenſe with the fanciful viſions of Plato, thus endeavouring to reconcile things totally incongruous: ſecondly, they aſcribe to their great maſter innumerable opinions which he did not hold, by making him continually dogmatiſe, where he only means to diſcuſs. To the ſame objections thoſe more modern writers are liable, who have drawn their knowledge of Ariſtotle's philoſophy from any other than the original fountain.

CHAP. I.

eye of hiſtory, but whoſe picture, beyond that of all other great characters, has been moſt miſerably mangled.

Ariſtotle's birth-place, Stagira.

Ariſtotle, who flouriſhed in Athens when Athens was the ornament of Greece, and Greece, under Alexander, the firſt country on earth, was born at Stagira towards the beginning of the ninety-ninth olympiad, eighty-five years after the birth of Socrates [b], and three hundred and eighty-four before the birth of Chriſt. The city of Stagira [c] ſtood on the coaſt of Thrace, in a diſtrict called the Chalcidic region, and near to the innermoſt receſs of the Strymonic gulf [d]. It was originally built by the Andrians [e], afterwards enlarged by a colony from Lubœan Chalcis [f], and long numbered among the Greek cities of Thrace, until the conqueſts of Philip of Macedon extended the name of his country far beyond the river Strymon, to the

Its hiſtory,

confines of mount Rhodope [g]. Stagira, as well as the neighbouring

Socrates drank the hemlock, according to moſt authors, the firſt year of the ninety-fifth olympiad; and, according to Diodorus Siculus, the firſt year of the ninety-ſeventh. Socrates therefore died at leaſt eight years before Ariſtotle was born. The latter was one year older than Philip, and three years older than Demoſthenes. Vid. Dionyſ. Halicarn. Epiſt. ad Ammæum. This chronology is clearly aſcertained by various critics. See Bayle's Dictionary, article "Ariſtotle." I know not therefore why Lord Monboddo and the late Mr. Harris (two modern writers who have paid great attention to Ariſtotle's works) ſhould ſay, and frequently repeat, on no better authority than that of the Life of Ariſtotle aſcribed to Ammonius, or Johannes Philoponus, that the Stagirite was three years a ſcholar of Socrates.

[c] Strabo Excerpt. ex lib. vii. p. 331. He calls the place Stageirus.

[d] Ptolemei Geograph. According to his diviſion, Stagira was in the Amphaxetide diſtrict of Macedon.

[e] Herodot. l. vii. c. 115.; & Thucydid. l. iv. p. 311. [f] Juſtin. l. viii. c. 13.

[g] Thence the frivolous diſpute among modern biographers, whether Ariſtotle, who was really a Greek, ought to be deemed a Macedonian or a Thracian. See Stanley and Brucker's Lives of Ariſtotle.

bouring Greek cities, enjoyed the precarious dignity of independent government: it was the ally of Athens in the Peloponneſian war, and, like other nominal allies, experienced the ſtern dominion of that tyrannical republic. It afterwards became ſubject to the city and commonwealth of Olynthus; which, having ſubdued Stagira and the whole region of Chalcidicé, was itſelf beſieged by Philip of Macedon; and, with all its dependencies, reduced by the arms or arts of that politic prince, in the firſt year of the 108th olympiad, and 348 years before the Chriſtian æra [h]. That the reſiſtance of Stagira was obſtinate, may be inferred from the ſeverity of its puniſhment; the conqueror raſed it to the ground [i]. Ariſtotle, who was then in his thirty-ſeventh year, had been removed from Stagira almoſt in his childhood; and he appears not, in that long interval, to have ever reſided in, and even rarely to have viſited, it [k]. But the misfortunes which fell on that city gave him an opportunity of ſhewing ſuch ardent affection for his birthplace, as is the indubitable proof of a feeling heart. Through his influence with Alexander the Great, Stagira was rebuilt [l]; both its uſeful defences and its ornamental edifices were reſtored; its wandering citizens were collected, and reinſtated in their poſſeſſions; Ariſtotle himſelf regulated their government by wiſe laws;

[h] Hiſtory of Ancient Greece, vol. iv. c. xxxv.

[i] Plutarch. adverſus Colot. p. 1126.; & de Exil. p. 605.

[k] Dionyſ. Halicarn. Epiſt. ad Ammæum. Ammonius & Diogen. Laert. in Ariſtot.

[l] Plin. Nat. Hiſt. l. vii. c. 29.; & Valer. Maxim. l. v. c. 6. Plutarch prefers to all the pleaſures of the Epicurean, the delights which Ariſtotle muſt have felt when he rebuilt his native city, and placed in their hereditary ſeats his expatriated countrymen. Plutarch. adverſ. Epicur. p. 1097. He aſcribes the rebuilding of Stagira to Ariſtotle's influence with Philip.

CHAP. I.

laws; and the Stagirites instituted a festival, to commemorate the generosity of Alexander, their admired sovereign, and the patriotism of Aristotle, their illustrious townsman [m].

connected with that of Aristotle and his family.

The city of Stagira indeed owes its celebrity wholly to Aristotle and his family; and, if its name is still familiar to modern ears, this proceeds merely from its having communicated to our philosopher the appellation of Stagirite [n]. His father Nicomachus, who was the physician and friend [o] of Amyntas, king of Macedon, derived his descent, through a long line of medical ancestors, from Æsculapius, the companion of the Argonauts, whose skill in the healing art had raised him to a seat among the gods [p]. Nicomachus improved a branch of knowledge, which was the inheritance of his family, by writing six books on natural philosophy and medicine [q]. To the same illustrious origin which distinguished Nicomachus, the testimony of one ancient biographer [r] (but his only) traces up the blood of Phestis, Aristotle's mother; who, whatever was her parentage, certainly acknowledged for her country [s] the middle district of Eubœa, which lies within twelve miles of the Attic coast. Aristotle was deprived of his parents in early youth [t]; yet it is an agreeable, and not altogether an unwarranted conjecture, that by his father Nicomachus he was inspired with that ardent love for the study of nature, which made him long be regarded as her best

[m] Plutarch. advers. Colot. p. 1126.; & Ammonius in Vit. Aristot.

[n] Strabo Excerp. ex lib. vii. p. 331.

[o] He was held by Amyntas, ω φιλυ χρεια. Diogen. Laert. in Aristot.

[p] Lucian. Jupiter Tragædus; & Suidas in Nicomach.

[q] Idem ibid.

[r] Ammon. Vit. Aristot.

[s] Dionys. Halic. Epist. ad Ammæum.

[t] Diogen. Laert. in Aristot.

best and chosen interpreter [u]; while from his mother Phestis he first imbibed that pure and sweet Atticism which every where pervades his writings.

CHAP. I.

Aristotle's education at Atarneus,

Aristotle also inherited from his parents a large fortune; and their early loss was supplied and compensated by the kind attentions of Proxenus, a citizen of Atarneus in Mysia, who received the young Stagirite into his family, and skilfully directed his education [x]. These important obligations our philosopher, in whose character gratitude appears to have been a prominent feature, amply repaid to Nicanor the son of Proxenus, whom he adopted, educated, and enriched [y]. At the age of seventeen [z], the young Stagirite was attracted by the love of learning to Athens, and particularly by the desire of hearing Plato in the Academy, the best school of science as well as of morals then existing in the world; and where the most assiduous student might find competitors worthy of exciting his emulation and sharpening his diligence. Plato early observed of him, that he required the rein rather than the spur [a]. His industry in perusing and copying manuscripts was unexampled, and almost incredible; he was named, by way of excellence, "the student or reader [b]." Plato often called him the "soul of his school [c];" and, when Aristotle happened to be absent from his prelections, often complained that he spoke to a *deaf audience* [d]. As the student

and at Athens.

His literary industry,

[u] Αριϛοτελης της φυσεως γραμματευς ην. Anonym. apud Suid. in Aristot. Literally, "Nature's secretary."

[x] Diogen. Laert. in Aristot. [y] Idem ibid.

[z] Dionys. Epist. ad Ammæum. Diogen. Laert. ibid. [a] Idem ibid.

[b] Diogen. Laert. ibid.

[c] Or rather the mind or intellect, νους της διατριβης. Idem ibid.

[d] Philoponus de Eternit. Mund. advers. Proclum, vi. 27.

CHAP. I.

ſtudent advanced in years, his acuteneſs was as extraordinary in canvaſſing opinions, as his induſtry had been unrivalled in collecting them [e]: his capacious mind embraced the whole circle of ſcience; and, notwithſtanding his pertinacity in rejecting every principle or tenet which he could not on reflection approve, his very ſingular merit failed not to recommend him to the diſcerning admiration of Plato, with whom he continued to reſide twenty years, even to his maſter's death; alike careleſs of the honours of a court, to which the rank and connections of his family might have opened to him the road in Macedon; and indifferent to the glory of a name, which his great abilities might early have attained, by eſtabliſhing a ſeparate ſchool, and founding a new ſect in philoſophy [f].

His perſon, and ſuppoſed foibles.

At the ſame time that Ariſtotle applied ſo aſſiduouſly to the embelliſhment of his mind, he was not neglectful, we are told, of whatever might adorn his perſon. His figure was not advantageous; he was of a ſhort ſtature, his eyes were remarkably ſmall, his limbs were diſproportionably ſlender, and he liſped or ſtammered in his ſpeech [g]. For his ungracious perſon Ariſtotle is ſaid to have been anxious to compenſate by the finery and elegance of his dreſs: his mantle was ſplendid; he wore rings of great value; and he was foppiſh enough (ſuch is the language of antiquity) to ſhave both his head and his face, while the other ſcholars of Plato kept their long hair and beards.

Reflections thereon.

To ſome learned men, the omiſſion of ſuch particulars might appear

[e] Diogen. Laert. ubi ſupra.

[f] επι σχολῆς ἡγεμενος, επι ιδιαν πεποιηκως αἱρεσιν. Dionyſ. Epiſt. ad Ammæum.

[g] Diogen. Laert. in Ariſtot. Plutarch. de Diſcrim. Adulat. & Amic. p. 53. ſays, "that many imitated Ariſtotle's ſtuttering, as they did Alexander's wry neck."

appear unpardonable; yet, in a life of Ariſtotle, ſuch particulars are totally unworthy of being told, ſince his love for oſtentatious finery (probably much exaggerated by his enemies) was in him merely an acceſſory, which neither altered his character, nor weakened that ardent paſſion for knowledge which reigned ſole miſtreſs of his ſoul. In men born for great intellectual atchievements, this paſſion muſt, at ſome period of their lives, ſuppreſs and ſtifle every other; and, while it continues to do ſo, their real happineſs is probably at its higheſt pitch. The purſuit of ſcience indeed, not having any natural limitations, might be ſuppoſed to invigorate with manhood, to confirm itſelf through cuſtom, and to operate through life with unceaſing or increaſing energy. But this delightful progreſs is liable to be interrupted by other cauſes than the decline of health and the decay of curioſity; for great exertions are not more certainly rewarded by celebrity, than celebrity is puniſhed with envy, which will ſometimes rankle in ſecret malice, and ſometimes vent itſelf in open reproach: wrongs will provoke reſentment; injuries will be offered and retorted; and, a ſtate of hoſtility commencing, the philoſopher, in defending his opinions and his fame, becomes a prey to the wretched anxieties incident to the vulgar ſcrambles of ſordid intereſt and ſenſeleſs ambition. Of this melancholy remark, both the life and the death of Ariſtotle will afford, as we ſhall ſee hereafter, very forcible illuſtrations.

Ariſtotle's gratitude to Plato.

Plato died in the firſt year of the 108th olympiad, and 338 years before the Chriſtian æra. He was ſucceeded in the academy by Speuſippus, the ſon of his ſiſter Potona; a man far inferior to the Stagirite in abilities; and however well he might be acquainted with the theory, not ſtrongly confirmed in the

CHAP. I.

the practice, of moral virtue, ſince he was too often and too eaſily vanquiſhed both by anger and pleaſure [h]. Ariſtotle appears not to have taken offence that, in the ſucceſſion to his admired maſter, the ſtrong claim of merit ſhould have been ſacrificed to the partialities of blood. In ſome of the lateſt of his writings, he ſpeaks of Plato with a degree of reſpect approaching to reverence. Soon after that philoſopher's deceaſe, Ariſtotle wrote verſes in his praiſe, and erected altars to his honour [i]: and the connections which he himſelf had already formed with ſome of the moſt illuſtrious as well as the moſt extraordinary perſonages of his own or any age, might naturally inſpire him with the deſign of leaving Athens, after he had loſt the philoſopher and friend whoſe fame had firſt drawn him thither, and whoſe inſtructive ſociety had ſo long retained him in that celebrated city.

His reſidence with Hermeias. The ſingular hiſtory of that prince.

One of the memorable characters with whom Ariſtotle maintained a cloſe and uninterrupted correſpondence was Hermeias, ſtiled, in the language of thoſe days, tyrant of Aſſus and Atarneus; a man whoſe life forcibly illuſtrates the ſtrange viciſſitudes of fortune. Hermeias is called a ſlave and a eunuch [k]; but he was a ſlave whoſe ſpirit was not to be broken, and a eunuch whoſe mind was not to be emaſculated. Through the bounty of a wealthy patron, he had been enabled early to gratify his natural taſte for philoſophy; and having become a fellow-ſtudent with Ariſtotle at Athens, ſoon united with him in the bands of affectionate eſteem, which finally cemented into firm

[h] Diogen. Laert. in Speuſipp.

[i] Idem; & Ammonius in Ariſtot.

[k] Ευνουχος ων και δουλος ηρχεν Ερμειας. His maſter's name was Eubulus, a prince and philoſopher of Bithynia. Suidas.

firm and unalterable friendſhip. Ariſtotle through life purſued the calm and ſecure paths of ſcience, but Hermeias ventured to climb the dangerous heights of ambition. His enterpriſing ſpirit, ſeconded by good fortune, raiſed him to the ſovereignty of Aſſus and Atarneus, Greek cities of Myſia, the former ſituate in the diſtrict of Troas, the latter in that of Æolis, and both of them, like moſt Grecian colonies on the Aſiatic coaſt but looſely dependant on the Perſian empire. Hermeias availed himſelf of the weakneſs or diſtance of the armies of Artaxerxes, and of the reſources with which his own ambition was ſupplied by a wealthy banker, to gain poſſeſſion of thoſe ſtrong-holds, with all their dependencies; and endeavoured to juſtify this bold uſurpation of the ſceptre, by the manly firmneſs with which he held it [l]. Upon the invitation of his royal friend, Ariſtotle, almoſt immediately after Plato's death, reviſited Atarneus [m], the ſame city in which he had ſpent the happy years of his youth under the kind protection of Proxenus; and might we indulge the conjecture that this worthy Atarnean ſtill lived, our philoſopher's voyage to Æolis muſt have been ſtrongly recommended by his deſire of repaying the favours of a man whom his gratitude always regarded as a ſecond father, and of thus propping, by his friendly aid, the declining age of his early guardian.

Deſtroyed by Mentor the Rhodian.

Ariſtotle found at Atarneus the wiſh of Plato realiſed; he beheld, in his friend Hermeias, philoſophy ſeated on a throne. In that city he reſided near three years, enjoying the inexpreſſible happineſs of ſeeing his enlightened political maxims illuſtrated in the virtuous reign of his fellow-ſtudent and ſovereign.

[l] Diodor. Sicul. l. xvi. ſect. 122.

[m] Dionyſ. Epiſt. ad Ammæum.

CHAP. I.

reign. But, to render his condition enviable, an eſſential requiſite was wanting, namely, that of ſecurity. Artaxerxes, whoſe ſucceſs againſt the rebels in Egypt had exceeded his moſt ſanguine hopes, could no longer brook the diſmemberment of the fair coaſt of Myſia, through the uſurpation of a ſlave and a eunuch. Mentor [n], a Greek, and kinſman of Memnon the Rhodian, a general ſo famous in the Perſian annals, had ſignaliſed his zeal and valour in the Egyptian war. He was one of thoſe crafty and unprincipled Greeks, whom the ambitious hopes of raiſing a ſplendid fortune often drew to a ſtandard naturally hoſtile to their country; and his recent merit with Artaxerxes recommended him as the fitteſt inſtrument to be employed in chaſtiſing the Myſian uſurper. This employment he did not decline, although the man whom he was commiſſioned to deſtroy had formerly been numbered among his friends [o]. Mentor marched with a powerful army to the weſtern coaſt. He might have effected his purpoſe by open force; but to accompliſh it by ſtratagem, was both more eaſy in itſelf, and more ſuitable to his character. He had been connected with Hermeias by the ſacred ties of hoſpitality; the ſanctity of this connection was revered by the greateſt profligates of antiquity; but the impious Mentor knew no religion but obedience to his maſter's commands. He employed his former intimacy with Hermeias as the means of decoying that unwary prince to an interview:

[n] Ariſtotle himſelf brands with infamy this ſucceſsful knave, by contraſting his profligate dexterity with the real virtue of prudence. Αλλα δεινος μεν και ὁ φαυλος λεγεται, &c. "A ſcoundrel may be clever; for example, Mentor, who ſeemed to be very clever, but ſurely was not prudent; for it belongs to prudence to deſire and prefer only the beſt ends, and to carry ſuch only into execution: but cleverneſs implies barely that fertility in reſource, and dexterity in execution, by which any purpoſes, whether good or bad, may be fitly and ſpeedily accompliſhed." *Magn. Moral.* l. i. c. 25. p. 171.

[o] Diodor. Sicul. l. xvi. ſect. 122.

CHAP. I.

His singular and cruel artifices.

view: Mentor seized his person, and sent him privately to Upper Asia, where, by order of Artaxerxes, he was hanged as a traitor [p]. The cruel artifices of Mentor ended not with this tragedy. Having possessed himself of the ring which the unfortunate Hermeias usually employed as his signet, he sealed with it his own dispatches, and immediately sent them to the cities that acknowledged the sovereignty of a man, whose mild exercise of power tended, in the minds of his subjects, to justify the irregular means by which he had acquired it. In these dispatches Mentor signified that, through his own intercession, Hermeias had obtained peace and pardon from the great king. The magistrates of the revolted cities easily gave credit to intelligence most agreeable to their wishes; they opened their gates without suspicion to Mentor's soldiers, who instantly made themselves masters both of those Mysian strong-holds, which might have made a long and vigorous resistance to the Persian arms, and of the powerful garrisons by which they were defended [q]. One further deception crowned the successful perfidy of Mentor. He affected to treat the conquered places with unexampled moderation. He was particularly careful to keep in their offices the same collectors of revenues and intendants who had been employed by Hermeias. Those officers, when they were first apprised of the danger which threatened their master, concealed their treasures under ground, or deposited them with their friends; but when they found themselves treated with so much unexpected generosity by the invader, they resumed their wonted confidence, and conveyed back into their own coffers their long-accumulated wealth; of which circumstance Mentor was

no

[p] Diodor. ubi supra. Helladius apud Phot. Biblioth. p. 866. Polyaen. Stratag. vi. 48.
[q] Diodor. ubi supra.

CHAP. I.

no fooner informed by his emiffaries, than he feized both the effects and the perfons of thofe too credulous collectors [r].

Ariftotle efcapes to Lefbos.

The veil of moderation which Mentor's policy had affumed in his firft tranfactions at Atarneus, enabled Ariftotle to avoid the punifhment which too naturally fell on the ambition of his friend. By a feafonable flight he efcaped to Mitylene in the ifle of Lefbos, in company with Pythias, the kinfwoman and adopted heirefs of the king of Affus and Atarneus, but now miferably fallen from the lofty expectations in which her youth had been educated. But this fad reverfe of fortune only endeared her the more to Ariftotle, who married the fair compa-

His marriage with Pythias.

nion of his flight in his thirty-feventh year [s]; which is precifely that age pointed out by himfelf as the fitteft, on the male fide, for entering into wedlock [t]. Pythias died fhortly afterwards, leaving an infant daughter, whom Ariftotle named after a wife tenderly beloved, and who repaid his affection with the moft tender fenfibility. It was her laft requeft that, when Ariftotle (which might the Fates long avert!) fhould die, her own bones might be difinterred, and carefully inclofed within the monument of her admired hufband [u].

Is invited to Macedon.

The Stagirite paffed but a fhort time in the foft ifland of Lefbos, in the tender indulgence either of love or of melancholy. During his refidence in Athens, he had ftrengthened his hereditary friendfhip with Philip of Macedon, a prince one year younger than himfelf, who, having lived from the age of fifteen

[r] We learn this particular, which is neceffary to explain what follows in the text, from Ariftotle himfelf, in his curious treatife De Cura Rei familiaris, p. 508.

[s] Comp. Dionyf. Epift. ad Ammæum; & Diogen. Laert. in Ariftot.

[t] Politic. l. vii. fect. 16.

[u] Diogen. Laert. ubi fupra.

fifteen to that of two-and-twenty in Thebes and the neighbouring cities, ascended the throne of his ancestors in the twenty-third year of his age. The busy scenes of war and negociation in which Philip was immediately after his accession engaged by necessity, and in which he continued to be involved during his whole reign by ambition, seem never to have interrupted his correspondence with the friends of his youth; with those who either possessed his affection, or who merited his admiration [u]. In the fifth year of his reign his son Alexander was born; an event which he notified to Aristotle in terms implying much previous communication between them: "Know that a son is born to us. We thank the gods for their gift, but especially for bestowing it at the time when Aristotle lives; assuring ourselves that, educated by you, he will be worthy of us, and worthy of inheriting our kingdom [x]." If this letter was written at the æra of Alexander's birth, it must have found Aristotle at Athens in his twenty-ninth year, still a diligent student in the school of Plato. But it is certain that the Stagirite did not assume the office of preceptor to the son of Philip till fourteen years afterwards, when the opening character of this young prince seemed as greatly to merit, as peculiarly to require, the assistance of so able an instructor [y]. In the second year of the 109th

Philip's letter to him.

[u] History of ancient Greece, vol. iv. c. 33.

[x] Aulus Gellius, l. ix. c. 3.

[y] The chronology is clearly ascertained by Dionysius of Halicarnassus's letter to Ammæus; yet the accurate Quintilian, because it served to enforce his argument, says, "An Philippus, Macedonum rex," &c. "Would Philip, king of the Macedonians, have thought fit that Aristotle, the greatest philosopher of the age, should have been employed in teaching his son Alexander the first rudiments of learning, or would Aristotle himself have accepted of such an office, had he not believed it of the utmost importance to the success of our future studies, that their first foundation should be laid by a teacher of consummate skill?" QUINTIL. *Instit.* l. i. c. 1.

CHAP. I.

109th olympiad, Ariſtotle, probably in conſequence of a new invitation from Philip, ſailed from the iſle of Leſbos, in which he had reſided near two years, eſcaped the dangers of the Athenian fleet, which then carried on war againſt Macedon, and arrived at the court of Pella [z], to undertake one of the few employments not unworthy of an author qualified to inſtruct and benefit the lateſt ages of the world.

His merit and ſucceſs in the education of Alexander.

In the education of Alexander, the Stagirite ſpent near eight years; during which long period, in an office of much delicacy, he enjoyed the rare advantage of giving the higheſt ſatisfaction to his employers, while he excited the warmeſt gratitude in his pupil [a]. The temper of Alexander, prone to every generous affection, loved and eſteemed many; but Ariſtotle is the only one of his friends whoſe ſuperior genius he appears unceaſingly to have viewed with undiminiſhed admiration, and whom he ſeems to have treated through life with uniform and unalterable reſpect. By Philip and his proud queen Olympias, our philoſopher was honoured with every mark of diſtinction which greatneſs can beſtow on illuſtrious merit. Philip placed his ſtatue near to his own: he was admitted to the councils of his ſovereign, where his advice was often uſeful, always honourable; and where his kind interceſſion benefited many individuals, and many communities [b]. On one occaſion the Athenians rewarded his good ſervices, by erecting his ſtatue in the citadel [c]: and his letters, both to Philip and to Alexander, atteſted his unremitting exertions in the cauſe of his friends and of the publick, as well as his manly freedom in admoniſhing kings of their

Honours beſtowed on him by Philip.

[z] Dionyſ. Halicarn. ubi ſupra.

[a] Plutarch. in Alexand. tom. i. p. 668.; & adverſ. Colot. t. ii. p. 1126.

[b] Ammonius Vit. Ariſtot.

[c] Pauſanias Eliac.

CHAP. I.

their duty [d]. But the ruling passions of Philip and Alexander, the interested policy of the one, and the lofty ambition of the other, were too strong and too ungovernable to be restrained by the power of reason, speaking through the voice of their admired philosopher. The ambition of Alexander had early taken root; and the peculiarities of his character had displayed themselves, in a very public and very important transaction, which happened several months before the Stagirite arrived at the court of Pella. During Philip's Illyrian expedition, Macedon was honoured with an embassy from the Great King. In the absence of his father, Alexander, scarcely fourteen years old, received the ambassadors; and his conversation with those illustrious strangers, at a period in history when the public conferences of great personages consisted not merely in words of ceremony, afforded a just subject of praise and wonder. Instead of admiring their external appearance, or asking them such superficial questions as corresponded with the unripeness of his years, he inquired into the nature of the Persian government; the character of Ochus, who then reigned; the strength and composition of his armies; the distance of his place of residence from the western coast; the state of the intermediate country, and particularly of the high roads leading to the great capitals of Susa and Babylon [e]. To his premature love of aggrandizement, Alexander already added singular dexterity and unexampled boldness in his exercises, particularly in horsemanship; the most fervid affections, invincible courage, and unbending dignity [f].

Peculiarities of Alexander's character.

In

Ammonius, ibid. See also the fragments still remaining in Du Valle's edition, p. 1102. & seq. [e] Plutarch. in Alexand. [f] Idem ibid.

CHAP. I.

The plan followed by Ariſtotle in his education.

In training ſuch a youth, the Stagirite had a rich field to cultivate; but he could only hope to give a new direction to paſſions, which it was too late to moderate or control. In his treatiſe on Politics, he has carefully delineated the plan of education beſt adapted to perſons of the higheſt rank in ſociety; and, in performing the taſk aſſigned to him by Philip, this plan was to be ſkilfully modified, by adjuſting it to the peculiar circumſtances and extraordinary character of his pupil. Alexander's loftineſs could not be conquered, but it might be made to combat on the ſide of virtue: if he was angry, it was proved to him that anger was the effect of inſult, and the mark of inferiority [s]. His love for military glory, which, while it is the idol of the multitude, will always be the paſſion of the great, could neither be reſtrained nor moderated; but, to rival this tyrant of his breaſt, ſtill more exalted affections were inſpired, which rendered Alexander as much ſuperior to conquerors, as conquerors deem themſelves ſuperior to the loweſt of the vulgar. Agreeably to a maxim inculcated in that book of Ariſtotle's Politics which relates to education, the two years immediately following puberty conſtitute that important period of life, which is peculiarly adapted for improving and ſtrengthening the bodily frame, and for acquiring that corporeal vigour which is one main ſpring of mental energy. During this intereſting period of youth, with the proper management of which the future happineſs of the whole of life is ſo intimately connected, Ariſtotle obſerves that the intellectual powers ought indeed to be kept in play, but not too ſtrenuouſly exerciſed, ſince powerful exertions of the mind and body cannot be made at once, nor

[s] Ælian. Var. Hiſt. l. xii. c. 54.

nor the habits of making them be ſimultaneouſly acquired. In conformity with this principle, Alexander was encouraged to proceed with alacrity in his exerciſes, till he acquired in them unrivalled proficiency; after which, the whole bent of his mind was directed to the moſt profound principles of ſcience.

Ariſtotle's acroatic philoſophy.

It is the opinion of many, that a ſlight tincture of learning is ſufficient for accompliſhing a prince. Both Philip and Ariſtotle thought otherwiſe; and the ardent curioſity of Alexander himſelf was not to be ſatisfied with ſuch ſuperficial and meagre inſtructions as have been ſometimes triumphantly publiſhed for the uſe of perſons deſtined to reign. The young Macedonian's mind was therefore to be ſharpened by whatever is moſt nice in diſtinction, and to be exalted by whatever is moſt lofty in ſpeculation[h]; that his faculties, by expanding and invigorating amidſt objects of the higheſt intellection, might thereby be rendered capable of comprehending ordinary matters the more readily and the more perfectly[i]. This recondite philoſophy, which was delivered by the Stagirite, firſt to his royal pupil, and afterwards to his hearers in the Lyceum, received the epithet of *acroatic*[k], to diſtinguiſh thoſe parts of his lectures which

[h] Plutarch. in Alexand.

[i] Ariſtot. de Anima, l. iii. c. 5 & 6. & Ethic. Nicom. l. x. c. 7 & 8.

[k] This diviſion of Ariſtotle's works into *acroatic* and *exoteric*, has given riſe to a variety of opinions and diſputes; which all have their ſource in the different accounts given by Plutarch and Aulus Gellius, on one hand; and by Strabo, Cicero, and Ammonius, on the other. The former writers (Plutarch. in Alexand.; & Aulus Gellius, l. xx. c. 4.) maintain that the acroatic, or, as they call them, the acroamatic works, differed from the exoteric in the nature of their ſubjects, which conſiſted in natural philoſophy and logic; whereas the ſubjects of the exoteric were rhetoric, ethics, and politics.

CHAP. I.

which were confined to a ſelect audience, from other parts called exoteric, becauſe delivered to the public at large. It has been ſuppoſed that, in thoſe two kinds of lectures, the Stagirite maintained contradictory doctrines on the ſubjects of religion and morality. But the fact is far otherwiſe: his practical tenets were uniformly the ſame in both; but his exoteric or popular treatiſes nearly reſembled the philoſophical dialogues of Plato or Cicero; whereas his acroatic writings (which will be explained in the following chapter) contained, in a conciſe energetic ſtyle peculiar to himſelf, thoſe deep and broad principles on which all ſolid ſcience is built, and, independently of which, the moſt operoſe reaſonings, and the moſt intricate combinations, are but matters of coarſe mechanical practice[1]. The ſublimity of this abſtract and recondite philoſophy admirably accorded with the loftineſs of Alexander's mind; and how highly he continued to prize it, amidſt the tumultuary occupations of war and government,

Highly prized by Alexander.

politics. But the opinions of both Plutarch and Gellius (for they do not entirely coincide) are refuted by Ariſtotle's references, as we ſhall ſee hereafter, from his *Ethic* to his exoteric works. The latter claſs of writers (Strabo, l. xiii. p. 608.; Cicero ad Attic. xiii. 19.; & Ammonius Herm. ad Catægor. Ariſtot.) maintain, that the acroatic works were diſtinguiſhed from the exoteric, not by the difference of the ſubjects, but by the different manner of treating them; the former being diſcourſes, the latter dialogues.

[1] Simplicius and Philoponus allow other writings beſides the dialogues to have been exoteric, as hiſtorical diſquiſitions, and whatever elſe did not require for underſtanding them intenſe thought in the reader. Simplicius ſays that Ariſtotle was purpoſely obſcure in his acroatic writings: "ut ſegniores ab eorum ſtudio repelleret & dehortaretur." Simplic. ad Auſcult. Phyſic. fol. ii. This would have been a very unworthy motive in the Stagirite: but the truth is, that the obſcurity of Ariſtotle's works proceeds from a corrupt text. When the text is pure, his writings are as eaſily intelligible, as a mere ſyllabus of lectures on moſt abſtruſe ſubjects can well be rendered.

vernment, appears from the following letter, written ſoon after the battle of Gaugamela, and while he was yet in purſuit of Darius: "Alexander wiſhing all happineſs to Ariſtotle. You have not done right in publiſhing your acroatic works. Wherein ſhall we be diſtinguiſhed above others, if the learning, in which we were inſtructed, be communicated to the public. I would rather ſurpaſs other men in knowledge than in power. Farewell [n]." Ariſtotle, not conſidering this letter as merely complimental, anſwered it as follows: "You wrote to me concerning my acroatic works, that they ought not to have been publiſhed. Know that in one ſenſe this ſtill is the caſe, ſince they can be fully underſtood by thoſe only who have heard my lectures [n]." Of thoſe much-valued writings, the theological part, if at all publiſhed, was probably moſt involved in a ſublime obſcurity. To have maintained, in plain and popular language, the unity and perfections of the Deity, muſt have excited againſt the Stagirite an earlier religious perſecution than that which really overtook him. Yet in this pure theology Alexander was carefully inſtructed; as his preceptor reminded him in the midſt of his unexampled victories and unbounded conqueſts, concluding a letter with this memorable admonition; that "thoſe who entertain juſt notions of the Deity are better entitled to be high-minded, than thoſe who ſubdue kingdoms [o]."

Ariſtotle's genius for poetry.

Ariſtotle's love of philoſophy did not, like that of Plato, ſet him at variance with poetry. He frequently cites the poets, particularly

[m] Aulus Gellius, l. xx. c. 5.

[n] Idem ibid. If theſe letters be aſcribed to their right authors, they prove in what light Ariſtotle regarded his acroatic works; he conſidered them merely as text-books.

[o] Plutarch. in Alexand.

particularly Homer; and he prepared for his pupil a correct copy of the Iliad, which that admirer of kindred heroes always carried with him in a caſket, whence this tranſcript was called "the Iliad of the Caſket [p]." The Stagirite was not only the beſt critic in poetry, but himſelf a poet of the firſt eminence. Few of his verſes indeed have reached modern times; but the few which remain prove him worthy of ſounding the lyre of Pindar [q]; and it is not the leaſt ſingularity attending this extraordinary man, that with the niceſt and moſt ſubtile powers of diſcrimination and analyſis, he united a vigorous and rich vein of poetic fancy.

The nature of his inſtructions to Alexander in ethics and politics.

Ariſtotle carefully inſtructed his pupil in ethics and politics. He wrote to him, long afterwards, a treatiſe on government; and exhorted him to adjuſt the meaſure of his authority to the various character of his ſubjects; agreeably to a doctrine which he frequently maintains in his political works, that different nations require different modes of government, reſpectively adapted to their various turns of mind, and different habits of thinking [r]. From the ethic writings of Ariſtotle which ſtill remain, and which are the moſt practically uſeful of any that pagan antiquity can boaſt, it is eaſy to detect that wicked calumny of his enemies, "that, for ſordid and ſelfiſh purpoſes, he accommodated the tenets of his philoſophy to the baſe morals of courts [s]." It may be ſafely affirmed that, if Alexander is

[p] Plutarch. In Alexand. vol. i. p. 688.

[q] Menag. Obſervat. in Diogen. Laert. l. v. p. 189.

[r] Plutarch. in Alexand.

[s] This abſurdity is brought forward and inſiſted on by Brucker, Hiſtor. Philoſoph. vol. i. p. 797. Nothing can be more erroneous or more unintelligible than Brucker's account of Ariſtotle's philoſophy. I have heard it ſaid in his own country, that this laborious German did not underſtand Greek!

is diſtinguiſhed above other princes for the love of knowledge and virtue, he was chiefly indebted for this advantage to his preceptor: the ſeeds of his haughtineſs and ambition were ſown before Ariſtotle was called to direct his education; his excellencies therefore may be aſcribed to our philoſopher; his imperfections to himſelf, to Philip, above all to the intoxicating effects of unbounded proſperity. This is the language of antiquity, and even of thoſe writers who are the leaſt partial to the fame of the Stagirite.

Ariſtotle recommends Calliſthenes to Alexander. His character and behaviour.

After the moſt intimate communication during the ſpace of eight years [x], the pupil and the preceptor ſeparated for ever, to purſue, in a career of almoſt equal length, the moſt oppoſite paths to the ſame immortal renown; the one by arms, the other by philoſophy; the one by gratifying the moſt immoderate luſt of power, the other by teaching to deſpiſe this and all ſimilar gratifications. During his eaſtern triumphs, terminated in the courſe of ten years by his premature death, Alexander (as we ſhall have occaſion to relate) gave many illuſtrious proofs of gratitude to the virtuous director of his youth. One incident, and one only, ſeems to have occaſioned ſome diſguſt between them. At leaving the Court of Pella, Ariſtotle recommended, as worthy of accompanying Alexander in his Perſian expedition, his own kinſman Calliſthenes, an Olynthian; a learned

See the proofs of this in Plutarch, p. 668. Alexander ſpared the houſe of Pindar, in the ſack of Thebes; and the town of Ereſſus in Leſbos, in his war with the Perſians, becauſe it was the birth-place of Theophraſtus and Phanias, Ariſtotle's diſciples. In the midſt of his expedition, he wrote to Athens for the works of the tragic poets, with the dithyrambics of Teleſtus and Philoxenus, and the hiſtory of Philiſtus.

[u] Αριϛοτελης τα οιοντα συμβυλευων Αλεξανδρῳ πολλοις ωφελιμος ην. Ælian. Var. Hiſt. l. xii. c. 54.

[x] Dionyſ. Halicarn.; & Diogen. Laert. ubi ſupra.

CHAP. I.

learned and certainly an honeſt man, but of a moroſe unaccommodating temper, pertinaciouſly attached to the old ſyſtem of republicaniſm, which the father of Alexander had overturned in Greece; equally daring and inflexible in his purpoſes, and unſeaſonably bold in his ſpeech [y]. Ariſtotle himſelf perceived and lamented his faults, and admoniſhed him in a line of Homer, "that his unbridled tongue might occaſion his early death [z]." The prophecy was fulfilled. Calliſthenes, not reflecting that "he who has once condeſcended" (in the words of Arrian) "to be the attendant of a king, ought never to be wanting in due deference to his will," rudely and outrageouſly oppoſed Alexander's reſolution of exacting the ſame marks of homage from the Greeks which were cheerfully paid to him by the Perſians [a]. The manner of Calliſthenes's puniſhment and death is related more variouſly [b] than almoſt any hiſtorical event of ſuch public notoriety; but moſt writers concur in opinion, that he met with the juſt reward of his raſhneſs and arrogance. This tranſaction, it is aſſerted, much eſtranged Alexander from his ancient preceptor. The aſſertion however is not accompanied with any ſolid proof [c]; and the abſurd calumny, that Ariſtotle not only regarded this pretended diſpleaſure

Suppoſed rupture between Ariſtotle and Alexander.

[y] Arrian. Exped. Alexand. l. iv. c. 8.

[z] Ωκυμορος δη μοι τεκος; εσσεαι οἱ ἀγορευεις. Il. xviii. 95.

[a] Arrian. ubi ſupra.

[b] By Arrian, Curtius, Juſtin, Diogenes Laertius, Philoſtratus, and Suidas.

[c] Alexander's reſentment is inferred from a vague and haſty expreſſion in a letter to Antipater; "Τον δε σοφιστην εγω κολασω, και τους εκπεμψαντας αυτον—I will puniſh the Sophiſt (meaning Calliſthenes) and thoſe who ſent him." Plutarch. in Alexand. p. 696. Alexander, it is true, ſent preſents to Xenocrates; but ſo did Antipater, who always remained Ariſtotle's ſincere and confidential friend.

pleaſure as an injury, but even proceeded to the wickedneſs of joining in a conſpiracy againſt Alexander's life, is warranted by nothing in hiſtory, but a hearſay preſerved in Plutarch[d], and the affected credit given to the monſtrous report by the monſter Caracalla, for the unworthy purpoſe of juſtifying his own violence in deſtroying the ſchools of the Ariſtotelian philoſophers in Alexandria, the burning their books, and depriving them of all thoſe privileges and revenues which they enjoyed through the munificence of the Ptolemies, Alexander's Egyptian ſucceſſors[e].

Plan of Ariſtotle's life in Athens.

Having taken leave of the Macedonian capital, Ariſtotle returned to his beloved Athens; where he ſpent thirteen[f] years, almoſt the whole remainder of his life, inſtructing his diſciples, and improving the various branches of his philoſophy. His *acroatic* lectures were given in the morning to thoſe who were his regular pupils[g]. A conſiderable part of them is ſtill preſerved in his works, which form an abſtract or ſyllabus of treatiſes on the moſt important branches of philoſophy. His *exoteric* diſcourſes were held after ſupper with occaſional viſitors, and formed the amuſement of his evening walks[h]; for he thought "exerciſe peculiarly uſeful after table for animating and invigorating the natural heat and ſtrength, which the too rapid ſucceſſion of ſleep to food ſeemed fitted to relax and encumber[i]." Before his arrival at Athens, Sheuſippus was dead; and

[d] "Thoſe who ſay that Ariſtotle adviſed Antipater to deſtroy Alexander by poiſon, cite for their authority a certain Agnothemis, who heard it from king Antigonus." Plut. in Alexand. p. 707.

[e] Dion in Caracall.

[f] Dionyſ. Epiſt. ad Ammæum.

[g] Aulus Gellius, l. xx. c. 5.

[h] Idem ibid.

[i] Plutarch, Conjug. Præcept. p. 133.

and Xenocrates, whose dull gravity and rigid austerity a man of Aristotle's character could not much admire, had taken possession of the academy [k]. The Stagirite, therefore, settled in a *gymnasium* in the suburbs, well shaded with trees, near to which the soldiers used to exercise, and adorned by the temple of Lycian Apollo, from whose *peripaton*, or walk, Aristotle and his followers were called Peripatetics [l]. It is reported that he opened his school, observing, "That it would be shameful for himself to be silent while Xenocrates publicly taught [m]." Aristotle is not likely to have uttered such a presumptuous boast; but if it was really made, even this arrogant speech was certainly very fully justified by the fame which the Lyceum speedily acquired, which the Stagirite himself maintained unimpaired through life, and which was ably supported by his disciple and successor Theophrastus.

Such is the genuine history of Aristotle's life, in the most important passages of which all the ancient writers [n], who have expressly treated his biography, unitedly concur. By arranging the subject, therefore, according to our present method, both my

[k] Diogen. Laert. in Xenocrat.

[l] Menagius ad Diogen. Laert. l. v. sect. 2.

[m] Diogen. Laert. in Aristot. But Cicero, Quintilian, and Dionysius Halicarn. read "Isocrates" instead of "Xenocrates." The reading in the text is the more probable, for Isocrates and Aristotle, following very different pursuits, were not naturally rivals; besides, the former is said to have died soon after the battle of Chæronæa in extreme old age, and Aristotle did not return to Athens till three years after that decisive engagement. Compare my Life of Isocrates, and the History of Ancient Greece, vol. iv. c. 33.

[n] Dionysius of Halicarnassus, Diogenes Laertius, and Ammonius: the ancient Latin translation of this last, first published by Nunnesius (Helmestadij 1767), contains some additional circumstances, but those of little value, and of doubtful authority.

my own labour will be abridged, and the reader's time will be ſaved; for the calumnies againſt Ariſtotle will be no ſooner mentioned than they will refute themſelves, and they could not paſs unnoticed, becauſe they are perpetuated in the ſarcaſms of Lucian [o], and the lying whiſpers of Athenæus [p], which have been too often miſtaken, even by the learned, for true hiſtory.

Calumnies againſt Ariſtotle.

The abſurd reports that Ariſtotle firſt ſerved in the army, that he there diſſipated his fortune by low profligacy, and then followed for bread the trade of an apothecary [q], may be confidently rejected by thoſe who know, on unqueſtionable authority, that he became, at the early age of ſeventeen, a diligent ſtudent in the academy at Athens, where he remained during the long period of twenty years. The reader who has ſeen the teſtimonies of his gratitude to Plato, will not eaſily be perſuaded that he could treat this revered maſter with the groſſeſt brutality [r]; and let him who reads the Ethics to Nicomachus aſk his own heart, whether it is likely that the author of ſuch a treatiſe ſhould, inſtead of reſtraining and correcting, have flattered

[o] Lucian treats both Ariſtotle and his pupil with equal injuſtice. Vid. Dialog. Diogen. & Alexand. et Alexand. & Philip.

[p] Athenæus Deipnos. l. viii. p. 354.

[q] Athenæus ubi ſupra, and Ariſtocles apud Euſebium. Their report reſts on a ſuppoſititious letter of Epicurus on Study, and the aſſertion of Timæus of Tauromenon in Sicily; an author nicknamed Epitimæus, the Detractor. Diodorus Siculus, l. v. c. 1. Athenæus, l. vi. p. 272.

[r] Αριστοτελης ημας απελακτισε—"Ariſtotle has kicked at us;" a ſtrong metaphor. Diogenes Laert. l. v. ſect. 2. Ælian Var. Hiſtor. l. iii. c. 19. aſcribes both to Plato and to Ariſtotle a behaviour totally inconſiſtent with every thing that we know of their characters. Comp. Ælian, Var. Hiſt. l. iv. c. 19. Photius, Biblioth. c. 279. Auguſtin. de Civitate Dei, l. viii. c. 12. Such contradictory reports mutually deſtroy each other.

CHAP. I.

flattered[a] and fomented the vices of Alexander. Inſtead of farther examining theſe wild fictions, which ſtand in direct contradiction to the matters of fact above related, it is of more importance to inquire whence ſuch improbable tales could have originated; eſpecially as this inquiry will bring us to the events which immediately preceded our philoſopher's death.

Wherein they originated.

From innumerable paſſages in the moral and political works of which we have preſumed to offer the tranſlation to the public, it will appear that Ariſtotle regarded with equal contempt vain pretenders to real ſcience, and real profeſſors of ſciences which he deemed vain and frivolous. His theological opinions, alſo, were far too refined for the groſſneſs of paganiſm. He ſought only for truth, and was careleſs of the obſtacles which ſtood in his way to attaining it, whether they were found in the errors of philoſophers, or in the prejudices of the vulgar. Such a man, in ſuch a city as Athens, where, ſince the days of Socrates, the learned taught publicly and converſed freely with all deſcriptions of perſons, could not fail to have many rivals and many enemies. Sophiſts and ſcioliſts, ſoothſayers and ſatiriſts, and that worſt of banes, ſatirical hiſtorians[t], heaped obloquy on a character, the ornament of his own age, and deſtined to be the inſtructor of poſterity. But the name of Alexander, which then filled the world, was duly reſpected, even in the turbulent democracy of Athens; and it was not till the year following the

[a] Lucian, Dial. Diogen. & Alexand.

[t] Ariſtocles (apud Euſebium) ſays, that Ariſtotle was attacked by a hoſt of writers, "whoſe books and memories have periſhed more completely than their bodies." Even his fellow ſtudent, Ariſtoxenus, who had treated him moſt reſpectfully while he lived, heaped the moſt illiberal reproaches on his memory, becauſe he preferred to himſelf Theophraſtus for his ſucceſſor. Suidas in Ariſtoxen. & Ariſtocles apud Euſebium.

the death of that incomparable prince, that the rancorous malignity, which had been long ſuppreſſed, burſt forth againſt Ariſtotle with irreſiſtible violence. He was accuſed of irreligion before the Areopagus by the hierophant Eurymedon, abetted by Demophilus, a man of weight in the republic; and both of them inſtigated to this cruel proſecution by our philoſopher's declared enemies[u]. The heads of the accuſation were, "that Ariſtotle had commemorated the virtues both of his wife Pythias and of his friend Hermeias, with ſuch ceremonies and honours as the piety of Athens juſtly reſerved for the majeſty of the gods." To Hermeias, indeed, he erected a ſtatue at Delphi; he alſo wrote an ode in his praiſe. Both the inſcription and the ode have come down to modern times; the former ſimply relating "the unworthy and treacherous death of Hermeias;" and the latter "extolling virtue above all earthly poſſeſſions; and eſpecially that generous patriotiſm, for the ſake of which the native of Atarneus, rivalling the merit of Hercules and Achilles, had willingly relinquiſhed the light of the ſun; whoſe fame therefore would never be forgotten by the Muſes, daughters of memory; and as often as it was ſung would redound to the glory of *Hoſpitable Jove*[x], and the honour of firm friendſhip[y]." From the frivolouſneſs of the accuſation reſpecting Hermeias, which was conſidered as the chief article of the impeachment, we may warrantably conjecture that the reproach of worſhipping Pythias with honours due to Eleuſinian Ceres, was altogether groundleſs: but in a philoſopher, whoſe intellectual rather than his moral virtues have been the object of panegyric, we may remark with pleaſure both the ſtrength of his friendſhip,

His accuſation at Athens.

[u] Diogen. Laert, l. v. ſect. 4 & 5.

[x] See above, p. 11.   [y] Laertius in Ariſtot. Athenæus, xv. p. 697.

CHAP. I.

ſhip, and the ſincere tenderneſs of his love, ſince both affections muſt have been expreſſed with an amiable enthuſiaſm, to enable even the malice of his enemies to interpret them into the crime of idolatry.

His tenets ignorantly calumniated.

It muſt not be diſſembled that the accuſation, and conſequent condemnation of Ariſtotle by the Areopagus, has been aſcribed to a different cauſe from that above aſſigned, and referred merely to the impiety of his tenets. He is ſaid by thoſe who have careleſsly examined his works, to have denied a Providence, and thence to have inferred the inefficacy of prayers and ſacrifices: doctrines, it is obſerved, which could not but enrage the prieſthood, as totally ſubverſive of its functions, eſtabliſhments, and revenues [y]. But never was any accuſation urged more falſely or more ignorantly. Ariſtotle, as it will be ſhewn hereafter, enumerates the prieſthood among the functions or offices eſſentially requiſite to the exiſtence of every community. In writing to Alexander he ſays, that thoſe are not entitled to be high-minded who conquer kingdoms, but rather thoſe who have learned to form juſt notions of the gods [z]; and in his life, as well as in his works, he uniformly ſhewed his veneration for religion in general, by treating, with great tenderneſs [a], even that diſtorted image of it reflected from the puerile ſuperſtitions of his country [b].

He

[y] Origines contra Celſum & Bruckeri, Hiſtor. Critic. vol. i. p. 790.

[z] Plutarch in Alexand.

[a] This tenderneſs, however, did not, probably, ſatisfy the Athenian prieſts; who, as it will appear from the following analyſis of his works, had more to apprehend from his real piety, than to fear from his pretended irreligion.

[b] Diogen. Laert. l. v. ſect. 16. But the beſt proof of this will appear hereafter, when we come to examine Ariſtotle's works.

He is ſaid to have written his own defence, and to have inveighed, in a ſtrong metaphor, againſt the increaſing degeneracy of the Athenians [c]. His diſcourſe, of which the boldneſs would only have inflamed the blind zeal of his weak or wicked judges, was not delivered in court; ſince he eſcaped his trial by ſeaſonably quitting Athens for Chalcis in Eubœa, ſaying, in alluſion to the death of Socrates, that he was unwilling to afford to the Athenians a ſecond opportunity of ſinning againſt philoſophy [d]. He ſurvived his retreat to the ſhores of the Euripus, ſcarcely a twelvemonth; perſecution and baniſhment having probably ſhortened his days [e].

His retreat to Chalcis, and death.

His teſtament, preſerved in Diogenes Laertius, accords with the circumſtances related concerning his life, and practically illuſtrates the liberal maxims of his philoſophy. Antipater, the confidential miniſter of Philip, regent of Macedon both under Alexander and after his demiſe, is appointed the executor of this teſtament, with an authority paramount, as it ſhould ſeem, to

His teſtament.

[c] Laert. l. v. ſect. 16. Ογχη επ ογχη γηρασκει. Homer's deſcription of the gardens of Alcinous. "The fig rotting on the fig," alludes to the Athenian ſycophants, ſo called originally from informing againſt the exporters of figs.

[d] Ælian, iii. 36.

[e] St. Juſtin (in admon. ad gentes) and Gregory of Naxianzen (contra Julian.) ſay that he died through the uneaſineſs of diſcontent at not being able to explain the cauſe of the tides of the Euripus; upon which authority the puerile ſtory is engrafted of his throwing himſelf into that arm of the ſea, ſaying, "You ſhall contain me, ſince I cannot comprehend you." Others ſay that he ended his life by poiſon to eſcape the vengeance of the Athenians (Rapin's Comparaiſon de Platon & d' Ariſtote). Such unwarranted reports would not be worthy of mention, did they not afford an opportunity of obſerving the extreme improbability that Ariſtotle ſhould have been guilty of ſuicide, ſince he always ſpeaks of it as of a ſhameful and cowardly crime.

CHAP. I.

to that of the other persons who are afterwards conjoined with him in the same trust. To his wife Herpylis, (for he had married a second time,) Aristotle, besides other property in money and slaves, leaves the choice of two houses, the one in Chalcis, the other his paternal mansion at Stagira; and desires, that whichever of them she might prefer, should be properly furnished for her reception. He commends her domestic virtues; and requests his friends that, mindful of her behaviour towards him, they would distinguish her by the kindest attention; and should she again think of a husband, that they would be careful to provide for her a suitable marriage. To Nicomachus, the son of this Herpylis, and to Pythias, the daughter of his first wife, he bequeathed the remainder of his fortune, with the exception of his library and writings, which he left to his favourite scholar Theophrastus [f]. He desires that his daughter, when she attained a marriageable age, should be given to Nicanor, the son of his ancient benefactor Proxenus; and failing Nicanor, that his esteemed disciple Theophrastus should accept her hand and fortune. The bones of his first wife Pythias, he ordered to be disinterred, and again buried with his own, as she herself had requested. None of his slaves are to be sold; they are all of them either emancipated by his will, or ordered to be manumitted by his heirs, whenever they seem worthy of liberty; an injunction conformable to the maxims inculcated in his "Politics," that slaves of all descriptions ought to be set free, whenever they merited freedom, and are qualified for enjoying it. He concludes with a testimony of external deference at least for the religion of his country, by ordering that the dedications which he had vowed for the safety of

[f] Strabo, xiii. 413.

CHAP. I.

of Nicanor, ſhould be preſented at Stagira to Jupiter and Minerva, the ſaviours.

Thus lived and thus died, in his 63d year, Ariſtotle the Stagirite. His enlightened humanity was often ſeaſoned by pleaſantry. Many ſtrokes of genuine humour, little ſuſpected by his commentators, will be found in his political writings. His ſmart ſayings and quick repartees were long remembered and admired by thoſe incapable of appreciating his weightier merits. Some of theſe ſayings, though apparently not the moſt memorable, are preſerved in Diogenes Laertius; of which the following may ſerve for a ſpecimen. Being aſked, What, of all things, ſooneſt grows old?—Gratitude. What advantage have you reaped from ſtudy?—That of doing through choice what others do through fear. What is friendſhip?—One ſoul in two bodies. Why do we never tire of the company of the beautiful?—The queſtion of a blind man! Such apoththegms would be unworthy of mention, had they not, by their perpetual recurrence in our philoſopher's converſation, ſhewn a mind free and unincumbered amidſt the abſtruſeſt ſtudies; and, together with the moſt intenſe thought, a readineſs of wit, which never failed to repel ſneerers, and to abaſh arrogance[g]. He exhibited a character as a man, worthy of his pre-eminence as a philoſopher; inhabiting courts, without meanneſs and without ſelfiſhneſs; living in ſchools, without pride and without auſterity[h]; cultivating with ardent affection every domeſtic and every ſocial virtue, while with indefatigable induſtry he reared that wonderful edifice of ſcience, the plan of which we are ſtill enabled to delineate from his imperfect and mutilated writings.

His ſayings.

The

[g] Diogen. Laert. in Ariſtot. & Diogen.

[h] Plutarch. de Virtut. Moral. p. 448.

The extraordinary fate of his writings.

The extraordinary and unmerited fate of theſe writings, while it excites the curioſity, muſt provoke the indignation of every friend to ſcience. Few of them were publiſhed in his lifetime; the greater part nearly periſhed through neglect; and the remainder has been ſo groſsly miſapplied, that doubts have ariſen whether its preſervation ought to be regarded as a benefit. Ariſtotle's manuſcripts and library were bequeathed to Theophraſtus, the moſt illuſtrious of his pupils. Theophraſtus again bequeathed them to his own ſcholar Neleus, who carrying them to Scepſis, a city of the ancient Troas, left them to his heirs in the undiſtinguiſhed maſs of his property. The heirs of Neleus, men ignorant of literature and careleſs of books [h], totally neglected the intellectual treaſure that had moſt unworthily devolved to them, until they heard that the king of Pergamus, under whoſe dominion they lived, was employing much attention and much reſearch in collecting a large library [i]. With the caution incident to the ſubjects of a deſpot, who often have recourſe to concealment in order to avoid robbery, they hid their books under ground; and the writings of Ariſtotle, as well as the vaſt collection of materials from which they had been compoſed, thus remained in a ſubterranean manſion for many generations, a prey to dampneſs and to worms [k].

At

[h] Strabo, lib. xiii. p. 608 & 609. Bayle gives too ſtrong a meaning to ἰδιώταις ἀνθρώποις, when he calls them "gens idiots:" ἰδιώτης means one who confines his attention to the private affairs of life, in oppoſition to philoſophers and ſtateſmen.

[i] Strabo, lib. xiii. p. 608.

[k] Athenæus, l. i. p. 3. ſays, that Neleus ſold Ariſtotle's books to Ptolemy Philadelphus; and Bayle (article Tyrannion) endeavours with Patricius (Diſcuſſ. Peripatet. t. i. p. 29.) to reconcile this account with that of Strabo, by ſuppoſing that Neleus indeed ſold Ariſtotle's library and works to king Ptolemy, but not before he had taken the precaution of having the whole carefully copied. According to thoſe writers, the

books

At length they were releaſed from their priſon, or rather raiſed from the grave, and ſold for a large ſum, together with the works of Theophraſtus, to Apellicon of Athens, a lover of books rather than a ſcholar [l]; through whoſe labour and expence the work of reſtoring Ariſtotle's manuſcripts, though performed in the ſame city in which they had been originally written, was very imperfectly executed. To this, not only the ignorance of the editors, but both the condition and the nature of the writings themſelves did not a little contribute. The moſt conſiderable part of his acroatic works, which are almoſt the whole of thoſe now remaining, conſiſt of little better than text books, containing the detached heads of his diſcourſes; and, through want of connexion in the matter, peculiarly liable to corruption from tranſcribers, and highly unſuſceptible of conjectural emendation.

Publiſhed at Rome by Andronycus of Rhodes.

What became of Ariſtotle's original manuſcript, we are not informed; but the copy made for Apellicon was, together with his whole library, ſeized by Sylla, the Roman conqueror of Athens, and by him tranſmitted to Rome [m]. Ariſtotle's works excited

books thus copied, and not the originals, ſuffered the unworthy treatment mentioned in the text. This ſuppoſition ſeems highly improbable; for not to mention the difficulty of copying, in a ſhort time, many thouſand volumes, it cannot be believed that Ptolemy, had he been in poſſeſſion of the genuine works of Ariſtotle, would have purchaſed at a high price thoſe counterfeits, which had no other connection with that philoſopher than bearing his forged name on their title-page. (Ammonius ad Categor ſub init.) Had a correct copy of the Stagirite's works adorned the library of Alexandria under the firſt Ptolemies, his genuine philoſophy would have ſtruck deeper root, and made farther progreſs than it ever did, in that Egyptian capital. Voſſius (de Sect. Philoſoph. c. xvi. p. 89.) endeavours to prove that Athenæus's words (which are certainly incorrect) imply that Neleus retained Ariſtotle's works when he ſold all the reſt.

[l] Strabo ſays, "rather than a philoſopher."

[m] Plutarch in Sylla.

CHAP. I.

excited the attention of Tyrannion, a native of Amysus in Pontus, who had been taken prisoner by Lucullus in the Mithridatic war, and insolently manumitted [n], as Plutarch says, by Muraena, Lucullus's lieutenant. Tyrannion procured the manuscript by paying court to Sylla's librarian; and communicated the use of it to Andronycus of Rhodes, who flourished as a philosopher at Rome, in the time of Cicero and Pompey; and who, having undertaken the task of arranging and correcting those long injured writings, finally performed the duty of a skilful editor .

Their number and magnitude.

Though the works which formed the object of Andronycus's labours had suffered such injuries as the utmost diligence and sagacity could not completely repair [p], yet in consequence of those labours the Peripatetic philosophy began to resume the lustre of which it had been deprived since the days of Theophrastus; and the later adherents to that sect, as they became acquainted with the real tenets of their master, far surpassed the

[n] Plutarch speaks with the dignity becoming a man of letters, who feels himself superior to the prejudices of his times: "That to give liberty by manumission to a man of Tyrannion's education and merit, was to rob him of that liberty which he naturally and essentially possessed." Plutarch in Lucull. p. 504. I have melted into one sentence ὃν γαρ εξιον (read αξιου) Λουκουλλος ανδρα δια παιδειαν εσπουδασμενον—and αφαιρεσις γαρ ην της ὑπαρχουσης ἡ της δοκουσης ελευθεριας δοσις.

[o] Plutarch in Syll. Porphyr. in Vitâ Plotini. Boetius in Procemio libri de interpret. Strabo only says that Tyrannion, in the manner mentioned in the text, got possession of the manuscript; which was copied for the Roman booksellers by careless transcribers, who did not even take the pains of comparing their copies with the original: a negligence, he observes, too common among the transcribers both in Rome and Alexandria.

[p] Even after this publication, Aristotle's followers were obliged τα πολλα εικοτως λεγειν δια το πληθος των αμαρτιων, "often to guess at his meaning, through the faultiness of his text." Strabo, in the place above cited.

the fame and merit of their ignorant and obſcure predeceſſors[q]. From the æra of Andronycus's publication to that of the invention of printing, a ſucceſſion of reſpectable writers on civil and ſacred ſubjects (not excepting the venerable fathers of the Chriſtian church) confirm, by their citations and criticiſms, the authenticity of moſt of the treatiſes ſtill bearing Ariſtotle's name; and of more than ten thouſand[r] commentators, who have endeavoured to illuſtrate different parts of his works, there are incomparably fewer than might have been expected, whoſe vanity has courted the praiſe of ſuperior diſcernment by rejecting any conſiderable portion of them as ſpurious[s]. According to the moſt credible accounts, therefore, he compoſed above four-hundred[t] different treatiſes, of which only forty-

[q] Strabo, l. xiii. p. 609. He obſerves, "that the Peripatetic philoſophers ſucceeding Theophraſtus had, till this time, but few of their maſter's works, and thoſe few chiefly of the exoteric kind; ſo that they were more converſant about words than things; and inſtead of reaſoning accurately and profoundly, were contented with diſplaying their ſkill in dialectic and rhetoric." I have thus paraphraſed the obſcurity of the original φιλοσοφειν πραγματικως and θεσεις ληκυθιζειν, becauſe Strabo, who had himſelf diligently ſtudied Ariſtotle's philoſophy (Strabo, l. xvi. p. 757.), uſes the word πραγματικως, moſt probably, in the ſame ſenſe in which it occurs in Ariſtotle, as ſynonymous with ακριβως, κατα αληθειαν; and in oppoſition to διαλεκτικως and το διαλεγεσθαι λογικως.

[r] Patricius Diſcuſſ. Peripatet.

[s] Compare Diogenes Laertius in Vit. Ariſtot. Patric. Diſcuſſ. Peripatetic. Fabricius Bibliothec. Græc. & Bruckerus Hiſtor. Philoſ. artic. Ariſtot.

[t] Diogenes Laertius (in Vit. Ariſtot.) makes Ariſtotle's volumes amount to four hundred; Patricius Venetus, a learned profeſſor of Padua in the ſixteenth century, endeavours to prove that they amounted to nearly double that number. (Patric. Diſcuſſ. Peripat.) The laborious Fabricius employs one hundred pages of his ſecond volume in enumerating and aſcertaining Ariſtotle's remains; which ſtill exceed four times the collective bulk of the Iliad and Odyſſey. The whole works of Ariſtotle, therefore, muſt have contained a quantity of proſe, equal to ſixteen times 28,088 verſes; a fact

CHAP. I.

forty-eight [a] have been tranſmitted to the preſent age. But many of theſe laſt conſiſt of ſeveral books, and the whole of his remains together ſtill form a golden chain of Greek erudition, exceeding four times the collective bulk of the Iliad and Odyſſey.

a fact the more extraordinary, ſince the greater part of his writings are merely elegant and comprehenſive text books, containing the heads of his lectures; laborious, but clear reaſonings; and often original diſcoveries in the moſt difficult branches of ſcience. The following paſſage concerning him in the French Encyclopedie, article Ariſtotéliſme, muſt excite a ſmile of ſomething more than ſurpriſe. "Le nombre de ſes ouvrages eſt prodigieux; on en peut voir les titres en Diogene Laerce .... encore ne ſommes nous pas ſûrs de les avoir tous: il eſt même probable que nous en avons perdu pluſieurs," &c.

[a] The treatiſes de Plantis & de Mundo are rejected by moſt writers. The former is, indeed, of little value; the latter, of the greateſt; but I do not cite it as an authority, becauſe it is my ambition to place my account of his philoſophy beyond the reach of cavil.

CHAP. II.

A NEW ANALYSIS OF ARISTOTLE'S SPECULATIVE WORKS.

ARGUMENT.

Senſation—Its nature explained—Imagination and memory—Aſſociation of perceptions—Reminiſcence—Intellect—Its power and dignity—Ariſtotle's organon—Origin of general terms—Categories—Diviſion and Definition—Propoſitions—Syllogiſms—Their nature and uſe—Second analytics—Topics—Ariſtotle's organon perverted and miſapplied—Demonſtration—Ariſtotle's metaphyſics—Proper arrangement thereof—Truth vindicated—Introduction to the firſt philoſophy—Its hiſtory—Refutation of the doctrine of ideas—Elements—Analyſis of the bodies ſo called—Their perpetual tranſmutations—Doctrine of atoms refuted—Motion or change—Its different kinds—Works of nature—How her operations are performed—Matter—Form—Privation—The ſpecific form or ſight—State of capacity and energy—Ariſtotle's aſtronomy—The earth and its productions—Hiſtory of animals—Philoſophy of natural hiſtory—His book on energy—The firſt energy eternally and ſubſtantially active—His attributes—Antiquity of the doctrine that Deity is the ſource of being—Inculcated in Ariſtotle's exoteric works—Objections to Ariſtotle's philoſophy—Anſwers thereto.

CHAP. II.

The different branches into which it is divided.

THE Works of Ariſtotle derive their importance and ſplendour, neither from their number nor their magnitude, but from their variety and their aim. Diſdaining the conqueſt of particular provinces, he daringly invaded the whole empire of

CHAP. II.

of philosophy; and his persevering and generally successful exertions in this bold enterprise excites the justest admiration of his genius and industry. The heavens and the earth; things human and divine; God, man, and nature; under these comprehensive divisions of whatever is the object of human thought, the Stagirite distributes the different articles of his truly philosophical Encyclopædia; of which time has yet spared to us the distinct outline, with many groups imperfectly sketched, and others totally defaced, yet filled up in some of its most essential parts with exquisite skill, and delineated throughout with unexampled boldness and inimitable precision.

In endeavouring to communicate to the reader, in few words, a clear and correct notion of the condition in which Aristotle found, and in which he left philosophy, it will be impossible strictly to adhere to the capricious order in which his Works have been arranged by his editors. Agreeably to his own maxim, I shall begin, not with what is absolutely first either in time or in dignity, but with what is first in relation to man; that is, with what is first in the order of his thoughts or conceptions; endeavouring, in my discourse throughout, to preserve the modesty and impartiality of an historian, and to be as faithful in explaining my author's opinions, as cautious in interposing my own judgment.

The sources of human knowledge.

It is the doctrine of Aristotle, a doctrine long and obstinately disputed, but now very generally admitted, that all our direct knowledge originates in perceptions of sense [a]. Of the five senses,

[a] De Anima, l. iii. c. ix. p. 656. εν τοις ειδεσι τοις αισθητοις τα νοητα εστι . . . και δια τουτο ουτε αισθανομενος μηθεν ουθεν αν μαθοι, ουδε ξυνιοι. τα δε πρωτα νοηματα, τινι διοισει του μη φαντασματα ειναι; η ουδε ταυτα φαντασματα, αλλ' ουκ ανευ φαντασματων; but I no where find in Aristotle the words universally ascribed to him, "Nihil est in intellectu, quid non prius fuerit in sensu."

ſenſes, that of touch, he obſerves, is generally diffuſed through the whole animal frame, and cannot therefore be deſtroyed without deſtroying the animal[b]. The ſenſe of taſte Ariſtotle regards as a particular kind of touch, requiſite for the purpoſe of nutrition, and therefore eſſential to life[c]. But the three other ſenſes, always reſiding in particular organs, are in ſome animals altogether wanting, in others extremely imperfect; and even in thoſe animals in whom they are moſt vigorous, are often, without deſtruction to the animal itſelf, overwhelmed, weakened, or totally deſtroyed, by the too powerful operation of their reſpective objects[d].

Senſation.

Colours and ſounds are perceived reſpectively by the eye and the ear, and by them only; motions and figures are conveyed to the mind through the inſtrumentality of more ſenſes than one; and a third claſs of perceptions are communicated and impreſſed through the united energy of all the ſenſes[e]. Thoſe of touch and of taſte ſeem to be nearly a-kin, becauſe external objects ſeem to operate on them by direct and immediate application. This, however, is not probably the caſe; becauſe, were it true, the analogy of nature would here be violated, ſince it is found by experiment, that external objects, directly and immediately applied to the organs of the three other ſenſes, totally obſtruct the motions on which their power of ſenſation depends, and

[b] Compar. Ariſtot. de Anima, l. ii. c. iii. p. 633. and c. xi. p. 624. & ſeq.

[c] ὁ δε χυμος εν τι των απτων εϛι. Comp. l. ii. de Anima, c. iii. p. 633, and c. 10, p. 643. & ſeq.

[d] De Anima, l. ii. c. 6, 7, 8, 9.
ἡ τȣ αισθητȣ ενεργεια εν τῳ αισθητικῳ; and again, ἡ δε τȣ αισθητȣ ενεργεια και της αισθησεως ἡ αυτη μεν εϛι και μια. De Anima, l. iii. c. i. p. 648.

[e] De Anima, l. ii. c. vi. p. 638.

CHAP. II.

and render their reſpective objects, ſounds, colours, and odours, altogether imperceptible [f]. By a rapid and continuous agitation of the air, ſonorous bodies affect the ear; through the intervention of light, colours are diſtinguiſhed by the eye; and odours are communicated in a ſubtile vapour, which muſt in ſome animals, before perception can have place, be accompanied with the act of inſpiring by the noſtrils [g]. Agreeably to this analogy, it is probable that the fleſhy and tender part of our external frame, which ſeems to us to be endowed with ſuch a delicate ſenſe of touch, is nothing more than the medium through which the perceptions of hardneſs, ſoftneſs, and other qualities of that kind, are conveyed and communicated [h].

Its nature explained.

The real qualities of external objects are ſuppoſed to be made known to us by our ſenſes; but in fact thoſe qualities, ſuch as they are by us conceived and denominated, have not any actual exiſtence until they are perceived [i]. Previouſly to this, they exiſt only in power or capacity; which, in the language of Ariſtotle, here means that they exiſt only in their cauſes [k];

cauſes

[f] εαν γαρ τις θῃ το εχον χρωμα επ' αυτην την οψιν, ουκ οψεται . . . ὁ δε αυτος λογος και περι ψοφου και οσμης εστι, &c. De Anima, l. ii. c. vii. p. 639.

[g] De Anima, l. ii. c. ix. p. 643.

[h] De Anima; c. xi. p. 641. How far is this conjecture connected with the diſcovery of the nerves and their functions? And to how many diſcoveries might the ſhrewd gueſſes of Ariſtotle, attentively examined, ſtill give birth?

[i] ἡ δε του αισθητου ενεργεια και της αισθησεως ἡ αυτη μεν εστι και μια. De Anima, l. iii. c. i. p. 638. And again, αναγκη ἁμα φθειρεσθαι και σωζεσθαι την ουτω λεγομενην ακοην και ψοφον, χυμον και γευσιν, και τα αλλα ὁμοιως. De Anima, l. iii. c. i. p. 649.

[k] Compare διχως γαρ λεγομενης της αισθησεως και του αισθητου, των μεν κατα δυναμιν, των δε κατ' ενεργειαν, &c. De Anima, l. iii. c. i. p. 649. And το μεν ουν μητε τα αισθητα ειναι, μητε τα αισθηματα, ισως αληθες. του γαρ αισθανομενου παθος τουτο εστι· το δε τα υποκειμενα μη ειναι ἁ ποιει την αισθησιν, και ανευ αισθησεως, αδυνατον. Metaphyſ. l. iv. c. v. p. 879.

causes which, though themselves imperceptible, have the power of moving and agitating our organs [l], and thereby of producing in them that variety of sensations, which relieves man from solitude, and connects him with the external world. To beings differently constituted, or to man himself, enjoying a direct and immediate intimacy with the causes of his perceptions, this world would probably assume an appearance altogether different from that which it now wears; for all sensation directly and immediately depends, not merely on the nature of its external causes, but on that also of the motions and changes produced in the organs of sense. Aristotle, therefore, justly reproves Democritus for saying, that if no medium were interposed, a pismire would be visible in the heavens [m]; asserting, on the contrary, that if vacuity alone intervened, nothing possibly could be seen, because all vision is performed by changes or motions in the organ of sight; and all such changes or motions imply an interposed medium [n].

Between the perceptions of the eye and of the ear there is a striking analogy. Bodies are only visible by their colour; and colour is only perceptible in light; and unless different motions were excited by light in the eye, colour and the distinctions of colour would no more be visible, than, independently of different vibrations communicated to the ear, sound, and the distinctions of

[l] ἡ δὲ λεγομένη αἴσθησις, ὡς ἐνέργεια, κίνησίς τις διὰ τοῦ σώματος τῆς ψυχῆς ἐστι. De Somn. & Vigilia, c. i. p. 685. ἡ δὲ αἴσθησις ἐν τῷ κινεῖσθαί τε καὶ πάσχειν συμβαίνει. De Anima. l. ii. c. 5. p. 636.

[m] De Anima, l. ii. c. viii. p. 639.

[n] De Sensu & Sensili, c. ii. p. 665.

CHAP. II.

of sound, would be audible [o]. When the vibrations in a given time are many, the sensation of sharpness or shrillness follows; when the vibrations are, in the same time, comparatively few, the sensation of flatness is the result: but the first sound does not excite many vibrations because it is shrill or sharp, but it is sharp because it excites many vibrations; and the second sound does not excite few vibrations because it is flat or grave, but it is grave because it excites few vibrations [p].

Imagination and memory.

The powers of imagination and memory owe their origin to the senses, and are common to man with many other animals. As sensation is carried on by means of certain motions excited in our organs, so imagination and memory, which are the copies of sensation, exert their energy by means of similar but fainter motions, representatives of the former [q]. That independently of external causes such motions are produced, is demonstrable from what happens in sleep [r]. In some kinds of madness too, the phantoms of the brain are mistaken for realities [s]; and, in other kinds, realities are mistaken for phantoms [t]. But when our

[o] De Anima, l. ii. c. viii. p. 641. See also l. ii. c. vii. p. 638. The intrepid ignorance of Voltaire might maintain, that Aristotle considered light as a quality merely; and that luminous and coloured bodies had qualities exactly such as they excited the ideas of in us. (Voltaire's Newtonian Philosophy.) But how could the learned Warburton assent to this erroneous account of the Peripatetic philosophy? See Divine Legation of Moses, &c. b. iv. sect. 6.

[p] De Anima, l. ii. c. viii. p. 641.

[q] ἡ δε φαντασια εϛι αισθησις τις ασθενης. Rhetor. l. i. c. xi. p. 536. The same doctrine is maintained De Anima, l. iii. c. 4. p. 652. and De Memor. & Reminiscent. c. i. p. 680. c. ii. 682 & 683.

[r] De Anima, l. iii. c. iv. p. 651.

[s] Of this see an extraordinary example in Mirabil. Auscult. p. 1152.

[t] De Anima, l. iii. c. iv. p. 652. and De Mem. & Reminisc. c. i. p. 680.

CHAP. II.

our ſenſes are ſound and awake, we can eaſily diſtinguiſh between perceptions ariſing from external cauſes, and thoſe called into being by the mere agency of our internal conſtitution; and in many caſes we can diſcover and explain the laws by which the energy of this conſtitution operates [v]. For the perceptions of imagination and memory, though not rigidly governed, like thoſe of ſenſe, by the power and preſence of external objects, do not, however, float at random, but are ſubjected to a certain order and progreſſion, conformably to eſtabliſhed laws of aſſociation, which Ariſtotle was the firſt philoſopher that attempted to inveſtigate, to enumerate, and to explain [w]. He inveſtigated them in analiſing the complex act of reminiſcence or recollection, in which the principles of aſſociation operate under the immediate direction of the human will. He enumerated them, as far as ſeemed requiſite to the ſubject which he was then treating, by ſaying that they might be reduced to the four following heads: proximity in time; contiguity in place; reſemblance or ſimilarity; contrariety or contraſt [x]: And he explains them by ſhewing, that in every

Aſſociation of ideas or perceptions.

[v] De Memor. & Reminiſcent. c. i. p. 680. [w] Ibid. c. 2. p. 681.

[x] Mr. Hume ſays, "I do not find that any philoſopher has attempted to enumerate or claſs all the principles of aſſociation; a ſubject, however, that ſeems very worthy of curioſity. To me there appears to be only three principles of connexion among ideas; reſemblance, contiguity in time or place, and cauſe or effect." Eſſays, ſect. iii. of the Aſſociation of Ideas, vol. ii. p. 24. Mr. Hume might be ignorant that Ariſtotle had attempted to enumerate the principles of aſſociation; but it is an unpardonable error in logic, to aſſign cauſe and effect as one of thoſe principles, ſince cauſe and effect, as far as aſſociation is concerned, reſolves itſelf into contiguity in time or place; and according to Mr. Hume's doctrine, the very idea of cauſe ariſes ſolely from theſe connexions. Eſſays, vol. ii. pp. 34, 35. 88. 107. It may be remarked that "the aſſociation of ideas" is a modern expreſſion. Ariſtotle did not need it, ſince the thing meant by it is referred by him to cuſtom. τῳ γαρ ἐθει ακολυθεσι αἱ κινησεις αλληλαις, ἡδε μετα τηνδε. De Memor. p. 682.

CHAP. II.

every act of recollection we are conscious of *hunting about, as it were, among our thoughts*, until we hit on some one which is intimately connected with that which we wish to recall; or, in other words, that we produce in succession a multitude of vibrations or motions in our organs, until we hit on some one of them intimately connected with that of which we are in quest; and which has the power of reviving this last, because the one motion is either excited nearly at the same time with the other, or is entirely the same in kind with it, or so nearly the same, that the minute difference between them is speedily overpowered and lost, and from near agreement finally reduced to perfect coincidence. Thus far our author proceeds in unfolding the mechanism of sensation, fancy [y], memory, and recollection; or, in other words, in ascertaining the laws which regulate the union of mind and matter, without attempting the fruitless task of explaining in what manner those totally heterogeneous [z] substances are united.

Every exercise of recollection, he observes, is a species of investigation, in which the mind may be conscious of its own activity in directing the current of its thoughts, in turning them from one channel to another, in rejecting those which hold by no tie to the perception or image of which it is in quest, and in preferring, examining, and contemplating in all their relations

[y] Fancy is here *used* in its strict and original meaning; not, as in books of rhetoric and criticism, for the power of combining ideas or images by creative genius, agreeably to the dictates of correct judgment and refined taste.

[z] Aristotle carefully distinguishes the percipient power from the motions accompanying perception. αναγκη αρα εν τι ειναι της ψυχης, ᾧ απαντα αισθανεται, καθαπερ ειρηται προτερον, αλλο δε γενος δια αλλω. De Sensu, c. vii. p. 675. See also De Anima, l. iii. c. x. p. 656.

tions those which, by their connexion with this perception or image, have a natural tendency to rouse the one or to revive the other [a].

Reminiscence the first boundary between man and other animals.

It is the characteristic of animals, in contradistinction to the inanimate parts of nature, to be endowed with sensation; and whatever is endowed with sensation must have perceptions of pain and pleasure; and whatever has such perceptions must feel the impulse of appetite; the great moving principle in all animated beings [b]. But in the exercise of reminiscence, which is the immoveable boundary between man and other animals, he, and he alone, recognises the divine principle of reason or intellect co-operating with the coarser powers of fancy or memory; since every act of reminiscence, as above explained [c], implies comparison; and every the slightest comparison, expressed in the simplest proposition, indicates a substance different and separable from matter, a substance totally inconceivable by man in his present state, where the gross perceptions of sense are the only foundation and sole materials of all others, how lofty soever and refined; but a substance, notwithstanding, of whose existence we are assured by our consciousness of its energies [d].

To

[a] τȣτο δε γινεται κινȣντα πολλας, ἑως αν τῃ αυτην κινηση κινησιν, ᾗ ακολȣθησει το πραγμα. De Memor. & Reminiscent. c. 2. p. 682. He adds, anticipating the philosophy of Hobbes and Hartley, τȣ δε απο τȣ αυτȣ ενιοτε μεν μνησθηναι, ενιοτε δε μη, αιτιον, ὁτι εστι πλειω ενδεχεται κινηθηναι απο της αυτης αρχης—ὡσπερ γαρ φυσις ηδη το εθος, &c. ibid. "But the cause that the same thing recalls sometimes one perception, and sometimes another, is, that different motions may spring from the same principle; for custom is like nature," &c.

[b] De Anima, l. ii. c. iii. p. 633. & seq.

[c] De Memor. & Reminisc. c. ii. p. 683.

[d] Com. De Anima, l. i. c. v. p. 625. and c. ix. p. 629.

CHAP. II.

Proof of an intellectual principle in man.

To illustrate this further by an example, Aristotle says, let the comparison or proposition be one of the simplest imaginable, that whiteness is not sweetness[e]. These sensible qualities which the vulgar ascribe to external objects, the philosopher knows, as above explained, to depend on certain motions communicated to his internal organs, motions vivid and forcible when first produced by sensation, more faint and languid when afterwards revived by imagination or memory[f]. But the comparison of any two objects necessarily implies, that they should be both present in the same indivisible point of time, to one and the same comparing power. Yet their presence to the senses, the fancy, or the memory, is known to consist in nothing else but certain motions produced in our bodily organs. If the comparison, therefore, could be made by any of them, it would follow that this organ was susceptible of different and contrary motions,

[e] De Anima, l. iii. c. ii. p. 649.

[f] De Memor. & Reminiscent. c. i. p. 680. and De Anima, l. iii. c. iv. p. 652. Sensible qualities as perceived by the mind, Aristotle calls, therefore, παθηματα εν τη ψυχη, of which, he says, words are the signs: De Interpret. c. i. p. 37: Meaning, thereby, that language expresses things as they are perceived, not as they really are. το μεν ουν μητε τα αισθητα ειναι, μητε τα αισθηματα, ισως αληθες· του γαρ αισθανομενου παθος τουτο εστι· το δε τα ὑποκειμενα μη ειναι ἁ ποιει την αισθησιν αδυνατον. ου γαρ δη ἡ αισθησις αυτη ἑαυτης εστιν, αλλα εστι τι ετερον παρα την αισθησιν, ὁ αναγκη προτερον ειναι της αισθησεως. το γαρ κινουν, του κινουμενου φυσει προτερον εστι· κἂν ει λεγεται προς αλληλα ταυτα, ουθεν ἡττον. Metaph. l. iv. c. v. p. 879. "To say that things perceptible by sense, and the objects of our perceptions, do not exist, is perhaps true; for these are merely the affections of the percipient: but that there should not be certain causes producing sensation, and existing independently of it, is impossible; for sensation is not its own work, but there is something beside sensation necessarily prior to it, since the principle of motion is necessarily prior to the movement communicated; and not the less, that these things are relatives." The existence of imperceptible, and therefore unknown causes of our sensations, is maintained by Aristotle against the ancient sceptics; in whose errors he refuted, by anticipation, those of Hobbes, Berkeley, Hume, &c. as we shall see hereafter.

CHAP. II.

motions, precifely at the fame indivifible inftant; for it is neceffary that the fame fimple power fhould comprehend at once the fweetnefs and whitenefs, or whatever elfe be the fenfations compared, fince if it comprehended them diftributively, by its parts however minute, or fucceffively in particles of time however fhort, it could no more draw the refult of the comparifon, than if the one fenfation was recognifed by one man, and the other by another, or one of them recognifed in the laft century, and another in the prefent. The perception of truth, therefore, being altogether unrelated to time and fpace, muft be totally diffimilar to any corporeal operation, and fo effentially one fimple energy, that it cannot without abfurdity be fuppofed capable of divifion. But all the motions and actions of body being performed in fpace and time, are therefore indefinitely divifible; and although their fmallnefs or quicknefs foon efcapes the perception of fenfe, and foon eludes the grafp of fancy, yet the intellect ftill purfues and detects them, knowing that they can never vanifh into nothing by their indefinite minutenefs. By our divifions and fubdivifions without limit, we ftill leave, in the fmalleft particle, body with its properties; and after all the fteps that poffibly can be taken, remain precifely as diftant from the goal, as at our firft fetting out. This goal, therefore, it is impoffible for us ultimately to attain; but in the language of geometers, infinite will be ftill interpofed between operations divifible and indivifible, between perceptions of fenfe and perceptions of reafon, between the nature and properties of mind and the nature and properties of matter. It is not fenfe or fancy, but mind alone, that recognifes itfelf; and this intellectual fubftance of which we muft be contented in our prefent ftate merely to know the exiftence,

The power and dignity of this principle.

CHAP. II.

and to exerciſe the energies, is that which characteriſes and ennobles the creature man, and which gives him a reſemblance to his Maker. It is this which, ſeparated from body, is then only, properly what it is[g], immortal and divine; which does not

[g] De Anima, l. iii. c. 6. which paſſage is commented by Plutarch from Ariſtotle himſelf. Vid. Plut. de Conſol. ad Apollon. p. 115. Where he ſays, that the dead are happy and bleſſed; and that to ſpeak ill of them falſely is to blaſpheme againſt thoſe far ſuperior to ourſelves. This work of Ariſtotle's was a Dialogue, written in honour of Eudemus of Cyprus. It is mentioned by Plutarch in Dion. p. 967. The paſſage above alluded to in the work De Anima is ſtrangely perverted by Ariſtotle's commentators; whoſe erroneous interpretation is adopted by Warburton in the following paſſage, as bold in aſſertion as defective in proof. "Ariſtotle thought of the ſoul like the reſt, as we learn from a paſſage quoted by Cudworth * out of his Nicomachean Ethics; where having ſpoke of the ſenſitive ſouls, and declared them mortal, he goes on in this manner: 'It remains that the mind or intellect, and that alone pre-exiſting, enter from without, and be only divine †.' But then he diſtinguiſhes again concerning this mind or intellect, and makes it two-fold, agent and patient, the former of which he concludes to be immortal, and the latter corruptible. The agent intellect is only immortal and eternal, but the paſſive is corruptible. Cudworth thinks this a very doubtful and obſcure paſſage, and imagines Ariſtotle was led to write thus unintelligibly by his doctrine of forms and qualities, whereby corporeal and incorporeal ſubſtances are confounded together. But had that great man reflected on the general doctrine of the το ἓν, he would have ſeen the paſſage was plain and eaſy; and that Ariſtotle, from the common principle of the human ſoul's being part of the divine ſubſtance, here draws a concluſion againſt a future ſtate of ſeparate exiſtence, which, though it now appears all the philoſophers embraced, yet all were not, as we ſaid, ſo forward to avow. The obvious meaning of the words then is this: "The agent intellect (ſays he) is only immortal and eternal, but the paſſive corruptible, *i. e.* the particular ſenſations of the ſoul will ceaſe after death, and the ſubſtance of it will be reſolved into the ſoul of the univerſe; for it was Ariſtotle's opinion, who compared the ſoul to a *tabula raſa*, that human ſenſations and reflections were paſſions. Theſe, therefore, are what he finely calls the paſſive intelligent, which he ſays ſhall ceaſe, or is corruptible. What he meant by the agent intelligent, we learn from his commentators,

* Intellectual Syſtem, p. 55.

† λειπεται δε τον νουν μονον θυραθεν επεισιεναι, και θειον ειναι μονον.

not decay with our corporeal powers; and whofe energies are fo totally different from thofe of organifed matter, that whereas our

commentators, who interpret it to fignify, as Cudworth here acknowledges, the divine intellect; which glofs Ariftotle himfelf fully juftifies, in calling it θειον, divine*." On this paffage I would firft obferve, that though I had frequently read the *Nicomachean Ethics*, I could not meet with the words cited by Warburton; and for this good reafon, that fuch words are not there to be found. In the firft edition of Cudworth's Intellectual Syftem, that great Author is very negligent in citing his authorities; and in the fecond edition publifhed by Birch, we are referred to Ariftotle de Generatione & Corruptione, l. ii. c. 3. The paffage quoted, however, is not to be found there, nor in any part of the work on Generation and Corruption. It is to be found, indeed, in the Phyfical Aufcultations; and words to the fame purpofe occur in the fifth chapter of the firft book de Anima. ὁ δε νους εοικεν εγγινεσθαι, ουσια τις ουσα, και ου φθειρεσθαι. "It is likely that the mind is a fubftance exifting in the body, and not liable to be deftroyed with the body." From this and feveral other paffages, where Ariftotle always fpeaks with the greateft modefty on the fubject of the human intellect, qualifying his words with a "perhaps," "it is likely," Warburton had no right to conclude that Ariftotle maintained the pre-exiftence of the mind as a part of the Divinity. The argument which he brings in fupport of this affertion, "that Ariftotle calls the active intelligent, Divine," is not conclufive, becaufe Ariftotle, with other Greek writers, might ufe the epithet "Divine" as fynonymous with excellent, as the Lacedæmonians, when they admired any one greatly, called him Σειος (inftead of θειος) ανηρ. Ethic. Nicom. l. vii. c. 1. But the Stagirite feldom ufes any word which he does not accurately define, and when he calls the intellect *divine*, or what *is moft divine in us*; Ethic. Nicom. l. x. c. 7; fub init. he tells us plainly what he means by thefe expreffions, which he fays can have no other fenfe, but either that thought, *i. e.* the energy of intellect, from which only it derives its excellence and dignity, exifts moft perfectly in the divine nature; or, fecondly, becaufe intellect enables us, imperfectly indeed, to comprehend that nature. The learned Reader may compare the following paffages, Ariftot. Metaphyf. l. i. c. ii. p. 841. De Anima, l. i. c. v. p. 625. and Metaphyf. l. xiv. c. ix. p. 1004. That *intelligence in capacity is prior in time to intelligence in energy, in the individual, but not abfolutely*, means merely that the human mind is capable of intelligence before it becomes actually intelligent; but that all intelligence in capacity is derived from intelligence in energy, that is, from God.

* Divine Legation, vol. i. book iii. fect. 4.

 Metaphyf.

CHAP. II.

our ſenſes are eaſily fatigued, overpowered, and deſtroyed by the force and intenſity of objects ſenſible[h], the intellect is rouſed, quickened, and invigorated by the force and intenſity of objects intelligible; inſtead of being overſtrained or blunted, it ſharpens and fortifies amidſt obſtinate exertions; and finds in

Metaphyſ. l. ix. c. viii. p. 938. & ſeq. and the laſt chapters both of his Phyſics and Metaphyſics. That the mind when ſeparated from the body *is only what it is*, means that it then aſſumes its true nature, activity, and dignity, and is then better and happier than it was before, in which Ariſtotle ſays that many agreed with him. ειπερ βελτιον τῳ νῳ μη μετα σωματος ειναι, καθαπερ ειωθε λεγεσθαι, και πολλοις συνδοκει. Ariſtot. de Anima, I. i. c. iii. p. 623. That it then *perpetually energiſes*, not needing the aſſiſtance of memory, is explained by what Ariſtotle ſays on memory, in his book on that ſubject, c. ii. p. 681. & ſeq. in which he ſhews that memory depends on aſſociation of perceptions, and that aſſociation again depends on motion; whereas the intellect is ſimple, impaſſive; and, exiſting independently of ſpace, incapable of motion; except by way of acceſſion or appendage, as a ſailor is moved in a ſhip. De Anima, l. i. c. 3.

Since writing the above note, I find that Lord Monboddo cites and tranſlates part of the paſſage which I have endeavoured to explain; but his Lordſhip, I think, conſtrues it wrong. On the words ου μνημονευομεν δε, ὁτι τουτο μεν απαθες· ὁ δε παθητικος νους φθαρτος, και ανευ τουτου ουθεν νοει, he obſerves, "that what Ariſtotle here ſays of the mind's thinking of nothing without the paſſive intellect refers to the progreſſion from the ſtate of mere capacity in which the intellect is, before it is impreſſed by external objects; which impreſſion is abſolutely neceſſary for its operating in this our preſent ſtate." His Lordſhip here condeſcends to ſpeak rather like a follower of Locke or Hume than as the diſciple of Ariſtotle; and the text will not at all bear his interpretation, for the ανευ τουτου can only refer to the active intellect, without which Ariſtotle ſays the paſſive thinks of nothing. Plutarch expreſſes Ariſtotle's meaning in popular language. παιδεια δε των εν ἡμιν μονον εστι αθανατον και θειον, &c. "That of all things belonging to man, the improvement of his mind alone is immortal and divine;—neither to be aſſailed by fortune nor ſhaken by calumny; not to be deſtroyed by diſeaſe nor weakened by old age." Plutarch de Liber. Educand. p. 5. Edit. Xyland. My explication of the obſcure paſſages in Ariſtotle concerning the ſoul is confirmed by what he himſelf ſays on the ſubject of education in the 15th chapter of the ſeventh book of his Politics. The Reader will find the paſſage in the following tranſlation, book iv. c. 15. Ancient Metaphyſics, v. ii. b. iii. c. iv. p. 165.

[h] De Anima, l. ii. c. xii. p. 646.

CHAP. II.

in ſuch alone its beſt improvement and moſt exquiſite delight[i].

Ariſtotle's Works referred to three heads.

Having recogniſed the dignity and the powers of man, Ariſtotle, in his works throughout, examines how thoſe powers have been exerciſed in rearing the fair fabric of ſcience, which it was his own ambition to complete and to adorn. Adverſe accidents interrupted, as we have ſeen, from poſterity the full benefit of his labours; yet the treatiſes which emerged amidſt the general wreck of his writings, beſt arrange themſelves under the three-fold diviſion of the objects of human thought; God, Nature, and Man: which diviſion he himſelf ſeems continually to keep in view. Whatever reaſonings relate to theology, though ſcattered in different treatiſes, may be referred, therefore, to his Metaphyſics; a name unknown, indeed, to Ariſtotle, but given to his theological works by his editors, and importing that the fourteen books which bear it, ſhould immediately follow his numerous treatiſes on the ſubject of phyſics or natural philoſophy; that we may not reſt ſatisfied with the knowledge of bare effects, but proceed to the inveſtigation of cauſes, and of the Deity himſelf, the primary cauſe of all[k]. His hiſtories of the heavens and of the earth; of animals, plants, and minerals; and even of man, conſidered merely as a material and ſentient Being, may conformably with modern language be arranged under the head of Nature; though, in Ariſtotle's own acceptation, that term has a more limited ſenſe; and, for a reaſon which will appear

I. God.

II. Nature.

[i] De Anima, l. iii. cc. 5, 6, 7, 8. p. 653. et ſeq. and Ethic. Nicom. l. x. cc. 7 and 8.

[k] Metaph. l. xiii. c. 7. p. 988.

appear hereafter, is confined to terreſtrial objects, and thoſe exiſting between this earth and the lunar ſphere. Upon the

III. Man.

Philoſophy of Man[l], as our Author calls it, that is, of Man conſidered as a ſocial and rational Being, endowed with ſentiment, affection, and intellect, Ariſtotle's writings are as clear and copious as they are ſolid and ſatisfactory. His treatiſes on Logic, Ethics, and Politics, as well as his books on Rhetoric and Poetry, may all be referred to this one head, and viewed as connected parts of one great ſyſtem of knowledge, to which, after the moſt patient examination, it will be found that the labours of his ſucceſſors and detractors have made but ſlender additions.

The proper ſubject of his Organon.

In endeavouring conciſely, but clearly, to communicate to my Readers the reſult of our Author's reaſonings and diſcoveries under the three heads above mentioned, I ſhall begin, for a reaſon which will preſently appear, with that work of his, recently the moſt decried of all, but long extravagantly magnified as the great engine of diſcovery, and ſole inſtrument[m] of univerſal ſcience. Ariſtotle himſelf never viewed it in this falſe and flattering light, nor ever beſtowed on it thoſe pompous titles. The various tracts compoſing the Organon, as it is called, are not even given by him as parts of one and the ſame work.

[l] ἡ περι τα ανθρωπινα φιλοσοφια. Ethic. Nicom. l. x. c. ult.

[m] The word οργανον, organum, is found in Diogenes Laertius (l. i. ſect. 28.); where Ariſtotle's philoſophy is divided into practical and ſpeculative: the practical comprehending his Ethics and Politics; the ſpeculative, Natural Philoſophy and Logic. Diogenes, however, does not uſe the word in the ſenſe in which it was afterwards taken by Ariſtotle's commentators. Beſides, when Laertius ſays, that logic is a part of ſpeculative philoſophy, he contradicts Ariſtotle himſelf, who divides ſpeculative philoſophy into the three branches of Mathematics, Phyſics, and Theology. Metaph. l. vi. c. i. p. 904.

work [n]. They all relate, however, to one and the ſame ſubject; ſince dialectic [o], in the ſtrict and proper ſenſe, is merely the art of dialogue, that is, the art of converſing. Ariſtotle's Organon, therefore, rightly underſtood, is nothing more than an endeavour to teach the rational and ſkilful employment of that characteriſtic faculty of man, by which he expreſſes, through appropriate ſigns [p], not only his perceptions of ſenſe, but what is indefinitely more various, the compariſons, abſtractions, and concluſions of his own mind concerning them. It is in this ſenſe that logic, or dialectic, in the order of communicating liberal and univerſal knowledge, ought to precede the more abſtruſe and loftier branches of philoſophy, becauſe, by carefully analyſing the ſigns by which internal operations, as well as external objects, are expreſſed, we remount at once to the origin and ſource both of our notions and of our perceptions; diſcover their intimate connections with each other; and unfold, even to the unexperienced minds of youth, a vaſt intellectual

[n] Even the different works muſt have been arranged otherwiſe than they now ſtand, ſince in ſome of the firſt of them we find references to thoſe now publiſhed as the laſt.

[o] Dialectic is the word often uſed by Ariſtotle himſelf to denote what is commonly called his Logic, or the ſubject of the books compoſing his Organon. Vid. Metaph. l. xiv. c. 4. Rhetor. l. i. c. ii.

[p] των δε ονοματων εκαστον συμβολον εστι. "Each word or name is a ſymbol or ſign." De Senſu & Senſili. l. i. c. i. p. 663. The whole paſſage, beginning with αυτων δε τουτων κρεισσων, and ending with the words juſt cited, may be abridged as follows: "Hearing is the ſenſe moſt inſtrumental to knowledge, not eſſentially or in itſelf, for the ſenſe of ſeeing diſcovers to us more of the differences of things; but becauſe ſound, which is the object of hearing, is the vehicle of language; which is compoſed of words, each of which is a ſign." Vid. etiam De Interpret. l. i. c. i. p. 36 and 37.

CHAP. II.

intellectual treaſure, of which, without being aware of it, they were already in poſſeſſion [q].

His analyſis of language.

Agreeably to theſe principles, the Stagirite defines diſcourſe, or ſpeech, to be ſound ſignificant by compact, of which the parts alſo are ſignificant [r]; all diſcourſe which ſimply affirms or denies, he reſolves into arguments, arguments into propoſitions, and propoſitions into words; which laſt are the ultimate elements of language, becauſe, though ſignificant themſelves, their parts are not ſignificant [s]. Sounds ſignificant by compact are either nouns, that is, names denoting things without any reference to time; or verbs, whoſe ſignification is accompanied with the appendage of time [t]. Nouns are either proper names or appellatives; a proper name denotes one individual only; an appellative denotes various individuals, and often various kinds or claſſes of individuals. The formation of appellatives is, according to Ariſtotle, the united work of abſtraction and aſſociation [u]; abſtraction, by which we ſeparate the combinations

Origin of general terms.

[q] Comp. Ariſtot. Topic. l. i. c. ii. p. 181. & Ariſtot. de Anima, l. iii. c. ix. p. 656.

[r] De Interpret. l. i. c. iv. p. 38.

[s] To obviate objections ariſing from the ſignificant parts of compound words, Ariſtotle ſays, εν δε τοις διπλοις, σημαινει μεν τι, αλλα ου καθ' αυτο . . . The ſyllables are ſignificant, but not eſſentially; ſince the whole word is ſignificant by compact; for however ſubtilely words may be analyſed, they will ultimately reſolve themſelves, not into οργανα, but into συμβολα; not into natural inſtruments, but into conventional ſigns. De Interpret. c. iv. p. 38.

[t] Ibid. c. iii. Thoſe parts of verbs, therefore, which do not imply time are merely nouns. Ibid.

[u] Compare Metaph. l. xi. c. 2. pp. 955, 956. Ibid. c. xii. pp. 957, 958. Analyt. Poſterior, l. ii. c. xix. p. 179. & ſeq. De Memor. & Reminiſc. p. 181. & ſeq.

tions of ſenſe, and conſider a complex object in one view, without attending to the other aſpects under which it may be examined [w]; aſſociation, by which perceptions that are ſimilar naturally revive each other in unbroken ſucceſſion; and, in conſequence of their ſimilarity, are expreſſed by a common name, or appellative, which is equally applicable to them all [x]. In reference to this common name, which is merely a ſign that different objects have been compared together, and found to agree in one or more reſpects with each other, different individuals are ſaid to belong to the ſame ſpecies, and different ſpecies are ſaid to belong to the ſame genus; for in order to explain the nature of things, and to ſee their agreements and differences, it

[w] Metaph. l. xi. c. iii. pp. 956, 957.

[x] δηλον δη ὁτι ἡμιν τα πρωτα επαγωγη γνωριζειν αναγκαιον· και γαρ και ἡ αισθησις ὑτω το καθολυ εμποιει. The author here maintains, that even general principles can only be gathered by induction from perceptions of ſenſe, or from repeated acts of memory coaleſcing into one experience (αἱ γαρ πολλαι μνημαι τῳ αριθμῳ εμπειρια μια εϛι). And the compariſon by which this intellectual operation is explained equally applies to that by which "τα καθολυ," "abſtract notions," gathered from repeated ſenſations, are generaliſed and embodied in language. "In a flying army, when one man ſtops, the next to him will often ſtop alſo, and ſo on in ſucceſſion, until the whole will ſometimes ſtand firm. The ſame thing happens in the irregular flow of our thoughts. The ſteady contemplation of any individual object in that aſpect in which it agrees with other individuals, will recall many ſimilar objects to the mind; the ſtability of the one will communicate ſtability to the others, and thus give birth to what are called Univerſals, that is, to general terms, equally applicable to an indefinite number of individuals." ϛαντος γαρ των αδιαφορων ἑνος, πρωτον μεν εν τῃ ψυχῃ καθολυ· και γαρ αισθανεται μεν το καθεκαϛον, ἡ δε αισθησις τυ καθολυ εϛι. When Ariſtotle ſays that we perceive, by ſenſe, the univerſal, he means that we view the object under that aſpect in which it agrees with other objects; and the contemplation of it under that aſpect only, or, in other words, the conſidering certain appearances of it apart from the reſt, produces in the mind an abſtract notion, of which, though itſelf be particular, the name is general. Metaph. ibid.

CHAP. II.

it is not neceſſary to ſuppoſe the exiſtence of general ideas, but it is neceſſary that one word or term ſhould, in the ſame ſenſe, be applicable to many individuals, and alſo that one word or term ſhould, in the ſame ſenſe, be applicable to many ſpecies [y].

Their importance.

Independently of this power in man, of expreſſing things that are alike by a common ſign, his knowledge would be confined to the coarſe and complex intimations of ſenſe; he could not form even the moſt common notion of all, namely, that of number, ſince objects could not be enumerated, unleſs they were previouſly referred to the ſame genus or claſs, that is, unleſs they were expreſſed by one common ſign. They muſt be ſo many trees, ſo many animals, or at leaſt ſo many beings; and thus generically united, before they can be ſpecifically or even numerically diſtinguiſhed. For this reaſon Ariſtotle obſerves, that "one" and "being" are, of all terms, the moſt univerſal; they are applicable to all other general terms; they can be ſaid in the ſame ſenſe of them all, but no other term can be correctly ſaid of them, becauſe no other term expreſſes the full extent of their meaning [z]; or, in other words, is uſed as a ſign for all the variety of things which they are employed to denote.

The categories.

Next to them, in point of univerſality, the ten categories immediately follow. Theſe moſt comprehenſive ſigns of things are called, in Latin, Predicaments, becauſe they can be ſaid, or predicated, in the ſame ſenſe of all other terms, as well as of all the objects denoted by them; whereas no other term can be correctly ſaid of them, becauſe no other is employed

[y] Analyt. Poſter. l. i. c. xi. p. 141. ibid. c. xxiv. p. 155.

[z] Metaph. l. x. c. 2. p. 945. The το ἱν και το ὀν, "unity and being," agree, he obſerves, in the univerſality of their ſignification. They contain all the categories, but are not included in any of them.

CHAP. II.

employed to expreſs the full extent of their meaning. They are; ſubſtance, quality, quantity, relation, time, place, action, paſſion, poſition, and habit[a]. All the objects of human thought that can be expreſſed by ſingle words, arrange themſelves under one or other of theſe general terms. Ariſtotle (not indeed in his "Categories," but in his works collectively) explains the nature and properties of each; and thus opens to the inquiſitive mind a wide field of various knowledge, ſince the properties of each predicament belong to all the objects, or claſſes of objects, comprehended under[b] it, and the properties of the whole united extend to all things in the univerſe. But to avoid the reproach of bewildering his reader in barren generalities, the philoſopher frequently applies his reaſonings concerning ſigns to the things ſignified by them; perpetually inculcating, that individuals only have a real exiſtence, and that what are called in the Pythagorean

[a] ἐςι δε ταυτα τον αριθμον δεκα· τι εςι, ποσον, ποιον, προς τι, που, ποτε, κεισθαι, εχειν, ποιειν, πασχειν. Topic, l. i. c. 9. p. 285. What is here called τι εςι, the author elſewhere calls ſubſtance, as Categor. c. iv. p. 15; where he ſays, that all ſingle words denote either ſubſtances, or quantity, or quality, &c. This tenfold diviſion had been made before Ariſtotle's time, and explained by the Pythagoreans, particularly by Archytas of Tarentum, in his book περι τυ παντος, "concerning the Univerſe." A great part of that work, in its primitive Doric, is preſerved in Simplicius' Commentary on Ariſtotle's Categories. But Archytas and the other Pythagoreans conſidered as "the principles of things," what Ariſtotle calls σχηματα κατηγοριας, "figures or forms of predication," and λογυς καθολυ, "univerſal denominations." Thus alſo they were conſidered by Archytas the Peripatetic (Boeth. in Predicam. p. 112.), whom Mr. Harris (Philoſoph. Arrangements, c. ii. p. 31.) confounds with Archytas the Pythagorean. The conſidering of theſe comprehenſive genera as the principles and cauſes of the univerſe with the Pythagoreans, or merely as univerſal denominations with Ariſtotle, conſtitutes as wide a difference as that between a viſionary and a philoſopher.

[b] Categor. c. v. to c. ix. incluſively.

CHAP. II.

Pythagorean or Platonic philosophy, numbers, ideas, immutable and eternal essences, are merely the work of human thought expressed and embodied in language [c]. This doctrine is nearly allied

[c] Categor: c. v. p. 17. "That if individuals, or the first substances, were not, nothing else could be;" so that, instead of ideas, &c. making them, every thing that exists is made by and from them. And again, ειδη μεν ουν ειναι, η εν τι παρα τα πολλα, ουκ αναγκη, ει αποδειξις εσται· ειναι μεντοι εν κατα πολλα αληθες ειπειν αναγκη . . . δει αρα τι εν και το αυτο, επι πλειονων ειναι, μη ομονυμον. "For the purpose of demonstration, it is not necessary to suppose the existence of general ideas, but only that one general term can be applied with truth, and in the same sense, to many individuals." Analyt. Poster. l. i. c. xi. p. 141. Compare cxxiv. p. 155. Ετι δε ουδεμια αναγκη τι ειναι τουτο παρα ταυτα, ότι εν δηλοι, ουδεν μαλλον η επι των αλλων, όσα μη τι σημαινει, αλλ' η ποιον, η προς τι, η ποιειν· ει δε αρα, ουχ ἡ αποδειξις αιτια, αλλ' ὁ ακουων. "It is not necessary to suppose, that the general term, denoting any class of substances, expresses any thing beside the different particulars to which it applies, any more than the general terms denoting qualities, relations, or actions. One general term stands as the sign for a variety of particulars considered under one and the same aspect; but to suppose that this term requires one substantial archetype, or idea, as general as itself, is the hearer's fault; such a supposition not being necessary for the purpose of demonstration." The simplicity and solidity of Aristotle's philosophy was early destroyed by confounding it with Platonism. The evil has been perpetuated from age to age, by his commentators and pretended followers; not excepting the latest of them all, Mr. Harris and Lord Monboddo, who perpetually ascribe to the Stagirite the doctrine of general ideas, which, in the passages above cited, he formally denies. Those last-mentioned writers acknowledge that Aristotle opposed Plato, in denying the separate and substantial existence of ideas, but maintain, that he asserted their existence originally in the divine intellect, forming what we call the intellectual world. "From thence proceeds the material world, which is a copy of these forms or ideas. The first kind of ideas, the Peripatetics called προ των πολλων, "before the many;" the other kind they called εν τοις πολλοις, "in the many;" and these last are the substantial forms of the Peripatetics; that is, the form which gives the substance or essence to the thing. And, last of all, come the ideas in our minds, which, being formed from the many, and only in consequence of their existing in the many, are said to be επι τοις πολλοις, "after the many." Monboddo Ancient Metaph. vol. i. p. 466. Mr. Harris, in describing this triple order of ideas, speaks to the same purpose. "By mind we mean something which, when it acts,

allied to another of Ariſtotle's above explained, that all our direct knowledge originates in perceptions of ſenſe; and in both

acts, knows what it is going to do; ſomething ſtored with ideas of its intended works, agreeably to which ideas theſe works are faſhioned. Hermes, book iii. c. iv. p. 380. Again, To work and to know what one is about is to have an idea of what one is doing; to poſſeſs a form internal, correſponding to the external, to which external it ſerves for an exemplar or pattern. Here then we have an intelligible form which is prior to the ſenſible form." Ibid. p. 376. The ſame authors abound in repetitions of the ſame doctrine, which ſeems indeed to have been univerſally that of Ariſtotle's commentators. But what ſays the author himſelf. I ſhall repeat his own words, leſt I ſhould incur the reproach of ſpeaking harſhly. το δε λεγειν παραδειγματα ειναι και μετεχειν αυτων τα αλλα, κενολογειν εϛι, και μεταφορας λεγειν ποιητικας. τι γαρ εϛι το εργαζομενον προς τας ιδεας αποβλεπον; ενδεχεται τι ειναι και γιγνεσθαι ὁτιουν και μη εικαζομενον. Metaph. l. xi. c. 5. p. 959. "To call ideas exemplars or patterns, and to ſay that other things are made in imitation, or by participation of them, is mere empty ſound and poetical metaphor. Whoever conſidered in working an idea as his model? Things may exiſt or be made that never had an exemplar or archetype." According to Ariſtotle, "the definition is the idea of the thing, and the definition is compoſed of words." ὁ λογος ειδος τȣ πραγματος . . . και ὁ λογος συγκειται εξ ονοματων. Comp. De Anima, l. i. c. i. p. 618. and De Senſu, c. i. p. 663. I cannot conclude this note without obſerving, that ſomething nearly akin to Ariſtotle's doctrine concerning the categories or univerſals was revived, in the darkneſs of the eleventh century, by the ſect called Nominaliſts, which had for its author Roſcellinus, a native of Brittany and Canon of Compiegne. But the Stagirite's genuine tenets were generally unknown in that century, and ſo little underſtood afterwards, (being ſtudied only in corrupt verſions, Arabic and Latin,) that the ſect of the Nominaliſts, after the complete triumph of the ſuppoſed Ariſtotelian philoſophy in the twelfth and ſucceeding centuries, were regarded as raſh innovators and philoſophical heretics. Their opinions, however, agreed more nearly with thoſe of Ariſtotle than the opinions of thoſe who believed themſelves the Stagirite's moſt obſequious followers; although the language of the Nominaliſts ſeems to have been extremely liable to be perverted to the purpoſes of ſcepticiſm, as taking away the ſpecific diſtinctions of things; and is in fact thus perverted by Hobbes, Berkeley, Hume, and their innumerable followers. But Ariſtotle's language is not liable to this abuſe; he every where maintains the ſtability of truth, and the reality of thoſe ſpecific diſtinctions which general terms are employed to expreſs. He agrees with the Nominaliſts, for example, that the words "horſe" and "dog" have not any correſpondent archetypes or ideas in the mind, as

CHAP. II.

both these capital points, the Learned, after innumerable disputes, carried on with singular eagerness through many centuries, have generally embraced his opinion; and, what is most remarkable, chiefly since the time that undue deference ceased to be paid to his writings, and that his name was no longer superstitiously venerated by those who either read what they did not understand, or who affected to admire what they had never taken the trouble to read.

The

as general as themselves, but he maintains that these words imply the result of the comparison of different individuals agreeing in the same ειδος, the same show or appearance; for the sight, as he observes, is that of all the senses which enables us to perceive the greatest number of the agreements and differences of things, and is therefore most generally useful in classing them; or, in other words, in distinguishing those which are alike by a sign common to them all; that is, by a general name. Metaph. l. iv. c. 7. p. 881. Comp. De Sensu, c. i. p. 662. and Metaph. l. i. c. i. p. 838. To prevent the possibility of mistake or obscurity in the above note, it is necessary to observe, that the word "idea" in English is popularly used, not merely to denote an object of thought, but thought itself. To deny ideas in this latter sense is to deny thinking. But this is not the philosophical meaning of the word, as understood by the pretended followers of Aristotle, any more than by Locke in his Essay on the Human Understanding; by whom, ideas are said to be the objects immediately present to the mind in thinking. Essay, b. i. c. i. p. 13. Now Aristotle, in the following passage, expressly denies the presence or existence of any object in the mind, when it theorises or thinks, distinct from the act of the mind itself. επι των θεωρητικων, ὁ λογος το πραγμα, και ἡ νοησις· ουχ ἑτερου ουν οντος του νοουμενου και του νου, ὁσα μη ὑλην εχει, το αυτο εςαι· και ἡ νοησις του νοουμενου μια. Metaph. l. xiv. c. ix. p. 1004. In another passage he says, ἡ ψυχη πως εςι τα οντα. "The mind is after a sort all things." De Anima, l. iii. c. ix. p. 656. What is meant by τα καθολου, "generals, universals, ideas," as the words are translated by his pretended followers, he states clearly thus: Επει δ' εςι, τα μεν καθολου των πραγματων· τα δε καθ' εκαςον· λεγω δε καθολου μεν, ὁ επι πλειονων πεφυκε κατηγορεισθαι· καθ' εκαςον δε, ὁ μη· οἱον ανθρωπος, των καθολου· καλλιας δε, των καθ' εκαςον, &c. De Interpret. c. vii. p. 39. "The distinction is to be made between universals and particulars; universals, which can be predicated of many, as the term "Man;" particulars, as "Callias," the proper name of an individual."

CHAP. II.

Division and definition.

The reduction of things to genera or classes, by applying to them common names, is the foundation of division and definition, which have been called by a just metaphor the firm Handles of Science. Each of the categories, or classes, above mentioned, that of substance for example, may be variously divided according to the intent of the division, which may be undertaken for explaining the works of art or of nature; for delineating the institutions of civil policy, or describing the structure of plants and animals; in a word, for examining any object, whether material or intellectual, about which human thought is conversant. But for whatever purpose the division is intended, it can be perspicuous and satisfactory only when it descends from the more general classes, or terms, to those which are less general, until it arrives at the lowest species of all, which rejects all further partition but into individuals only[d]. The intermediate terms between the highest genus and this lowest species, stand each of them in two distinct relations, and therefore receive two different names, that of genus with respect to the less general terms which they contain, and that of species with respect to the more general terms under which they are contained[e]. Such is Aristotle's own doctrine concerning classification

[d] Analyt. Poster. l. ii. c. xiii. p. 175.

[e] Compare Categor. c. ii. p. 15. and Analyt. Prior. c. i. p. 52. The subject has been strangely perplexed by mistaking Aristotle's language, which is in itself highly perspicuous. το δε εν όλῳ ειναι έτερον ἑτερῳ, και το κατα παντος κατηγορεισθαι θατερου θατερῳ, τ' αυτον εςι· λεγομεν δε το κατα παντος κατηγορεισθαι, όταν μηδεν η του ὑποκειμενου λαβειν, κατα ὁ θατερον ου λεχθησεται. "To say that one term is contained in another is the same as saying, that the second can be predicated of the first in the full extent of its signification; and one term is predicated of another in the full extent of its signification, when there is no

CHAP. II.

claſſification and diviſion; a doctrine continually exemplified in his works throughout, moral as well as phyſical; and admirably illuſtrated by ſome modern writers, eſpecially on the ſubjects of natural hiſtory.

Propoſitions.

Having explained the uſes and functions of ſingle words, the author proceeds to examine their combinations into propoſitions, and the combinations of propoſitions into reaſoning or diſcourſe. According to the meaſure of our deſires or exigencies, our power or inability, language is variouſly moulded into commands, prayers, or wiſhes; but for the purpoſes of inſtruction or argument, it requires the form of an enunciative propoſition, which is defined by Ariſtotle "the affirming or denying one thing of another." But all that can be directly affirmed of any ſubject is, either that it belongs to a certain claſs, or that it is poſſeſſed of certain qualities. Thoſe qualities are either ſuch as neceſſarily inhere in the thing itſelf while it remains what it is, or retains its diſtinctive name; or ſecondly, qualities neceſſarily proceeding from the former; or thirdly, qualities which do not uniformly belong to the ſubject, nor proceed from thoſe uniformly belonging to it, but which accede to it

no particular denoted by the ſubject, to which the predicate does not apply." This remark, which is the foundation of all Ariſtotle's logic, has been ſadly miſtaken by many. Among others, the learned and truly reſpectable Dr. Reid writes as follows: "The being in a ſubject, and the being truly predicated of a ſubject, are uſed by Ariſtotle in his Analytics as ſynonymous phraſes. And this variation of ſtyle has led ſome perſons to think that the Categories were not written by Ariſtotle." See Kaim's Sketches, vol. iii. p. 316. But the two phraſes of "being in a ſubject," and "being predicated of it," are ſo far from being uſed as ſynonymous, that the meaning of the one is directly the reverſe of the meaning of the other.

it merely by way of adjunct or appendage [f]. Thus we can ſay of man, that he is an animal, which is the claſs to which he belongs; that he is an animal capable of reaſon, which is the quality neceſſarily inherent in him, while he deſerves his diſtinctive name; that he is capable of learning grammar or geometry, which are qualities neceſſarily flowing from the former; but when we proceed farther, and aſcribe to him qualities not neceſſarily flowing from thoſe inherent in the ſpecies, although they may be found in many individuals, and even many nations, it is plain that theſe qualities are mere acceſſions or appendages to his diſtinctive name or ſpecific character.

The ſpecific difference.

To define a thing, or to define a term, (for when words are conſidered as ſigns, theſe expreſſions are ſynonymous,) is to tell, as preciſely and perſpicuouſly as poſſible, what that thing is, or what that term ſignifies. This can only be done by aſcertaining the claſs to which the object to be defined immediately belongs, and the quality or qualities which, neceſſarily inhering in it, uniformly diſtinguiſhes that object from other objects belonging to the ſame claſs or genus. That quality, therefore, or thoſe qualities form what is called the ſpecific difference; becauſe they diſtinguiſh the ſpecies in queſtion from the other ſpecies in the ſame genus, or the object in queſtion from the other objects that moſt nearly reſemble it. Thus, to define

[f] Topic. l. i. c. viii. p. 285. The Greek word συμβεβηκος is, as far as I know, univerſally tranſlated "accident;" συμβεβηκοτα, in the plural, "accidents;" from which, "Accidence," denoting the little book that explains the properties of the eight parts of ſpeech, is generally held to be a corruption. But accident, in its proper ſenſe of what is caſual or fortuitous, has nothing to do with the one or the other; and Ariſtotle's meaning of συμβεβηκος ought to be expreſſed by a Latin or Engliſh word derived, not from 'accĭdo,' but from 'accēdo.'

CHAP. II.

define the number three, or the triad, we may ſay or predicate of it, that it is a quantity, and that kind of quantity called number, and that kind of number called an odd number; but each of theſe predicates, and all of them united, have a ſignification far more extenſive than that of the ſubject; ſince there are other quantities beſide number, and other numbers beſide odd numbers, and many other odd numbers beſide three. How then are we to proceed to find the exact definition of the triad? We muſt continue to combine ſtill more of thoſe predicates, until the whole of them unitedly will apply to the number three, and to it only; although each of them taken ſeparately, and even any number of them ſhort of the whole, have a far more extenſive ſignification. Thus, with the predicates "number" and "odd" we muſt join that of "firſt," defining the triad "the firſt odd number;" for though the predicate "firſt" applies to the number "two" as well as to "three," yet "the firſt odd number" applies to "three" only[g]. It may be neceſſary here to remark, that, in the accurate language of Ariſtotle, unity is not number, but the element of number[h]; all numbers are compoſed of units, but they themſelves are indiviſible and ultimate elements, incapable as units of farther reſolution[i]. For coarſe practical purpoſes, arithmeticians talk of the parts of unit; but when they do this, they have always previouſly converted unity into number; as when we ſpeak of the tenth of an inch, we muſt neceſſarily have firſt changed the one inch into ten portions; the inch therefore, before it can be divided, ceaſes to be an unit, and is converted into ten.

Ac-

[g] Analyt. Poſter. l. ii. c. xiii. p. 173. & ſeq.

[h] διοτι το ἑν αριθμου αρχη, η αριθμος. Metaph. l. x. c. i. p. 943.

[i] ουτε γαρ του εσχατου, εσχατωτερον ειη αν τι. Ibid. c. iv. p. 946; and again, αντικειται το ἑν και τα πολλα, ὡς αδιαιρετον και διαιρετον. Ibid. c. iii. p. 945.

According to Aristotle, definitions are the fountains of all science[k]; but those fountains are pure only when they originate in an accurate examination and patient comparison of the perceptible qualities of individual objects; for it is in that case only, that our words being the correct signs of things, the conclusions drawn from our intellectual operations on the signs, exactly apply to the things signified by them. We must cautiously proceed, therefore, from particulars to generals[l], that we may not be cheated by words[m]; endeavouring to discover, in each object of our examination, that principal and paramount property in which all its other inherent qualities unite and terminate[n]. To this property we must assign a name, when an appropriate name for it is wanting; and in the invention of this name, we must respect the analogies of language[o], that the same relations may be preserved among words which subsist among the things which they denote[p]. The name, thus invented, is called the specific difference; which, in the objects to which it applies, is not always that quality which is most palpable or most striking; for many other qualities are often actually

[k] αι αρχαι των αποδειξεων, όι ορισμοι. Analyt. Poster. l. ii. c. 3. p. 164. Compare Analyt. Poster. l. ii. c. xvii. p. 178.

[l] δια δει απο των καθεκαστον επι τα καθολυ μεταβαινειν. Analyt. Poster. l. ii. c. xiii. p. 176.

[m] άι όμωνυμιαι λανθανουσι μαλλον εν τοις καθολυ. Ibid.

[n] Analyt. Poster. l. ii. c. xiv. p. 176. & Topic. l. i. c. iv. p. 182.

[o] όυτω δε ῥαςα αν ισως τις λαβοι όις μη κειται ονοματα, ει απο των πρωτων, και τοις προς ά αντιςρεφουσι, τιθειη τα ονοματα. Categor. c. vii. p. 23.

[p] Comp. Metaph. l. iv. c. vii. p. 881. ό γαρ λογος, ὁ το ονομα σημειον, ορισμος γινεται του πραγματος, & Metaph. l. vii. c. iv. p. 908. c. vi. p. 911. & seq.

CHAP. II.

actually discovered in them, before we distinguish that most important and most general one, which is implied in all the rest, and which forms, as it were, the basis on which they all stand[q]. This paramount property exists independently in its subject; but none of the other properties can subsist independently of the specific difference, which is therefore the principle in which they originate, and the source from which they flow. In many objects with whose sensible qualities we are most conversant, this source is concealed; yet to remount to it, when possible, is the main business of philosophy, since the more our knowledge is generalised, it will be the more satisfactory, and therefore the more delightful .

The patient examination of objects, and the accurate definition of terms, are continually employed by our philosopher, as the best means for arranging perceptions into science. These, and not syllogisms, are the sole instruments used by himself in the deepest and most various researches that ever exercised the ingenuity of man. Yet his art of syllogism (an art ignorantly depreciated in the present age, and more absurdly magnified in preceding times beyond its real worth) is not therefore useless, although its real uses, as will presently appear, are altogether different from the purposes to which it was long most injudiciously applied. The art of syllogism was entirely Aristotle's invention; and in appreciating his merit as a philosopher, it becomes

[q] το δε ταξαι ὡς δει ἐϛαι, και το πρωτον λαβῃ. τουτο δε ἐϛαι, αν ληφθη, ὁ πασιν ακολουθει, ἐκεινῳ δε μη παντα. Analyt. Poster. l. ii. c. xiii. p. 175. The word ακολουθει is used in the same sense, when he says (as quoted above) that ἑν & ὀν, "unity and being," is implied in all the Categories.

[r] Analyt. Poster. l. i. c. xxiv. p. 155.

comes neceſſary to examine his firſt Analytics, in which that art is contained, that we may be enabled to decide whether the ſuppoſed improvements of his ſyſtem by ſome writers be not ignorant perverſions, and the objections made to the whole of it by others be not ſenſeleſs cavils. CHAP. II.

It was formerly obſerved that every propoſition, affirming or denying one thing of another, muſt affirm or deny that the ſubject of which we ſpeak belongs to a certain claſs, or that it is endowed with certain qualities *. But to affirm one term of another, when both of them are taken in the full extent of their ſignification, is merely to ſay that there is not any ſpecies or any individual contained under the name of the ſubject, to which the name of the predicate does not apply. It matters not whether thoſe names denote ſubſtances or qualities, or any other of the ten predicaments. Whatever they denote, the name of the ſpecies, according to the principles on which all languages are conſtructed, may ſtill be predicated of every individual, and the name of the genus of every ſpecies. When the definition of any term is predicated of that term, the definition and word defined, having exactly the ſame ſignification, they

* The Author proves this by obſerving, that every ſubject muſt either reciprocate with its predicate, or not. If the ſubject reciprocates with the predicate, that is, if the ſubject can in its turn be predicated of it, then the predicate muſt have been either the definition or the property of the ſubject: if the ſubject does not reciprocate, then the predicate muſt have been either ſomething contained in the definition, namely the genus or ſpecific difference, or ſomething not contained in the definition, but acceding to it as an appendage. Theſe relations of genus, difference, &c. which the predicates can ſtand in to their ſubject are called, in the Scholaſtic Philoſophy, the Predicables. They are the only things that can be affirmed or denied of any ſubject, categorically; which means, in the language of Ariſtotle, that can be affirmed of any ſubject merely by the interpoſition of the ſubſtantive verb between two terms. Topic. c. viii. p. 285.

CHAP. II.

they both necessarily apply to exactly the same number of things, and are therefore of exactly the same extent. But in all propositions not identical, but which affirm or deny one thing of another, the predicate is according to the structure of all languages, naturally more extensive than the subject[t]; because, as before observed, to predicate one term of another is merely to say that there is not any thing contained under the name of the subject to which that of the predicate does not apply. The predicate, therefore, in every proposition is called the major term; the subject, the minor term; and these terms are conjoined in discourse by the substantive verb "is," called therefore the copula. When we say "the wall is white," the substantive verb is expressed; the same verb is understood, when we say "Achilles runs;" because the word "runs" may be resolved into "is running;" being in fact merely an abbreviation of it for the purpose of communicating the rapidity of our thoughts with suitable rapidity of speech[u]. To prevent imposition arising from the abuse of words, it is necessary to be able quickly to discern whether one term can be justly predicated of another. Aristotle, for this purpose, invented the syllogism, which consists in comparing both the subject and the predicate of any proposition with what is called the middle term, because its natural place is the middle between the other two terms, called therefore the extremes. Let the question be proposed, whether temperance be a habit? I readily find a middle term which is contained under the more extensive appellation of habit, and which itself contains the more limited appellation of temperance. The terms, therefore, stand in

Nature and use of syllogism.

[t] Categor. c. v. p. 17.

[u] ουδεν γαρ διαφερει το ανθρωπος υγιαινων εστι, η το ανθρωπος υγιαινει, &c. Metaph. l. v. c. 7. p. 889.

in this order: Habit, virtue, temperance; or, in the form of propositions,

Virtue is a habit,

Temperance is a virtue;

therefore temperance is a habit. Now the whole cogency of this argument depends on that great principle which presides in the formation of language, that things, which have a common nature, receive a common name. They may differ in many important particulars, yet having received one common appellation from the particular in which they all agree, the term denoting the genus may be predicated of every species, and every individual contained under it. Whatever is affirmed or denied of a more general term, may therefore be affirmed or denied of all the more particular terms, as well as of all the individual things to which its signification extends. In the language of Aristotle, this is expressed by his calling those things synonymous which have the same name in the same sense. Thus "man" and "ox" are, according to him, synonymous, because the name of animal is equally applicable to both [x]; an observation which must sound harshly to those English readers who have derived their knowledge of Greek through the circuitous channel of France.

Wonderful variety in a subject seemingly so simple.

On the basis of this one simple truth, itself founded in the natural and universal texture of language, Aristotle has reared a lofty

[x] Categor. c. i. p. 14. Words, synonymous in the modern sense, have nothing to do with philosophy, whose terms, if accurate, cannot be interchangeable. Their proper place is poetry; accordingly we find that Aristotle, in his now imperfect treatise on that subject, had treated of συνωνυμα ὠν πλειω τα ονοματα, λογος δε ὁ αυτος, that is, "of various words meaning the same thing;" which agrees with the modern acceptation Simplicius in Categor. fol. viii.

CHAP. II.

lofty and various ſtructure of abſtract ſcience, clearly expreſſed, and fully demonſtrated. To convince ourſelves of the wonderful variety in a ſubject, ſeemingly ſo ſimple, it is ſufficient to obſerve, that the middle term may either be the ſubject of both the premiſſes; or the predicate of both; or, as in the ſyllogiſm given above, the ſubject of the major premiſs, in which it is compared with the major extreme, and the predicate of the minor premiſs, in which it is compared with the minor extreme. Theſe various arrangements form what are called the three figures of ſyllogiſm[y]; and in each of theſe three figures, every one of the three propoſitions may be either affirmative or negative; and each of the affirmative and negative propoſitions may be either univerſal or particular; univerſal, when their ſubject is taken in the full extent of its meaning, as "all men are mortal;" particular, when their ſubject in its ſignification is reſtricted to a part of the things which its name properly denotes, as "ſome men are wiſe." If we expreſs theſe four kinds of propoſitions, the univerſal affirmative, the univerſal negative, the particular affirmative, and the particular negative, by the four vowels, a, e, i, o, we ſhall find that they will afford ſixty-four different combinations by threes, which are called the different modes in each figure; and therefore one hundred and ninety-two combinations in the three figures collectively. But the variety does not end here; for propoſitions themſelves are either

[y] It may be proper to remark, that in books of logic there is a fourth figure which is ſaid to have been invented by Galen the phyſician. In this Galenical figure, as it is called, the middle term is predicated of the major, and the minor term is predicated of the middle. In this abſurd figure, the more general term is placed as the ſubject of the more particular. The natural arrangement of the terms is thus totally reverſed. But every ſyllogiſm in this figure, when properly expreſſed, naturally falls under Ariſtotle's firſt figure.

either pure or modal. A pure propoſition ſimply affirms or denies one thing of another; a modal propoſition affirms or denies with the addition of neceſſity or contingency, poſſibility or impoſſibility. When we conſider, therefore, the numerous combinations that will reſult from theſe new elements variouſly joined with the old, and that every new combination forms a diſtinct ſyllogiſm, it is impoſſible not to admire the perſevering induſtry that could contemplate each ſeparately, and examine how the truth of the concluſion was affected by each ſpecific arrangement.

All ſyllogiſms reduced to thoſe of the firſt figure.

From this induction, the moſt copious and complete that any ſpeculation ever exhibited, Ariſtotle infers that all concluſive ſyllogiſms whatever may be reduced to concluſive modes in the firſt figure[*]; of all which, the truth reſts immediately on the grammatical principle above explained; and of which, therefore, the ſyllogiſm already given may ſerve for an example. When the three terms of a ſyllogiſm, therefore, are accurately defined, and the three propoſitions compoſing it are properly arranged, the juſtneſs of its concluſion may always be perceived by a rapid glance of the mind diſcerning, by means of the minor premiſs, or the propoſition in which the ſubject of the concluſion is compared with the middle term, whether the major premiſs, or propoſition in which the predicate of the concluſion is compared with the ſame middle term, neceſſarily infers the concluſion. For enabling the mind readily to draw this inference in the caſe of all ſyllogiſms whatever, whether their concluſions be affirmative or negative, univerſal or particular, and how awkwardly ſoever their terms may have been arranged, the Author

[*] Comp. Analyt. Prior. c. vii. p. 60. and c. xxiii. p. 79.

CHAP. II.

Author has recourſe to no other rules or axioms than thoſe which concern what is called converſion and oppoſition; and that moſt extenſive principle of reaſon which infers the truth of any propoſition by ſhewing, that to ſuppoſe it falſe leads to an abſurdity. To convert a propoſition, is to make its ſubject and its predicate change places. This may often be done ſafely, becauſe in many propoſitions the converſe will retain that truth which was in the propoſition to be converted. All univerſal negatives, for example, can always be completely converted. If no A is B, no B is A; for if B could be predicated of any thing called A, for example of C, then C would fall under the names both of A and of B, which is contrary to the firſt ſuppoſition, that no A is B; or that B cannot be predicated of any thing called A [a]. When one term, therefore, is univerſally denied of another, that other may, without heſitation, be univerſally denied of the firſt. An univerſal affirmative propoſition does not admit of a complete converſion, becauſe, according to what was formerly obſerved, in every ſuch propoſition the predicate muſt apply to all the ſpecies and individuals expreſſed by the name of the ſubject, but the ſubject needs not therefore apply to all the ſpecies and individuals contained under the name of the predicate. But an univerſal affirmative, though it rejects a complete, yet admits of a partial converſion. Thus if every A is B, ſome B muſt be A; for if no B is A, then no A is B, as juſt proved in the caſe of univerſal negatives. Particular affirmatives admit of a complete converſion; for if ſome A is B, then ſome B is A; ſince, when no B is A, no A is B, as formerly proved in the caſe of univerſal negatives. Particular negatives do not at all admit of converſion, either complete or partial

Rules of converſion.

[a] Analyt. Prior. c. ii. p. 52

partial. Thus, ſome A is not B cannot be converted by ſaying that ſome B is not A, becauſe, though the name of a ſpecies does not apply to ſome things comprehended under the name of its genus, it does not thence follow that the name of the genus does not apply to all the individuals comprehended under the name of the ſpecies[b]. The rules concerning conversion then are, that univerſal negatives, as well as particular affirmatives, may be converted completely; that univerſal affirmatives can only be converted partially; and that particular negatives are totally incapable of converſion. Theſe rules, perhaps, may all be reſolved into one and the ſame primitive truth, of which they are only different expreſſions; yet theſe different expreſſions will on many occaſions render the perception of that truth more diſtinct, and the application of it more eaſy as well as more expeditious. The ſame thing holds here, as with reſpect to the axioms of geometry, concerning the whole and its parts, equality and inequality, greater and leſſer, ſince the comprehenſion of any one of thoſe terms neceſſarily implies the comprehenſion of them all. Yet geometers find it uſeful to repreſent the ſame elementary truth under a variety of forms, that it may be more forcibly impreſſed, and more readily applied; and

[b] The doctrines of Ariſtotle's Organon have been ſtrangely perplexed by confounding the grammatical principles on which that work is built with mathematical axioms. All the modern ſyſtems of logic that have fallen into my hands, employ in demonſtrating the theory of ſyllogiſm theſe two axioms, "Things agreeing with the ſame third agree with each other:" "When one thing agrees with the third, and the other does not, they do not agree with each other." But Ariſtotle tells us, that theſe axioms do not at all apply to the predication of terms, the one of the other; except when thoſe terms denote mathematical quantities. The reaſon why they do apply to mathematical quantities he ſays is, becauſe in them, ἡ ισοτης, ἑνοτης, "equality is ſameneſs;" and in them, equality is ſameneſs, becauſe ὁ λογος ὁ της πρωτης ουσιας εἱς εστι. The definition of any particular object denoted by the one, is preciſely the ſame with the definition of any particular object denoted by the other. Metaph. l. x. c. iii. p. 845.

CHAP. II.

and the indefinite number of mathematical theorems ultimately refolve themfelves into a few fimple propofitions, which may themfelves perhaps be confidered as only different expreffions of one and the fame original conception of the mind.

Rules of oppofition.

Upon this great principle of tranflating the fame truth into different words, in order to render it more familiar to our thoughts, Ariftotle next examines the doctrine of oppofition. Propofitions may be oppofite or contrary, which are not contradictory; becaufe the truth of the one does not always infer the falfehood of the other. Thus, "all men are white," "no man is white," are contrary propofitions, and both of them falfe. "Some men are white," "fome men are not white," are contrary propofitions, and both of them true. But if I fay, "all men are white," "fome men are not white," the truth of the one propofition infers the falfehood of the other; becaufe in this laft cafe only the predicate "whitenefs" is affirmed of the whole fpecies, and denied of fome individuals belonging to it; which is inconfiftent with the great principle on which all language and all reafoning is founded [e].

In

[e] De Interpret. c. vii. p. 39. & feq. and Analyt. Prior. c. xv. p. 117. & feq. To fhew how grofsly Ariftotle's logic has been miftaken, and with what contempt of reafon and grammar, as well as of good manners, the character of this philofopher has been affailed, I fhall cite the following paffage from a late author (Lord Kaims) of confiderable reputation, and of very confiderable merit: "His (Ariftotle's) artificial mode of reafoning is no lefs fuperficial than intricate. The propofitions he attempts to prove by fyllogifm are all felf-evident. Take for example the following propofition, 'that man has the power of felf-motion.' To prove this, he affumes the following maxim, upon which indeed every one of his fyllogifms are founded, 'that whatever is true of a number of particulars joined together holds true of every one feparately." Lord Kaims' Sketches, vol. iii. p. 306. It would have been charitable in this acute author to have pointed out the paffage where Ariftotle maintains, that becaufe it is true of a number of particulars joined together, that they are an hundred or a thoufand, the fame holds true of every one of them feparately. It is impoffible to reftrain indignation at fuch unmeaning jargon, poured out againft the moft accurate of all writers.

CHAP. II.

The design of Aristotle's first Analytics misunderstood.

In the first Analytics, Aristotle shews what is that arrangement of terms in each proposition, and that arrangement of propositions in each syllogism, which constitutes a necessary connection between the premisses and the conclusion. When this connection takes place, the syllogism is perfect in point of form; and when the form is perfect, the conclusion necessarily follows from the premisses, whatever be the signification of the terms of which they are composed. These terms, therefore, he commonly expresses by the letters of the alphabet, for the purpose of shewing that our assent to the conclusion results, not from comparing the things signified, but merely from considering the relation which the signs (whether words or letters) bear to each other. Those [a], therefore, totally misconceive the meaning of Aristotle's logic, who think that, by employing letters instead of words, he has darkened the subject; since the more abstract and general his signs are, they must be the better adapted to shew that the inference results from considering them alone, without at all regarding the things which they signify.

His second Analytics.

The *form* of syllogisms may be perfect when there is much imperfection in their *matter;* that is, in the premisses from which the conclusion is derived; and which may be either certain or probable, or only seem to be probable, as a face may seem to be beautiful which is only painted. In his second Analytics, Aristotle treats of what he calls Demonstrative Syllogisms, because their premisses are certain. In his Topics, he treats of what he calls Dialectical Syllogisms, because their premisses are only

[a] A truly respectable philosopher says, in speaking of this subject, "Aristotle's rules are illustrated, or rather in my opinion purposely darkened, by putting letters of the alphabet for the several terms." Reid's Appendix to Kaims's Sketches, vol. iii. p. 631.

CHAP. II.

only probable; and, in his Refutations of Sophiſtry, he treats of thoſe deceitful ſyllogiſms whoſe premiſſes ſeem to be, but which are not really, probable. As ſophiſtry conſiſts, not only in reaſoning from falſe principles, but in reaſoning unfairly from principles that are true, the Author refers all ſuch erroneous deductions to one head, which he calls "a miſtake of the queſtion;" becauſe, in all of them, the "concluſion or anſwer" will be found to come out otherwiſe than it ought to do when drawn agreeably to the rules of juſt inference[c].

His Topics.

The four claſſes of predicates above explained, Genus, Difference, Property, and Appendage, are applicable to ſingle things or ſingle terms, conſidered ſeparately; there are other predicates which are applicable only to more things or more terms than one, conſidered conjunctly. Theſe conjunct predicates the Author reduces to four claſſes; Agreement, Diverſity, Oppoſition, and Order; under which heads, as well as thoſe firſt-mentioned, he examines in his Topics all the probable arguments by which our affirmations or negations may be either confirmed or invalidated; thus ſupplying a vaſt intellectual magazine, which, when compared with the ſlender additions made to it by ſubſequent writers, atteſts both the unwearied ardour of his application, and the incomparable richneſs of his invention.

His Organon perverted and miſapplied.

In as few words as ſeemed conſiſtent with perſpicuity, I have thus endeavoured to explain the nature and deſign of Ariſtotle's Organon; a work which has often been as ſhamefully miſrepreſented, as it was long moſt groſsly miſapplied. In that ſcholaſtic jargon, which inſolently uſurped during many centuries the name

[c] De Sophiſt. Elench. c. vi. p. 287.

name of Philosophy, syllogisms were perverted to purposes for which their inventor declares them totally unfit, and employed on subjects in which his uniform practice shews that he considered them as altogether useless. Our acquaintance with the properties of things, he perpetually inculcates, must be acquired by patient observation, generalised by comparison and induction; but when this foundation is once laid, the words by which our generalizations are expressed, deserve not merely to be regarded as the materials in which our knowledge is embodied, or the channels by which it is communicated, but to be considered in the two following respects, as the principles or sources from which new knowledge may be derived. First, by means of a skilful arrangement of accurate and well-chosen terms, many processes of reasoning may be performed by discerning the relations and analogies of words, with a certainty as great, and with a rapidity far greater, than these processes could possibly be carried on, were we obliged, in every step of our progress, to fix our attention on things. Every general term is considered by Aristotle as the abridgment of a definition[f], and every definition is denominated by him a Collection[g], because it is the result always of observation and comparison, and often of many observations and many comparisons. The improvements in mathematics have advanced from age to age, chiefly by improving the language, that is, the signs, by which mathematical truths are expressed; and the most important discoveries have been made in that noble science, by continually simplifying the objects of our comparisons; or, in other

Its real uses. 1. As an analytic art.

[f] διαφερει δε ουδεν, ουδ᾽ ει πλειω τις φαιη σημαινειν, μονον δε ώρισμενα. τεθειη γαρ αν᾽ επ᾽ ἑκαστῳ λογῳ, ἑτερον ονομα. Metaph. l. iv. c. iv. p. 873.

[g] ει δε μη τεθειη, αλλ᾽ απειρα σημαινειν φαιη, φανερον ὁτι ουκ αν ειη λογος. Ibid.

CHAP. II.

other words, by finding clear expreffions for ratios, including the refults of many others. In all other fciences, this inveftigation is of the utmoft importance; and, in many of them, our knowledge will be found to advance almoft exactly in proportion to the fuccefs with which our language is improved. When terms, therefore, are formed and applied with that propriety which perpetually fhines in the Stagirite's writings, his general formulas of reafoning afford an analytic art, which may be employed as an engine for raifing new truths on thofe previoufly eftablifhed; and if modern languages do not afford the fame advantage precifely in the fame degree, it is not from the inefficacy of words as figns, but from the inefficacy of figns ill chofen and ill arranged; from impropriety of application, contempt of analogy, and abufe of metaphor.

As ftrengthening the affociating principles, and thereby multiplying the energies of thought.

Under another afpect, nearly connected with the former, yet really diftinct from it, Ariftotle's Analytics, and ftill more his Topics, have the moft direct and moft efficacious tendency to invigorate and fharpen the underftanding; and even to animate and cherifh the feeds of invention and genius. The properties and relations of external objects, whether actually prefent to the fenfes, or treafured up in the memory, are confined, both as to their kind and number, within narrow limits. But our abftractions, comparifons, and conclufions refpecting thofe objects, expreffed and embodied in words, are of a much wider and almoft boundlefs extent. According to that law of mental action by which our Author proves that the current of thought is moved and regulated [h], the relations and analogies of words

[h] See the remarks above made concerning what is commonly called "the affociation of ideas." "Ideas are more powerfully affociated," (to ufe modern language,) "in proportion to the attention with which they are fimultaneoufly examined and obferved."

words, therefore, will appear to form the main ſpring of intellectual energy; and their connections and dependencies, as compared and claſſed by Ariſtotle in his Topics, muſt have a direct tendency to invigorate and expand the thinking faculty; to revive and brighten thoſe aſſociating bands that might otherwiſe have been effaced; to ſuggeſt thoſe principles of reaſoning which would not otherwiſe occur; and thus to prevent that deception and error which moſt commonly proceeds from partial and incomplete views of our ſubject; from weakneſs of combination, and narrowneſs of comprehenſion. To ſay, therefore, that this part of our Author's Works is converſant entirely about *words*, is not to depreciate or reproach it; for Ariſtotle well knew that our knowledge of *things* chiefly depending on the proper application of language as an inſtrument[1] of thought, the true art of reaſoning is nothing but a language accurately defined and ſkilfully arranged; an opinion which, after many idle declamations againſt his barren generalities and verbal trifling, philoſophers have begun very generally to adopt. Let it always, however, be remembered, that the Author who firſt taught this doctrine, had previouſly endeavoured to prove that all our notions, as well as the ſigns by which they are expreſſed, originate in perceptions of ſenſe; and

obſerved." In Ariſtotle's language, the action of thought depends on the attentive examination of things, and of words which are their ſigns. When not only the things themſelves, but the ſigns expreſſing them, are thus examined, the connections between theſe things will take faſter hold of the mind; the perception of them will be more vivid, and the recollection of them more eaſy and more expeditious. But words are the ſigns not merely of perceptible objects and their qualities, but of the compariſons, abſtractions, and concluſions of the mind with reſpect to thoſe objects and their qualities. An attentive examination of the relations and analogies of words ſerves, therefore, not only to ſtrengthen old aſſociations, but to produce many new ones.

[1] Topic, l. i. c. 15. Metaph. ubi ſupra, and l. v. paſſim.

CHAP. II.

and that the principles on which languages are first constructed, as well as every step in their progress to perfection, all ultimately depend on inductions from observation; in one word, on experience merely.

Of Truth Demonstrative.

To abridge Aristotle's Works is to treat them unfairly, because (where his text is correct) no author expresses his meaning in fewer or more appropriate words. Yet, as it is the purpose of this discourse to afford such specimens of every part of his writings, as may satisfy the curiosity of one class of readers, while it augments or inspires that of another, I shall collect within a narrow compass his observations on Truth Demonstrative, that is, on Science; and follow him in his application of those principles to the loftiest, and, as commonly treated, the most abstruse science, that ever exercised the human intellect.

All instruction, and all intellectual discipline, he observes, proceeds on principles already known and established. This is manifestly the case in mathematics, in the arts, and in every kind of reasoning, which is universally carried on either by syllogism or by induction; the former proving to us, that a particular proposition is true, because it is deducible from a general one, already known to us; and the latter demonstrating a general truth, because it holds in all particular cases. Orators persuade by examples or arguments, examples being a rhetorical or coarser kind of induction, as arguments are a rhetorical or coarser kind of syllogism.

Wherein it consists.

Truth is the exact conformity of human conception with the real nature of things[k]. Demonstrative truth, therefore, can apply

[k] το δε κυριωτατον ον, αληθες η ψευδος· τυτο δ' επι των πραγματων εςι συγκεισθαι η διαιρεισθαι . . εψευςαι δε ὁ εναντιως εχων, η τα πραγματα ποτε εςι, η υκ εςι. Metaph. l. ix. c. x. p. 941. Vid. etiam Metaph. l. v. c. xxix. p. 901.

CHAP. II.

apply only to thoſe things which neceſſarily exiſt after a certain manner, and whoſe ſtate is unalterable: and we know thoſe things when we know their cauſes: thus, we know a mathematical propoſition, when we know the cauſes that make it true; that is, when we know all the intermediate propoſitions up to the firſt principles, or axioms, on which it is ultimately built. Demonſtration cannot be indefinitely extended, becauſe the certainty, and even probability of every kind of reaſoning would be deſtroyed, were we to call in queſtion thoſe firſt principles which, in matters of ſcience, are recogniſed by what Ariſtotle calls Intellect, and in matters of practice by what he calls Common Senſe [1].

Rules concerning it.

In demonſtration, the premiſſes are the cauſes of the concluſion, and therefore prior to it. We cannot, therefore, demonſtrate things in a circle, ſupporting the premiſſes by the concluſion; becauſe this would be to ſuppoſe, that the one propoſition could be both prior and poſterior to the other. In all demonſtration, the firſt principles muſt be neceſſary, immutable, and therefore eternal truths, becauſe thoſe qualities could not belong to the concluſion, unleſs they belonged to the premiſſes, which are its cauſes. An affirmative demonſtration is preferable to a negative one, and a direct demonſtration of any truth to that drawn from the abſurdity of ſuppoſing it falſe; becauſe, other things remaining the ſame, the ſhorteſt demonſtration is always the beſt. Ariſtotle debates the queſtion, whether an univerſal demonſtration is better than a particular one; and, as his remarks on this ſubject form an apology for the univerſality and abſtractedneſs of his own reaſonings in many parts of his Works,

[1] αλλα αισθησις ουχ ἡ των ιδιων. Ethic. Nicom. c. vi. p. 8.

CHAP. II.

Universal and particular; which preferable.

Works, I shall subjoin a translation, or paraphrase, of the whole chapter[a]. "1st, To some a particular demonstration may seem preferable, because we know any object better by examining itself, than by examining the class to which it belongs. Thus, that the three angles of an isoskeles triangle are equal to two rights, may be thought more convincing when proved with regard to the isoskeles itself, than when proved with regard to triangles in general, to which class of figures the isoskeles belongs; and therefore the particular demonstration may appear better than a general one. 2d, If individuals only have a real existence in nature, and every demonstration supposes the existence of its subject, a general demonstration must be worse than a particular one, because it leads us to suppose the existence of nonentities.

The former more informing and more satisfactory.

In answer to these objections let it be remarked, that the first does not apply, because if the property of having the three angles equal to two rights belongs to the isoskeles, not as it is an isoskeles, but as it is a triangle, he who demonstrates this truth respecting the isoskeles only, less examines the object in itself, than he who demonstrates the same truth respecting triangles in general: for the definition of a triangle enters into that of an isoskeles; and because it is a triangle, the isoskeles has its angles equal to two rights; so that he who demonstrates universally, better shews the cause and reason of the conclusion, than he who demonstrates particularly; and he shews it from considering the object itself, that is, the definition of the object, and that part of the definition from which the conclusion results. Again, if universals are merely words, denoting certain classes or species, to all the individuals of which they equally apply,

[a] Analytic Posterior, l. i. c. xxiv. p. 154, &. seq.

apply, there is no reason to say that they are nonentities when applied to those objects or individuals. Their existence is even firmer than that of any *portion* of the individuals signified by them, which is continually liable to corruption or change; whereas the general name denoting the whole species is not liable to either, but has a precise and permanent meaning as long as any objects of that species continue to exist. But to suppose that universals, because they are employed in demonstration, have any existence independently of the objects or individuals which they denote, is a mistake chargeable, not on those who employ such terms, but on those who misconceive their use[a].

The more universal the demonstration of any proposition is rendered, it becomes at the same time the more informing and the

[a] Had the learned Lord Monboddo proceeded to read this sentence, perhaps he would not have quoted that immediately preceding it, to prove that Aristotle thought, that "ideas, considered as in the divine mind, have an existence, and an existence more real than particulars, because they are eternal and unchangeable." Monboddo's Ancient Metaphysics, vol. i. p. 470.

Aristotle speaks with great caution concerning the divine mind, nor ever says that any thing exists *in* it. Of ideas or examplars he speaks often, and always contemptuously, as of metaphors and vain flourishes. Analyt. Post. l. i. c. xxii. p. 151. Metaph. l. i. c. vii. p. 853. So that it is plain what he would have thought of the distinction, προ των πολλων, η τοις πολλοις, επι τοις πολλοις; which was adopted by his followers, and is so much insisted on, as the great doctrine of the Peripatetics, by Lord Monboddo and Mr. Harris. The following passage may be quoted to shew what Aristotle thought of the προ των πολλων; "those eternal exemplars." αυτο γαρ ανθρωπον φασιν ειναι, και αυτο ἱππον και ὑγιειαν, αλλο δε ουδεν· παραπλησιον μεν ποιουντες τοις θεους μεν ειναι φασκουσι ανθρωποειδεις δε. ουτε γαρ εκεινοι ουδεν αλλο εποιουν η ανθρωπους αιδιους, ουτε ουτοι τα ειδη αλλα η αισθητα αιδια. "They who maintained the eternal existence of such exemplars, as the ideas of man, horse, health, acted exactly like to those who maintained there were Gods, but that the Gods were of a human shape. The Gods of such theologians were nothing more than eternal or incorruptible men; and the ideas of such philosophers nothing more than eternal or incorruptible objects of sense." Metaphys. l. iii. c. xi. p. 861.

CHAP. II.

the more ſatisfactory; the more informing, becauſe it comprehends the greater number of particular truths; and the more ſatisfactory, becauſe it demonſtrates theſe truths from their firſt and ultimate cauſe; at leaſt, approximates nearer to this cauſe in exact proportion to its greater univerſality. To deſcend from generals is alſo more natural; becauſe, in matters of ſcience, they are the ſource and fountain of particulars. It has alſo more dignity, becauſe generals are the work of intellect, whereas the more particular propoſitions are, the more nearly they approach to perceptions of ſenſe, in which, when ſtrictly particular, they ultimately terminate.

Ariſtotle's Metaphyſics

From this part of Ariſtotle's Logic, there is an eaſy tranſition to what has been called his Metaphyſics; a name unknown, as above obſerved, to the Author himſelf, and given to his moſt abſtract philoſophical works by his editors, from an opinion that thoſe books ought to be ſtudied immediately after his Phyſics, or Treatiſes on Natural Philoſophy. Conſidered under one particular aſpect, thoſe books may be properly thus arranged [a]; becauſe, as we ſhall ſee hereafter, the ſtudy of nature, conducted according to Ariſtotle's principles, neceſſarily leads to Deity, and to the moſt delightful of all contemplations, that of the Divine Goodneſs. But, viewed in the full extent of their relations, Ariſtotle's Metaphyſics are intimately connected with every branch of human ſcience, whether natural or moral, ſince their real ſubject (which has been groſsly miſtaken through a prepoſterous arrangement of the treatiſes which they compriſe) is the vindication of the exiſtence and nature of truth againſt the cavils of Sophiſts, and thoſe now called Metaphyſicians;

extend to every branch of human ſcience.

[a] Topic, l. i. c. 2.

CHAP. II.

ſicians; and this doctrine concerning truth illuſtrated in the demonſtration of the being of one God, in oppoſition to Atheiſts on one hand, and Polytheiſts on the other. The whole of Ariſtotle's metaphyſical works may be referred to one or other of thoſe two heads; ſince to them the greater part of his treatiſes relate immediately, and the ſmaller part will appear to be merely preparatory, to their diſcuſſion.

Begin with a Philoſophical Vocabulary.

The unſkilfulneſs of his editors [p] has placed near the middle of the work, a book plainly preparatory, ſince it merely exhibits the different acceptation of the terms of which he has occaſion afterwards to make uſe. This fifth book of his Metaphyſics, which ought undoubtedly to ſtand as the firſt, contains in thirty chapters, an accurate philoſophical vocabulary, which Ariſtotle thought peculiarly requiſite as an introduction to the firſt and moſt comprehenſive [q] of all ſciences, that of which truth in general was the ſubject, ſince the terms employed in it having neceſſarily a variety of meanings, it was impoſſible to uſe thoſe ſigns properly, without preciſely aſcertaining the things which they ſignified. Wonder and admiration, he obſerves, are the paſſions naturally excited by the contemplation of the univerſe, whoſe ſublime obſcurity, while it fixes the attention, inflames the curioſity of man, and makes him ambitious to know and comprehend ſo intereſting and magnificent a ſpectacle. But it is impoſſible to know any thing without

[p] Dr. Morton of the Britiſh Muſeum, who has long ſtudied the writings of Ariſtotle with equal diligence and ſucceſs, firſt ſhewed to me, that Samuel Petit, in the fourth book of his *Miſcellanea*, had already placed Ariſtotle's Metaphyſics in nearly the ſame order in which I alſo had arranged them.

[q] αλλα ἡ μεν γεωμετρια και ἡ αστρολογια περι τινα φυσιν ιδιαν εισι· εκεινη δε (ἡ πρωτη φιλοσοφια, ſeu θεολογικη,) καθολυ πασων κοινη. Metaphyſ. l. vi. c. i. p. 904.

CHAP. II.

illustrated in words, cause or principle.

without knowing its causes and principles. Aristotle, therefore, begins his vocabulary with an explanation of those terms; he observes, that all causes are principles; and defines a principle to be that from which any thing exists, is made, or is known. The notion of a cause always includes that of priority, which is the specific quality belonging to all the different acceptations of the word principle. Aristotle enumerates four kinds of causes, the same word being taken in Greek in four different meanings. 1. The material cause, that is, the matter from which any thing is made; as brass of the statue, and silver of the goblet; and which are evidently causes, since, independently of them, neither the statue nor the goblet could exist. The brass and the silver have also their material causes, namely the substances from which those metals are composed; and in the works both of nature and of art, the first component substances, which are so simple as not to admit of any further resolution, are called Elements. 2. The formal cause, which is that specific form or shape, or quality, most commonly distinguished by sight, which characterises each particular object, and gives to it an appropriate nature and essence. It is from their agreement in the same form or essence, that different objects receive a common name; of which name, this form or essence is therefore the proper definition. In losing their appropriate form, objects lose their name and nature; this form, therefore, is a cause of those objects, since, independently of it, they would not be at all, or would not continue to exist. 3. The efficient cause is the principle of motion or change; or, in other words, the maker; which term sufficiently explains itself. 4. The final cause, that is, the end or purpose for which any thing is made, and, independently of which

The material, formal, efficient, final.

CHAP. II.

which end or purpofe, the maker could not have exerted his power or fkill; and therefore his work would never have commenced; that is, the thing made would never have exifted[1]. Of thefe four caufes, the two firft are always inherent in the object caufed: in works of art, the two laft caufes are always feparate from this object; we fhall fee in the fequel, whether this is alfo the cafe with refpect to the works of nature.

The fecond book confiders words as ftanding in oppofition to each other.

Ariftotle's enumeration of the different meanings of the word "caufe," which muft be carefully diftinguifhed in all parts of his philofophy, may ferve as a fpecimen of that book, which was intitled "An Explanation of Words with various Significations." That book is naturally followed by the tenth, which ought therefore to ftand as the fecond; becaufe, in it, words are confidered, not fimply in themfelves, but as ftanding in the relation of oppofition or contrariety to each other. It is briefly intitled "The Selection of Contraries," and treats of one and many; likenefs and unlikenefs; contraries in the fame genus, as "white" and "black;" and contraries which are not in the fame genus, as "corruptible" and "incorruptible." The firft kind of contraries may fubfift at different times in the fame fubject;

[1] Juftnefs of thought is infeparably connected with propriety of language. The feveral caufes enumerated by Ariftotle, the names of which found awkwardly in Englifh, were expreffed briefly in Greek, each by a particular prepofition. The material was the ἐξ οὗ; the formal, the καθ' ὅ; the efficient, the ὑφ' οὗ; and the final, the διὰ ὅ: befides which, the Greeks indicated the means, or inftrument, by which any thing is done, or made, by διὰ οὗ; and the model after which it was made, by πρὸς ὅ. This model, or exemplar, was confidered as a caufe by the Pythagoreans and Platonifts; the former of whom maintained, that all perceptible things were imitations of *numbers*; and the latter, that they owed their exiftence to the participation of *ideas*: but wherein either this imitation or this participation confifted, thefe philofophers, Ariftotle obferves, omitted to fhew.

CHAP. II.

ſubject; the ſecond, never can; becauſe the firſt kind are merely appendages to the ſubject in which they ſubſiſt, and may therefore be ſeparated from it; but the ſecond are eſſentials[a].

The third book treats of ſcience.

The ſecond and fourth books treat of truth and ſcience; they ought to be conſidered as one, and to ſtand the third in order; ſince they naturally follow the definitions laid down in the firſt and ſecond. His treatiſe on ſcience opens with great modeſty. Its difficulty, he obſerves, ariſes not merely from the ſubject, but from ourſelves, whoſe intellectual ſight (as happens to the eyes of bats) is blinded by what is brighteſt. Much thanks are due, not only to thoſe who have eſtabliſhed truths worthy of being adopted, but to thoſe alſo who have given us opinions worthy of being conſidered. They ſet our faculties to work; and even their errors are uſeful to their ſucceſſors. Had Phrynis never lived, we ſhould not now enjoy the charming melodies of his ſcholar Timotheus[b].

Of ſpeculative philoſophy, truth is the end; and each object participates of truth more or leſs, in proportion as it more or leſs participates of reality. Truth, therefore, is to be found in things eternal and unalterable, rather than in their contraries; becauſe ſuch things are not dependent for their reality on other things, but all others on them.

There cannot be an infinite progreſſion of cauſes.

There muſt be ſome principle or firſt cauſe of whatever really exiſts; for if this were not the caſe, there would be an infinite progreſſion of cauſes. But this infinite progreſſion is impoſſible: 1. With regard to material cauſes; that fleſh, for inſtance, ſhould be made of earth, earth of air, air of fire; and that to this

[a] Metaphyſ. l. x. c. ix. and x. p. 951. & ſeq. [b] Metaphyſ. l. ii. c. i. p. 856.

this ſeries of productions there ſhould be no end. 2. As to the efficient cauſe or principle of motion; that man, for inſtance, ſhould be actuated by the air, the air moved by the ſun, the ſun by ſtrife, in endleſs ſucceſſion. 3. As to the final cauſe; that exerciſe, for inſtance, ſhould be taken for the ſake of health, and health choſen for the ſake of happineſs, and happineſs itſelf for the ſake of ſome farther object. 4. As to the formal cauſe; that the characteriſing properties of things ſhould be derived one from the other without ultimately terminating in one common ſource. For in all thoſe four caſes alike, to ſuppoſe an infinite ſucceſſion of cauſes, is to ſay that things exiſt without any cauſe at all; ſince, in this infinite chain, every link is merely the effect of the link preceding it, and when the chain is endleſs, there is no firſt link, and therefore no cauſe. Were we deſired to tell which of three things is the cauſe of the other two, we ſhould name the firſt of the three. We could not ſay the laſt, for it is the cauſe of nothing; neither could we ſay the ſecond, for it is the cauſe of one thing only; and though conſidered in relation to that one, it be really a cauſe; yet conſidered in relation to the whole, it is merely an effect; and in the ſame manner all the intermediate links are effects, how numerous ſoever they may be ſuppoſed. The very term "final cauſe" expreſſes an end and boundary; and if there was not ſomething ultimately deſirable on its own account, for the ſake of which other things are deſirable as means, all deſire and all volition would neceſſarily ceaſe; and all intellection would be deſtroyed, if the properties of things could be continually traced up to other properties ſtill more eſſential; that is, if formal cauſes might be traced back in infinite progreſſion, there

 would

CHAP. II.

would be no firmneſs for the intellect to reſt on; in other words, no underſtanding [l].

The exiſtence of truth vindicated.

Democritus had ſaid, that truth either did not exiſt; or that, by man at leaſt, it was not to be diſcovered. In the ſame ſpirit of ſcepticiſm, Protagoras maintained that man was the meaſure of all things; which were true or falſe, good or bad, merely according to his conception of them. It is melancholy, Ariſtotle obſerves, to hear thoſe who might be expected beſt to ſee what is true, ſince they moſt ſought and loved it, maintain ſuch opinions; becauſe, were they well founded, to aim at philoſophy would be to court diſappointment, and to purſue truth as puerile a folly as that of attempting to catch birds in their flight. But the misfortune of thoſe philoſophers is, that they confine their inquiries merely to ſenſible and ſublunary objects, which from their own nature, as well as that of the ſenſes by which they are perceived, are indefinite and variable, liable to decay and corruption, and continually appearing under different aſpects to different men; and even to the ſame man, according to the point from which he views them, and the actual diſpoſition of his organs. But theſe variations as to the objects of perception by ſenſe, take place chiefly in ſublunary things, the whole maſs of which is ſo inconſiderable in magnitude, that it bears not any proportion to the univerſe at large, where all is permanent and invariable, and the ſtability of whoſe arrangement ought to convince us, that there is an eternal arranging cauſe [m], and ſome manner at leaſt of firmneſs and conſtancy in the

[l] ἡ νοησις εοικεν ηρεμησει τινι και επιστασει, μαλλον η κινησει. De Anim. l. i. c. 3. νοησαι δε ουκ εστι μη στησαντα. Metaphyſ. l. ii. c. ii. p. 857.

[m] πως γαρ εσται ταξις, μη τινος οντος αιδιου, &c. p. 983. Natural. Auſcult. l. ii. c. vi. p. 335. and c. iv. p. 332.

the world by which we are surrounded[x]. Even here, it belongs to the eye to judge of colours, to the ear to judge of founds, and to the other fenfes to judge of their refpective objects; and they judge exactly alike, when fimilarly difpofed and fimilarly circumftanced. If fublunary things are generated, and perifh, there muft be fome material caufe from which they are generated; and fomething that exifts immutably, even while the deftruction of one fubftance is the production of another. The fceptics are not convinced by their own arguments. None of them, while in Libya, becaufe he can conceive himfelf in Athens, thinks of walking into the Odeum[y]. They confide more in their eyes, with regard to near than remote objects. As to taftes and colours, they prefer the judgment of perfons in health to thofe of perfons in ficknefs; and when they are themfelves indifpofed, they will have more confidence in the prediction of a phyfician than in that of a perfon ignorant of the healing art. But fenfible objects are neither the whole nor the principal of things. There are, as fhall be proved hereafter, exiftences firm and immoveable, and altogether imperceptible to corporeal organs. That our fenfes do not fhew us things as they really are, is perhaps true, but that there fhould not be fome caufe of our fenfation, exifting independently of the fenfations themfelves, is impoffible; becaufe, whatever is produced by motion fuppofes a moving power[z], which exifts independently, and is prior to the thing moved, in the order of caufality and nature[a].

It

[x] Metaph. l. iv. c. v. p. 879.

[y] The Theatre of Mufic at Athens. [z] Idem ibid.

[a] The moving power does not infer the exiftence of the thing moved, μη αντιςρεφει κατα την τε ειναι ακολεθησιν, but the latter infers the former. Ariftot. Predicam.

CHAP. II.

It is the mifery of the fceptics ftill vainly to reafon, while they deftroy the only bafe on which all folid reafoning muft ftand. Some of them do this through ignorance, and others through obftinacy. The latter ftand in need, not of conviction, but correction, for the oppofers of fome truths ought to be chaftifed, not confuted; as thofe who deny that we ought to reverence the Gods, or to refpect our parents. But it is the groffeft ignorance not to know, that all truths cannot be demonftrated; for it is impoffible that demonftrations fhould run back to infinity, without ftopping at certain principles or firft truths, which are called felf-evident, becaufe more certain and more neceffary in themfelves than any arguments that could be produced in proof of them. To deny a firft caufe, we have already proved, is to deny all caufation: to deny axioms, is, for the fame reafon, to deny all demonftration, and to fubvert the principles on which both reafoning and language are built [b]. The very nature of words infers, that the things fignified by them, have a certain determinate mode of exiftence; for words, even the moft comprehenfive, are nothing elfe than figns denoting that certain properties are characteriftic of certain fubjects. How numerous foever thefe properties may be, provided they be not infinite, they are ftill capable of being collected under one name; but if the properties were totally indefinite, there could not be any collection. Each term, therefore, affirms fomething definitely refpecting the object which it denotes [c]; and to fay with the fceptics, truth is merely apparent, or that the fame thing may be both affirmed and denied

[b] Metaph. l. iv. c. iv. p. 874.

[c] ὁ γαρ λογος, οὗ τὸ ονομα σημειον, ορισμος γιγνεται του πραγματος, p. 881.

denied concerning the ſame object at the ſame time, is to maintain that it is impoſſible for man, either to reaſon within himſelf, or to diſcourſe with his fellow-creatures [d]. CHAP. II.

The ſubject continued.

The exiſtence of truth may be evinced, from the various ſhades of error, which gradually receding from the regions of light, finally darken into perfect obſcurity. As truth conſiſts in the agreement of human conception with the nature of things, the brighteſt truths reſult from thoſe ſciences which treat of things ſimple and invariable. In this view, arithmetic and geometry have long held the pre-eminence. The geometer abſtracts from body heat and cold, hardneſs, ſoftneſs, gravity, levity, and all other perceptible contrarieties; and contemplates it only under the two properties of magnitude and continuity; concerning which he demonſtrates innumerable affections, aſcertaining either the magnitudes themſelves, or their proportions to each other. His theorems therefore are more convincing than thoſe of the natural philoſopher, whoſe ſpeculations are more complex [e], as comprehending a greater variety of objects. But there is a ſcience preceding geometry in ſimplicity as well as dignity; which, inſtead of contemplating properties and their affections, contemplates being and its

[d] δει τοινυν των ονοματων ἑκαϛον ειναι γνωριμον, και δηλουν ἑν τι, και μη πολλα, μονον δε ἑν· καν πλειονα σημαινη, φανερον ποιειν ἐφ' ὁ φερει τουνομα τουτων· ὁ δη λεγων ειναι τουτο, και μη ειναι, τουτο ὁ λεγει ειναι φησιν, ου φησιν. ωϛε ὁ σημαινει τουνομα, τουτο ου φησι σημαινειν, p. 984. When it is ſaid that each name ſhould denote one, Ariſtotle means ἑν, as explained p. 888. τα δε πρωτως λεγομενα ἑν, ὧν η ουσια μια· μια δε η συνεχεια η ειδει η λογῳ. That unity is aſcribed to things whoſe ſubſtance is one; one in continuity, form, or definition; one in form or appearance, is what our eyes tell us is one; one in definition, is what our reaſon tells us is one; the ſpecific quality being ſometimes viſible, ſometimes intelligible. See above, p. 66.

[e] ἀκριβεϛαται των επιϛημων αἱ μαλιϛα των πρωτων εισι· αἱ γαρ εξ ελαττονων ακριβεϛεραι των εκ προσθεσεως λεγομενων, οἱον αριθμητικη γεωμετριας, &c. p. 842.

CHAP. II.

its properties[f]. This ſcience may be juſtly called the firſt philoſophy, and theology: it may be called the firſt philoſophy, becauſe all other ſciences imply it, and borrow from it their principles[g]; and it may be called theology, becauſe all the claſſes of being, as quantity, quality, and relation, finally reſt on ſubſtance; and God is the firſt, the one neceſſary and independent ſubſtance, whoſe non-exiſtence implies a contradiction, and from contemplating whoſe nature our knowledge of being and its properties is ultimately derived[h].

Ariſtotle's introduction to his hiſtory of the firſt philoſophy, or theology.

Having given to his readers a glimpſe of this ſublime ſubject, our author proceeds in examining the principles of things according to his uſual method; firſt explaining the ſentiments of his predeceſſors in ſcience, before he endeavours to eſtabliſh his own ſyſtem. The book publiſhed as the firſt, and that publiſhed as the third, treat of principles; and together form only one diſcourſe, which ought to ſtand as book the fourth. The elaborate exordium of this book ſeems to account for its being conſidered as the beginning of the whole treatiſe. "That all men," our author obſerves, "are naturally fond of knowledge, is proved from the pleaſure which they univerſally take in the exerciſe of their ſenſes; which exerciſe they love on its own account, independently of any end or uſe. But of all our ſenſes, the ſight is that which we moſt delight to exerciſe, and that independently of its aſſiſtance in the buſineſs of life; for even when we have nothing to do, we prefer this exerciſe to all other employments; the cauſe of which is, that the eye affords to us more knowledge, and makes us acquainted with more of the

[f] Metaph. l. iv. c. i. p. 869. and Metaph. l. xiii. c. iii. p. 983.

[g] Metaph. l. iv. c. ii. p. 871. & ſeq.

[h] Metaph. l. iv. c. iii. p. 872.

the differences of things, than any of the other ſenſes. All animals are endowed with ſenſation; but in ſome only, ſenſation is followed by memory. Thoſe who are endowed with memory, are ſuſceptible of inſtruction; and even without inſtruction, (ſince incapable of hearing,) attain a wonderful degree of ſagacity, as appears in bees, and in ſome reſembling tribes. The powers of hearing and remembering infer the capacity of being taught by inſtruction as well as by experience; of which capacity inferior animals participate in a ſmall degree, but which in man is exalted into art and ſcience. His experience, alſo, ariſes from memory; many particular remembrances combining into our experience. From experience, again, both art and ſcience are derived; art being nothing more than the general reſult of various experience; as when we obſerve that a certain medicine is beneficial to Socrates, to Callias, and many others, we infer that it will alſo be ſo, to all others labouring under a ſimilar malady. In each particular caſe, therefore, we can aſſign a cauſe why the medicine ſhould be adminiſtered; and the man of art is preferred to the mere empiric, becauſe he can thus explain the reaſons of his practice, and communicate his ſkill to others. The practice of the empiric, however, may often be far more ſucceſsful; and even his ſkill in the healing art may be far greater; for if his knowledge is derived only from individuals, it is with individuals only he has to do. Arts, therefore, are admired rather for their ingenuity than utility; and the farther they are removed from the common uſes of life, our admiration of them is the greater. Such arts, indeed, are the lateſt in invention; for men muſt be provided with neceſſaries and accommodations, before they can attain that freedom of mind which is requiſite

CHAP. II.

for ſpeculation. The mathematical ſtudies, therefore, firſt aſſumed a ſyſtematic form among the prieſts of Egypt, who enjoyed independent leiſure. We make theſe obſervations to ſhow how men are led from ſenſe and memory to experience; from experience to art, and from practical arts to ſpeculative ſciences; till they finally reach the moſt lofty ſpeculations of all, concerning the firſt principles of the univerſe.

The nature and dignity of this ſcience.

The ſcience containing theſe ſpeculations is called wiſdom; and thoſe by whom it is cultivated, are eminently diſtinguiſhed as the wiſe. The particulars in which it differs from other ſciences are, that it is the moſt univerſal, the moſt difficult, the moſt accurate; and, merely for its own ſake, of all ſciences the moſt deſirable. It is the moſt univerſal, becauſe the knowledge of firſt principles is the ſource of all other knowledge; it is the moſt difficult, becauſe it is of all ſciences the fartheſt removed from ſenſation; it is the moſt accurate, becauſe its object is the moſt ſimple, being unaccompanied with any acceſſaries; as geometry is more ſimple than phyſics, and arithmetic than geometry. It is alſo the moſt deſirable on its own account, ſince in proportion as men poſſeſs all other goods of the mind and body, they become moſt ambitious of attaining this knowledge; which is coveted, loved, and ſought merely for itſelf, independently of any further end than the pleaſure of enjoying it. A freeman, in oppoſition to a ſlave, lives for himſelf, not for another; ſo this ſcience is of all the moſt liberal, terminating completely in itſelf. It may therefore be deemed above the rank of humanity, (ſince men are naturally ſlaves to innumerable wants,) and a ſcience fit only for gods; ſo that if the gods, as the poets ſay, are capable of envy, this ſcience ought to draw down the divine diſpleaſure on thoſe

who

who cultivate it. But the Divinity cannot poſſibly be ſubject to envy; and the poets, even by the common proverb, are acknowledged to be liars. This ſcience, therefore, is moſt valuable, becauſe, in two reſpects, the moſt divine; firſt, as the Divinity being a cauſe or principle, is therefore its object; ſecondly, as the Divinity, to whom the univerſe is but one great truth, alone fully comprehends it. Although all other ſciences are more neceſſary than this, yet none is better.

Its hiſtory.

With this preface Ariſtotle introduces his hiſtory of what he calls wiſdom, theology, and the firſt philoſophy; and then proceeds to ſhow that of the two great ſchools, the Ionian and the Italic, the philoſophers of the former were attentive ſolely to groſs material cauſes, whereas thoſe of the latter wandered in the chimerical regions of ideas and numbers; ſubſtituting for the real cauſes of things metaphyſical abſtractions, which were the mere creatures of their own intellect. The materialiſts differed widely from each other. Thales maintained water to be the firſt principle of things; probably, as our Author ſays, obſerving that the nouriſhment, as well as the ſeeds, of moſt natural objects are moiſt; and that heat, perhaps life, is produced by fermentation. He might alſo allege the opinions of divines and poets long before his own age, who conſidered Oceanus and Tethys as the fathers of generation; and who make the gods ſwear by Styx, that is by water, as the moſt to be revered of all things, becauſe the moſt ancient. Anaximenes and Diogenes perceived that water might be reſolved into air; and therefore maintained air to be the original principle of bodies. The cauſe of fire was defended by Hippaſus and Heracleitus, who ſaw all things expanded, animated, and revived by heat; and differing from each other in proportion as they

CHAP. II.

participated of the different degrees of the caloric, from the extreme of condenſation to that of rarefaction. Empedocles conſidering all theſe three ſubſtances as principles, added to them earth as a fourth principle; and called theſe four the elements, becauſe he ſuppoſed that all things were compoſed of them, that all things might be reſolved into them, and that they themſelves were ſimple, indeſtructible, and totally incapable of farther reſolution[1]. Anaxagoras introduced the obſcure doctrine of the omæomeria, or the production of bodies from indefinitely ſmall organic particles, exactly reſembling the bodies themſelves; and therefore maintained principles to be infinite.

In this inveſtigation, which reſpected only the material cauſe, philoſophers were naturally led to inquire what made theſe principles or elements (whether one, many, or infinite) change their actual ſtate. In works of art, they perceived that the materials were totally inactive; that the iron did not make itſelf into a ſaw, nor the braſs into a ſtatue. To anſwer this queſtion, ſome maintained, contrary to experience, that all things were one, and unalterable. Others aſcribed an active power to fire, which produced all the changes which we behold, by its operation on the other elements. But of the order and beauty which prevail in the univerſe, neither fire nor any ſimilar ſubſtance could be ſuſpected of being the cauſe; nor was it poſſible that ſuch regular effects ſhould reſult from blind chance. Philoſophers were again compelled therefore, by the force of truth itſelf, to look for ſome higher principle; when one, far wiſer than the reſt, like a ſober man among drunken babblers, pronounced mind to be the primary cauſe of the

Metaph. lib. i. c. iv. p. 844, & ſeq.

the beauty and harmony of the universe. This opinion was asserted in plain language by Anaxagoras of Clazomene; but the first author of it was his countryman Hermotimus[k]. Yet Anaxagoras himself, though he employs mind as a machine for making the world, introduces it, however, only when compelled by necessity; and prefers having recourse rather to every other cause in explaining the phænomena of nature[l].

Fifth book, concerning ideas as causes of the universe.

We shall not follow Aristotle further in examining the tenets of the Ionian school; much less are we inclined to enter into his sixth, seventh, and eleventh books; where he examines, with a degree of attention, of which the subject would now appear totally unworthy, the *numbers* of Pythagoras, and the *ideas* of Plato; those intellectual abstractions which the wildness of philosophy had converted into the primary causes of the universe; thus substituting shadows for realities. These three books properly constitute one, which ought to stand as the fifth, and be intitled, Concerning Ideas or Universals considered as Causes of the Universe.

The proper arrangement of the five remaining books.

In his eighth book, he explains his own doctrine concerning natural philosophy; that is, concerning things liable to motion or change; which subject is treated more fully in his eight books of Physicks, and in his treatise concerning Generation and Corruption. This eighth book ought therefore to stand as the sixth. The seventh book, which is now printed as the ninth, treats of Energy; a word, as we shall see, of mighty import in the Aristotelian philosophy; from the explanation of which he naturally passes to the three concluding books of his Metaphysics, the thirteenth, fourteenth, and twelfth, which treat of a being totally distinct from matter; necessary, eternal, infinite in

k Metaph. l. i. c. iii. p. 844.

l Ibid. l. i. c. iv. p. 844.

CHAP. II.

in perfection[l]; one ſubſtantially and numerically, the primary cauſe of motion, himſelf immoveable[m]. Theſe three laſt books, which ought to ſtand as the eighth, ninth, and tenth of what is now called his Metaphyſics, are intitled, by Ariſtotle himſelf, his Works concerning Philoſophy[n]; meaning thereby, as he elſewhere explains it, the firſt philoſophy or theology[o].

Ariſtotle's natural philoſophy.

In travelling over the vaſt ſpace which ſtill lies before us, we ſhall follow the order preſcribed by our Author; beginning therefore with the Philoſophy of Nature, which is treated in various parts of his works, where the ſame doctrines are repeated nearly in the ſame words. In his Analyſis of Material Objects, his reſearches penetrate far beyond thoſe vulgar and ſpurious elements, firſt propoſed by Empedocles, earth, water, fire, and air; which are ſo far from being ſimple and unalterable, that they may be converted with great faeility, and are in fact perpetually changing the one into the other[p]. But, in relation to human perception, Empedocles' diviſion is not without merit; ſince the ſenſe of touch, the moſt ſure and ſcientific of all our ſenſes, acquaints us with only four different qualities of bodies, diſtinguiſhed by the names hot, cold, moiſt, and dry. Ariſtotle endeavours to prove, by induction, that all other differences perceived by the touch, reſolve themſelves into theſe four; whereas no one of theſe four can be reſolved into any of the other three.

His analyſis of the ſuppoſed elements.

The qualities, therefore, above mentioned, may be regarded as the fitteſt for diſtinguiſhing the different kinds of bodies from each other; and theſe four qualities, in their moſt ſimple combination with each other, will thus form the characteriſtics[q] of the elements

[m] ἱν μεν αρα και λογῳ και αριθμῳ, το πρωτον κινουν ακινητον ον. See p. 1001 and 1003.

[n] Ethic. Eadem, l. i. c. viii.

[o] Metaphyſics, l. vi. c. i. p. 904.

[p] Degenerat. & Corrupt. l. ii. c. iii. p. 517.

[q] Ibid. p. 515, 516.

CHAP. II.

elements as discovered by the sense of touch. But these qualities combined by two, that is, in the manner the most simple, form only four combinations. The elements, therefore, are four. The combination of coldness with dryness is called earth; of coldness with humidity, water; of heat with dryness, fire; of heat with humidity, air. Those elements are most easily convertible, which have one quality in common. Thus water is changed into air, when the quality of cold is destroyed by the caloric [r]. What was before water has now the two characteristics of air, viz. humidity and heat; and, when the latter it added in due proportion, the water evaporates, and mounts to the sky, where it remains, until a new cause again deprives the air of its heat, and makes it fall to the ground in rain. In the same manner, fire may be converted into air, and air into fire; for fire is warm and dry, and air is warm and moist; and the element will therefore be denominated either fire or air, according to the prevalence of the dryness or humidity. Water, too, will be easily converted into earth; since both being cold, but the former moist, and the latter dry, the moisture need only to be overcome by the dryness to make water earth; and dryness need only to be overcome by moisture to make earth water. When the elements possess not any common quality, their transmutation is more slow and difficult. To make water into fire, it is necessary that both its cold and its moisture should be overcome by the contrary principles of heat and dryness; and to make air into earth, or earth into air, the two characteristic qualities of both elements must also be changed. These changes, however, are continually happening around us; the air being first converted into

Their continual transmutations.

[r] More properly calorific. Το θερμαντικον—Το δε δυναμενον θερμον ειναι, παροντος τυ θερμαντικυ και πλησιαζοντος, αναγκη θερμαινεσθαι. "What has the capacity of receiving heat, must be heated by the approach and presence of the caloric." P. 508.

CHAP. II.

into water, and the water into earth. Fire alſo is viſibly generated; for flame, which is a ſpecies of fire, conſiſts of nothing but burning ſmoke, which itſelf is compoſed of air and earth[s].

The perpetual changes of the elements and their compounds produce the ever-varying ſpectacle which we behold around us, and are themſelves produced by the revolutions of the heavenly bodies acting in concert with thoſe laws of motion which God has impreſſed on his lower works[t]. Earth naturally tends to the centre of the univerſe; water riſes above earth; air above water; and fire above air. A gravitating principle, therefore, belongs properly to earth; and an anti-gravitating, to fire; which always ſeeks the extremities; and is therefore the great miniſter of the Almighty in moulding the forms of things[u]. The intermediate elements of air and water have only a relative gravity, being heavier than fire, and lighter than earth[v]; and this relative gravity diſappears when they are either in, or below, their proper place[x]: yet that air itſelf is heavy, appears evidently from this, that a bladder filled with air is heavier than when it was void of that element[y].

From

[s] De Generat. et Corrupt. l. ii. c. iv. p. 518.

[t] συνεπληρωσε το ὁλον ὁ θεος εντελεχειαν ποιησας την γενεσιν· ὁυτω γαρ μαλιϛα συνειροιτο το ειναι διο το εγγυτατω ειναι της ουσιας το γιγνεσθαι αει την γενεσιν. Ibid. p. 525.

[u] De Generat. & Corrupt. l. ii. c. viii. p. 523.

[v] De Coelo, l. i. c. viii. p. 444.

[x] De Cœlo, p. 490. et ſeq.

[y] De Coelo, l. iv. c. iv. p. 490. The brevity of the expreſſion renders it doubtful whether the experiment was made by exhauſting or by accumulating the air. While writing this paſſage, a book fell in my way of a very eminent profeſſor, Dr. Adam Smith, in which I met with the following paſſage: "Thoſe facts and experiments, which demonſtrate the weight of the air, and which no ſuperior ſagacity, but chance alone, preſented to the moderns, were altogether unknown to them (the ancients before the time of Archimedes)." Smith's Eſſays on Philoſophical Subjects, p. 101.

CHAP. II.

The immediate causes of the mixed properties of bodies, and of natural phænomena.

From the active[z] principles of heat and cold, and the passive[a] ones of dryness and humidity, the density, rarity, hardness, softness, tenacity, friability, in one word, all the mixed properties of bodies are derived[b]; and from them are compounded the highest meteors of heaven[c], as well as the metals and minerals in the bosom of the earth[d]. The hardest of those fossils are produced from dry exhalations or humid vapours; which are the material causes of those permanent substances, and the efficient causes of the most tremendous convulsions; for the earthquakes are not caused, as Democritus suspected, merely by the agency of water bursting the too narrow caverns in which it had been accumulated and pent up, but by the agency of heat, which, converting this water into vapour, gives to it a power of overthrowing the weightiest mountains which resist its expansion[e].

Refutation of the doctrine of atoms.

Aristotle's doctrine concerning the transmutation of the elements, vulgarly so called, (a doctrine long held visionary by his pretended followers,) is countenanced by recent experiments[f], which

[z] Meteor. l. iv. c. i. p. 584.

[a] Ibid.

[b] De Generat. & Corrupt. p. 515.

[c] De Meteor. l. ii. c. iv. p. 558.

[d] De Meteor. l. iii. c. vi. p. 583.

[e] Ibid. p. 566. & seq.

[f] I have just read a small German volume, intitled, "Antiphlogistische Chemie," by Johann. And. Scherer, Vienna, 1792, 8vo. which is written with the purpose of proving, that the most important of the discoveries which have established the antiphlogistic system, called on the Continent the system of Lavoisier, had been made by our countryman Mayow upwards of an hundred years ago. This wonderful young man, for he died at the age of 34, was acquainted (as his words are quoted by Scherer) with the composition of the atmosphere; the nature of what is now called vital or dephlogisticated air; the origin and common nature of acids; the doctrines of combustion, fermentation, respiration, &c. as explained by Lavoisier, and other authors of the antiphlogistic system of chemistry. Scherer makes the comparison with great fairness, stating the modern doctrines in his own German text, and placing Mayow's Latin in notes at the bottom of the page, from an edition of his works published at the Hague

 in

CHAP. II.

which ſhow that water may be reſolved into different gaſes, or airs; that atmoſpheric air itſelf is capable of reſolution; and that the moſt ſubtile fluids enter into the compoſition of ſolid bodies, which may again, by the agency of the calorific, be changed into fluids. But our Author did not reſt ſatisfied with any diſcoveries that mere experiment could make, nor with any analogical deductions from ſuch diſcoveries, of which the moſt celebrated was the Syſtem of Atoms, as explained by Democritus. That philoſopher, whom Ariſtotle often cites and refutes, but on whom he beſtows the juſt praiſe of unextinguiſhable curioſity and indefatigable induſtry[g], thought it an invincible argument in favour of his atoms, that if body was infinitely diviſible, it would finally vaniſh into nothing. Ariſtotle denies both the poſition and the inference. The error of Democritus, he obſerves, aroſe from thinking, that, becauſe a body might be divided *any where*, it might therefore be divided *every where*. In a line, a point may be taken *any where*, but points cannot be taken *every where*, becauſe one point cannot be contiguous to another[h]. Bodies, therefore, cannot actually be divided to infinity, and therefore cannot vaniſh into nothing; but as the minuteſt

in 1681, intitled, "Johannis Mayow, Londinenſis, &c. Opera omnia Medico-Phyſica." Mayow was born in London in 1645, where he died in 1679. He was a Fellow of All Souls College, Oxford. In 1668 he publiſhed there "Tractatus duo de Reſpiratione & de Rachitide;" and, in 1674, he publiſhed the ſame five Treatiſes, which were afterwards republiſhed at the Hague. This work contains, beſides the two tracts above mentioned, I. "Tractatus de Sal-nitro et Spiritu Nitro Aerio," (which he calls Spiritus Vitalis Igneus, p. 1. and Aer Purus Vitalis, p. 281, the name which is likely to prevail.) II. "De Reſpiratione Fœtus in Utero." III. "De Motu Muſculorum & Spiritibus Animalibus."

[g] οὗτος δὲ Δημόκριτος ἔοικε μὲν περὶ ἁπάντων φροντίσαι, p. 494. De Generat. & Corrupt. p. 2.

[h] De Gener. & Corrupt. l. i. c. ii. p. 497.

minuteſt particle ſtill poſſeſſes all the properties of body, it is ſtill capable of diviſion, and therefore not an atom [i].

Of change, and its different ſpecies.

According to our univerſal experience reſpecting the viciſſitudes of ſublunary things, our Author obſerves, that there are no realiſings of non-entity, and no abſolute reductions of exiſtence into nothing. Theſe viciſſitudes or changes may all be reduced to the four following [k]: 1. A change of place, called lation, the firſt and moſt ſimple ſpecies of change, which is implied in all the three following kinds. 2. A change of quantity, which muſt conſiſt either in augmentation or in diminution. 3. A change of quality, called alteration; as from hard to ſoft, from health to ſickneſs. 4. A change in ſubſtance, which conſiſts in generation and corruption [l]; and which is ſufficiently exemplified in what is above obſerved concerning the tranſmutations of the elements. When any regularly organized object changes its place, its quantity, or its quality, the object itſelf, it is plain, ſtill remains the ſame eſſentially, though altered in its acceſſories. But when it changes in ſubſtance, that is in the unknown cauſe from which all its preceptible qualities proceed, is there reaſon to believe that the continuity of exiſtence is broken, and that one thing is totally annihilated, and another actually created? Ariſtotle thinks not; and that in this change, as well as in every other, there is ſomething that departs, ſomething that accedes, and ſomething

Lation.

Change as to quantity.

Alteration.

Generation and corruption.

[i] The obſcurity of this paſſage will be removed, by conſidering what he afterwards proves, that our notion of infinity is entirely negative; and that to ſuppoſe body actually divided to infinity, implies a contradiction, κατα ενεργειαν μεν ουδεν εστι απειρον, δυναμει δε επι την διαιρεσιν. Ibid. p. 499.

[k] De Generation. & Corrupt. l. i. c. xxxiv. p. 498. &. ſeq. & Phyſic. Auſcult. l. iii. c. i. p. 340.

[l] Idem ibid.

CHAP. II.

something that still remains; a something, indeed, that escapes sense, and even eludes fancy, but of which we get a glimpse [m] from reason, as of a shadowy and obscure existence, susceptible of all qualities, but unendowed with any. What iron is to the saw, or marble to the statue, precisely the same is this *first matter* to all the natural productions which diversify and adorn the earth. It possesses not in itself any characteristic or essentiating quality; never existing therefore apart; but before it quits one form, constantly assuming another [n]. As the secondary elements, and all the compounds formed of them, are moulded into works of art by the hand of man, that instrument of instruments, to which human nature owes so much of its accommodation and comfort, so this primary element is moulded by the hand of God into what are called the works of nature; none of which exist in a rude chaotic state, but of which each is distinguished by its peculiar characteristic; and all admirably adapted

The first matter.

[m] εξ απαντων των γιγνομενων τουτο εστι λαβειν, αν τις επιβλεψη, ωσπερ λεγομεν, ότι δει αιει τι υποκεισθαι το γιγνομενον. Natural. Auscult. l. i. c. viii. p. 324.

[n] ημεις δε φαμεν ὑλην τινα των σωματων των αισθητων, αλλα ταυτην ου χωριστην, αλλα αιει μετ' εναντιωσεως, εξ ἡς γινεται τα καλουμενα στοιχεια . . . ου γαρ το θερμον ὑλη τῳ ψυχρῳ· ουδε τουτο τῳ θερμῳ· αλλα το ὑποκειμενον αμφοιν. ωστε πρωτον μεν το δυναμει σωμα αισθητον αρχη· δευτερον δε, αι εναντιωσεις· λεγω δε οιον θερμοτης και ψυχροτης· τριτον δε ηδη πυρ και ὑδωρ. ταυτα μεν γαρ μεταβαλλει εις αλληλα· αι δε εναντιωσεις, ου μεταβαλλουσι. De Generat. & Corrupt. l. ii. c. i. p. 515. "We say that perceptible bodies have for their principle a certain stuff or matter, which exists not separately, but is always endowed with some one of the contraries, hot or cold, moist or dry; and from these two, matter and one of the contraries, the elements are composed. For heat supplies not the materials for cold, nor cold for heat; but there is a certain subject susceptible of either of these contraries. So that this subject-matter is the first constituent principle, or element of perceptible bodies; the second, the contraries of which this matter is susceptible; the third, the compound elements of fire, water, &c.; which, as we have said, change into each other; but the contraries do not so change." See also De Generat. & Corrupt. l. i. c. 6.

adapted to answer their respective ends. This peculiar characteristic, by which objects are distinguished, Aristotle calls their appearance or form, because the sight, of all our senses, is that which gives us most information concerning the differences of things.

What is meant by the works of nature.

Works of art are easily distinguished by their outward shape; but the primary form of physical productions lies within; for all their sensible differences result from that internal principle determining their motion to or from a certain state, and of rest during a certain time in that state; which principle is called their nature. Of this nature we see, for example, the effects in plants, when they fix their roots in the earth, rear their stems, expand their leaves, and scatter their seeds; which operations, were these organised bodies endowed with intelligence, could not be more skilfully performed for the preservation of the individual, and the propagation of the kind °. Plants, therefore, act,

° Natur. Auscult. l. ii. c. viii. p. 336. &. seq ατοπον δε το μη οιεσθαι ἑνεκα του γινεσθαι εαν μη ιδωσι το κινουν βουλευσαμενον· και τοι και ἡ τεχνη ου βουλευεται· και γαρ ει ενην εν τῳ ξυλῳ ἡ ναυπηγικη, ὁμοιως αν τῃ φυσει εποιει· ὡστε ει εν τῃ τεχνῃ ενεστι ἡ ἑνεκα του, και εν τῃ φυσει ενεστι. μαλιστα δε δηλον, ὁταν τις ιατρευῃ αυτος ἑαυτον· τουτῳ γαρ εοικεν ἡ φυσις. Ibid. p. 338. " It is absurd to think, that because we do not see the moving principle actually deliberating, that it therefore acts at random, and not with an end in view. Art, then, we must say, acts at random; for if the art of ship-building was in wood, it would not act more judiciously *for making a ship*, than nature *does for nourishing, preserving, and propagating a tree*. If there is design in art, there must also be design in nature. This is most plain when a man, being a physician, cures himself. Nature acts like this man. But nature, as well as art, sometimes acts beside or beyond her intention; and sometimes fails in the execution of her own purposes. De Republica. l. i. c. vi. p. 302. By the compound word αυτοματον, (ὁταν αυτο ματην γινηται,) Aristotle expresses nature effecting either more or less than the specific ends or purposes to which her respective operations invariably tend. Natural. Auscult. l. ii. c. vi. p. 335. This, he observes, happens through the concurrence or accession of causes or circumstances, (indefinite in number, since things innumerable may accede to

CHAP. II.

act, not indeed with, but by intelligence, in consequence of that nature or form which they have received from the first cause of motion and order[p]. The constituent principles of things, therefore, are matter and form; and in all the changes which they undergo, there is a form which departs, a form which accedes, and a substance which remains, namely the first matter. Unless this doctrine is admitted, the continuity of existence would, in this lower world, be perpetually interrupted; each destruction would be an annihilation, and each production an evocation of non-entity into existence. The first matter being totally inactive, all change must proceed from matter endowed with form. But things exactly similar cannot produce any change on each other, because having all properties in common,

to the same thing, and causes innumerable may concur with the same cause; Natural. Auscult. l. ii. c. iii. p. 331.) vitiating Nature's operations and deforming her works. Nature operating κατα συμβεβηκος, and thereby producing effects not in her intention, is called αυτοματον, or chance; and art operating κατα συμβεβηκος, and producing effects not in her intention, is called τυχη, or fortune. Chance, or fortune, therefore, cannot have any existence independently of intention or design. Aristotle, therefore, concludes sublimely, that "if the heavens themselves were the work of chance, this would only prove that intelligence had been the cause of many still nobler works, and was the cause of the universe itself." Natural. Auscult. l. ii. c. vi. p. 335. Chance and fortune, therefore, are merely abridged expressions to denote nature and art producing unintentional and therefore unusual effects. Comp. Natural. Auscult. l. ii. c. iv. v. vi.; Metaph. l. v. c. xxx. and l. vi. c. ii. Ethic. Nichom. l. vi. c. iv. Magn. Moral. l. ii. c. vii. How unjustly is our Author treated by modern writers, (vid. Brucker. Histor. Philosoph. in Aristotel. passim, & Voyage du Jeune Anacharsis, vol. v. c. lxiv. p. 349.) when they arraign his impiety, on account of his doctrine of chance and fortune! Our inimitable Poet far better expresses the sense of his philosophy:

> Shall burning Ætna, if a sage requires,
> Forget to thunder, and recall her fires.
>
> Ethic. Epist. iv. ver. 123, & seq.

[p] τῳ χρονῳ αει προλαμβανει ενεργεια ἑτερα προ ἑτερας ἑως της τῳ αει κινουντος πρωτως. "There is a continual progression of efficient moving principles up to the first mover." Metaph. l. ix. c. viii. p. 939.

CHAP. II.

common, the one cannot communicate any thing to the other, nor act on that other any more than on itself[q]. Neither do things disparate, that is, totally dissimilar, admit of any reciprocal action. Whiteness has no action on straightness, any more than hardness has on bitterness; because neither of those qualities tends to exclude the qualities to which they are respectively opposed; and both the whiteness and straightness, as well as the hardness and bitterness, may subsist harmoniously in the same subject. By the accession of whiteness, therefore, the subject is not altered as to its straightness, nor by the accession of any one quality is it altered as to any other quality totally dissimilar to the former. To effect this alteration or change, the qualities or forms must be incapable of remaining in the same subject, which no sooner admits the one, than it rejects the other. But this is the nature of what are called contraries, heat and cold, moist and dry, black and white, straightness and crookedness, order and confusion; and of all those things which belong to one common genus, but are of a different species, that is, as formerly explained, which are similar in one respect[r], and dissimilar in another. By the reciprocal actions and sufferings of those contraries, in their utmost extremes and their intermediate states, all the changes are effected which we behold in the world around us. One flavour destroys

How her operations are performed.

Contraries.

[q] ὑπο αλληλων γὰρ πασχειν τ'αναντια αδυνατον. Natural. Auscult. p. 325. De General. & Corrupt. l. i. c. vii. p. 506. The subject in which the contraries inhere is properly acted upon, and changed from the one contrary to the other; from cold to hot, white to black. When Aristotle speaks of the actions and passions of forms, qualities, or contraries, he always supposes them clothed with matter. Ibid.

[r] The materials of white, black; order, confusion, &c. are the same. εςι δη των οντων τα μεν ποιητικα, τα δε ὑπο τετων παθητικα. τα μεν εν αντιςρεφει, ὁσων ἡ αυτη ὑλη εςι, και ποιητικα αλληλων, και παθητικα ὑπο αλληλων. De Generat. & Corrupt. l. i. c. x. p. 507.

CHAP. II.

destroys a flavour that is contrary to it, one colour its contrary, and complexly one body acts on a body endowed with many contrary qualities. Aristotle claims not for his own discovery, that contraries are the elements of generation and corruption, and of all the lesser changes observable in material objects. That doctrine, he observes, was first established by the school of Pythagoras[s], which arranged contraries into two classes; the better, and the worse: as light, darkness; good, evil; finite, infinite: and thenceforth adopted by all philosophers, compelled thereto by the force of truth[t]. One of these contraries, it was observed, departs as soon as the other accedes; three things, therefore, are concerned in every mutation or change, the matter which still remains one and the same; the contrary which accedes, called in general form; and the contrary which departs, which Aristotle calls in general privation[u]. This term, like many others employed by our author, is merely a sign to mark a thing indefinite and unknown; for the contrary which accedes, or, in other words, the characterising quality, is something certain and definite; but the form which departed in order to make room for this characterising quality, and without the departure of which the change could not have been effected, is, in a great measure, uncertain and indefinite: thus there is but one form of health, and innumerable forms of sickness; one form of order, innumerable forms of confusion; or in things more simple, each body has its definite colour or colours; but it may have been changed to any of these colours, for instance,

Form, and privation.

[s] οἱ δὲ Πυθαγορειοι, και ποσαι και τινες αἱ εναντιωσεις, απεφηναντο, &c. Metaphys. l. i. c. v. p. 846.

[t] Natural. Auscult. l. i. c. v.

[u] Ibid. l. i. c. viii. p. 325. των εναντιων ἡ ἑτερα συστοιχια στερησις. Aristot. Metaph. passim.

CHAP. II.

inſtance, to black, either from its contrary white, or from any of the intermediate ſhades between thoſe oppoſite extremes *.

In the changes which material ſubſtances undergo, they reciprocally act on each other; in other words, both ſubſtances are agents, and both patients. This is illuſtrated by what happens in mixture; which, according to Ariſtotle, conſiſts in this, that two ſubſtances, acting on each other, produce a third ſubſtance ſpecifically different from either; and of which each, the minuteſt part, is ſpecifically different from each, the minuteſt part, of either of the compoſing ingredients. Leucippus and Democritus, the fathers of the mechanical philoſophy, endeavoured to explain mixture as well as all other natural appearances by atoms and a vacuum, commenſurate pores, the motions, figures, and poſitions of the minute particles of matter. But Ariſtotle juſtly obſerves, that if mixture depended merely on mechanical cauſes, there would be no ſuch thing to the keen ſight of Lynceus, which could always diſtinguiſh theſe compoſing ingredients, how minutely ſoever they were ſubdivided, from each other; and eaſily perceive that what, to our obtuſe ſenſes, appeared to be the production of a new ſubſtance, was nothing more

* Natural. Auſcult. l. i. c. vi. p. 331. Ariſtotle maintained a definite number of colours againſt the atomic philoſophers, who made them depend on the indefinite variety of the figures and diſpoſitions of minute corpuſcles, τα ειδη των χρωματων εϛι ωρισμενα και ȣκ απειρα. De Senſu & Senſiti, c. iii. p. 667. He conſidered colours alſo as bearing the ſame relation to light, which ſharpneſs and flatneſs do to ſound: ωσπερ γαρ ανευ φωτος ȣχ οραται τα χρωματα; ȣτω ȣδε ανευ ψοφȣ το οξυ και το βαρυ. De Anima, l. ii. c. viii. p. 641. How ſtrangely were his doctrines perverted by the ſcholaſtics! And how nearly did they in themſelves approach to inductions from experiments with which he was not acquainted!

CHAP. II.

more than the minute ſubdiviſion and new arrangement of two old ones [x].

Tranſition to his theology.

Subſtances endowed with different characteriſing qualities, in other words, different forms which have the ſame matter, are fitted for reciprocally acting on each other. But there is a higher order of forms, which act, without ſuffering; and of which, the higheſt of all muſt *neceſſarily* be impaſſive. A patient is ſaid, with equal propriety, to be cured, either by the phyſician's ſkill, or by the medicines preſcribed. The medicines, while they act, are alſo acted upon; are warmed, cooled, or undergo ſome ſuch alteration. But the phyſician's ſkill ſuffers nothing from the effect produced on the patient; and by this compariſon, Ariſtotle ſays we may conceive why, of ſubſtances not immerged in the ſame matter, the one may produce a change on the other, without being reciprocally affected by it.

The form, ſpecies, or ſight.

To know phyſical objects is to know their cauſes; the efficient and final, which are principles external to thoſe objects; and the material and formal, which, exiſting in the objects themſelves, are the elements into which they muſt intellectually be reſolved. The formal cauſe is that by which each object is characteriſed and diſtinguiſhed; and from which, as from a perennial and abundant ſpring, its ſenſible qualities, as well as latent powers, perpetually flow. Ariſtotle did not think that, in the preſent ſtate of our exiſtence, we could remount to this fruitful ſource, and behold things as they are [y]; but in all his inquiries it is conſtantly his endeavour to approximate as nearly as poſſible to

[x] De Generat. & Corrupt. l. i. c. x. p. 507. Ariſtotle illuſtrates his doctrine by obſervations on the mixture of metals, one of which is noticed by my ingenious friend Dr. Pearſon. See Philoſoph. Tranſ. for the year 1796, p. 432.

[y] Metaph. l. ii. c. i. p. 856.

CHAP. II.

to this *species*, *form*, or *sight*, which words he often employs merely as signs for things sought; and to discover in each object that essentiating characteristic, whether substance or property, on which its perceptible qualities depend[a]. Familiar with the correct geometry of his times, he discerned the concatenation of truths, which being linked indissolubly together, unite the most distant and seemingly unconnected extremes. Of each object he investigates the true definition; and of each science, the *principal* theorem; because the foundation and bond of union of its parts; justly thinking, that the variety of our apparent knowledge is often the proof of our real ignorance; and that true science improves in proportion as many particular propositions resolve themselves into one general truth. Under the influence of this generalising spirit, the true spirit of philosophy, he is carried sometimes beyond the bounds prescribed to the human intellect; but his errors are always those of a man of genius; and what adventurer in science ever successfully contended in the field of truth, without sometimes being tempted to launch on the ocean of conjecture?

Of the laws regulating this lower world.

Nothing in nature, he observes, exists in a totally crude and absolutely unorganised state; but it is the inward organization, or invisible form, which moulds the external shape of bodies; and imposes on the motion, producing their various figures and appearances,

[a] Metaphys. l. vii. c. ii, xi, xiii. It is worthy of remark, that Aristotle *did* precisely that which he is blamed by Bacon, Hobbes, Malbranche, &c. for not doing; and declared it impossible to do that which he is blamed for having attempted. By examining, comparing, and classing the perceptible qualities of things, he endeavoured to make them known by a definition, affirming this examination to be the only method by which they could be known and defined. επειδαν γαρ εχομεν αποδιδοναι κατα την φαντασιαν περι των συμβεβηκοτων, η των παντων, η των πλειϛων, τοτε περι της ουσιας ἑξομεν τι λεγειν ὁτι μαλιϛα. Ibid.

CHAP. II.

appearances, the laws and limits of its action. In exerting this inherent power of forms, fire seems to be their principal minister[a]; for fire, the most subtile of material principles, and of which light seems to be a modification[b], always diffuses itself through bodies, and seeks their extremities, by which their outward conformation is delineated and defined. There are forms of a peculiar nature, as we shall prove hereafter, that seem to be totally separable from matter, because they are capable of energies and pleasures totally unrelated to any of its properties; but the forms of most physical objects are inseparably combined with the material principle, because independently of it, they would not answer any possible end. Of what use would be the nutritive power of plants, were there not some material substance to be nourished? To what purpose would serve the fierce instincts of the lion, separated from his fangs, his paws, and his brawny members? It is highly unreasonable, therefore, to believe the Pythagorean and Platonic doctrine concerning the separate existence of those substantial forms[c]; and not less unreasonable to admit the opinion so strongly inculcated by some poets and philosophers, that such forms migrate from one body to another[d].

In

[a] De Part. Animal. l. ii. c. vii. p. 986.

[b] πυρος η τοιουτου τινος παρουσια εν τῳ διαφανει. De Anima, l. ii. c. vii. p. 638.

[c] Natural. Auscult. l. ii. c. ii. p. 329.

[d] De Anima, l. i. c. iii. p. 624. It is pleasant to find Hobbes, in the 4th chapter of his Leviathan, and in many other parts of his works, combating, under the name of Aristotle's philosophy, abstract essences, substantial forms, and innumerable other doctrines, metaphysical as well as moral and political, with nearly the same arguments by which Aristotle, their supposed author, had long before victoriously refuted them. Malbranche and the French philosophers in general treat the Stagyrite with not less unfairness, and speak of his opinions with not less ignorance. I scarcely except

14 Rapin,

CHAP. II.

The ſtate of capacity and energy between which all objects in it fluctuate.

In the language of Ariſtotle, the word "nature" is confined to that part of the univerſe ſituate within the lunar ſphere; which, according to a philoſophy preceding his own times, was regarded as the intermediate iſthmus ſeparating terreſtrial and periſhing, from celeſtial and immortal, things[e]. In its primitive and proper ſenſe, nature peculiarly applies to this lower world, which is the region of perpetual change, and in which all things are continually fluctuating between the extremes of generation and corruption; whereas the heavenly bodies, whether originally created, or the eternal production of an eternal cauſe[f], appear, as far as our experience reaches, to perform their unwearied motions exempted from the viciſſitudes of renovation or decay. Every thing therefore in nature, that is, in this lower world, may be conceived as exiſting in two different ſtates; ſo called, though variable, becauſe relatively more ſtable than the other changes to which they are liable. The firſt ſtate of their exiſtence, both abſolutely[g], and in the order of human conception,

Rapin, whoſe account of Ariſtotle, hitherto regarded as the beſt, is diſgraced by great inaccuracies. It is not eaſy to conceive how a writer, who had not acquired his notion of Ariſtotle's writings at ſecond hand, ſhould ſo totally miſtake their aim as Rapin does in ſpeaking of the Ethics to Eudemus. See Comparaiſon de Platon & Ariſtotle, p. 345. Edit. Amſterdam. 1686.

[e] Gale's Opuſcula Mythol. p. 516.

[f] ὡςε το τη γενεσει ὑςερον, τη φυσει προτερον ειναι. Natural. Auſcult. l. viii. c. x. p. 422: and we ſhall ſee hereafter that things exiſting in capacity muſt proceed univerſally from things exiſting in energy.

[g] No tenet of the Peripatetic philoſophy is thought more clearly aſcertained than the eternity of the world; and this tenet, I believe, is univerſally aſcribed to Ariſtotle by all writers whatever, both ancient and modern. The brevity and energy of our author's ſtyle, often gives to him indeed the appearance of dogmatiſing where he is only inveſtigating; but, in the following paſſage, he ſpeaks concerning the eternity of the

CHAP. II.

ception, is that of their maturity and perfection; in the ftate of a tree, a horfe, and a man. But with refpect to the individuals of thofe, as well as all other claffes, though they always univerfally proceed from other individuals in a ftate of maturity, it will be found that they all undergo innumerable changes, before they attain, by flow and infenfible degrees, the perfection of their nature. As the rude marble is gradually formed by art into a beautiful or majeftic ftatue, fo feeds and embryos, fcarcely perceptible to the fenfes, expand, by affimilating their proper nourifhment, into the wonderfully organifed productions called plants and animals. Such progreffive and ever varying natures may be confidered therefore as exifting either in a ftate of capacity for attaining a certain form and maturity, a thing as different from abfolute incapacity as fleep is from death; or in a ftate of actuality and perfection, which qualifies them for performing their refpective functions, and exerting their peculiar energies. What then is change or motion in its moft comprehenfive and philofophical fenfe? It is the paffage from a ftate of imperfection to perfection, from capacity

the world with the fame becoming modefty that he fhows on other fubjects unfathomable to mere reafon. Having mentioned that principle in the works of nature, analogous to art in the productions of man, which makes the ftems of plants fhoot upwards, while their roots fix deeply in the earth; which gives to animals their determinate organifation and proper fhape, diftinguifhable in their refpective members, adapted to fpecific and falutary purpofes, he proceeds thus: μαλλον εικος τον ουρανον γεγενησθαι ὑπο τοιαυτης αιτιας, ει γεγονε, και ειναι δια τοιαυτην αιτιαν μαλλον η τα ζωα τα θνητα· το γε εν τεταγμενον και ὡρισμενον πολυ μαλλον φαινεται εν τοις ουρανοις, η περι ἡμας. De Part. Animal. l. i. p. 970. "It is more likely that the heavens were produced by fuch a caufe, if indeed they were produced, and that they fubfift through the efficacy of fuch a caufe, than perifhing animals, fince definite arrangement and regular harmony are confpicuous far more in celeftial than in terreftrial things." Befides this, when Ariftotle's doctrine of time is underftood, we fhall fee that he means by the eternity of the world fomething very different from the fenfe commonly affixed to thofe words.

pacity to energy; or, the reverſe of this, from energy to mere capacity. For this reaſon Ariſtotle, anticipating the ſubtile principles which gave birth to the ſublime geometry of Newton and Leibnitz, expreſſes an object in itſelf too fugitive for words to repreſent, by the limits or extremes between which it fluctuates; calling motion the perfection of mere capacity, becauſe the immediate end at which mere capacity aims; and an imperfect energy or actuality, becauſe until the productive motion ſtops, the object is only approximating to its moſt perceptible and moſt perfect ſtate [h].

Motion defined.

Ariſtotle obſerves, that the four kinds of change or motion, formerly deſcribed, all finally reſolve themſelves into lation, or change of place [i]; and that place is only a modification of ſpace, that

Space and time.

[h] Ariſtot. Naturaſ. Auſcult. l. iii. c. i, ii, iii. p. 339. & ſeqq. Had Mr. Locke known what Ariſtotle meant by motion, his candour would not have allowed him to ſpeak of this definition as he does in the following paſſage: "What more exquiſite jargon could the wit of man invent than this definition, 'the act of a being in power, as far forth as in power?' which would puzzle any rational man, to whom it was not already known by its famous abſurdity, to gueſs what word it could ever be ſuppoſed to be the explication of. If Tully, aſking a Dutchman what *beweeginge* was, ſhould have received this anſwer in his own language, that it was "actus cutis in potentia, quatenus in potentia," I aſk whether any one can imagine he would thereby have underſtood what the word *beweeginge* ſignified, or have gueſſed what idea a Dutchman ordinarily had in his mind, and would ſignify to another, when he uſed that ſound?" Eſſay on the Human Underſtanding, vol. ii. b. iii. c. 4. p. 26. But Ariſtotle, who had taught before Mr. Locke that, what the latter calls ſimple ideas, could not be defined, ("φανερον τοινυν, ὅτι επι των ἁπλων ουκ εστι ζητησις, ουδε διδαξις, αλλα ετερος τροπος της ζητησεως των τοιουτων." Metaphyſ. l. vii. c. xvii. p. 925. Vid. etiam, pp. 910 & 929.) would have more eaſily explained to Mr. L. his own definition of motion, than Mr. L. could have explained to Ariſtotle what he meant by the idea of a triangle, which is neither rectangular, obtuſangular, nor acute-angular, but at once none and all of theſe together—the ſuppoſed exiſtence of which ideas, and an infinity of others of the ſame kind, is the principal baſis of the whole Eſſay on Human Underſtanding.

[i] Natural. Auſcult. l. viii. c. x. p. 421. Metaph. l. xiv. c. vii. p. 1002.

that unſubſtantial being of which no other definition can be given but that it is the recipient of body[k]. As our conception of ſpace originates in that of body, and our conception of motion in that of ſpace, ſo our conception of time originates in that of motion; and particularly in thoſe regular and equable motions carried on in the heavens, the parts of which, from their perfect ſimilarity to each other, are correct meaſures of the continuous and ſucceſſive quantity called Time, with which they are conceived to co-exiſt. Time therefore may be defined the perceived number of ſucceſſive movements; for as number aſcertains the greater or leſſer quantity of things numbered, ſo time aſcertains the greater or leſſer quantity of motion performed[l]. An inſtant is not a part, but the boundary of time[m]; whoſe elements are the perceptible intervals bounded by inſtants[n]. If body, therefore, had a beginning, ſo muſt ſpace, motion, and time, which are conceived merely as affections of body, or of each other[o]. If body cannot be ſuppoſed infinitely extended, without ſuppoſing a contradiction, (for what quantity can actually exiſt of which the magnitude cannot be aſcertained and expreſſed?) ſo neither can any of its properties; and therefore motion cannot be infinite; nor time, which is conceived ſolely as the meaſure of motion, a mere fiction of the fancy, poſſeſſing no real exiſtence independently of us and our thoughts. The very eſſence of infinity, again, conſiſts in privation; it is a word denoting not a conception, but the negation of all conception; ſo that the errors committed on this ſubject by the ancients, and repeated by ſome modern philoſophers, and

[k] Natural. Auſcult. l. iv. c. i, ii. &c. p. 351—364.

[l] Ibid. p. 367.

[m] Phyſ. Auſc. p. 397.

[n] Ibid. l. iv. c. xiv. &c. p. 364—373.

[o] Metaph. l. v. c. xiii. p. 894.

CHAP. II.

and even ſome modern mathematicians [p], proceed from their realiſing a non-entity, and aſſigning a poſitive archetype, or what they call an idea, to a word, which is merely a ſign that no ſuch archetype or idea exiſts. Body and ſpace cannot be conceived as infinite either in greatneſs or littleneſs; and although its adjunct of motion or time is imagined to be ſo conceived, this ariſes from a mere illuſion of the fancy, which, not retaining the parts of time firſt taken, continually adds new parts, but without increaſing the whole; ſince the former parts are continually annihilated, as the latter are created [q]. To realiſe infinity muſt, in all our reaſonings, neceſſarily lead to abſurdity; thus, to give our Author's example, to ſuppoſe an infinite progreſſion of cauſes in making and arranging the world, is the ſame thing as ſuppoſing it made or arranged without any cauſe at all [r].

It

[p] "La grandeur (ſays the admired Fontenelle) eſt ſuſceptible d'augmentation ſans fin. Elle n'eſt donc pas & ne peut être ſuppoſée dans le même cas, que ſi elle n'étoit pas ſuſceptible d'augmentation ſans fin: or ſi elle n'étoit pas ſuſceptible d'augmentation ſans fin, elle reſteroit toujours finie; donc étant ſuſceptible d'augmentation ſans fin, elle peut être ſuppoſée infinie." See the ſame reaſoning throughout his treatiſe, intitled, Elémens de la Geometrie de l'Infini. It is eaſy to perceive how much this ingenious man, and his innumerable followers, might have been benefited by reading the third book of Ariſtotle's Phyſics, c. iv. to chapter xiii. both incluſive, p. 342—350. ουκ αφαιρειται δε ὁ λογος ουδε τους μαθηματικους την θεωριαν, αναιρων ουτως ειναι το απειρον, ὡςτ' ενεργεια ειναι επι την αυξησιν ὡς αδιεξιτητον· ουδε γαρ νυν δεονται του απειρου, ουδε χρωνται, αλλα μονον ειναι ὁσην αν βουλωνται πεπερασμενην· τῳ δε μεγιςῳ μεγεθει τον αυτον εςι τετμησθαι λογον ὁπηλικονουν μεγεθος ἑτερον, ὡςε προς μεν το δειξαι εκεινοις ουθεν διοισει· το δε ειναι, εν τοις ουσι εςαι μεγεθεσι. Ibid. c. xii. p. 350. "We do not deſtroy the ſpeculations of mathematicians, when we aſſert that infinite magnitude cannot exiſt. For in theſe ſpeculations, they neither employ nor need to employ infinite, but only a finite magnitude as great as they pleaſe; and the ſmalleſt may be divided in the ſame proportions with the greateſt. For finding proportions, therefore, it is not neceſſary to ſuppoſe the exiſtence of what is impoſſible."

[q] Metaph. l. v. c. xiii. p. 350.

[r] Ibid. l. ii. c. ii. p. 857.

CHAP. II.

Ariſtotle's aſtronomy.

It is both the glory and the ſhame of Ariſtotle's abſtract philoſophy, that his general concluſions are correct, when ſome of the arguments, by which he maintains them, are faulty. This is peculiarly manifeſt in the uſe which he makes of the erroneous ſyſtem of aſtronomy, which prevailed in his own age, to vindicate the doctrines contained in his books of Phyſics. His treatiſe concerning the Heavens, indeed, deſcribes with perſpicuity and preciſion the celeſtial phænomena; while, at the ſame time, it informs us of the ſublime notions given by the firſt Pythagoreans and their contemporaries, of the diſtances, figures, motions, and magnitudes of the planets [s]; that the moon abounded with inhabitants; that the milky-way conſiſted of contiguous cluſters of ſtars [t]; and, conjecturing what it is the boaſt of modern aſtronomy to have confirmed, that the ſame principle which makes the heavenly bodies approach to their centre, perpetually impels them in their orbits, by proportionably increaſing their celerity [u]. Ariſtotle's own ſagacity led him to perceive that, in the revolutions of the heavenly bodies, all was regular, eaſy, and harmonious; and to reject with diſdain thoſe childiſh fictions, by which the moving principles of the univerſe were degraded by a ſuppoſed analogy with the laborious exertions of mortals in ſublunary and periſhing ſcenes [w]. But he did not think the aſtronomical theory of the Pythagoreans ſufficiently juſtified by obſervation: teleſcopes were not to be invented till a far later period; and to thoſe who held Ariſtotle's doctrine concerning ſpace and time, the argument in favour of the earth's motion, reſulting from the otherwiſe inconceivable velocity of the heavens,

[s] De Cœlo, l. ii. c. xiii. p. 465.

[t] Meteor. l. i. c. viii.

[u] De Cœlo, l. ii. c. i. p. 452. Comp. c. xiii. p. 465. & l. i. c. viii. pp. 443, 444. & l. ii. c. ix. p. 462.

[w] Ibid. p. 451. & c. vi. p. 458.

heavens, is not calculated to afford conviction. The earth, therefore, as the heaviest of bodies, he places at the centre; around which, the sun, moon, planets, and fixed stars perpetually performed their respective revolutions[x]; the only kind of motion or change to which these etherial[y] substances, unchangeable in their essence, were supposed to be liable; whereas the earth and all its productions, the metals and minerals in its bowels, the plants and animals on its surface, together with the vapours and meteors between that surface and the lunar sphere, were obnoxious to a great variety of complicated motions, which changed their characterising qualities or essence, and rendered the dissolution of one object the production of another. On the hypothesis, therefore, of the stability of the earth and the daily revolution of the heavens, Aristotle argues, that the material universe cannot be infinite; because, could a radius be infinitely extended from the earth's centre to the remotest body in the universe, that body could never perform a complete circular revolution[z]; since an infinite extent of space could not be passed over in a definite time. Space therefore cannot be infinite, because space is only the receptacle of body, the place where body may subsist; and, if space is not infinite, neither is motion, which depends on space; nor time, which depends on motion. Unalterable and divine substances exist, therefore, in a manner totally unfathomable to our present faculties. In this manner, the first Supreme Deity exists *necessarily*[a]; neither generated in space,

[x] De Cœlo, l. ii. passim.

[y] Meteor. l. i. c. iii. p. 530.

[z] De Cœlo, l. i. c. v. p. 437.

[a] καθαπερ εν τοις εγκυκλιοις φιλοσοφημασι περι τα θεια πολλακις προφαινεται τοις λογοις, ὅτι το θειον αμεταβλητον αναγκαιον ειναι το πρωτον και ακροτατον, p. 446.

CHAP. II.

ſpace, nor growing old in time, unchangeable and impaſſive, enjoying the beſt and moſt perfect life through all eternity [b].

Ariſtotle makes amends for his airy ſpeculations in aſtronomy, by well explaining, in oppoſition to Democritus, the true principles of corpuſcular attraction, which gives to the earth its globular form [c]. This, he obſerves, is further aſcertained by the phænomenon of lunar eclipſes, in which the bounding line is always perceived to be circular. The earth therefore, he ſays, is plainly a ſphere, and but a ſmall [d] one, compared with many others, its periphery not exceeding 37,000 miles [e]. He ſpeaks with ſuch raptures, as the calmeſt of philoſophers could feel, of the beauty and grandeur of the heavenly motions, whoſe celerities, how frightful ſoever to fancy, yet being harmoniſed by proportion, might be ſteadily contemplated by the intellect [f]. Had he known the diſcoveries of Galileo and Kepler, he might perhaps have been a Newton. But aſtronomy being one of thoſe ſciences which requires long-continued obſervation for its baſis, was left by Ariſtotle in the ſame imperfect ſtate in which he found it; and yet, by the perverſeneſs of ſtupidity, it was that part of his works which, in the ages of darkneſs, was moſt warmly admired, and moſt obſtinately and moſt ſuperſtitiouſly defended.

His doctrine concerning the earth and its productions.

From the magnitudes and motions of the heavenly bodies, Ariſtotle deſcended to a humbler ſubject, the productions of the earth; which are connected, however, with man, by far more numerous [g] and powerful relations, namely, thoſe of his daily wants. This globe which we inhabit ſeems to have undergone various

[b] De Cœlo, c. ix. p. 446. [c] Ibid. l. iv. c. vi. p. 492. & l. ii. c. xiv. p. 470.
[d] Meteor. l. i. c. iii. p. 529. [e] Ibid. p. 471. [f] Ibid. p. 451 & 463.
[g] De Part. Animal. l. i. c. v. p. 974.

various revolutions, to have been overwhelmed by inundations and ſhattered by convulſions, which ſwept away nations with their cities and their arts; ſo that the moſt valuable inventions have innumerable times been loſt, and times innumerable been recovered. Of the productions with which our earth abounds, many give indications of theſe direful viciſſitudes; and many appear to have emerged from the wreck of ſome dreadful cataſtrophe. Both as the hiſtorian and the interpreter of nature, our Author endeavoured to embrace and exhauſt the complete ſcience of the globe; and if we may judge of thoſe parts of his works which are loſt or imperfect, by thoſe which have come down to us entire, it muſt have been no eaſy matter to determine whether moſt admiration was due to his deſcriptions of the great maſſes of nature, ſeas, rivers, mountains, and meteors [h], or to his minute diligence in treating the ſeveral objects of the animal, vegetable, and mineral kingdoms. His books on plants and minerals no longer remain [i]; but both his hiſtory of animals, and his philoſophy reſpecting that hiſtory, have come down to us in a far more perfect ſtate than any other portion of his writings concerning natural knowledge.

His hiſtory of animals and other works relative to that ſubject.

On the ſubject of Zoology, his treatiſes are comprifed in fifty books, of which twenty-five are happily preſerved among his works. The hiſtory of animals occupies nine books; the following ſixteen are employed in explaining their general affections or properties, and their principal parts or members. Four books

[h] Meteor. l. i. c. i. p. 518. See the great views which he there gives of his undertakings.

[i] The two ſhort books on plants, p. 1007—1030. vol. ii. edit. du Val. are ſpurious. In the laſt chapter of the third book of his Meteorology, he ſays he is to proceed to give an account of all the different foſſils and metals; but that account nowhere appears.

CHAP. II.

books treat of their parts; five treat of generation; the remainder, of their ſenſations and motions, inſpiration and reſpiration, ſleeping, waking, youth, old age, life, and death; in the knowledge of which particulars, the liberal ſtudy of Zoology, or, in Ariſtotle's language, its philoſophy, appears to him principally to conſiſt. As he extends that term to its full and proper ſenſe, denoting by it the knowledge of whatever has animal life, the firſt four books of his hiſtory, beginning with what is moſt ſtriking and palpable, the outward conformation of animals, divides and diſtinguiſhes, in relation to this complex object, and in compariſon with the human form, as that which is moſt familiarly known, the inhabitants of the earth, the water, and the air, from the enormous whale and maſſy elephant to the ſcarcely perceptible productions of duſt and rottenneſs[k], enumerating and defining with incomparable accuracy the agreements, differences, and analogies that prevail, in point of external organization, among all living tribes, and ſometimes referring to his treatiſes on Comparative Anatomy, which are now unfortunately loſt. In the three following books, he examines the different claſſes of animals with reſpect to the commencement, duration, and term of their generative powers. His eighth book examines their habitation and nouriſhment; and the concluding

[k] Buffon (vol. iii. p. 223.) carries Ariſtotle's ſyſtem of ſpontaneous generation much farther than the author intended, when he makes him ſay that "the firſt men ſprung from the earth in the form of worms." Our author is conſtantly miſrepreſented by being made to ſpeak abſolutely, when he ſpeaks merely hypothetically. His words are ειπερ εγιγνοντο ποτε γηγενεις. De General. l. iii. c. ii. And we ſhall find hereafter, that the reſult of all Ariſtotle's inquiries into nature is a concluſion directly oppoſite to the following of Mr. Buffon, namely, "qu'il y a peut être autant d'étres, ſoit vivans, ſoit végétaux, qu'il ſe reproduiſent par l'aſſemblage fortuit de molecules organiques, qu'il y a d'animaux ou de végétaux qui peuvent ſe reproduire par une ſucceſſion conſtante de générations." Supplement à l'Hiſt. Nat. tom. viii. p. 18.

CHAP. II.

cluding book of the hiſtory contains their manners and habits, enumerates their friends and enemies, and explains the ordinary means by which each claſs provides for its preſervation and defence. In taking this wide ſurvey of animated nature, Ariſtotle pretends not to comprehend its indefinitely varied branches (ſince infinites of every kind ſpurn the limits of ſcience); but in the multitude of important and well-aſcertained facts which he relates, and which is incomparably greater than can be found in any work of equal compaſs, it is his main purpoſe to illuſtrate the general heads above mentioned, and to explain the properties or affections common to the greateſt or moſt diſtinguiſhed portion of the whole animal kingdom. To theſe general heads or common properties, he conſtantly has reſpect in the hiſtorical part of his work; ſo that his minuteſt obſervations reſpecting the minuteſt inſects and leaſt-organized animals, will be often found to elucidate or confirm ſome important law of the animal œconomy[1].

His philoſophy of natural hiſtory.

His Syſtem, that is, in the popular ſenſe of the word, his nomenclature, is indeed imperfect. The world created by a microſcope, had not any exiſtence for the philoſophers of antiquity; and, by the improvements of this invention, new worlds perhaps may be brought to light in endleſs ſucceſſion. But in the chain of being, mortal eyes, however aſſiſted, can contemplate only the middle links, of which, though our glaſſes have ſhewn to us a greater number than were ſeen by Ariſtotle,

[1] Take the following example: The σηπια is a ſpecies of the Mollia, (fiſhes ſo called becauſe their ſoft parts are without, and their hard within,) which was long degraded by modern naturaliſts to the rank of ſea plants. Ariſtotle remarks, with regard to this ſpecies, that when the female is attacked, the male boldly defends her; but when an attack is made on the male, the female conſults her own ſafety by flight. Females, except in defence of their young, are leſs courageous than males, and leſs forward to give aſſiſtance. Hiſtor. Animal. l. ix. c. i. p. 922. & ſeq.

CHAP. II.

Ariſtotle, yet have they not brought us nearer to what ought to be the reſult of beholding the extremity of the chain. This reſult, the hiſtory of nature in animals, the Stagyrite, by the intellectual eye of reaſon and analogy[m], endeavoured to reach and reveal; analyſing, defining, demonſtrating; ſometimes penetrating deeply into nature's myſteries; ſometimes encountering difficulties which the human intellect is unable to ſurmount; often foiled in his exertions, yet always renewing the combat with reanimated hope. Knowledge, he thought, was more likely to be ſtruck out from the colliſion of error than to emerge ſpontaneouſly from confuſion[n]; and while his theories are attacked and defended, exploded and revived, the facts which he collected with unexampled diligence, and which he relates with inimitable preciſion, will for ever ſupport his fame, and inſtruct the moſt diſtant ages of poſterity. Our wider ſurvey of the globe has indeed increaſed our acquaintance with quadrupeds; and the invention of glaſſes has multiplied to our eyes the ever-diminiſhing tribes of inſects, and enabled us to examine more accurately their germs and organs; yet it will not be eaſy to prove that modern writers have added any thing of importance to Ariſtotle's obſervations on birds, or that any of their works diſplay even an equal degree of knowledge on the ſubject of fiſhes[o].

It

[m] The expreſſion of an anonymous writer preſerved in Suidas, is bold in the extreme: Αριστοτελης γραμματευς ην της φυσεως, τον καλαμον αποβρεχων εις νουν. "Ariſtotle was Nature's ſecretary, having dipped his pen in intellect." Suid. in Αριστοτελης.

[n] Metaph. paſſim.

[o] In proof of this, I ſhall cite the teſtimony of an author, which derives great weight from the accuracy of his own obſervations, and the importance of his own diſcoveries. "Queſti fatti finora rapportati in ordine allo ſuiluppo delle ouva nei peſci ſpinoſi, ſono

CHAP. II.

By what means he was enabled to render this philosophy so complete.

It may seem extraordinary that, on a branch of science, which, like all other parts of natural history, is naturally progressive, our author should have attained such accurate and extensive knowledge in so early an age of the world. But Aristotle was the friend of a man as extraordinary as himself, from whom he received two favours, which, to a mind like his, must

sono quelli pochi che ho potuto osservare nelle rare occasioni che mi si son presentati delle loro covate gattate, & gia suiluppantisi. E percio la serie di tali fatti e di multo interrotta, ne' continuata come a giorni nostri e' quella dello sviluppo del feto nelle uova della gallina. E quando io reflettendo su di questa mancanza, scorro la Storia degli Animali di Aristotele, non posso non essere da stupore preso, in esso leggendo veduti quei fatti, che a noi non si son potuti che a stento manifestare; & relevati poi con tutta la nettezza, & posti in parallelo coi fatti gia' riconosciuti nelfeto di gallo: & tanto maggiormente in me cresce lo stupore, quanto che allora uso non vi era degli instrumenti microscopici, che a tempi nostri abbiamo grandemente perfezzionati. E quindi non posso che di sdegno accendarmi contra dei moderni Izaiologi, vedendo per lor balordaggine trascurato quanto la veneranda antiquità avea scritto sa questo particulare, & a quello sostituite false osservazioni, illuzioni assurde ed incoerenti." "These are the few observations concerning the development of the eggs of shell-fish, which I have been able to make on the few occasions on which I found the impregnated gems in the act of disclosure; observations of which the series has been greatly interrupted, nor continued to the present times, like those which relate to eggs of birds. When I consider this defect, and turn to Aristotle's History of Animals, I am seized with astonishment at finding, that he should have fully and distinctly seen the facts which we have been able only very imperfectly to perceive; that he should have described them with the utmost precision, and compared them with the well-known observations concerning the eggs of birds. My astonishment is the greater, when I reflect that he was unassisted by microscopes, which instruments have in our days been greatly perfected; and I cannot therefore repress my indignation against those modern Ichthyologists, whose stupidity, neglecting the lights thrown on their subject by venerable antiquity, has substituted in their stead false observations, absurd and incongruous inferences." Memorie Sulla Generazione dei Pesci, di Philippo Cavolini. Compare p. 55. and p. 92. with Aristotle's History of Animals, b. vi. c. viii. and c. xiii. To the petulant questions in Athenæus, l. viii. p. 352. "From whom did Aristotle learn the minute particularities which he tells of fishes? From Proteus or Nereus?" No, (we may answer with If. Casaubon,) but from fishermen. Vid. Casaubon Animadvers. in Athenæum, l. viii. p. 388.

CHAP. II.

must have been of inestimable value. Alexander enabled him to rebuild and adorn his native city, for the benefit of his contemporaries[p], and to improve science for the benefit of posterity[q]. Upon his first entering Babylon, that inimitable prince eagerly demanded, for the use of his preceptor, the astronomical tables preserved in that ancient capital above nineteen centuries, and remounting 2234 years beyond the Christian æra[r]; and Pliny labours to describe with what ardour and zeal the same illustrious conqueror, during the course of his expedition, collected as presents to be sent to Aristotle, at the expence of 200,000l.[s], and by the activity of several thousand men, whatever rarities were to be found in parks or ponds, in aviaries or hives, or were to be procured by hunting, fishing, and fowling, in the wide extent of Asia. Such were the resources of Aristotle for writing the history of animals, besides the assistance of a great library, which Strabo says that, to the best of his knowledge, he was the first person that knew properly how to arrange[t]. By combining with the descriptions in his books the observation of those living wonders transported from the East, Aristotle, who preferred a philosophical residence in Athens to the honour of personal attendance on the master of the world, composed, in the tranquillity of the Lyceum, his immortal work, which a Pliny professes to abridge[u], and a Buffon despairs to rival[w].

In the wide survey which our author takes of the heavens and of the earth, as well as in the minute diligence with which he

[p] Plin. l. vii. c. 29.

[q] Idem, l. viii. c. 16.

[r] Porphyrius apud Simplicium in Aristot. de Cœlo.

[s] Comp. Plin. ubi supra, & Athenæum, p. 398. edit. Casaub.

[t] πρωτος ὧν ισμεν συναγαγων βιβλια, και διδαξας τους εν αιγυπτῳ βασιλεας βιβλιοθηκης συνταξιν. Strabo, l. xiii. p. 609.

[u] Plin. ubi supra.

[w] Histoire Naturelle, t. i. p. 63. & seq.

he examines the productions of the latter, whether inanimate or living, it is his perpetual aim to remount from effects to causes, and to lead us from perceptible qualities to those invisible principles by which they are produced. These principles, not being objects of sense, can be discovered only by making fair inferences from observation and experience. In this manner Aristotle treats, in three books, a subject which naturally follows his history of animals, investigating those principles on which their nutrition, sensation, and appetite, with all their perceptible powers and actions, depend. In this treatise, intitled "Concerning the Soul," his language is perpetually and necessarily metaphorical, because words, in their origin, being universally expressive merely of perceptions of sense, metaphors become indispensable in expressing the deductions of reason. Of material as well as intellectual substances our knowledge, he observes, results entirely from their perceptible qualities, that is, from what our universal experience teaches us to regard merely as the effects of hidden causes, scarcely conceivable to ourselves, and of which our notions are totally incommunicable to other men but by images and comparisons drawn from sensible objects. When Aristotle speaks philosophically of fire, he calls it "the power of communicating heat." In the same manner, the hidden causes necessary for explaining the properties and actions of animals, he calls "the nutritive, sentient, motive, and rational," that is, the collecting "power;" and as, from the phenomena of body, he inferred the existence of a substance called Matter; so, from the phenomena of sensation, reason, and intelligence, he inferred the existence of a substance called Mind; of which latter substance our knowledge is equally

The soul or mind in its most general sense.

 certain

certain with that of the former[x]. But as ſome of the moſt noted philoſophers before him had attempted to explain every thing by matter and its properties[y], Ariſtotle, on the other hand, thinks that it is by mind chiefly that all natural productions are characteriſed and diſtinguiſhed; meaning, by mind, that inward principle and inviſible form whoſe effects are diſplayed in the external organization of things, as well as in their perceptible properties and actions. In this ſenſe, therefore, the terms "form" and "mind" are applied to whatever characteriſes and diſtinguiſhes, whether that be merely a ſpecific and principal quality; or whether it be a ſubſtance inſeparable from matter, becauſe ſeparately unfit for any end or uſe[z]; or whether it be a ſubſtance capable of actions and pleaſures peculiar to itſelf, and ſo totally different from thoſe of body, and any of its variable affections, that, when ſeparated from this mortal frame, it will then, and then only, aſſume its natural activity, perfection, and dignity[a].

The book intitled "Concerning Energy," connects his natural philoſophy with his theology.

The doctrine of the mind naturally brings Ariſtotle to what is publiſhed as the ninth book of his Metaphyſics, but which, as above mentioned, ought to ſtand as the ſeventh. It is intitled "Concerning Energy," a word of mighty import in our author's philoſophy, ſince his doctrine on that ſubject is a link in the grand chain, by which he connects the earth with the heavens, and nature with the Deity. The ſtate of energy, as oppoſed

[x] δηλον δε και ὅτι ἡ μεν ψυχη ουσια ἡ πρωτη, το δε σωμα ὑλη· ὁδε ανθρωπος η το ζωον το εξ αμφοιν. Metaph. l. vii. c. xi. p. 919. and l. i. De Anima, c. v. p. 625.

[y] Metaph. l. viii. c. ii. p. 927.

[z] Ibid. l. viii. c. iii. p. 929.

[a] De Anima, l. i. c. iii. p. 623. and c. v. p. 625. and Metaph. l. xiv. c. ix. p. 1004.

CHAP. II.

opposed to that of capacity, was already explained; but it may be a matter of some curiosity more minutely to examine distinctions, independently of which this great philosopher thought it impossible to mount up from things visible and perishing to things invisible and eternal. Energy, then, as the word denotes, is always said in reference to action; and that is said to exist in energy, which executes its peculiar work, or performs its peculiar function [b]. The state of energy is the most perfect state of existence in which any object can be exhibited; as a master thinks he has perfected his scholar when he shews him performing skilfully the proper work of the art in which he was instructed [c]. Though energy always implies action, yet all actions are not energies. The actions of building, carving, healing, learning, respectively terminate i a house, a statue, health, and science. But the actions of thought, of life, and of happiness, (which is a kind of life,) have not any natural limit, but may proceed eternally revolving on themselves, perfect without addition, complete in every instant [d]. That things essentially different may be distinguished by different names, Aristotle calls limited actions, motions; the unlimited, energies; observing, that in the scale of being there is a continual ascent from mere powers and capacities to motions or imperfect energies, properly so called, because terminating in nothing more excellent than themselves [e]. Those operations, which terminate in a certain work, are only perfect in the work or production in which they are fixed and concentrated; as painting

The nature of energy explained.

[b] Metaph. l. ix. c. viii. p. 339. Comp. Metaph. l. ix. c. vi. p. 936.

[c] Idem ibid. [d] Metaph. l. ix. c. vi. p. 937.

[e] Comp. Metaph. l. xiii. c. ix. p. 990. & p. 991. and Metaph. l. ix. c. viii. p. 938.

CHAP. II.

painting in the picture, building in the edifice [f]. But energies not terminating in any work or production, are complete and perfect in themselves. The former belong in a certain sense to the work in which they are embodied [g]; the latter can belong only to the energising principle, which, when unceasingly active, as the first efficient cause was proved necessarily to be, is simple, unmixed, and pure energy [h].

The first energy eternally and substantially active.

On such a principle as this, eternally and substantially active, both the heavens and the earth depend [i]. He is the spring of motion, the fountain of life, the source of order and of beauty [k]. All our observations and all our reasonings lead us irresistibly to this conclusion; for in all the motions or changes of body or matter, there must always be one part acted upon as well as another that acts, otherwise no action, and therefore no motion, could possibly take place. But when we separate this acting part from the inert mass with which it is united, the same reasoning will still apply to it; it cannot be self-moved wholly [l], and the part which gives the impulse must always be different from that which receives it [m]. By our divisions and subdivisions without end, we shall therefore never come nearer to a solution than at first setting out, but shall always be compelled to consider matter as something fit to be moved, changed, or acted upon, but

[f] Comp. Metaph. l. xiii. c. ix. p. 990. & p. 991. and Metaph. l. ix. c. viii. p. 938.

[g] Metaph. l. ix. c. vi. p. 936.

[h] ὁ γαρ νυς ενεργεια. Metaph. l. xiv. c. vi. p. 999.

[i] εκ τοιαυτης αρα αρχης ηρτηται ὁ υρανος και ἡ φυσις. l. xiv. c. vii. p. 1000. and Physic. Auscult. l. viii. c. vii. p. 418.

[k] το πρωτον παντων κινει παντα. Metaph. l. xiv. c. iv. p. 998. Comp. c. vi. p. 999. and l. xii. c. iii. p. 975. and l. ix. c. viii. p. 930.

[l] Physic. Auscult. l. iii. c. i. p. 340.

[m] Ibid. l. viii. c. vi. p. 417.

CHAP. II.

His attributes.

but conſtantly deriving its motion, change, or activity from ſome foreign cauſe[n]. The prime mover, then, is neceſſarily [o]immaterial; and therefore indiviſible, immoveable, impaſſive, and invariable[p]; ever actuating this viſible ſyſtem, as is plain from the phænomena, according to the beſt principles both of intellection and volition, which exactly coincide[q], when traced up to Deity, their ultimate ſource. The phenomena of the univerſe are not unconnected and epiſodical, like an ill-written tragedy; but all of them regulated and adjuſted with conſummate harmony[r]. The Divinity, who comprehends and directs the whole, is not himſelf diviſible in parts, nor comprehenſible by magnitude, ſince all magnitude may be meaſured[s]; and what finite magnitude can exert infinite power[t]? He ever is what he is[u], exiſting in energy before time began, ſince time is only an affection of motion, of which God is the author[w]. That kind of life which the beſt and happieſt of men lead occaſionally, in the unobſtructed exerciſe of their higheſt powers, belongs eternally to God in a degree that ſhould excite admiration in proportion as it ſurpaſſes comprehenſion[x].

This

[n] Phyſic. Auſcult. l. viii. c. vi. p. 417.

[o] Ibid. l. viii. c. vi. p. 416. & ſeq.

[p] Metaph. l. xiv. c. vii. p. 1000. and 1001.

[q] τετων (in reference to the ορεκτον and νοητον) τα πρωτα τα αυτα. Comp. Metaph. l. ix. c. ix. and l. xiv. c. vii.

[r] ουκ εοικε η φυσις επεισοδιωδης . . ωσπερ μοχθηρα τραγωδια. Metaph. l. xii. c. iii. p. 975.

[s] Metaph. l. xiii. c. x. p. 991. [t] Ibid. l. xiv. c. vii. p. 1001.

[u] δει αρα ειναι αρχην τοιαυτην ἡς ἡ ουσια ενεργεια. Metaph. l. xiv. c. vi. p. 999. Comp. De Cœlo, l. ii. c. xiii. p. 466.

[w] Metaph. l. xiii. c. viii. p. 992. and το κινουν αιδιον, και προτερον του κινουμενου. και — προτερον ουσιας, ουσιαν αναγκαιον ειναι. Metaph. l. xiv. c. viii. p. 1002.

[x] ει δε μαλλον, ετι θαυμασιωτερον. l. xiv. c. vii. p. 1001.

CHAP. II.

That Deity the ſource of Being handed down from antiquity.

This doctrine was delivered down from the ancients, and remains with their poſterity, in the form of a fable; which, with many additions to it, has been employed for the ſervice of legiſlation, and for bridling the paſſions of the multitude [y]. The Gods have thence been repreſented as endowed with human forms, and agitated by human paſſions; from which ſtrange ſuppoſitions, many conſequences not leſs ſtrange have very naturally been derived. Yet, from the motley maſs of fiction, if we ſeparate this ſingle propoſition, that Deity is the firſt of ſubſtances, it will appear to be divinely ſaid; and to have been ſaved, as a precious remnant, in the wreck of arts and philoſophy, which, it is probable, have often flouriſhed, and often fallen to decay [z].

Ariſtotle refutes the materialiſts and metaphyſicians.

Such is Ariſtotle's doctrine in his books intitled "Concerning Philoſophy;" the far greater part of which is employed in refuting two claſſes of writers, who may very properly be called the Materialiſts and the Metaphyſicians. The former contenting themſelves with the properties and laws of matter and motion, beyond which they thought it impoſſible to penetrate, miſtook effects for cauſes, and confounded the maker [a] with his works: The latter, who were the more modern, and alſo the more faſhionable of the two, perverted logical analyſis by applying it to phyſical ſubjects [b]; and ſubſtituting words for things, ſought

[y] Metaph. l. xiv. c. viii. p. 1003. [z] Idem Ibid.

[a] το κινουν ποιει, l. xiv. c. x. p. 1006. This muſt ſound harſh to thoſe who do not underſtand Ariſtotle's notion of the eternity of the world, in the ſenſe in which it is above explained.

[b] Compar. Metaph. l. xii. c. iv. p. 977. l. xiii. c. ii. p. 981. & ſeq. and l. xiv. c. i. p. 995.

CHAP. II.

ſought for firſt cauſes in numbers, ideas, contraries, and other metaphyſical abſtractions; or, in Ariſtotle's language, general terms; which, the more general they become, diverge the wider[c] in their nature from energies, the only ſubſtantial and efficient principles in the univerſe[d]; and all proceeding from the firſt energy or ſubſtance, who is both ſpecifically and numerically one[e]. This doctrine perfectly agrees with that beautiful harmony diſcernible in the works of the firſt mover; which are all of them connected by the moſt intimate relations[f]; and whoſe arrangements uniformly conſpire to one great and ſalutary end[g]: For the perfection, excellence, and beauty, diſcernible in the univerſe, are to be aſcribed to its Maker, not leſs than the regular arrangement of a well diſciplined army is aſcribed to its general[h]. This doctrine only is conſiſtent:

Goodneſs of God.

> " One rules alone, one, only one, bears ſway;
> " *His* are the laws, and Him let all obey[i]."

This

[c] Compar. Metaph. l. xiii. c. ii. p. 982. and l. xiv. c. v. p. 998.

[d] Comp. l. xiii. c. vii. p. 988. and l. xiv. c. ii, iii. p. 996.

[e] ἱν μεν αρα και λογῳ και αριθμῳ το πρωτον κινει ακινητον ον. l. xiv. c. viii. p. 1003. Things are one ſpecifically or λογῳ, when they are collected into one count, and expreſſed by one word or κατηγορημα, the definition of which applies equally to them all. Material things may be one ſpecifically, though many numerically: but this cannot hold as to energies; ſo that if there were as many different heavens as there are different men, the firſt neceſſary being would ſtill be numerically, as well as ſpecifically, one. Compar. Phyſ. Auſcult. l. viii. c. vii. p. 418. & ſeq.

[f] ουχ ὁυτως εχει, ὡστε μη ειναι θατερον θατερῳ, l. xiv. c. x. p. 1005. & Phyſ. Auſcult. l. viii. c. vii. p. 418.

[g] προς μεν γαρ ἑν, ἁπαντα συντεταχται. Ibid.

[h] Comp. l. xii. c. iv. p. 976. & l. xiv. c. x. p. 1004. Pliny, l. ii. c. i. & l. xxvii. c. ii. ſtrangely miſtakes his great maſter in natural hiſtory. The ſame errors he commits elſewhere in ſpeaking of God, Nature, the world, &c.

[i] Iliad, l. i. v. 204. quoted Metaph. l. xiv. c. ult. p. 1006. Cicero greatly miſ-

repreſents

CHAP. II.

The same doctrine inculcated in his exoteric or popular works.

This system of theology, not less satisfactory than sublime, Aristotle tells us that he had often inculcated, not merely in his acroatic works, which were lectures confined solely to his pupils, but also in his exoteric or popular writings, intended for the instruction of the public[k]. If this assertion cannot be disproved, his character will be rescued from the charge of dishonesty, in teaching a double doctrine, one to his pupils, and another to the world. Cicero[l] indeed says, that the Greek philosophers (meaning our author in particular) did not "seem always to hold the same language in their popular and in their more accurate works;" which variation was, surely, to be expected; since, in the former, they often reasoned, as Aristotle himself tells us, loosely or according to vulgar conception, and in the latter strictly or philosophically. But as to the fundamental points of his most important doctrines, Aristotle frequently refers from those of his books, "which were distinguished by pregnant brevity, closeness of thought, and quickness of transitions[m]," to his more expanded, more perspicuous, and more popular productions[n]. Much circumspection indeed became

represents his original. Inde deinde illi tot Dij si numeramus etiam Cœlum, Deum," &c. De Natur. Deor. l. i. c. xiii.

[k] καθαπερ εν τοις εγκυκλιοις φιλοσοφημασι περι τα θεια πολλακις προφαινεται τοις λογοις ότι το θειον αμεταβλητον ειναι το πρωτον και ακροτατον. De Cœlo, l. i. c. ix. p. 446.

[l] De Fin. l. v. c. v.

[m] Simplicius (ad Categor. in Procem.) thus characterises the acroatic, in contradistinction to the exoteric works, "ἡ βραχυλογια, ἡ των εννοιων πυκνοτης, και το της φρασεως συνεστραμμενον. To the last clause I have given a sense more conformable to truth than that which the words naturally present.

[n] Simplicius Comment. in Aristot. de Cœlo, fol. 67. Ethic. Nicom. l. i. c. iii. & xiii. l. vi. c. iv. Ethic. Eudem. l. i. c. viii. l. ii. c. i. De Republ. l. iii. c. vi. & l. vii. c. i.

became a philoſopher, deteſting ſuperſtition and deteſting democracy, yet living and teaching in the boſom of Athens; a city ſhamefully deformed by whatever is moſt abject in the one, and moſt wild in the other. But there is not a ſhadow of proof that, in any part of his writings, he encouraged or approved either of thoſe groſs popular deluſions; though it is highly probable that he arraigned their folly and abſurdity with more freedom in the Lyceum, than his prudence would have allowed him to expreſs in the Pantheon or the Forum.

The objection made to Ariſtotle's philoſophy, as not built on experiment.

An objection very commonly made to Ariſtotle's philoſophy is, that he is regardleſs of experience, and too fond of hypotheſis. In the whole extent in which this reproach is uſually urged by his detractors, it betrays ignorance in the extreme; ſince the principles of every one of his treatiſes are drawn ſolely from experience; and, in almoſt every ſtep that he takes, to experience he continually recurs for trying and confirming his concluſions. That he was not ſparing of experiments, in the modern ſenſe of the word, upon thoſe ſubjects on which he thought that a philoſopher might conſiſtently make uſe of them, is evident from his mechanical queſtions, his problems, his diſcourſes on the general properties or affections of animated nature, and, above all, from his doctrine of ſenſation, memory, recollection, and other powers of the ſoul or mind; which is entirely experimental. But Ariſtotle was contented with catching Nature in the fact, without attempting, after the modern faſhion, to put her to the torture; and in rejecting experiments operoſe, toilſome, or painful, either to their objects or their authors, he was juſtified by the habits of thinking, almoſt univerſally prevalent in his age and country. Educated in free and martial republics, careleſs of wealth, becauſe uncorrupted by

CHAP. II.

luxury, the whole tribe of ancient philosophers dedicated themselves to agreeable only and liberal pursuits, with too proud a disdain of arts merely useful or lucrative. They ranked with the first class of citizens; and, as such, were not to be lightly subjected to unwholesome or disgusting employments. To bend over a furnace, inhaling noxious steams; to torture animals, or to touch dead bodies, appeared to them operations not more misbecoming their humanity, than unsuitable to their dignity. For such discoveries as the heating and mixing of bodies offers to inquisitive curiosity, the naturalists of Greece trusted to slaves and mercenary mechanics, whose poverty or avarice tempted them to work in metals and minerals; and to produce, by unwearied labour, those coloured and sculptured ornaments, those gems, rings, cups, and vases, and other admired but frivolous elegancies, of which (in the opinion of good judges * of art) our boasted chemistry cannot produce the materials; nor, were the materials at hand, supply us with instruments fit to shape. The work-shops of tradesmen then revealed those mysteries which are now sought for in colleges and laboratories; and useful knowledge, perhaps, was not the less likely to be advanced, while the arts were confined to artists only; nor facts the more likely to be perverted, in order to support favourite theories, before the empiric had yet assumed the name, and usurped the functions, of the philosopher.

His philosophical language

To the Stagirite, it appeared to be the proper business of philosophy, not to multiply or collect facts, but to arrange and to

* I remember a strong expression of the late Mr. Wedgewood, in speaking of the Portland Vase, that the making of it "implied a science of chemistry, of which we have not yet the elements."

to explain them. This can only be done through the medium of a well-defined and highly cultivated language; and the language of Ariſtotle will be found the moſt copious and complete, and at the ſame time the moſt preciſe and elegant, ever employed by any philoſopher; ſerving at once as the readieſt channel of conveyance, and the fitteſt inſtrument for diſcovery. In his phyſical, as well as in his moral works, facts known and aſcertained are reduced to their ſimpleſt expreſſions, and thoſe doubtfully inferred, or barely ſuſpected, are, according to the true ſpirit of analyſis, denoted by words merely expreſſive of relations to things previouſly known. It is true that, in ages of ignorance, when Ariſtotle's ſuppoſed tenets were read in barbarous and diſguſting tranſlations, the terms employed by him, as ſigns of things ſought, and which, unleſs marked by ſigns, could never poſſibly be diſcovered, were as groſsly miſtaken, as they have been ſince ſhamefully miſrepreſented. In the ſcholaſtic philoſophy, that uſeleſs maſs of inſipid dulneſs, which inſolently arrogated to itſelf the name of Ariſtotleiſm, the ſchoolmen reſted in the names of occult qualities for explaining the phenomena both of mind and matter; and neglecting the repeated warnings of him whom they called their great maſter, and who well knew how liable the beſt things are to abuſe, they perverted the ſtudy of nature into metaphyſical ſubtlety and vain logomachy. But the ſame ſtupid ignorance which made them incapable of appreciating the Stagirite as a philoſopher, rendered them prone to worſhip him as a god. This imaginary divinity and his adorers were aſſailed by the giants of the ſixteenth century; who, in their rage to puniſh ſuch groſs intellectual idolatry, confounded the maſter with his diſciples, arraigned Ariſtotle for opinions which he had never held, degraded

miſtaken and preverted.

CHAP. II.

degraded him from honours which he had never usurped; and adopting his favourite method of analysis, endeavoured ungratefully and insidiously to destroy his well-earned fame with the instrument which he himself had formed and sharpened. But whatever unmerited disgrace may have been thereby reflected on some speculative doctrines, which I have here attempted briefly to explain, his practical philosophy, which may be read in the following translation, will still vindicate his fair claim to be regarded as one of the best instructors of mankind, on the more important subjects of Ethics and Politics.

ARISTOTLE's ETHICS.

BOOK I.

INTRODUCTION.

THE poet Gray writes thus in a letter to a friend: "For my part I read Ariſtotle, his poetics, politics, and morals; though I do not know well, which is which. In the firſt place, he is the hardeſt author by far I ever meddled with. Then he has a dry conciſeneſs, that makes one imagine one is peruſing a table of contents rather than a book: it taſtes for all the world like chopped hay, or rather like chopped logic; for he has a violent affection for that art, being in ſome ſort his own invention; ſo that he often loſes himſelf in little trifling diſtinctions and verbal niceties; and what is worſe, leaves you to extricate him as well as you can. Thirdly, he has ſuffered vaſtly from the tranſcribers, as all authors of great brevity neceſſarily muſt. Fourthly and laſtly, he has abundance of fine uncommon things, which make him well worth the pains he gives one." See Gray's Letters.

In this firſt book, our Author ſays "abundance of fine uncommon things," on the ſubjects of human nature, virtue, and happineſs. His mode of compoſition, however, is ſo totally different from that to which the caprice of faſhion has

given

given its temporary ſanction, that much labour and much ſkill muſt be employed, to adapt the form of his work to the taſte of modern readers; to whom both his method and his ſtyle, which formerly appeared to deſerve admiration [a], may now ſeem to demand apology. His method requires, that every ſubject of diſcuſſion ſhould be accurately defined, and completely divided; and that, how complex ſoever its nature may be, the compound ſhould be reſolved into its conſtituent elements; viewed in its birth and origin; and examined, in all its changes, varieties, augmentations, and diminutions. This mode of proceeding appeared to him peculiarly uſeful in moral and political queſtions, whoſe connections and relations are ſo intimate and ſo extenſive, that erroneous concluſions, on ſuch ſubjects, proceed far more frequently from narrowneſs of ſurvey, than from inaccuracy of reaſoning. In practical matters above all, this full and comprehenſive examination ſeemed indiſpenſably neceſſary, to prevent haſty deciſion, to inſpire cautious diſtruſt; and thus to arreſt the progreſs of paſſion and frenzy in a career which might leave them without retreat.

But, with whatever other advantages a treatiſe written with this ſtrictneſs and ſeverity of method may be accompanied, it certainly is not calculated to afford *gratuitous* information. To apprehend its meaning diſtinctly, and to perceive its full ſcope, demands much attention and much reflection on the part even of the reader. His patience is likely to be ſoon exhauſted by the too painful taſk; eſpecially if his taſte has been corrupted by thoſe flowery and fallacious productions of the times, whoſe authors (men of narrow views and ſelfiſh minds, and ſo long habituated

[a] Cicero Topic. c. i. p. 171. Edit. Olivet. & paſſim.

habituated to party politics, that they have loſt all reliſh, and almoſt all perception of truth,) are contented to confound and darken a whole region of ſcience, provided they can throw a falſe glare on one favourite and faſhionable ſpot. This darling topic they exert themſelves to beautify and illumine; adorning with eloquence and metaphors, and all the embroidery of declamation, the dangerous inference that is drawn from their erroneous, becauſe imperfect, argument. Nothing can be more ſmooth, or more eaſily followed by the reader, than the whole progreſs of their diſcourſe. But the very circumſtance which renders it ſo eaſy and ſo popular, alſo makes it of no value. The ſubject has been conſidered under one partial aſpect; a different view of it is taken; the incomplete theory is aſſaulted by another equally imperfect; and both of them ſo flimſy and cloud-built, that they are unable to withſtand even the ſoft impreſſions of their adverſe debility. Yet each party triumphs for a while in the bubble of its own creating, and vainly deems it irreſiſtible; a falſe confidence, that often gives birth to the greateſt practical errors. Ariſtotle's method is directly the reverſe: his works require attention, but they repay it; they will fully compenſate, in ſolid inſtruction, for their defect (if it may be called one) in point of deluſive entertainment.

The Stagirite's ſtyle is not leſs unfaſhionable than his method. It diſplays not any allurements to catch the reader's fancy; it diſdains every attempt to excite ſurpriſe, to provoke mirth, to inflame, ſooth, or gratify paſſion. The thirſt for knowledge is the only want which the Author profeſſes to ſupply; and this thirſt, he was of opinion, will ever be beſt quenched

BOOK I.

in the clear ſtream of unadorned reaſon; as that water is the pureſt and moſt ſalutary, which has neither taſte nor colour.

Ariſtotle did not, like his maſter Plato, baniſh poets from his Republic. He himſelf courted the Lyric muſe, and reached her loftieſt flights. But he never underſtood by what perverſity of purpoſe the agreeable illuſions of poetry could be aſſociated and mixed with the ſober ſcience of politics. In all practical matters, he knew the danger of ſaying any thing to the heart and paſſions, which would not bear to be examined by the light of the underſtanding. In tranſlating incomparably the moſt valuable part of his works, I have attempted therefore to imitate his preciſion and energy, as far as that can be done without leaving the fainteſt trace of his obſcurity. My aim throughout is to adhere rigidly to his ſenſe; to omit nothing which he ſays; to ſay nothing which he has omitted; but to endeavour, to the beſt of my abilities, to expreſs his meaning, agreeably as well as forcibly; ſince a mere verbal tranſlation would convey not only an inadequate, but often a very falſe, impreſſion of the Greek original.

Words, as our Author teaches, are both the ſigns of things, and the materials in which our compariſons, abſtractions, and concluſions concerning thoſe things are embodied. The words of one language, therefore, will often be very imperfectly expreſſed by thoſe of another; and the more complex their ſignifications are, the diverſities between them will naturally be the wider. To the terms employed in the ſciences of Ethics and Politics, this obſervation is peculiarly applicable. The original term, and that by which it is tranſlated, not compre-

hending

hending exactly the ſame identical notions, the Engliſh word which correſponds to the Greek in one of its meanings, will often not expreſs it in another. The phraſeology, therefore, muſt be occaſionally varied; and the ambition to attain propriety and excellence, will thus ſometimes give to a tranſlation, the appearance of looſeneſs and inaccuracy. In many caſes, exact equivalents to ſingle Greek words, are not to be found either in Engliſh, or in any other language. One term, therefore, muſt frequently be rendered by ſeveral; and the tranſlation neceſſarily degenerating into a paraphraſe, will often gain in perſpicuity and popularity, what it loſes in preciſion and energy [b]. From the philoſophical arrangement of the Greek tongue, and the ſingular fondneſs of Greek writers for abſtract and univerſal concluſions, words denoting the higher genera or claſſes, are employed by them on many occaſions, when terms more ſpecific would anſwer the purpoſe better, and ſound more gracefully, in Engliſh. With regard to this particular, I have ſometimes ventured to prefer to ſtrictneſs of verſion, a compliance with the genius of modern tongues, and with the taſte of modern readers.

My

[b] When the Greek language was more familiarly known than it is at preſent, Ariſtotle's ſtyle was acknowledged by the beſt critics to poſſeſs the higheſt of all merits, that of expreſſing his deep and various wiſdom always in the fitteſt terms. Dicendi quoque incredibili quadam cum copia, tum etiam ſuavitate. Cicero Topic. c. i. p. 171. Edit. Oliveti. Quintilian ſpeaks to the ſame purpoſe: Quid Ariſtotelem? quem dubito ſcientia rerum, an ſcriptorum copia, an eloquendi ſuavitate, an inventionum acumine, an varietate operum, clariorem puto. "Why need I mention Ariſtotle? concerning whom I am in doubt, whether he is rendered more illuſtrious by the magnitude and variety of his writings, his univerſal ſcience, the acuteneſs of his inventions, or the ſuavity of his diction." Quintil. Inſ. Orat. l. x. c. i. p. 224. Edit. Bipont.

My principal deſign and only ambition is to convey, in the preſent ſtate of public opinion with reſpect to fundamental principles, a clear notion of thoſe writings of the Stagirite which he intitled his "Philoſophy concerning Human Affairs [c]." His Ethics, I believe, no man can read without becoming the better; and his Politics, I think, no ſtateſman can ſtudy, without becoming the wiſer. But the corrupt and mutilated ſtate of his works compelled me, reluctantly, to uſe ſome freedom with their form, in order the more completely to preſerve their ſubſtance. In different books, and even in different chapters of the ſame book, the ſame thoughts often recur in nearly the ſame words. Theſe uſeleſs repetitions, proceeding commonly from the fault of unſkilful editors, I thought it my duty to retrench; and continually to aim at ſelecting that expreſſion in which the ſenſe is moſt fully conveyed. A tranſlation is a portrait; but that the portrait may pleaſe, the original ſhould be ſhown with its moſt becoming expreſſion, and in its beſt attitudes.

[c] η περι τα ανθρωπινα φιλοσοφια.

BOOK I.

ARGUMENT.

Human action—Operations and productions—Happiness—Opinions concerning it—It consists in virtuous energies—Proved by induction—Solon's saying concerning it explained—Analysis of our moral powers.

BOOK I. Chap. 1.

Human action terminates either in operations or in productions.

SINCE every art and every kind of knowledge, as well as all the actions and all the deliberations of men, constantly aim at something which they call good; good, in general, may be justly defined, "that which all desire." But among the various ends and purposes of our activity and pursuit, there is this important difference, that some consist merely in operations, and others chiefly in productions. Of those arts or actions of which production is the chief end, the work is more valuable than the operation by which it was produced; and, as there is a wide variety of arts and actions, there must be a correspondent variety of ends: of the medical art, health; of shipbuilding, a vessel; of generalship, victory; of œconomy, riches. It often happens that arts rise one above another in dignity, and that all those of an inferior sort are subservent to one principal, their natural and acknowledged sovereign. Thus bridle making is subservient to horsemanship; and horsemanship to war; and the end of the subservient art is plainly less valuable than that of the art to which it ministers, because the former is pursued merely for the sake of the latter. This holds universally, whe-

ther

BOOK I. Chap. 2.

It belongs to politics to investigate the chief end of man.

ther the ends of human action consist in operations or in productions.

But if there be an ultimate end of all human pursuit, an end desirable merely in itself, (and unless there be such an end, desire, proceeding to infinity, will terminate in a baseless vision,) this ultimate end must be what is called good; and of goods, the best. The knowledge of it, also, must greatly contribute to the benefit of life; serving, as a butt to bowmen, for the direction of our views and actions. Let us, therefore, endeavour to delineate it carefully, first premising that the investigation of it belongs to that master-science called politics; a science which regulates and appoints what are the other sciences, as well as what are the arts that ought to be introduced into cities, what kinds of them the different classes of citizens ought respectively to learn, and to what extent each in particular ought to be known and cultivated. The most honourable functions of a civil or military nature; those of the orator, financier, or general, are but instruments employed by politics for promoting human happiness; which, if precisely one and the same in states and individuals, must, with regard to the former, be more difficult both to produce and to maintain. How delightful is it to make individuals happy! but to effect the happiness of states is an employment still more divine. Such then is the aim of this work, which is entirely of a political nature [d].

It

[d] In the Magna Moralia, l. i. c. i. p. 145. the following reason is given why Ethics should be considered as a part of politics, οτι δε ουδεν εν τοις πολιτικοις δυνατον πραξαι ανευ του ποιον τινα ειναι, &c. "That it is impossible to do any thing in politics, without having men endowed with certain habits; wherefore Ethics," he observes, "are likely to be a part as well as the principle and source of politics."

The proper method of treating moral and political philosophy, and the fit character of its hearers.

It will be our endeavour to attain that accuracy which the nature of the ſubject admits; for perfection is not required in all the labours of the mind, any more than in all the works of the hand. Political juſtice or virtue ſeems liable to this uncertainty, that it depends rather on law than on nature. The good, or end, at which this virtue aims, ſeems to be not leſs doubtful; ſince much evil is frequently its reſult. Many are ruined by their wealth, and many by their courage. In matters ſo little ſtable we muſt be contented, therefore, with catching the general reſemblance of truth; and our concluſions will deſerve to be approved, if in moſt caſes they are found to hold true; for it is the part of wiſdom to be ſatisfied in each ſubject with that kind of evidence which the nature of the ſubject allows; it not being leſs abſurd to require demonſtrations from an orator, than to be contented with probabilities from a mathematician. Of performances in each ſcience, thoſe only can appreciate the merit by whom that ſcience has been ſtudied. From a work on politics, therefore, thoſe alone can derive much benefit who have acquired a general and practical knowledge of human nature. Youth is not the ſeaſon for ſuch a ſtudy; for youth is unexperienced in the buſineſs of life, which is both the ſource and the object of all ſound political reaſoning. It makes not any difference whether a man is young in point of years, or in point of character; for his inaptitude ariſes entirely from his boyiſh purſuits, and childiſh opinions. But to thoſe whoſe paſſions have been diſciplined by the maturity of years and reaſon, this kind of knowledge will afford both pleaſure and profit. Thus much concerning our ſubject, the mode of treating it, and the character of thoſe to whom our diſcourſe is addreſſed.

Let

BOOK I. Chap. 4.

Different opinions concerning happiness.

Let us resume, therefore, by inquiring, since all our thoughts and desires aim at some kind of good, what is the end of the science called politics: or, in other words, what is the principal of all those goods resulting from the proper direction of human action? Its name is universally[e] acknowledged; both the learned and the multitude call it happiness[f]. But as to the thing itself, there is a wide diversity of opinion between philosophers and the vulgar. The latter place happiness in things visible and palpable: in pleasure, wealth, honour; and, often changing their minds, they place it, when sick, in health; when poor, in riches; and when they reflect on their own ignorance, they deem those most happy who can boast their attainments in science. Some philosophers again think that besides all these particular and relative goods, there is a good in itself absolutely, the cause of this quality in other things, which deserve to be called good merely because they participate of this absolute goodness. It would be useless to enumerate all the opinions on this subject; let it suffice to mention the most prevalent, or the most reasonable. It ought not to escape our notice that, in all our inquiries, we may either proceed from principles, or mount up towards them. Plato, therefore, doubted which of the two was the best mode of investigation; as, in Olympic Stadium, whether the proper course proceeded from the judges to the goal, or from the goal to the judges[g]. In other sciences, we ought to begin from the things best known; either absolutely in themselves, from

[e] σχεδον ὑπο των πλειστων ὁμολογειται. "Almost acknowledged by the most," which seems merely a modest way of speaking, not tolerable in English.

[f] το δε ευ ζην και ευ πραττειν ταὐτον ὑπολαμβανουσι τῳ ευδαιμονειν. "To live well and to act well, they reckon synonymous with being happy." This sentence is omitted.

[g] See History of Ancient Greece, vol. i. c. v. p. 228.

BOOK I.

from the ſimplicity and ſtability of their nature; or relatively to the inquirer, becauſe moſt familiar to his ſenſes, his obſervation, and experience[g]. But in Politics, we ought to begin by operating on the moral nature of man, ſince the firſt requiſite is to have diſciples habituated to the practice of virtue. Such perſons either know, or will ſoon underſtand, principles[h]. But thoſe of a different character may attend to Heſiod.

The beſt and nobleſt of the human kind
Are thoſe endow'd with a deep-thinking mind;
Nor are *they* uſeleſs, who ſuch men obey,
Submitting ſtill to wiſdom's lawful ſway;
But he, who though unfit his ways to rule,
Yet will not to a wiſer go to ſchool,
That man is, ſure, a good-for-nothing fool[i].

Chap. 5.

Thoſe opinions examined.

To return from this digreſſion, men's notions of happineſs may eaſily be conjectured from the lives which they lead. The groſs vulgar of mankind think of nothing but pleaſure, and therefore lead a life of mere ſenſual enjoyment; conſtrained like ſlaves, and ſtupid as cattle. Their error is excuſable, ſince many of the great ſet them an example, which themſelves ſeem

[g] For the ſake of perſpicuity I have here expanded Ariſtotle's thought by borrowing expreſſions frequently repeated in his Analytics and Metaphyſics.

[h] Ariſtotle ſays, they know that the thing is, and therefore need not be taught its cauſe; they have a practical knowledge of virtue, which is better than its theory; and this practical knowledge is itſelf a principle inſtilled and confirmed by experience and cuſtom. See the end of chapter vii. It may be further obſerved, that our author, with his uſual modeſty, ſays, *perhaps* we ought to begin with the things beſt known to ourſelves; and *therefore* thoſe only are qualified to ſtudy politics with advantage, who have been previouſly trained to good morals. I have inverted the order, becauſe the latter is proved in chapter iii.

[i] Heſiod, Εργων, i. 293.

ſeem to have copied from the ſottiſh Sardanapalus. A ſecond plan of life is that purſued by men of activity and enterpriſe, who eagerly engage in the public concerns of their country, and have honour for their object. But this honour is a thing too ſuperficial and flimſy to be the happineſs of which we are in queſt. It ſeems to depend not leſs on thoſe who confer honours, than upon thoſe on whom they are conferred. But happineſs, we foreſee, muſt be ſomething independent and permanent. Beſides, theſe troubleſome honours are courted chiefly for the purpoſe of flattering ſelf-love, for removing our ſuſpicions of our own unworthineſs, and for rendering us in our own conceit virtuous and happy. For this reaſon we take moſt pride in being honoured by men of ſenſe, by thoſe who beſt know us, and for meritorious actions. Virtue, therefore, is plainly more valuable than honour, even in the eſtimation of thoſe by whom honour is moſt coveted; ſince the latter is purſued merely as the ſign and ſhadow of the former. But virtue alone does not conſtitute happineſs. A man poſſeſſed of virtue may be aſleep or inactive; he may never, through life, have an opportunity of exhibiting his good qualities; and notwithſtanding theſe qualities, he may frequently be involved in the greateſt diſaſters. Such a man was never, except for argument's ſake, pronounced happy. But enough on this ſubject, which has been already treated in our popular diſcourſes. A third plan of life is that of the ſpeculative philoſopher, which ſhall be examined in the ſequel. A life of money-making and commerce is plainly a ſtate of toil and trouble; and riches cannot be the good inquired after, becauſe they are deſired, not on their own account, but for the purpoſes which they anſwer; and are valuable, not as ends, but merely as inſtruments. The other ſchemes of happineſs

BOOK I.

happineſs are, therefore, preferable to that of the money-maker; but even thoſe, it appears, are defective; in confirmation of which many arguments may be produced, which we ſhall not at preſent urge.

Chap. 6.

Examination of Plato's opinion concerning the chief good; and refutation of the doctrine of ideas.

It may, perhaps, be better to conſider good, abſolute and univerſal; which, according to ſome philoſophers, is the only real good, by the mere participation of which other things are entitled to this epithet. To me the taſk of examining this opinion is unpleaſant and arduous, becauſe the doctrine of univerſals and ideas was introduced by thoſe for whom I have the greateſt friendſhip[k]. Yet a philoſopher ought to demoliſh even his own ſyſtems, when they ſtand in the way of truth; nor ought the ſacred name of friendſhip ever to obſtruct a thing ſtill more ſacred than itſelf. Thoſe who introduced the doctrine of ideas allow that it is not applicable to things prior in order the one to the other[l], and therefore not applicable to number. But the word "good" applies equally to ſubſtances, to modes, and to relations; although ſubſtances are certainly prior in order to modes and relations, which are the affections or appendages of ſubſtances. The word "good" therefore, when applied to both, is not taken in the ſame ſenſe; and therefore it does not

[k] The author means Plato. He ſays, in his Magna Moralia, p. 145, that Pythagoras firſt treated of virtue, but improperly; ſince he explained the ſcience of Ethics by that of numbers, confounding ſpeculations altogether heterogeneous. Socrates ſpoke better and more perſpicuouſly: but his theory is imperfect, becauſe he makes the virtues matters of ſcience; whereas ſcience belongs only to the intellect or rational part of the ſoul, while the virtues belong not only to that, but (as will be fully explained hereafter) to the irrational part, conſiſting in the paſſions and appetites. Plato followed, well diſtinguiſhing the rational and irrational principles, but perplexing and darkening the ſubject of Ethics, by mixing with it the doctrine of ideas.

[l] Eudem. Ethic. l. i. c. viii. p. 201.—See alſo Analyſis, p. 84. & ſeq.

BOOK I.

not denote any common idea. Good, indeed, is ſaid in as many ways as being: thus it is applied to God, and the human mind, which are ſubſtances; to the virtues, which are qualities; to utility, which is a relation; to mediocrity, which is a quantity; to the critical moment, which is time; and to a fit reſidence, which is place[m]. It is plain, therefore, that the word "good" applied to things ſo different, does not denote any one idea common to all thoſe claſſes or categories. If it did, all kinds of good would belong to one and the ſame ſcience. But we find that various ſciences are requiſite for aſcertaining the different kinds of good, even in one and the ſame category. Thus, the critical moment in war is aſcertained by a general; in diſeaſe, by a phyſician. The medical ſcience determines what is mediocrity with reſpect to diet; and the gymnaſtic, what is mediocrity in point of exerciſe. It is difficult to know wherein conſiſts the difference between the idea of a man and a man, ſince both muſt be defined by the ſame terms. The ſame obſervation applies to good, and the idea of good. The eternity aſcribed to the latter does not make any difference; for that which is white now, is as much white, as what has continued white for an indefinite length of time. The Pythagoreans reaſon better when they diſtinguiſh various kinds of good and evil[n]; in which they ſeem to be followed by Speuſippus[o]. But of this ſubject we ſhall treat hereafter. Some uncertainty ſeems ſtill

[m] Ariſtotle ſays, περα τοιαυτα, meaning the other categories, See above, p. 58.

[n] Ariſtotle ſays, they placed one in the co-arrangement of good. See above, p. 112.

[o] Ariſtotle is ſuppoſed to have taken it amiſs that Plato ſhould have preferred to him his own nephew Speuſippus, as his ſucceſſor in the academy; and this private pique is thought to have influenced him in his philoſophical oppoſition to his maſter's doctrines. Were this true, it might be expected that his oppoſition would not have been leſs marked to Speuſippus, whom he here goes out of his way to commend.

ftill to adhere to the obfervations above made, becaufe we have not fufficiently diftinguifhed the two kinds of goods; thofe which are loved and purfued for their own fake only, and thofe which are loved and purfued merely becaufe they are fitted to produce or preferve the former, or to ward off the contrary evils. Let us feparate therefore from things merely ufeful to fome further end, things called good in themfelves, and confider whether this epithet is beftowed on all of them precifely in the fame fenfe. What are thefe goods in themfelves, unlefs fuch things as we wifh to obtain and enjoy for their own fake only; pleafures, honours, the exercife of our fight or underftanding? Such things may be ufeful, but they are not merely ufeful, fince, independently of any purpofe which they anfwer, they are defired on their own account. Are all fuch things then called good, for the fame reafon that fnow and cerufe are both called white, becaufe they excite one and the fame fimple perception of whitenefs? This is not true; for pleafure is good in one fenfe, honour in another, intellection in a third; in each of the three, the word "good" has a different meaning; which would not be the cafe if the idea of good was as fimple and uniform as that of white; a doctrine that totally confounds the fpecific diftinctions of things. Why then is the fame appellation applied to fuch different objects? Not furely by chance; but becaufe thofe objects are fomehow related to each other, as proceeding from one caufe, tending to one end, or connected by fome analogy; as the underftanding is called the eye of the mind, having the fame relation to it, which the eye has to the body. But fuch nice fpeculations belong not to the prefent fubject [p]; for if there be

[p] Ariftotle fays, that it is not neceffary at prefent accurately to afcertain why different things are called good, any more than to treat accurately concerning the general idea of goodnefs.

BOOK I.

be a general idea of goodneſs, common to all things called good, and ſeparable from them, it is plain that this ſeparate goodneſs cannot be an object of human attainment, and therefore need not be an object of human purſuit. None of the arts or ſciences contemplate this general idea as their example or pattern[q]; or conſider it as affording the ſmalleſt aſſiſtance for attaining the different ends at which they reſpectively aim. Of what benefit would ſuch a contemplation be to the embroiderer or the architect? The phyſician does not conſider good in general, but the good, or health of man, or rather of that particular man who happens to be his patient; for with individuals only he has to do.

Chap. 7.

A delineation of the ſupreme good;

Let us return again to the ſought-for good, and try to find out what it can be. We ſee that it is a different thing in different arts and actions: one thing, for example, in the art of phyſic; another in the art of war. What then is the good peculiar to each? Is it not that for the ſake of which all the other operations of the art are performed; as in phyſic, health; in war, victory; in architecture, a houſe; and in all our actions and deliberations, the end at which they aim? If then there is an end or purpoſe in life itſelf, the good ſought for muſt conſiſt in this; and if more ends than one, in theſe. This inveſtigation therefore brings us back to the ſame concluſion as before; but we muſt endeavour, if poſſible, to render the matter ſtill more perſpicuous. Since there are various objects of our purſuit, ſome of which are deſired merely for the ſake of other things, and never rationally for their own, ſuch as riches, a flute,

[q] The author ſays, that though this general good be neither πρακτον nor κτητον; neither an object of human practice nor human attainment, yet it may be thought to ſerve as a παραδειγμα, or pattern; and therefore removes this objection, which he had propoſed to himſelf.

BOOK I.

flute, and whatever comes under the defcription of means or inftruments, it is plain that none of thefe can be the good of which we are in queft, and which muft be fomething complete and perfect in itfelf; for we call that more perfect which is defired on its own account, than that which is defired as a means towards fome further end: and that more perfect which is never defired but as an end, than that which is defired both as a means and as an end. Happinefs is never defired but for its own fake only. Honour, pleafure, intelligence, and every virtue, are defirable furely on their own account, but they are alfo defirable as means towards happinefs. But happinefs, we have faid, is never defired as a means, becaufe it is complete and all-fufficient in itfelf, which the good fought for ought to be; and all-fufficient, not merely for the individual, but for his parents, children, family, friends, and fellow-citizens, fince man is by nature a focial being; yet to this focial principle limits are affigned, for if it diverged to infinity [r], there would be a defire without an object [s]: but of this we fhall fpeak hereafter. That is all-fufficient, which, taken by itfelf, renders life an object of defire. Such we fay is happinefs, which, feparate and alone, is the moft defirable of all things; and therefore united with the leaft of other goods, ftill entitled to pre-eminence [t]; complete and perfect in itfelf, and the ultimate end of all our defigns and actions.

which confifts in virtuous energies.

But to call happinefs the beft thing in the world, (which none will difpute,) does not clearly explain wherein human happinefs confifts. This will beft appear, if we confider what is the peculiar work and proper bufinefs of a man. A mufician, a fculptor,

[r] Ariftotle fays, to his children's children, and the friends of his friends, in endlefs fucceffion.

[s] See above, p. 91.

[t] The good added to happinefs is ὑπεροχη των αγαθων, fuperabundant.

BOOK I.

ſculptor, and every other artiſt, has his reſpective operation and work, in the performance of which his main excellence lies; and can it be imagined, while ſhoemakers and carpenters have their proper taſks aſſigned to them, that Nature intended man for idleneſs? His eyes, and hands, and feet, and all his other parts, have their peculiar functions; and ſhall there be no function different from any, or all, of theſe, belonging to the whole? Wherein does this function conſiſt? To live, is common to him with plants. The mere power of growth and nutrition belongs not therefore to the preſent queſtion. The ſenſitive life follows next, which is common to man with horſes, oxen, and the whole animal kingdom. There remains then a life of rational action; whether he exerciſe reaſon himſelf, or obey the reaſon of another. In ſuch a life his real buſineſs conſiſts; and that man does his buſineſs the beſt [t], who acts moſt rationally through life; the virtue of each individual of a ſpecies, depending on the excellence with which he performs the work peculiar to that ſpecies alone. The proper good of man conſiſts then in virtuous energies [u], that is, in the exerciſe of virtue continued through life; for one ſwallow makes not a ſummer; neither does one day, or a ſhort time, conſtitute happineſs. Let this ſerve for a ſketch of good—that univerſally coveted object, which will afterwards be more fully delineated: for, it ſhould ſeem, that an accurate outline may eaſily be filled up; eſpecially with the aſſiſtance of time, from

[t] The author illuſtrates this, by ſaying that the buſineſs of a harper, and of a good harper, is the ſame; the difference between them ariſing only from the ſuperior excellence with which the latter performs his work.

[u] Ariſtotle here introduces his diſtinction between virtue and the energy of virtue. See above, p. 133. This ſenſe is expreſſed in the text, in language more familiar to the modern reader.

BOOK I.

from which arts derive their improvement. Let us remember alſo what was before obſerved, that more accuracy ſhould not be expected from an author, than is conſiſtent with the nature of his ſubject, and his deſign in treating it. Both the bricklayer and the mathematician are converſant with perpendiculars; but the former conſiders them only as uſeful in his work; the latter examines their nature and properties, becauſe abſtract truth is the object of his ſtudy. Unleſs the example of the bricklayer be followed in other matters, the principal ſubject will often be exceeded and obſcured by the mere acceſſories. Let it alſo be remembered, that we ought not to be over curious in the inveſtigation of cauſes; concerning ſome things it is ſufficient to know that they are, without knowing their reaſon. This is the caſe with thoſe firſt principles which reſult from perceptions of ſenſe, from induction, and from cuſtom [x]. We ought carefully to draw them from their reſpective ſources, and exert our utmoſt care that they be correctly aſcertained. This is of the higheſt importance in all our inquiries; in which, that which is begun well, is more than half ended; ſince much light is thereby diffuſed through every ſubſequent part of our ſpeculations.

Chap. 8.

This opinion conſiſtent with the properties aſcribed to happineſs.

We ſhall examine this chief good or happineſs, not merely in its definition, but in the properties rightly aſcribed to it. Truth only is conſiſtent; and if our notion of happineſs be juſt, it will not be diſcordant with thoſe properties. Goods are

[x] Our author adds, αλλαι δε αλλως, which may be tranſlated, "and other principles ariſe from other ſources." But this does not appear to me to be his meaning, becauſe I do not find any other ſources mentioned in any part of his works: The αλλαι αλλως muſt then mean that ſome of thoſe principles ariſe from one of thoſe ſources, and ſome from another, which is implied in the tranſlation.

BOOK I.

are divided into three kinds: thofe of the mind, thofe of the body, and thofe confifting in externals. We give the preference to the firft of the three, which we regard as the fovereign good; placing happinefs in mental energy; an opinion ancient and univerfal among philofophers. We do right alfo in placing the chief end and main purpofe of life in action. From this, it refults that happinefs is feated in the mind; a truth confirmed by the common fenfe of mankind embodied in language; "living well," or "doing well," being expreffions fynonymous with happinefs. In all their inquiries on the fubject, men feem to have been led to conclufions nearly refembling the notion of happinefs above given. Some place it in virtue, others in prudence, others in wifdom; fome join pleafure; others add externals; and thofe different opinions have either been long held by the greater part of mankind, or more recently introduced by moft refpectable philofophers. It is not credible, that either party fhould totally miftake the truth. Our notion nearly agrees with theirs who place happinefs in virtue; for we fay that it confifts in the action of virtue; that is, not merely in the poffeffion, but in the ufe[7]. The mere poffeffion is confiftent with a ftate of fleep, or liftlefs apathy, from which no good can refult. But the virtuous man, when he acts, muft act well, and be happy; as, in the Olympic games, the prize is gained only by the combatants; not by thofe, whatever their merits may be, who decline entering the lifts. To fuch men virtue is the higheft pleafure; for pleafure refides in the mind, and each is moft pleafed with what he moft loves. Thus the lover of horfes is pleafed with horfes; the lover of fhows, with fhows; and the lover of juftice is no lefs pleafed with juftice; and

[7] Ariftotle here oppofes habit to energy, as well as poffeffion to ufe.

and the lover of virtue, with virtue. The multitude, indeed, purſue different pleaſures, becauſe they do not rightly apprehend in what true pleaſure conſiſts. But pleaſure, ſtrictly ſo called, is the delight of a virtuous man, whoſe life needs not an-appendage of falſe joys, containing the perennial ſpring of true pleaſure in itſelf. For he is not a good man who delights not in good actions; and vain is the praiſe of juſtice, liberality, and other virtues, by thoſe who feel no gratification in their practice. In the eſtimation of a wiſe man, virtue is pleaſant becauſe it is honourable and good; his happineſs is one regular whole; not broken and disjointed like that in the Delian inſcription:

> "The faireſt good is juſtice; health, the beſt;
> "The ſweeteſt far, to taſte of what we love."

All theſe qualities belong to the beſt energies, in which, we ſay, happineſs conſiſts. The opinion of thoſe who add externals, is not ill-founded; ſince, independently of them, it is often impoſſible, at leaſt very difficult, to exhibit virtue in its full luſtre [a]. Many operations muſt be performed by inſtruments; under which name I include friends, wealth, and political power. The want of ſome advantages; for example, of honourable deſcent, of promiſing children, or of dignity of preſence;

[a] In the Ethics to Eudemus, b. i. c. ii. p. 196., Ariſtotle makes an important diſtinction between the things in which human happineſs conſiſts, and thoſe without which it cannot be completely enjoyed; εν τισι των ἡμετερων το ξην ευ· και τινων ανευ, τοις ανθρωποις ουκ ενδεχεται ειναι, &c. "Health is different from the things by which it is upheld, and life from thoſe by which it is rendered comfortable. The ſame holds with regard to all the actions and habits of men." The confounding happineſs with the externals, without which, in our dependent ſtate, it cannot be completely enjoyed, is conſidered by our author as one of the great ſources of immoral practice, as well as of erroneous theory.

BOOK I.

presence; deprives happiness of its splendour: and the man seems less qualified for attaining it, who is deformed in body, friendless, childless, and forlorn [a]. Wherefore some place happiness in external prosperity [b].

Chap. 9.

Which depends on our own exertions.

It comes then to be considered, whether happiness is acquired by instruction, custom, or some other kind of exercise; or merely by the dispensation of fortune and the gods. There is not any gift surely that might more reasonably be expected to descend from heaven, since, of all human possessions, happiness is the most valuable. But this question will be more fitly examined in another place. For happiness, even though it descend not from heaven, but be attained by study and exercise on earth, is yet most divine in itself; the end and prize of virtue, which all may gain by due exertion, who are not maimed in their minds. The acquiring of happiness by ourselves, is preferable to owing it to fortune [c]; it most probably therefore is thus acquired; since nature always effects her purposes by the best means; a point aimed at by art, and every intelligent cause, and which the best cause always attains: and to leave happiness, the fairest and best of things, to the disposal of fortune, would be a mark of negligence not discernible in any other of the arrangements of nature [d]. That happiness is acquired by ourselves,

[a] Aristotle adds, "or who having had good friends and promising children, has lost them."

[b] What is added, ενιοι δε την αρετην, "and some place it in virtue," seems superfluous.

[c] For this he assigns two reasons in the Ethics to Eudemus, b. i. c. iii. p. 197. ει δ᾽ εν τῳ, αυτον ποιον τινα ειναι, και τας κατ᾽ αυτον πραξεις, κοινοτερον αν ειη το αγαθον και θειοτερον, &c. "If good or happiness consists in the quality of our actions and characters, it must be both more common and more divine; more common, because a greater number may attain it; and more divine, because it will depend upon our own exertions." Idem ibid.

[d] There is, perhaps, an intentional obscurity in the whole of this passage. Aristotle does

BOOK I.

ourſelves, agrees alſo with its definition, "that it conſiſts in virtuous energies." Other things, we have ſaid, are neceſſary, as a certain length of time; and others are ſerviceable, as inſtruments. The ſame concluſion correſponds with what we ſaid in the beginning, namely, that politics aimed at promoting the higheſt felicity of man; the principal care, therefore, of all good ſtateſmen has always been, to form their fellow-citizens to virtue. Neither an ox nor a horſe, nor any other animal, is denominated happy; becauſe virtuous energies cannot be aſcribed to them. Nor is this epithet beſtowed on children, whoſe imperfect age affords only a promiſe of happineſs. But many are the viciſſitudes of life; and thoſe who have long been proſperous, may, towards the concluſion of their days, be involved in calamities rivalling the far-famed diſaſters of Priam. None will call thoſe happy, who, after ſuffering ſuch evils in life, die a wretched death.

Chap. 10.

Solon's ſaying, that none can be pronounced happy till dead.

Ought we, then, to adopt the ſentiments of Solon, "that no man can be called happy while he lives?" Is he therefore happy when he dies? or is not this too abſurd to be ſaid, eſpecially by thoſe who place happineſs in action? It does not appear that Solon had this meaning, but only that a man might, at death, be congratulated upon his eſcape from the evils and calamities of life. Yet this opinion is liable to contradiction; for a man when dead, is, with regard to proſperity and adverſity, in the ſame ſtate with a man who meets with either of them when alive,

does not expreſsly deny the interference of the gods; but afterwards, confounding this interference with fortune, ſays, that it is not reaſonable to believe that nature, or (as explained in other paſſages) the God of nature, ſhould commit ſuch an important object as human happineſs to the direction of ſo blind a guide as fortune. But in the ſtrict philoſophical ſenſe, happineſs, as well as all other things, is ultimately to be referred to the Deity as its cauſe. Metaphyſ. l. i. c. ii. p. 841.

BOOK I.

alive, without being ſenſible of them; and is in this manner ſtill within the reach of the good or bad fortune which befals his children and their deſcendants. And how unſtable is the proſperity of families? What vaſt degeneracy in the ſons of happy and illuſtrious fathers? Yet it ſeems abſurd to ſuppoſe the ſtate of the dead affected and altered by theſe revolutions, and not leſs abſurd to ſuppoſe that the happineſs of children ſhould not be ſhared by their parents. But the ſolution of the queſtion firſt propoſed, will enable us to ſolve the other difficulties.

This ſaying explained.

Solon ſaid that we muſt look to the end; meaning thereby, that we might then juſtly ſay, not that a man was, but that he had been, happy. Is it not therefore abſurd to think that, while he actually was happy, this epithet could not be applied to him, becauſe of the viciſſitudes of life to which he was expoſed? If happineſs changes with fortune, it will be as variable as the colours of the camelion. But this is not true: for the propriety of our conduct depends, not on our fortune, but on our manner of uſing it; and virtuous energies are the genuine ſource of happineſs, as the vicious are of miſery. This is atteſted by the queſtion juſt ſtarted concerning the importance of ſtability to happineſs.

The peculiar ſtability of virtuous energies.

Of all human things, habitual energies of virtue are the moſt ſtable; they are more permanent than even the ſciences; and of the virtues themſelves, the moſt valuable are the firmeſt; forming the continual meditation and delight of thoſe whom they adorn. For this reaſon, they alone are not liable to be forgotten or loſt; but are an immoveable property in the thoughts and life of a good man; who, whatever may befal him, will behave gracefully; approving his conduct exact, ſquare, and blameleſs. Slight misfortunes are unable to ſhakehis well-balanced happineſs; but, in in the uſe of a great proſperity, his excellence will ſhine more conſpicuous: and when perſecuted by painful and afflicting calamity, which not only impedes his preſent exertions, but darkens his future proſpects, his worth will irradiate the gloom, while he reſiſts and ſurmounts the ſevereſt ſufferings, not by ſtupid inſenſibility, but by generous magnanimity; for, if our own actions be the ſovereign arbiters of our lot, a virtuous man can never be wretched; becauſe he will never render himſelf an object either of hatred or contempt. Of the circumſtances in which he is placed, he will always make the beſt and moſt honourable uſe; as a good general, and a good artiſt, employs the forces, and the materials, with which they are reſpectively entruſted, always to the beſt advantage. A happineſs founded on ſuch a baſis, can never ſink into miſery; although it muſt be ſhaken by tragic misfortunes, from which it will not ſoon recover its natural ſtate. Yet, in conſequence of virtuous exertions, continued through a ſufficient length of time, a good man, competently furniſhed with the accommodations of life, will reſume his wonted ſerenity; and may be pronounced happy, notwithſtanding the viciſſitudes to which he is ſtill expoſed; at leaſt poſſeſſed of ſuch happineſs as is conſiſtent with the condition of humanity.

Chap. II.

How the dead are affected by the condition of the living.

We are not therefore to aſcribe happineſs only to the dead, (for thus Solon's ſentiment is commonly underſtood,) eſpecially ſince to ſuppoſe that the dead are totally inſenſible to the misfortunes of their kinſmen and friends on earth, is neither conformable to common opinion, nor conſiſtent with the ſocial principles belonging to human nature. It would be endleſs to enumerate and deſcribe the various forms of calamity and woe, by the differences of which even the living are very

differently

BOOK I.

differently affected; but the ſympathy of the dead with ſuch miſeries, bears leſs proportion to that of the living, than the ſympathy of ſpectators at the theatre bears to that of ſpectators in the real tragedies of life. It may deſerve conſideration, whether the dead at all participate in the good or bad fortune of their living friends; but if they do, it is reaſonable to think that the events of this world affect them too ſlightly, to render ſuch of them as are miſerable happy, or thoſe that are happy miſerable.

Chap. 12.

That happineſs is above praiſe.

Let us proceed then to determine whether happineſs be the object of praiſe, or rather of honour; for it is plain that its nature is not doubtful, and that it never can be blamed or deſpiſed. That only is an object of praiſe, which is endowed with certain qualities or habits, that naturally terminate in ſome ſalutary effect. For this reaſon we commend juſtice and courage, as well as ſtrength and ſwiftneſs, and every virtue; but the praiſes which belong to men, are ridiculous when applied to the gods, whoſe perfections are the objects of emotions of a higher nature; we bleſs and honour and magnify them; and even thoſe things which, from ſome reſemblance to them, are called divine. Happineſs, therefore, is exalted above praiſe, by the excellence and divinity of its nature. Wherefore Eudoxus[*] ingeniouſly defended the pretenſions of pleaſure to be called the ſovereign good; ſaying, that it was confeſſedly not the object of praiſe, and therefore ſomething better. But praiſe properly belongs to virtue, the only ſource of thoſe exertions of mind or body on which juſt encomiums are beſtowed; to examine which particularly, belongs to the ſubject of Rhetoric.

[*] Eudoxus, the ſcholar of Plato, and legiſlator of his countrymen, the Cnidians.—He is again mentioned by our author in the tenth book of his Ethics.

toric. This, then, is clear, that the value of happineſs is not relative, but abſolute; it is complete and perfect in itſelf; and, being the ultimate end to which all praiſe-worthy things are referred, is itſelf the object, not of praiſe, but of veneration and honour[f].

Chap. 13.

The knowledge of the mind a neceſſary preparation for moral ſcience.

But ſince happineſs reſults from virtuous energies, by examining the nature of virtue, we ſhall be more likely to underſtand that of happineſs. The true ſtateſman is chiefly ſolicitous about virtue, exerting himſelf to the utmoſt to inſpire his fellow-citizens with a reſpectful deference for good laws. Such were the legiſlators of Crete and of Sparta; and others, perhaps, who were animated by the ſame enlightened principles of public ſpirit. To inveſtigate the nature of virtue belongs to every liberal ſyſtem of politics, and therefore to our preſent ſubject, of which human happineſs is the end, and human virtue the means; underſtanding, thereby, the virtue of the mind, in the exerciſe of which happineſs conſiſts. The true ſtateſman therefore ought to know the mind, as much, or rather more, (becauſe his purſuit is ſtill more excellent,) than the phyſician does the body; and we ſee that the more liberal ſort of phyſicians beſtow no ſmall pains in gaining an accurate knowledge of the latter. To enter into ſpeculations, not connected with practice, is

[f] This ſubject is explained more clearly in the Ethics to Eudemus, b. i. c. i. p. 203. The author diſcriminates the words εγκωμιον επαινος and ευδαιμονισμος: the firſt of which applies to particular actions; the ſecond to habits; and the third to the ends and enjoyments which are thereby accompliſhed or attained. The Engliſh language does not admit of ſuch nice diſtinctions; and ευδαιμονισμος, "beatification," is an appropriate term in the Romiſh church, which could not, without doing violence, be diſtorted to a philoſophical ſenſe.

BOOK I.

is beside our present purpose. We shall make use of that distinction between powers rational and irrational, which is sufficiently explained in our popular discourses, without inquiring whether these two are separable from each other, like the parts of the body and every thing divisible, or whether they be two merely to the intellectual eye, though as incapable of corporeal division as are the convexity and concavity of the same circle [g]. The irrational powers of the soul are distinguishable into different kinds. Those which contribute to nutrition and growth are the same in man arrived at maturity, and in the child unborn, and even in plants. Any virtue belonging to them cannot be dignified with the epithet of human, since their energies are most perfect in sleep, during the total inactivity of those higher powers, by which men are peculiarly characterised and individually distinguished; wherefore it is said, that for nearly one half of their lives, the same lot befals the good and the bad, the happy and the miserable; except that, in consequence of some remains of wakeful motions, the dreams of the former will commonly be more agreeable. But enough of this, which is foreign to our present subject. There is another part of the soul, which, though irrational itself, is capable of combining with reason;

Our moral powers compounded of the rational and irrational principles of our nature.

[g] διαφερει δε ουδεν ουδε ει μεριστη ἡ ψυχη, ουδε ει αμερης· εχει μεντοι δυναμεις διαφορους. Eudem. l. ii. c. i. p. 204. Aristotle says, that it makes not any difference as to the present subject, whether the soul be divisible or indivisible; it is sufficient that it have distinct powers or faculties; that is, distinct principles to which all the complicated operations of the mind, and all the wide variety of human action may be traced. It will not be easy to point out what improvement has been made since the days of Aristotle, either in the investigation of those principles from the phenomena, or in the application of them when discovered, to explain the highly-diversified operations observable in the intellectual and moral world.

reafon; and, when thus combined, is virtuous and praife-worthy. This appears in perfons endowed with felf-command, but not completely confirmed in that habit. Reafon exhorts them to prefer the better part, but another power impels them to the contrary fide, and violently refifts reafon; in the fame manner as limbs affected by the palfy refufe obedience to our determinations, and affume one direction when we wifh them to move in another. A fimilar refifting power exifts in the mind, though the falfe motion impreffed by it is not perceptible to the fenfes. This power, though irrational[h], is capable of combining with reafon, and fubmitting to its control, as appears in men endowed with felf-command[i] or continency, and ftill more in thofe whofe minds are harmonifed by temperance. The appetites therefore are of a higher order than the mere powers of growth and nutrition, becaufe they are capable of liftening to reafon, as children do to their parents, whofe admonitions they underftand and obey, in a fenfe quite different from that in which they afterwards underftand and know mathematical truths. If we choofe to call alfo this part of the foul rational, there will then be two different principles of reafon in the mind, the firft of which poffeffes reafon abfolutely in itfelf, whereas the fecond is only capable of harkening to the reafon of another. On this diftinction,

BOOK I.

[h] This power, he fays, is fomething different from reafon, but how different it is unneceffary to inquire; which relates to what is explained above.

[i] Self-command or continency, in Greek εγκρατεια, implies that a man is impelled by corrupt appetites, which he has ftrength of mind fufficient to refift; temperance, in Greek σωφροσυνη, implies that his appetites have been fo thoroughly fubdued by cuftom and reafon, that they no longer have any tendency to rebel. This latter, in its higheft perfection, is that delightful harmony of foul in which our moral improvement terminates.

BOOK I.

diſtinction, the diviſion of the virtues into the intellectual and moral, is founded. Wiſdom, intelligence, and prudence belong to the former claſs; liberality and temperance to the latter. In reference to morals, we do not ſay that a man is wiſe or intelligent, but that he is meak or temperate. Good men are praiſed for good habits; and all praiſe-worthy habits are called virtues.

ARISTOTLE's ETHICS.

BOOK II.

INTRODUCTION.

THE most profound as well as the most elegant of all modern writers on the subject of political Ethics, the immortal Grotius, in his treatise on the laws of war and peace, observes, that Aristotle holds the first rank among philosophers, whether we estimate him by the perspicuity of his method, the acuteness of his distinctions, or the weight and solidity of his arguments [a]. This criticism is fully justified by the book before us, in which our author treats of the nature of moral virtue, shews by what means it is acquired, proves by an accurate induction that it consists in the habit of mediocrity, and lays down three practical rules for its attainment. This part of his work will bear that trial which he regards as the test of excellence; "it requires not any addition, and it will not admit of retrenchment." The objections made to it, as falling short of the purity and sublimity of Christian morality, will equally apply to all the discoveries of human reason, when compared with "that divine light which, coming into the world, gives, or offers, light to every man in it [b]. But the critics who make objections [c] to Aristotle, would urge

[a] Grotius in Prolegom. [b] John, c. i. v. 9.

[c] See some of them stated in Grotii Prolegom. de Jure Belli & Pacis.

BOOK II.

urge them with lefs confidence, if they attended to two remarks on which our author often infifts; firft, that practical matters admit not of fcientific or logical accuracy; fecondly, that the virtues of which he is in queft, are all of them merely relative to the condition and exigencies of man in political fociety, being thofe habits, acquired by our own exertion, in which, when confirmed, we fhall uniformly act our parts on the theatre of the world, ufefully, agreeably, and gracefully. In Ariftotle's philofophy, man is the judge of man; in Chriftianity, the judge of man is God. Philofophy confines itfelf to the perifhing interefts of the prefent world; Chriftianity, looking beyond thofe interefts, takes a loftier aim, infpires the mind with nobler motives, and promifes to adorn it with perfections, worthy of its ineftimably valuable rewards. Yet to the man of piety, it may be a matter of edification, to compare the virtue of philofophical firmnefs with the grace of Chriftian patience; and to obferve how nearly the rules difcovered by reafon and experience, as moft conducive to the happinefs of our prefent ftate, coincide with thofe precepts which are given in the Gofpel in order to fit us for a better.

BOOK II.

ARGUMENT.

Moral virtues acquired by exercise and custom—Consist in holding the mean between blameable extremes—Test of virtue—The virtues, habits—The nature of these habits ascertained—Why vices mistaken for virtues, and conversely—Practical rules for the attainment of virtue.

BOOK II. Chap. 1.

The moral virtues not implanted by nature.

VIRTUE being twofold, intellectual and moral, the former is produced and increased chiefly by instruction, and therefore requires experience and time; the latter is acquired by repeated acts or custom, from which, by a small change[d], its name is derived. None of the moral virtues, therefore, are implanted by nature; for properties given by nature, cannot be taken away or altered by custom; thus the gravity of a stone, which naturally carries it downward, cannot be changed into levity, which would carry it upward, were we to throw it in that direction ten thousand times; and fire, which naturally seeks the extremities, cannot be brought by custom to have a tendency towards the center: nor, in a word, can any law of nature be altered by custom. The moral virtues, therefore, are neither natural nor preternatural; we are born with capacities for acquiring them, but they can only be acquired by our own exertions. Powers, implanted by nature, precede in the order of existence their operations; which is manifest with regard to the senses. The powers of seeing and hearing are not acquired by repeated operations of those faculties; but, on the contrary, they existed in us before we exercised them, and continue to

Proof of this.

exist

[d] ηθος ab εθος.

BOOK II.

They are acquired by exercise and custom.

exist in us, though they should cease to be exercised. But the habit of moral virtue, like all other practical arts, can be acquired or preserved by practice only. By building, we become architects; by harping, musicians; and, in the same manner, by acts of justice, we become just; and by acts of courage, courageous. This is attested by what happens in whole nations; whose characters result from their conduct. All legislators wish to make virtuous and happy citizens: but they do not all attain this end; for the virtues are like the arts, acquired by a right, and destroyed by a wrong, practice. Architects and musicians thus become good or bad; and if this were not the case, instruction would be superfluous. The same holds in the virtues. By correctness, or the contrary, in our transactions with mankind, we become just or unjust; according to our behaviour in circumstances of danger, our characters are formed to courage or cowardice; and in proportion as we indulge or restrain the excitements to anger and pleasure, we become adorned with the habits of meekness and temperance, or deformed by those of passionateness and profligacy. In one word, such as our actions are, such will our habits become. Actions, therefore, ought to be most diligently attended to; and it is not a matter of small moment how we are trained from our youth; much depends on this, or rather all [c].

Chap. 2.

What are the rules by which our actions ought to be shaped in order to attain virtue.

Since the present treatise is not merely a theory, as other parts of our works, (for the inquiry is not "wherein virtue consists," but "how it may best be attained," without which the speculative knowledge of it is not of the smallest value,) we must begin by examining, by what rules our actions ought to be shaped, because by them our habits and characters are moulded. That our conduct ought to be agreeable to right reason, may be

[c] The same subject is treated in the Magna Moralia, l. i. c. vi.; and in the Eudemian Ethics, l. ii. c. ii.

be here assumed as an axiom; but it will afterwards be shewn what this right reason is, and what reference it has to the other virtues. Let us not forget, what was formerly observed, that practical matters admit not of logical precision; and that greater accuracy of language ought not to be expected, than is consistent with the nature of the subject. The propriety of action admits not of definite rules, any more than the exact quantity of food or exercise conducive to health. This observation holds true with regard to the science of morals as well as of medicines; but is peculiarly applicable to the particular cases belonging to both sciences; which cases are so dissimilar to each other, that it is impossible to include them under any common precept; and the man of morals, like the pilot and the physician, must comply with the exigencies of the moment, and vary his behaviour with the variation of circumstances. Notwithstanding this instability in the nature of the subject, we must endeavour to give some assistance to those who aim at virtue. First, then, it is worthy of remark, that propriety of conduct always consists in a mean or middle between two vicious extremes; and as the health and strength of our bodies visibly depend on a due proportion of food and exercise, equally remote from superabundance or penury; so is the health and vigour of our minds destroyed by superabundance or penury of those very things or qualities, by the due proportion of which those excellencies are acquired, maintained, or augmented. This we may perceive holds true with respect to courage, temperance, and every other virtue. He who flies from every danger, is a coward; he who rushes on every danger, is a madman; the man who indulges in every pleasure, is a voluptuary; and the man who, with rustic austerity, rejects the most allowable pleasures, may be justly charged with an insensibility misbecoming his nature. The virtues of courage and temperance, which are de-

That it consists in holding the mean between two vicious extremes.

This proved by induction.

BOOK II.

ſtroyed by exceſs or deficiency, are therefore preſerved by mediocrity; and on obſerving this golden mean depend not only the origin and increaſe of the virtues[f], but the energy or operation by which their proper work is effected; for as a ſtrong conſtitution, which is produced or confirmed by much food and much exerciſe, enables a man to bear with ſafety a great meaſure of either; ſo, by reſiſting the temptations of pleaſure, we acquire temperance; and having become temperate, we can reſiſt ſuch temptations: by reſiſting the emotions of fear amidſt dangers, we acquire courage; and having become courageous, we are able to face dangers.

Chap. 3.

The ſureſt teſt of virtue is the pleaſure felt in exerciſing it.

The pleaſure or pain reſulting from acts of virtue, affords the beſt criterion concerning the confirmation of the habit. He who abſtains from bodily pleaſures, and rejoices in his temperance, is truly poſſeſſed of this virtue; he who grieves at his abſtinence is, on the other hand, a voluptuary. A man of courage faces dangers with pleaſure, at leaſt without pain; a coward, always with the latter. Moral virtue is therefore occupied about regulating our pleaſures and pains; for the love of pleaſure ſtimulates us to profligacy, and fear of pain withholds us from the path of honour. Plato ſays well, that right education conſiſts in teaching us to rejoice, and to grieve, at ſuch things as are the proper objects of thoſe emotions. Virtue is ſeen in affections and actions, all of which are accompanied either with pleaſure or with pain; and therefore virtue is neceſſarily converſant about pains and pleaſures; as is proved alſo by the neceſſity of rewards and puniſhments, which are moral medicines; and, like all other medicines, in their nature contrary to the diſeaſes which they are fitted to cure. Beſides, every

[f] Ariſtotle adds, "their deſtruction," which is produced by a departure from this mean, ſo that their energies have the ſame cauſes with their generation, augmentation, and deſtruction; only with regard to the laſt, theſe cauſes act in a contrary direction.

every habit of the mind is intimately connected with those things by which it is rendered better or worse; which happens to virtue with regard to pleasure and pain; for our morals are vitiated by pursuing or avoiding either of them with undue ardour; at improper times, in improper places, or on improper occasions. The virtues, therefore, have been supposed to consist in apathy; erroneously indeed, because they consist in the due regulation, not in the total extinction, of passion; and passion properly directed, is productive of happiness; improperly, of misery. For, as there are three objects naturally preferred, namely, honour, profit, and pleasure; and three naturally shunned, namely, disgrace, loss, and pain; a virtuous man knows practically how to estimate the value of all those things in their relation to human happiness; a knowledge, of which the man enured to vicious habits is totally unsusceptible. But the two characters are principally distinguished by their various degrees of sensibility to the different kinds of pleasure; the love of which is implanted in all animals, and of which one kind or other necessarily accompanies every object of preference; both profit and honour being pursued as pleasures. Our natures indeed are deeply tinged, and as it were engrained, with the love of pleasure, which, being nourished and growing stronger with our frame, is most difficultly moderated; especially when it has become the standard by which things and actions are appreciated. The great business of morality, therefore, lies in restraining the undue pursuit of pleasure, and the undue aversion to pain. As Heracleitus says, it is more difficult to contend with pleasure than with anger; but the most difficult part is that best fitted for shewing the excellence of the performer. The moralist and statesman, therefore, must bend their utmost attention towards regulating the behaviour of those intrusted

BOOK II.

to their care, in thoſe particulars on which their merit or demerit chiefly depends. But enough has been ſaid to ſhew, that moral virtue is converſant about pains and pleaſures; that the actions from which it originally ſprings, either augment or deſtroy it, according as they are well or ill directed; and that the ſame good works to which its exiſtence is due, are thoſe in which it continues to be conſtantly employed.

Chap. 4.

Solution of a difficulty reſpecting the mode of acquiring virtue.

A doubt ariſes, why we ſhould ſay that men acquire juſtice by doing juſt actions, or become temperate by obſerving the rules of temperance; ſince, if they perform ſuch actions and obſerve ſuch rules, it ſhould ſeem that they muſt be already endowed with thoſe virtues; in the ſame manner as a man who writes or who performs according to the rules of grammar and muſic, is already a grammarian and a muſician. But this does not hold true even with reſpect to the arts; for a man may write grammar, merely by imitation, by chance, or by the direction of another; but to be a grammarian, he muſt himſelf underſtand the art. Beſides this, the perfection of works of art is in themſelves; but the whole merit of virtuous actions depends on the diſpoſition of the actor: firſt, that he performed them with knowledge; ſecondly, with deliberation and preference; thirdly, that he preferred and performed them on their own account; and laſtly, that he is firm and immovable in his virtuous reſolutions. The firſt of theſe requiſites only, viz. that of knowledge, is eſſential to the artiſt; but in conſtituting the character of a virtuous man, mere knowledge is of little avail, and the other three particulars of the greateſt: ſtability in virtuous practice reſults from repeated acts of virtue; in conſequence of which, not only thoſe acts are ſuch as a virtuous man would perform, but he who performs them is rightly diſpoſed, and virtuouſly affected. It is therefore truly ſaid, that we acquire juſtice and temperance

Four things requiſite to conſtitute a virtuous character.

temperance from acting justly and temperately; since, independently of our own actions, we never could acquire those virtues. But the multitude, neglecting practice, think to acquire virtue by theory; like those patients who consult physicians, but use none of their prescriptions. Such physic will not benefit the body; nor such philosophy the mind.

Chap. 5.

That the virtues are neither passions nor capacities, but habits.

We must next examine, whether virtue be a passion, a faculty, or a habit; for these are three distinct principles in the mind. By passion, I mean every emotion accompanied with pain or pleasure; as love, anger, fear, courage, envy, joy, friendship, hatred, tenderness, emulation, pity. By faculty, I mean, in this place, the capacity of being affected by those passions; by anger, grief, or pity. By habit, I mean the habitude or relation which our minds bear to those passions; as whether we are affected too much or too little by anger, both which are wrong; or affected by it moderately, on proper occasions, which only is right: the same observation applies to all other passions. Neither the virtues nor the vices therefore can be passions; because it is not in reference to the passions that we are denominated good or bad, and are regarded as the objects of praise or of blame. It is not our fear or anger simply, but the degree of those passions, that constitutes the propriety or impropriety of our conduct; and renders us the just objects of commendation or reproach. Besides, fear and anger, and all other passions, are emotions independent of our own deliberation and preference; but the virtues always imply an act of comparison, and the preference of one sort of conduct to another. Farther, we are said to be moved and impelled by passion, but our characters are disposed and settled by virtue; for which reason the virtues cannot be called capacities; and also, because we are neither praised nor blamed in reference to

our

BOOK II.

our being susceptive or capable of passion. These capacities, besides, are implanted by nature; which the virtues, as we have already proved, are not. Since then they are neither passions nor faculties, it remains that they should belong to that class called habits [g].

Chap. 6.

The nature of this habit ascertained.

It is not enough to say that virtue is a habit; we must further ascertain what is the nature of that habit. Every virtue, then, tends to constitute the perfection of that object to which it belongs, and to fit it for performing properly its peculiar functions. Thus, the virtue of the eye constitutes the perfection of that organ, and qualifies it for seeing distinctly: and the virtue of a horse constitutes the perfection of that animal, and qualifies him for running swiftly, for bearing his rider, and for disdaining fear at the approach of an enemy. The virtue of a man, therefore, must be that habit which constitutes the perfection of his nature; and fits him for performing properly his peculiar functions. How this habit is to be attained, we have explained already; but the matter will be rendered more perspicuous by further examining the nature of virtue. From every thing continuous and divisible, we may take the half, a greater part, or a lesser. The half may be considered as the mean proportional between the extremes of too much and too little, from which it is equally remote; and considered in relation to the object itself, this mean proportional is always one and the same; but considered in relation to man, this just mean continually varies, because the middle between the two vicious extremes of too much or too little is, in reference to him, that which is neither more nor less than propriety requires. Thus, if ten be the greater extreme, and two the lesser, six must be the arithmetical

[g] The same subject is treated in Magna Moral. l. i. c. v.; and in the Eudemian Ethics, l. ii. c. iii.

arithmetical mean, becaufe it exceeds the leffer, as much as it is exceeded by the greater. But in regulating human actions, which, like all other motions, are things continuous and divifible[h], the fame fimple rule will not apply: for two pounds may be too fmall an allowance, and ten too large; yet he who directs the regimen of the wreftlers, will not therefore prefcribe univerfally fix pounds, which might be too little for Milo the wreftler, though far too much for one beginning his exercifes: the fame thing holds as to the quantity of labour which he enjoins to be performed, in running, wreftling, and the other branches of the gymnaftic. Thus, he who is fkilful in directing actions of any other kind, will carefully avoid excefs or defect, but find out and prefer the golden mean; which is the object that every good artift always keeps in view, fince the higheft commendation of works of art confifts in faying that they admit neither of addition nor retrenchment. But virtue, which is the perfection of nature itfelf, is far fuperior to art, which only imitates her operations, in aiming at the juft mean between two vicious extremes. I fpeak here of moral virtue, which is converfant about paffions and actions, all of which admit of mediocrity, as well as of excefs or defect. Thus we may be too much or too little affected, with defire or averfion, courage or fear, anger or pity, pain or pleafure. Both extremes are bad; and the paffion is then only proper and correct, when we are affected fuitably to its caufes, its objects, and its ends: when this is the cafe, both the paffion, and the action proceeding from it, are juftly praifed as virtuous; becaufe they do not deviate from the mark at which they ought to aim. The Pythagoreans, therefore, did well in affigning definite to the co-arrangement of

That the virtues do not admit of excefs or of defect, nor the vices of mediocrity.

[h] ἡ μεν γαρ κινησις συνεχης· ἡ δε πραξις κινησις, Eudem. l. ii. c. iii. p. 205.

BOOK II.

of good, and indefinite to that of evil[h]; for there is but one right road; but the ways of error are innumerable. The former is as difficult as the latter is eaſy; it is difficult to hit the mark, but eaſy to miſs it;

"Virtue is ſtill the ſame, but vice has various forms."

The former, therefore, is the habit of preferring and obſerving mediocrity in our paſſions and actions, agreeably to the rules of right reaſon: virtue then, in its eſſence, is mediocrity; in its effect, it is excellence, and the higheſt excellence[i]. But neither all paſſions nor all actions admit of mediocrity; for there are many whoſe very names infer exceſs and blame; as the paſſions of impudence, malice, and envy; and the actions of adultery, theft, and murder. Such paſſions and ſuch actions are in themſelves deteſtable exceſſes: and for the ſame reaſon, there cannot be any mediocrity in cowardice, injuſtice, or intemperance; nor any exceſs or defect in the virtues of courage or wiſdom; nor univerſally can mediocrity or virtue admit of exceſs

[h] See Analyſis, p. 112.

[i] This is the cleareſt meaning I can affix to κατα το ευ ακροτης. But Ariſtotle when he calls virtue, in one ſenſe, an extreme, ſeems to allude to what is ſaid in his ſecond Analytics concerning the ὅροι συμπερασματικοι, the termini concluſorii, and the difference between them and definitions, ſhewing the eſſence, that is, the cauſe which makes any thing to be what it is. Thus, What is it to ſquare an oblong? This queſtion may be anſwered, or in other words, the ſquaring may be defined by ſaying, either that it is to find a ſquare equal to an oblong; or, that it is to find a line which is a geometrical mean between the ſides of the oblong. The former definition is called συμπερασματικος, becauſe when the mathematician demonſtrates, that the ſquare conſtructed on a line, which is the mean proportional between the ſides of the oblong, is equal to that oblong, he draws the concluſion, "a ſquare, therefore, is found equal to an oblong:" but the ſecond definition tells, not only that the ſquare is equal to the oblong, but the cauſe which makes it to be ſo. In the ſame manner, when we call virtue the higheſt excellence or perfection of any object, we only tell, in other words, what is meant by virtue; but when we call it mediocrity, we define it by its eſſence, and ſhew the cauſe which makes it to be the higheſt excellence.

BOOK II. Chap. 7.

excefs or defect; nor the vices, which are all of them extremes, admit of a virtuous mediocrity.

That all the virtues confift in mediocrity, proved by induction.

In practical morality, general principles are of little ufe, unlefs they be applied to particulars, in which all practice confifts, and by which all general principles muft, if true, be confirmed. Let the various paffions or emotions therefore be arranged in a diagram[k], and we fhall fee that the degree of them confiftent with propriety always lies in the middle between two blamable extremes. Thus, in encountering or avoiding dangers, courage holds the middle place between rafhnefs and timidity: in obeying or refifting folicitations to pleafure, temperance holds the middle place between voluptuoufnefs, and a vice which, being uncommon, is namelefs, but which we fhall call unfeeling apathy. In pecuniary matters, liberality is the mean between extravagance and parfimony. The prodigal is too carelefs in throwing away money, and at too little pains to acquire it. The mifer pays exceffive attention to the acquifition of money, and exceffive attention to the keeping of it. There are other qualities relating to money, as magnificence with its contrary extremes of niggardlinefs and wafteful profufion; which diftinctions will be afterwards explained[l]. As to honour and difhonour, magnanimity is the middle term between boaftful pride and mean-fpirited abafement; and there is another quality or habit which bears the fame proportion to magnanimity which liberality does to magnificence, confifting in the propriety of our affection with refpect to fmall and ordinary marks of honour,

[k] The diagram, or delineation, which is here wanting, may be partly fupplied from Ethic. Eudem. l. ii. c. iii. for even there it is extremely incomplete.

[l] In the firft chapters of the Fourth Book.

BOOK II.

nour, whereas magnanimity conſiſts in the propriety of our affection with reſpect to thoſe which are great and extraordinary. In the common intercourſe of life, men are diſtinguiſhed by too much or too little deſire of honour; the exceſs and the defect are both marked by names [m], but the intermediate and praiſeworthy degree of the affection is nameleſs; wherefore the extremes contend with each other about the middle place; and, as either happens to obtain it, we praiſe a decent pride or a becoming humility. The reaſon of this incongruity in our judgments will be afterwards explained: we proceed at preſent according to our propoſed plan. With regard to anger, ſome men are too ſuſceptible, and others too unſuſceptible of this paſſion; and others commonly indulge it only in that degree which is laudable. Theſe different diſpoſitions or habits are not accurately diſtinguiſhed by names. We ſhall call the intermediate and proper degree of the affection meekneſs; which inclines, however, more to the extreme of phlegmatic endurance, than to that of immoderate iraſcibility. There are three other virtues or proprieties, which, though different, are yet nearly allied to each other, and all of them diſtinguiſhable in the ordinary intercourſe of words and actions; bearing different relations, the one to truth, and the other to pleaſure; and that which relates to pleaſure, either confined to matters of paſtime and amuſement only, or comprehending all the complicated buſineſſes of life, whether they be gay or ſerious. Neither theſe proprieties themſelves, nor the various and contrary deviations from them, are accurately diſtinguiſhed by names; but it is neceſſary that they

[m] The perſons diſtinguiſhed by the exceſs and defect, were called φιλοτιμοι and αφιλοτιμοι: but there was only one of theſe adjectives, which afforded an abſtract φιλοτιμια, denoting the diſpoſition or habit.

they ſhould here be conſidered, in order to ſhew that the praiſeworthy habit in trivial as well as in important actions, always lies in the middle between two blameable extremes; and as names are wanting, we muſt, as in other caſes, take the liberty of making them, both for the ſake of perſpicuity, and to keep unbroken the connexion of our diſcourſe. In the habit or diſpoſition relative to the true exhibition of our characters in word and action, let the propriety or virtue which lies in the middle be called plain-dealing; and the impropriety or vice, by which we aſſume good qualities which do not belong to us, be called oſtentation; and that, by which we diveſt ourſelves of the good qualities with which we are really endowed, be called diſſimulation or irony. In matters relating to pleaſure and merriment, there is a virtue in facetiouſneſs; buffoonery is the impropriety on the one ſide, and ruſtic ſimplicity on the other. In the more ſerious concerns of life, but which have ſtill pleaſure for their object, the virtue of companionable friendlineſs is diſtinguiſhed, on the one hand, from quarrelſome moroſeneſs; and, on the other, both from unmeaning officiouſneſs, and intereſted flattery. Even in mere affections which do not exert themſelves either in words or deeds, modeſty is praiſed as holding the middle place between baſhful timidity, and frontleſs aſſurance. An honeſt indignation at the proſperity of the worthleſs is eaſily diſtinguiſhable, both from envy which pines at the proſperity of all alike, and from that depraved pleaſure which none but the moſt vicious can receive from beholding the unmerited ſucceſs of artful villany or ruffian violence[a]. But concerning thoſe habits,

[a] ἐπιχαιρεκακία in the Latin verſions is tranſlated *malevolentia*, which does not at all expreſs Ariſtotle's meaning: malevolence wiſhes ill to all mankind, even to the good, and therefore is grieved at their proſperity; but the vice here ſpoken of is that depraved

BOOK II.

habits, we ſhall treat more fully hereafter, and alſo concerning juſtice, which muſt be divided into two kinds, before we can diſtinguiſh wherein the propriety of each kind conſiſts; and likewiſe concerning the intellectual virtues.

Chap. 8.

Why vices are often miſtaken for virtues; and converſely.

Of thoſe three diſpoſitions or habits, of which that in the middle is only right, the extremes are contrary to, and at variance with, each other, and alſo with the virtue which lies between them. For as in a line divided into equal, and alſo unequal, parts, the half is great when compared with the ſmaller diviſion, but ſmall when compared with the greater; ſo of human paſſions and actions, their proper and moderate degree appears an exceſs or defect juſt as it happens to be compared with either extreme. To the fool-hardy, courage appears cowardice; and to the coward, raſhneſs*. The voluptuary deems temperance inſenſibility; and the ſpendthrift calls liberality avarice; each puſhing the extreme, which happens to form part of his own character, into the place of honour. It is worthy of remark, that the extremes are not only more contrary to each other than either of them is to the middle, but alſo that one of them often bears a falſe reſemblance to this middle, and is frequently miſtaken for it. Thus raſhneſs often paſſes for bravery, and profuſion for liberality: but cowardice is never miſtaken for courage, nor voluptuouſneſs for temperance; although temperance is

depraved pleaſure which wicked men take in beholding the ſucceſs of arts like to their own. In this ſenſe only, Ariſtotle could ſay νεμεσις εϛι μεσοτης φθονου και επιχαιρεκακιας, that indignation was the middle between envy and the vice here ſpecified: for envy grieves at proſperity well merited, but επιχαιρεκακια rejoices at proſperity unmerited; which are two extremes equally remote from that affection by which we rejoice at the proſperity of good men, and grieve at the proſperity of the wicked.

* Ariſtotle ſays, that the courageous man, compared with the coward, ſeems fool-hardy, and therefore the coward calls him raſh.

is ſometimes called inſenſibility, and inſenſibility temperance. This irregularity proceeds from two cauſes; firſt, the one extreme is really nearer than the other to that proper affection which lies between them. Raſhneſs is nearer than cowardice to the virtue of courage; and therefore cowardice, the moſt diſtant extreme, is moſt properly oppoſed to courage. The ſecond cauſe is, that mankind in general being more inclined to one extreme than the other, thoſe vices to which we are naturally moſt prone, are moſt the objects of our blame as well as of our attention. Thus, with regard to pleaſure, moſt men are prone to err rather on the ſide of indulgence, than on that of abſtinence. Voluptuouſneſs therefore is the vice naturally oppoſed to temperance [p].

Chap. 9. Practical rules for the attainment of propriety of affection and action.

Enough has been ſaid to ſhew that virtue conſiſts in mediocrity. But this middle point, either in paſſions or actions, it is not eaſy to hit; for, as a man muſt have ſome knowledge in geometry to find the centre of a circle, ſo it belongs not to thoſe ignorant of Ethics to obſerve the rules of propriety. Every one is capable of being angry, or of giving away money; but how much, when, to whom, in what manner, and for what end or purpoſe, are queſtions which it is not eaſy for every one to reſolve; and of which, as the proper ſolution is extremely rare, ſo it is highly praiſeworthy. He, therefore, who would not err widely from the point of propriety, muſt make it his firſt care to keep at a diſtance from the moſt blameable extreme; and as Calypſo adviſes,

> "Steer by the higher rock; leſt whirled around
> We ſink, beneath the circling eddy drown'd [q]."

In

p The ſame thoughts are expreſſed in other words, and illuſtrated by other examples, in the Ethics to Eudemus, l. ii. c. v.

q Pope's Iliad, b. xii. v. 263, 264. But Ulyſſes, and not Calypſo, ſays this, Il. xii. v. 108.

BOOK II.

In doing this we ſhall imitate the ſkilful pilot who, when he cannot hold the courſe which he deſires, ſails the neareſt to it poſſible; and of two evils prefers the leaſt. We ought next to conſider to which of the two extremes or faults we are moſt prone; for different men are more or leſs eaſily beſet by different faults or vices, and what theſe are by which each is moſt liable to be entangled, he will beſt diſcover by attending to the pleaſure which he has in indulging, or the pain in reſtraining them. In order to correct his character, he muſt bend it, in a contrary direction, as we ſtraighten a crooked ſtick; but, above all, he muſt beware of the blandiſhments of pleaſure, of which we are ſeldom impartial or uncorrupt judges: treating this fair enchantreſs, as the aged ſenators in Homer did the beautiful Helen, whoſe words on this occaſion cannot be too often repeated, nor their example too ſtrictly imitated.

> "They cry'd, no wonder, ſuch celeſtial charms
> For nine long years have ſet the world in arms;
> What winning graces! what majeſtic mien!
> She moves a goddeſs, and ſhe looks a queen!
> *Yet hence, Oh, Heaven! convey that fatal face,*
> *And from deſtruction ſave the Trojan race*[1]."

By thus baniſhing pleaſure, we ſhall be leſs liable to error. Such, briefly, are the precepts by which propriety of affection and action may be attained; a thing for which it is extremely difficult to lay down general rules, which are at all applicable to the indefinite variety of particular caſes; and to aſcertain, for inſtance, with whom we ought to be angry, how long, to what degree, and for what reaſons or purpoſes. Sometimes we praiſe the defect, and call inſenſibility meekneſs; ſometimes we praiſe the exceſs, and call iraſcibility manhood. He who deviates

[1] Iliad, iii. v. 203, &c.

deviates but a little from the middle point, commonly escapes blame; great deviations become perceptible, but the precise degrees of blame which they respectively merit cannot be accurately expressed in words; and in such practical matters*, common sense is the sole and ultimate judge. This only is certain, that mediocrity is always praiseworthy; and that, in order to attain it, we must, for the reasons above given, incline ourselves, according to circumstances, sometimes to the one extreme, and sometimes to the other.

* In things perceptible by sense, or objects of sensation, as contradistinguished from objects of intellection; in which latter only, accuracy is attainable. See above, p. 141.

ARISTOTLE's ETHICS.

BOOK III.

INTRODUCTION.

BOOK III.

IN this Book, Ariftotle examines the fpecific diftinctions between moral virtue and other habits of the mind. The habit of moral virtue implies the deliberate preference of one kind of conduct to another; and deliberate preference implies freedom of choice. Thofe actions are voluntary, which have their principle in ourfelves; thofe are involuntary, which proceed from an external caufe. Building on accurate definitions and folid diftinctions, the philofopher proves, with equal perfpicuity and energy, that our moral conduct is the proper object of praife or blame, of reward or punifhment. His reafonings and fpeculations foar above and fuperfede the abftrufe, or rather the frivolous queftion, introduced by his perverters the fchoolmen, concerning the freedom of the human will; a queftion which continued to be agitated, long after their other fubtilties were condemned to oblivion. With Ariftotle, all will is free-will; fince nothing can be more free than that which is voluntary: and although fome actions originating in ourfelves are confidered as of a mixed nature, becaufe they are performed reluctantly, though fpontaneoufly, this happens merely becaufe, of two evils, we naturally choofe the leaft: fuch actions, how contrary foever to our will in their own nature, being neverthelefs volun-

BOOK III.

tary in reference to the unfortunate circumſtances in which we happen to be placed.

His work, hitherto, proceeds with great regularity. He began by proving that the happineſs of man conſiſts in the exerciſe of the moral and intellectual virtues; or, in his own technical language, "that happineſs is energy directed in the line of virtue." As his definition of happineſs implies an acquaintance with the nature of virtue, and the knowledge of virtue implies that of the mind in which this habit reſides, he explains the different parts or principles of the mind, whether rational or irrational; ſhewing that both principles neceſſarily cooperate in the acquirement of good moral habits, as well as in the approbation of good moral characters. This ſyſtem is totally different from that which regards morality as founded ſolely or ultimately on feeling; whether a moral ſenſe, ſympathy, or any other modification of merely ſenſitive nature; an abſurd doctrine, liable to groſs and dangerous perverſion; and which has often been employed to juſtify, and even to produce the wildeſt practical errors. Having explained his theory of Ethics, the Author proceeds to the practice; and concludes this Book with the examination of courage and temperance.

BOOK III.

ARGUMENT.

Moral election and preference.—Our habits voluntary.—Courage.—Its different kinds distinguished.—Temperance.—Natural and adventitious wants.—Comparison of intemperance and cowardice.

BOOK III. Chap. 1.

What is meant by the epithet voluntary as applied to human actions.

VIRTUE is relative to passions and actions; of which, those only which are voluntary, are the objects of praise or blame; and those which are involuntary, are the objects always of pardon, and sometimes of pity. In treating of virtue, therefore, it is necessary clearly to explain what is meant by the epithets *voluntary* and *involuntary*; the force of which words ought to be fully understood by legislators, when they establish rewards and punishments. Those actions and those crimes, then, are involuntary, which are either done by compulsion, or committed through ignorance. We are said to act or move by compulsion, when the principle of action or motion is not in ourselves, but external; as when we are driven before the force of the wind, or impelled by strength greater than our own. But it is doubtful whether those evils are voluntary which we either encounter through motives of honour, or endure through the fear of greater calamities. Thus, if a tyrant commands us to commit some act of baseness, having in his power our parents and children, whose fate depends on our obedience; and when sailors or merchants in a storm throw their goods overboard to save their lives; such actions are of a mixed nature, but rather voluntary, because, at the moment of doing them, they are matters of choice; and the true motive to any action is that by which we are actuated at the time of performing it. Beſides, the principle of motion is in ourſelves, and may be exerted or not at pleaſure. Such actions, therefore, are voluntary in reference to the unfortunate circumſtances in which we are placed, though independently of thoſe circumſtances they are much againſt our will; and therefore, conſidered abſolutely, are involuntary.

Actions of this mixed kind are ſometimes the objects of high panegyric, when we boldly encounter pain and diſgrace for the ſake of great and honourable advantages: and when we decline this conflict, we often render ourſelves the objects of reproach. But to encounter difficulties and diſgrace without the expectancy of honour or advantage, is the part only of a fool. On other occaſions, though we receive not any praiſe, yet we meet with pardon, when our virtue yields to terrors too powerful for the weakneſs of humanity: but the degree in which it yields, is ſtill in our power; for there are ſome criminal acts to which neither threats nor violence can ever compel thoſe who, rather than commit them, would ſuffer the moſt wretched death. In Euripides' Alcmæon, the reaſons for which that hero ſays he is forced to commit matricide, are only worthy of ridicule.

It is difficult to determine what goods are to be preferred, and what evils are to be encountered; and ſtill more difficult in time of action and danger to adhere firmly to our predetermined reſolutions. For the moſt part, men are forced to ſuffer diſgrace, only for the ſake of avoiding pain; and as theſe evils are of a different kind, it is not eaſy fairly to compare, and exactly to appretiate them: but when pain is preferred to diſgrace, our manlineſs is praiſed; when diſgrace is preferred to pain, our effeminacy is blamed. On the whole then, what actions are compulſory? Are they thoſe only whoſe principle is external, and in which the immediate agent has not any voluntary ſhare? Or, ſhall we call thoſe actions compulſory, which, though matters of choice relatively to the unfortunate circumſtances in which we are placed, are yet, when conſidered in themſelves, abſolutely againſt our will? We ſay, that ſuch acts ought to be conſidered rather as voluntary, becauſe all actions being converſant about particulars only, muſt depend on circumſtances, and leave room for the preference of one motive to another. If it ſhould be ſaid that pleaſures and honours conſiſting in things external to ourſelves, the actions performed for their attainment, are alſo compulſory, all actions whatever would then deſerve this epithet, becauſe all proceed from ſuch motives. But it is abſurd to accuſe pleaſure, which cannot be the object either of puniſhment or blame; and not ourſelves, who are too eaſily ſeduced by it; and equally abſurd to conſider ourſelves as the cauſe of our good actions, and pleaſure as the cauſe of our bad ones. Thoſe actions only, therefore, are properly compulſory, whoſe principle lies without, and which are totally independent of our own voluntary co-operation.

We ſaid that crimes committed through ignorance are involuntary. But this aſſertion is not univerſally true; for thoſe only are involuntary, which produce pain and repentance. He who has committed a wickedneſs through ignorance, and feels no compunction for the act, cannot be ſaid indeed to have done voluntarily what he did not intend; nor, on the other hand, is his action involuntary, ſince he feels not any uneaſineſs for the commiſſion of it. But as *his* action is *involuntary* who repents; *his*, who repents not, may be called *not voluntary*: that things of different natures may be expreſſed by different names. A diſtinction is alſo to be made, between acting *through* ignorance

and

BOOK III.

and *with* ignorance. A man drunk, or in a paſſion, is guilty of violence *through* intoxication or anger, not *through* ignorance, though ignorantly; and every bad man is ignorant of what things it is his duty either to do or to avoid; an ignorance profound and univerſal, inſeparably connected with his pravity of will and election, and therefore inexcuſable. But in the particular actions, which, becauſe committed through ignorance, ſeem entitled to pardon or pity, it will often be uſeful to diſtinguiſh, between the agent and the action, its ſubject, end, the manner how, and the inſtrument with which it is performed. None but a madman can be ignorant with regard to all thoſe particulars. In whatever he has done, every one in his ſenſes muſt know that he himſelf was the agent; but he may not know that he was doing wrong; as thoſe who blab in ſpeaking, beg pardon for words which eſcaped them unintentionally; or, as Æſchylus[1] profaned the myſtical terms, not knowing them to be ſuch; and, in actions, a man ſhowing a catapult, diſcharged that formidable engine; and Meropé would have ſlain her own ſon, taking him for an enemy; poiſons have been given inſtead of remedies; ſome perſons have been killed by thoſe who inſtructed them in their exerciſes; and others have been ſlain with ſpears thought to be blunted, or with ſtones miſtaken for pumice. The reſult of ſuch actions being totally different from what the agents intended, they are juſtly deemed involuntary, when accompanied with pain and repentance; whereas thoſe actions ſeem moſt voluntary, which not only proceed from our own movements, but which are begun, carried on, and terminated

[1] Æſchylus was acquitted by the Areopagus for divulging ſome expreſſions uſed in the myſteries, having proved that he was not initiated, and therefore did not know what he ſaid. Clemens Alexandrin. ſtrom. ii.

BOOK III.

terminated with a clear perception or knowledge of their real nature and end. To which of the two claſſes then ſhall we aſcribe things done through anger or appetite? If we call them involuntary, brute animals, and children, who are yet incapable of reaſon, can never act voluntarily. But appetite and anger are principles of human nature, as well as reaſon itſelf; and when they prompt us to act amiſs, are not leſs voluntary than when they prompt us to act properly; to repel injuries, and to defend our perſons; to gratify hunger which promotes health, or to gratify curioſity which promotes knowledge. That which is involuntary is painful, but the gratification of our natural appetites is highly pleaſing. Beſides, what does it import us to ſay, that things done in paſſion are leſs voluntary than thoſe done on reflection, ſince guilty tranſports of paſſion ought to be as carefully avoided and ſhunned as deliberate villainy? The actions of man too often proceed from anger or concupiſcence; which irrational impulſes, being moving principles in the human frame, cannot, without abſurdity, be conſidered as involuntary [w].

Chap. 2. Of moral election and preference.

Having thus diſtinguiſhed actions and paſſions as voluntary and involuntary, we next proceed to treat of that intentional election or preference of one plan of conduct to another, which ſeems, ſtill more than actions themſelves, to compoſe the nature and eſſence of virtue, and to conſtitute the diſtinction of characters. This election or preference is not only voluntary, but ſomething more [x]; for it belongs not to brute animals and children,

[w] See Magna Moralia, b. i. c. xiii.; and Ethic. Eudem. b. ii. c. vii.

[x] επι πλειον το εκουσιον. "Voluntary," is an epithet of more extenſive application. It applies to actions that are not "deliberate." Moral election therefore implies ſomething more than merely what is "voluntary."

BOOK III.

children, whoſe actions are voluntary; nor to voluntary acts done ſuddenly, with ſuch precipitate haſte as leaves not any time for compariſon, election, or choice. Thoſe who name it inclination, paſſion, or opinion, ſeem to miſtake its nature. For the paſſions, whether founded in anger or concupiſcence, are common to man with the brute creation; but this election or preference is peculiar to himſelf. The intemperate man acts from paſſion, without election; but the man of true temperance acts from election, without paſſion[y]. The calm motive, by which he is actuated, is a thing ſo different from paſſion or deſire, that it is frequently ſet in direct oppoſition to them: but deſire cannot be oppoſed to deſire, nor any one paſſion to itſelf. Pleaſure and pain are the ultimate moving principles which ſet all the deſires and paſſions to work, but the actions of good men depending on a higher cauſe, do not obey their impulſe. Neither ought this intentional preference or election to be confounded with mere inclinations or wiſhes, though it appears to be nearly connected with them. We may wiſh for things impoſſible, as immortality; or things not depending on ourſelves, as that ſuch a player or wreſtler may gain the prize. But to prefer impoſſibilities, is the part only of a madman; and moral election or choice implies, that the goods preferred may be obtained by our own exertions. Beſides, our wiſhes relate principally to ends; our preferences, to means: we wiſh for health,

[y] ὁ ακρατης επιθυμων μεν πραττει, προαιρουμενος δε ου· ὁ εγκρατης δ' ανάπαλιν, προαιρουμενος μεν, επιθυμων δ' ου. "The intemperate man acts deſiring, not preferring; the temperate man (quite the reverſe) acts preferring, not deſiring." The full ſenſe of this paſſage will appear hereafter, when we come to treat of the important diſtinctions between temperance and ſelf-command on the one ſide, and intemperance, or weakneſs and wickedneſs, on the other: diſtinctions eſſential to a complete theory of Ethics, but which Ariſtotle is the only author that clearly explains.

health, we prefer the means neceſſary for attaining it; "to wiſh for happineſs," is correct language; "to prefer happineſs," is an expreſſion highly inaccurate: our preferences ſeem univerſally to relate to things within our own power. Moral preferences, therefore, are not merely opinions; which latter may relate to things impoſſible, eternal, and unchangeable; and which are characteriſed by the epithets "true" and "falſe," not by thoſe of "good" and "bad;" which apply only to our preferences or elections. Theſe laſt differ not only from opinion in general, but from every opinion in particular; for by no opinion whatever, and which is merely an opinion, are our characters marked as good or bad. Our preferences aſcertain the morality of our actions and habits. But our opinions merely tell us what it is that we chooſe or reject; wherein it may be uſeful or hurtful; and how it may prove either the one or the other. Our opinions are eſtimated by their truth, our preferences by their propriety; the former are unſtable like their cauſes, the latter are regulated by our own experience; and what opinion tells us to be the beſt road, is not always that which we chooſe to follow, our vices dragging us in an oppoſite direction[a]. To determine whether this moral preference is either preceded by, or accompanied with opinion, belongs not to the preſent queſtion, which conſiſts only in deciding whether theſe two be one and the ſame. We ſee that they are not. What then can this moral preference be, ſince it belongs not to any of the claſſes above mentioned? It plainly is voluntary, but alſo ſomething more, ſince it implies deliberation and reaſon; and, as its name indicates, is that which, after due

[a] —— Video meliora proboque
Deteriora ſequor. Hor.

BOOK III.

Chap. 3.

About what objects it is conversant.

due comparisons made by the understanding, the will prefers as best [a].

But it is worthy of consideration, whether all questions be the objects of such deliberations and comparisons, or some questions only. There are some points concerning which none but a fool or madman would hesitate a moment; and we are not said to deliberate concerning things eternal and unalterable, as the existence of the universe, or the incommensurability of the sides of a square with its diagonal. Neither do we deliberate concerning things merely fortuitous, as the finding of a treasure; nor concerning those which either naturally or necessarily always happen after the same manner, as the seasons of draughts and tempests; the rising, setting, and motions of the planets. Nor do all human affairs, that is, all those depending on the exertions of man, form a fit subject for our deliberation. The Lacedæmonians do not deliberate what is the constitution of government most suitable to the Scythians; because the conduct of the Lacedæmonians cannot have any efficacy in establishing it. The proper object of deliberation, therefore, consists in those practical matters, which depend on our own exertions; since these are the only things that remain unmentioned. Nature, necessity, fortune, intellect, are all of them considered as causes; but our deliberations bear a reference to those causes only which it is in our own power to influence and control. Things subjected to strict rules, admit not of deliberation; for example, in writing the letters of the alphabet, we have only to follow the practice prescribed. But the great field for deliberation

[a] See Ethics to Eudemus, b. ii. c. vii, viii, ix, x.; and Magn. Moral. b. i. c. xiii, xiv, xv, xvi, xvii, xviii.

beration lies in those practical arts which are uncertain and doubtful; physic, œconomy, and navigation, rather than the gymnastic; because the more precarious their operations are, the more patient deliberation is requisite; it is more necessary therefore in arts than in sciences; and must be constantly exercised about those things which, as they are not fortuitous, happen, for the most part, after the same manner; but concerning which, it is not easy for human wisdom to foresee how they will, in any given case, fall out. In matters of this kind, which are of high moment, we do not choose to act without the advice of counsellors, mistrusting our own sagacity. It was before observed, that we do not deliberate concerning ends, but concerning the means by which they may be attained. A physician never examines, whether he shall cure his patient; nor an orator, whether he shall persuade his audience; nor a statesman, whether he shall promote public prosperity. But the means through which those several purposes may be best attained, are the proper objects of their respective deliberations; which often extend to a long series of reasoning: for the immediate instruments, or agents, through which their designs may be effected, must often be procured by means of others more remote, and those, by others naturally prior; until they arrive finally at the first efficient cause; which, as in a mathematical investigation or analysis, is frequently the last in the order of discovery. The statesman, too, as well as the mathematician, when he comes to an impossibility, there stops; and tries some other road, which may lead to the end in view: as for example, if money be wanted, and cannot possibly be found, his schemes, which must be ineffectual without it, are immediately laid aside; but he does not desist from his purpose until he has

BOOK III.

examined not only his own resources but those of his friends; for what may be done by our friends, is in our own power, since they may be set to work by a principle in ourselves. Our deliberations, therefore, relate to instruments, to agents, to materials, and to means; and not only to the causes by which, but to the manner in which, our actions are to be performed, our conduct regulated, and our purposes effected. On the other hand, our ends and purposes themselves are never subjects of deliberation; neither are we said to deliberate concerning those particulars, which are merely perceptions of sense, as whether this bit of bread be well baked; neither can our deliberations be indefinite or endless, because this would imply a desire without an object. Moral preference, then, is not deliberation, but that which, after mature deliberation, is preferred as most agreeable to the commanding principles in our nature. In this preference, deliberation terminates; and from it, action commences. This natural progress appears in the Heroic Polities, faithfully delineated by Homer. The wisdom of the senate deliberates, and prefers, and declares its resolves to the people; who immediately carry them into execution. Moral preference, then, relates to those things only which may be accomplished by our own exertions; it is appetite or affection, combined with, and modified by, reason [b]; and, as above observed,

[b] The sagacious Polybius analyses with Aristotle the moral principle or faculty into reason or intellect, operating on the social and sympathetic nature of man. The passage is in the part of Polybius translated by Hampton, in whose words I shall give it. "From the union of the two sexes, to which all are naturally inclined, children are born. When any of these therefore, being arrived at perfect age, instead of yielding suitable returns of gratitude and assistance to those by whom they have been bred, on the contrary, attempt to injure them by words or actions, it is manifest that those who behold the wrong, after having also seen the sufferings and the anxious cares that were

observed, conversant, not about ends, but about the best means by which they may be attained.

BOOK III. Chap. 4.

The causes which move the will.

Volition, on the contrary, is, as above said, conversant only about ends; which consist, according to some, in real, and, according to others, in seeming, good. The opinion of those who think that the will is moved only by what is really good, involves this contradiction, that the volitions of a bad man are not voluntary; and the opinion of those who think that

were sustained by the parents in the nourishment and education of their children, must be greatly offended and displeased at such proceeding. For man, who, among all the various kinds of animals, is alone endowed with the faculty of reason, cannot, like the rest, pass over such actions with indifference; but will make reflection on what he sees; and comparing likewise the future with the present, will not fail to express his indignation at this injurious treatment; to which, as he foresees, he may also at some time be exposed. Thus again, when any one who has been succoured by another in the time of danger, instead of shewing the like kindness to this benefactor, endeavours at any time to destroy or hurt him; it is certain that all men must be shocked by such ingratitude, through sympathy with the resentment of their neighbour; and from an apprehension also, that the case may be their own. And from hence arises, in the mind of every man, a certain *notion* of the nature and force of duty, in which consists both the beginning and the end of justice. In like manner, the man, who, in defence of others, is seen to throw himself the foremost into every danger, and even to sustain the fury of the fiercest animals, never fails to obtain the loudest acclamations of applause and veneration from all the multitude; while he who shews a different conduct, is pursued with censure and reproach. And thus it is that the people begin to discern the nature of things honourable and base, and in what consists the difference between them; and to perceive that the former, on account of the advantage that attends them, are fit to be admired and imitated, and the latter to be detested and avoided." Polybius, l. vi. c. 6. The doctrine contained in this passage is expanded by Dr. Smith into a theory of moral sentiments. But he departs from his author in placing the perception of right and wrong in sentiment or feeling ultimately and simply. This also was the doctrine of Hutcheson, who ascribes our notions of virtue and vice to what he calls a moral sense *. Polybius, on the contrary, maintains with Aristotle, that these notions arise from reason or intellect operating on affection or appetite; or, in other words, that the moral faculty is a compound, and may be resolved into two simpler principles of the mind.

* Hutcheson's Moral Philosophy.

BOOK III.

that the will is moved only by ſeeming good, deſtroys all natural motives to volition, and makes it dependent merely on human caprice. If ſuch opinions muſt at firſt ſight be rejected, let us, then, ſay, that real good is the natural cauſe of volition, but that each individual prefers what ſeems good to himſelf; a good man, what is truly good; and a bad man, what he happens to think ſo; juſt as we ſee, in different habits and conſtitutions of body, the ſame things are not equally conducive to the health of all alike, but wholeſome things agree with healthy conſtitutions, whereas the ſickly often delight moſt in things naturally unwholeſome. In the ſame manner the moral conſtitution of a virtuous man, being congenial with truth, appreciates things by their real worth; for ſuch as our habits are, ſuch will be the eſtimates which we form of honour, pleaſure, and every object of deſire. This perhaps is the chief excellence of virtue, that it enables us to ſee the true value of things, and to meaſure them by a correct ſtandard. But the multitude, deceived by appearances, purſue pleaſures as the only good, and ſhun pain as the only evil.

Chap. 5.

That our habits are voluntary.

Ends are, then, the objects of volition; and the means of attaining them are the objects of deliberation and preference; which, being converſant only about ſuch things as are in our own power, the virtues immediately proceeding from them muſt alſo be in our own power, and voluntary, as well as the contrary vices. The poet's ſentiment therefore is but partially true:

"None chooſes wretchedneſs, or ſpurns delight[c]."

The

[c] ουδεις ἑκων πονηρος ουδ' ακων μακαρ. "Nobody is willingly wicked, or happy againſt his will." The ſentiment is aſcribed to an ancient tragedian. Ethic. Nicom. edit. Oxford, p. 108. and to Heſiod, "ν ταις μεγαλαις." Euſtrat. in Moral. Ariſtot. p. 62. The verſe originally meant that nobody was willingly *miſerable*, &c. that ſenſe being given to the word πονηρος in Heſiod. Suidas ſays, that Heſiod wrote a catalogue of illuſtrious women in five books, from which work Euſtratius conjectures this verſe may be copied.

BOOK III.

The latter clause cannot be disputed; but the former must be denied, otherwise we must reject the doctrine just established, that man is the author of his own actions; and that those things, whose principles or causes are in ourselves, are also in our own power. Yet these truths are attested by common sense and universal experience. Criminal actions are punished by law, when not committed either through compulsion or ignorance; in which cases they are pardoned, as not proceeding from ourselves. Praise-worthy actions, on the other hand, are encouraged and honoured; that as men are deterred from vice by the dread of punishment, they may be excited to virtue by the hope of reward. But were not our conduct voluntary, such persuasives to virtue would be useless and absurd; and there would be no more sense in exhorting a man to his duty, than in persuading him not to feel cold or heat, thirst or hunger. Crimes committed through ignorance are only excusable when the ignorance is involuntary; for when the cause of it lies in ourselves, it is then justly punishable; as in that ancient law which inflicts a double penalty on crimes done in drunkenness[d]. The ignorance of those laws, which all may know if they will, does not excuse the breach of them; and neglect is not pardonable, where attention ought to be bestowed. But perhaps we are incapable of attention. This however is our own fault; since the incapacity has been contracted by our continual carelessness; as the evils of injustice and intemperance are contracted by the daily commission of iniquity, and the daily indulgence in voluptuousness. For such as our actions are, such must our habits become; a truth confirmed by such universal experience, that to be ignorant of it betrays the grossest

[d] This, and other laws of the same tendency, will be considered in the "Politics."

grosseſt ſtupidity. It is plain therefore that our vices are voluntary; ſince we voluntarily do thoſe things which we know muſt produce them. But does it depend merely on our own wills to correct and reform our bad habits? It certainly does not; neither does it depend on the will of a patient, who has deſpiſed the adviſe of his phyſician, to recover that health which is loſt by his own profligacy. When we have thrown a ſtone, we cannot reſtrain its flight; but it depended entirely on ourſelves, whether we ſhould throw it or not. The villain and the voluptuary are therefore voluntarily ſuch; becauſe the cauſe of their turpitude lies ſolely in themſelves. Not only the vices of the mind, but even the imperfections of the body, are juſt ſubjects for reproach, when they are not natural, but produced through our own indolence or neglect. We pity blindneſs, lameneſs, or deformity, when they proceed from cauſes independent on thoſe afflicted with them; but they are juſt objects of reproach, when contracted through drunkenneſs or any other ſpecies of debauchery; and, in the ſame manner, all vices and imperfections are blameable which originate in ourſelves [e].

Objections anſwered.

But ſhould any endeavour to excuſe their wickedneſs, by ſaying that all men aſpire after apparent good, but that the appearances or phantaſms which make us aſſign to things this important epithet, ariſe not from our own ſuggeſtion, but depend on our conſtitution and character, it may be anſwered, that in as far as we ourſelves are the cauſes of this conſtitution and character, we alſo muſt be the cauſes of theſe phantaſms or appearances. But if the two former depend not at all on ourſelves, and villains, when they commit wickedneſs, do it merely through ignorance of the ends at which they ought to aim; and

[e] The Magna Moralia, and Ethics to Eudemus, as above.

and virtuous men, on the contrary, when they perform virtuous actions, do them merely through Nature's bounty in furnishing them with a moral or intellectual eye, which enables them to discern what is truly good; this surely would, in the latter, be the best and fairest of pre-eminences, a prerogative not adventitious but innate[f], not acquired by instruction or example, but growing up spontaneously with the admirable frame of their natural constitution. First of all, if this were the case, virtue would not be voluntary any more than vice, since both would solely depend on the original organization of our minds. But if we ourselves are in any degree the artificers of our own characters; and if it depends on our own voluntary acts, what sort of habits we shall form; and, if not entirely what ends we shall pursue, at least what means we shall use for their attainment; then both our virtue and our vices will be voluntary; and, as such, the former will be the objects of praise and reward, and the latter of blame and punishment.

Transition to the consideration of each virtue in particular.

We have thus given a sketch of the virtues in general, shewing that they are practical habits, consisting in mediocrity, dependent on ourselves, voluntary, and agreeable to right reason. Actions and habits are not precisely in the same sense voluntary; the former are voluntary throughout, from beginning to end; but the beginnings only of habits, which gain force, like maladies, by degrees, until they become irresistible; even these

[f] This word is used in other parts of Aristotle's works to distinguish natural powers from those acquired by our own exertions. Thus in his Metaph. l. ix. c. v. Απασων δη των δυναμεων ουσων, των μεν συγγενων, οιον των αισθησεων, των δε εθει, οιον της του αυλειν· των δε μαθησει, οιον της των τεχνων. "The most general division of powers is into three, which are innate, like the senses; those acquired by custom, like the power of playing on the flute; and those acquired by instruction, like many of the arts."

BOOK III.

these however are alſo voluntary, ſince their cauſes were ſuch, namely, the actions by which they were formed. We now proceed to conſider the ſeveral virtues in particular; wherein each conſiſts, to what object it relates, and in what manner it relates to them; whence their number will be manifeſt:—and firſt, concerning courage.

Chap. 6.

The definition and nature of courage.

This virtue, as we formerly obſerved, conſiſts in the moderation and propriety of our affections and actions in reference to thoſe cauſes and circumſtances which either excite fear, or inſpire confidence. Since whatever is evil is in ſome degree formidable[s], fear is defined "the dread of evil," and of evil of every kind, infamy, poverty, diſeaſe, friendleſſneſs, and death. But courage is not diſplayed in univerſal fearleſſneſs; for not to fear infamy is the part of impudence and baſeneſs; whereas the worthy and reſpectable character has always the keeneſt ſenſe of ſhame, and the ſtrongeſt averſion to diſgrace. Yet impudence ſometimes paſſes for courage; and may be ſo called, by a metaphor; ſince it reſembles that virtue in being equally fearleſs. Neither poverty nor diſeaſe, nor whatever proceeds not from any voluntary turpitude, ought, perhaps, to be much dreaded by thoſe who aſpire to the dignity of virtue; yet fearleſſneſs, as to ſuch objects, does not conſtitute what is properly called courage, though it ſometimes receives metaphorically that name: for thoſe who tremble at the ſound of war, may be liberal of their money, and fearleſs of poverty; thoſe, ſurely, are not cowards, who dread the inſults likely to fall on their wives or children; nor are thoſe to be dignified with the epithet of courageous, who, with the calm intrepidity of ſlaves, endure

[s] φοβυμεθα δε δηλονοτι τα φοβερα· ταυτα δ' εςι, ως απλως ειπειν, κακα. "We fear things formidable, which, to expreſs them in one word, are evils."

endure the prospect of disgraceful stripes. To what kind of terrors, then, does courage render us superior? To the greatest of all, the fear of death; for death seems of all things the most formidable; because, in common opinion, it is the ultimate limit of all our pains and pleasures, beyond which there is neither good nor evil. Yet courage is not alike shewn in contempt for every form of death. This virtue appears not conspicuous in disease or shipwreck, but in an honourable death in the field of battle, which is, of all, the fairest and most illustrious; as is attested by the honours with which it is rewarded, both by republics and kings. Courage, therefore, is peculiarly displayed in encountering death in battle, and in setting warlike dangers at defiance: not but that a brave man will be fearless during a storm at sea, or on a sick-bed; but his fortitude is different from that of sailors, who are rendered fearless through experience and custom; whereas he, perceiving no means of safety, submits with indignant[h] intrepidity to a death, from which no honour can be reaped, and in which no exertion of manhood can be displayed.

The

[h] εν ταις τοιαυταις δε φθοραις ουδετερον υπαρχει. Both Ulysses and Eneas thought with our author.

> With what a cloud the brows of Heaven are crown'd?
> What raging winds? What roaring waters round?
> 'Tis Jove himself the swelling tempest rears;
> Death, present death, on every side appears.
> Happy! thrice happy, who in battle slain,
> Prest, in Atrides' cause, the Trojan plain, &c. Odyss. V. v. 390.

And Æneas,

> O ter quaterque beati,
> Queis ante ora patrum, Trojæ sub mœnibus altis,
> Contigit oppetere, &c. Æneis, l. i. v. 98.

BOOK III. Chap. 7.

The ſame evils which terrify one perſon are not formidable to another; though there are ſome of ſuch an irreſiſtible nature, as to ſhake the firmeſt minds, and to inſpire fear into all poſſeſſed of underſtanding. But thoſe objects of terror which ſurpaſs not the ſtrength of human nature, differing from each other in magnitude, as well as do the grounds of confidence, courage will diſcriminate between real and apparent dangers; and make us meet the former as brave men ought, unſhaken and dauntleſs, ſubjecting the inſtinctive emotions of fear to the dictates of reaſon and of honour. For we betray our weakneſs, not only when we fear things really not formidable, but when we are affected in an undue degree, or at an improper time, by objects of real danger. A brave man avoids ſuch errors; and, eſtimating things by their real worth, prefers the grace and beauty of habitual fortitude to the deluſive ſecurity of deformed cowardice. Yet he is not leſs careful to avoid that exceſs of intrepidity, which, being rarely met with, is, like many other vices, without a name; though nothing but madneſs, or a moſt ſtupid inſenſibility, can make any man preſerve, amidſt earthquakes and inundations, that unſhaken compoſure, which has been aſcribed to the Celts[1]. An overweening eſtimate of the cauſes of confidence, and a conſequent exceſs of courage, is called audacity; a boaſtful ſpecies of bravery, and the mere ape of true manhood. What the brave man *is*, the raſh and audacious man wiſhes to *appear;* he courts and provokes unneceſſary dangers, but fails in the hour of trial; and is, for the moſt part, a bluſtering bully, who, under a ſemblance of pretended courage, conceals no inconſiderable portion of cowardice.

[1] Alexander, who perhaps knew them better than his preceptor, conſidered the "κελται or καλαται, or γαλαται," the Celts or Gauls, as an arrogant and boaſtful nation. Arrian. Exped. Alexand. l. i. p. 5.

cowardice. But the complete and genuine coward easily betrays himself, by fearing either things not formidable, or things formidable, in an undue degree; and his failing is the more manifest, because it is accompanied with plain indications of pain; he lives in continual alarm, and is therefore spiritless and dejected; whereas courage warms our breasts, and animates our hopes. Such then is the character of true courage, as opposed to audacity on one hand, and cowardice on the other. It holds the middle place between those vicious extremes; it is calm and sedate; and though it never provokes danger, is always ready to meet even death in an honourable cause. But to die, rather than endure manfully the pressure of poverty, or the stings of love, or any other cruel suffering, is the part of a coward; who basely flies from an enemy that he has not spirit to encounter; and ignominiously quits the field, where he might have sustained a strenuous and honourable conflict.

Chap. 8.

There are five kinds of courage, besides that properly so called. The first kind is the political, which most resembles that above described; because it is inspired by legal honours and rewards, and upheld by legal punishments and infamy. Courage therefore chiefly prevails, where cowardice is most stigmatised. Homer will supply us with examples; hear those of Hector and Diomed:

> Shall proud Polydamas before the gate
> Proclaim, his counsels are obeyed too late,
> Which timely followed but the former night,
> What numbers had been saved by Hector's flight[k]?

And Diomed,

> But ah, what grief! should haughty Hector boast,
> I fled inglorious to the guarded coast[l]?

This

[k] Il. xxii. v. 140. & seq. [l] Il. viii. v. 179. & seq.

This political courage most resembles genuine valour, because it originates in the love of glory and the shame of reproach, which are virtuous and honourable motives. Nearly alike to it, is that bravery which is inspired into soldiers by their generals; but inferior in merit, since engendered not by shame, but by fear; and by the dread not of disgrace but of punishment. For generals compel by threats; as Hector:

"On rushed bold Hector, gloomy as the night;
Forbids to plunder, animates the fight,
Points to the fleet; for by the Gods, who flies,
Who dares but linger, by this hand he dies;
No weeping sister his cold eye shall close,
No friendly hand his funeral pile compose.
Who stops to plunder at this signal hour,
The birds shall tear him, and the dogs devour [m]."

Those who advance, fearful of stripes, should they retreat; and those who stand their ground, in consequence of obstacles to their flight, all such lose the merit of bravery, because they are brave on compulsion. Experience and custom may produce likewise an artificial bravery; wherefore Socrates thought that courage was a matter of science. Each is most courageous in what he best understands; and therefore soldiers in battle, since they know the emptiness of many of the terrors with which the parade of war is accompanied. To the ignorant, therefore, they appear truly valiant; besides, their experience has taught them skilfully to employ their weapons, and by what means they may best defend themselves, and most effectually assault their enemies. They contend therefore with all the advantage which a practised prize-fighter enjoys over an ignorant rustic;

[m] Il. xv. v. 194. & seq.

rustic; or that men completely armed enjoy over naked troops; for in such combats, spirit and manhood yield to armed dexterity. But when the odds are against them, the courage of disciplined mercenaries speedily fails, and they are the first to fly; whereas the national troops remain and are slain; which recently happened at the Hermæus, where the Theban citizens preferred death to an ignominious safety, while their auxiliaries, though they behaved valiantly in the beginning of the action, no sooner discovered their inferiority in strength, than they basely betook themselves to flight; fearing death more than disgrace. Anger is often called to the assistance of manhood; and men seem courageous through passion, like wild beasts which turn, when wounded, and attack their pursuers; for both valour and anger makes us regardless of danger.—Whence Homer says:

> Inflaming thus the rage of all their hosts[a];

And

> Each Trojan bosom with new warmth he fires[b].

These passages imply, that the excitement of anger is auxiliary to courage; which, however, in man, ought to originate in a sense of honour, whereas in beasts it springs only from the smart of pain; for they turn on their pursuers, only when they are afraid or hurt; but, in their native woods or marshes, they venture not to approach human kind. Manly courage, therefore, cannot result from the irritation of pain, or from that blind passion which rushes, improvident, on unknown dangers. Even the unfeeling ass, when hungry, does not, through the fear of blows, forsake his pasture; and adulterers, impelled by lust, have exhibited signal examples of boldness;

[a] Il. xvi. v. 658. [b] Il. vi. v. 626.

BOOK III.

boldneſs; but ſuch things are far remote from true courage. Yet, of all paſſions, anger is the moſt nearly allied to this virtue, and would entirely accord with it, if directed by mature deliberation, and controlled by maxims of honour. Even in men, anger is painful, and revenge is ſweet: yet acting under the impulſe of ſuch paſſions, they are not courageous but quarrelſome; for neither reaſon nor moral principle has any ſhare in their behaviour; which has ſomething in it reſembling courage, but is not that virtue. Nor are perſons buoyed up by hope courageous; for they are confident of ſucceſs, only becauſe they have often conquered. This confidence, indeed, reſembles that of true courage; but it proceeds from a different principle, the opinion of ſuperiority, and the conſequent ſenſe of ſafety; and like the ſpurious valour of drunkards, (who are brave while ſucceſsful,) fails them under the ſlighteſt reverſe of fortune. But true courage ſurmounts real and known dangers, becauſe it is honourable to reſiſt them, and baſe to ſink under them. It is beſt ſeen in ſudden emergencies, becauſe, on ſuch occaſions, undiſturbed firmneſs cannot be aſſumed, but muſt be the reſult of confirmed manly habits. Perſons ignorant of the dangers which they encounter, have alſo a falſe ſemblance of courage; they are ſomewhat allied to thoſe buoyed up by hope, but are of a ſtamp ſtill inferior, their boldneſs being founded on miſtake, and therefore deſtitute of merit: for when they either know or ſuſpect the truth, they betake themſelves to ſhameful flight; as the Argives did, after encountering the Lacedæmonians, whom they miſtook for Scyonians. We have now deſcribed, who are truly courageous, and who only ſeem to be ſo.

Though

BOOK III. Chap. 9.

Though the office of courage consists in moderating the impulse of rash boldness, as well as the excess of cautious timidity, yet its principal business is employed about the latter; because it is more difficult, and therefore more praiseworthy, to endure pain, than to resist pleasure; and we endure pain when we silence the dictates of fear, and encounter real dangers with manly fortitude. Yet the end and essence of courage are truly pleasant, though the pleasure disappears amidst the crowd of painful circumstances with which it is accompanied. In the Gymnastic games, the prize-fighters contemplate with pleasure the crowns and honours with which their victories are rewarded: but their laborious exertions, and repeated wounds, are uneasy and painful. The splendour of the prize, which is small, is lost therefore in the gloomy magnitude of surrounding circumstances. The same thing happens as to courage. Death and wounds are painful to a brave man, and reluctantly encountered; yet he meets and defies them, because it is honourable to do so; and although the more distinguished he is in virtue, and therefore in happiness, he well knows that his loss in death will be the greater, and therefore the more deeply laments the dangers to which he is exposed; yet, on this account, his courage is only the more conspicuous in preferring a glorious death to a happy life. The exercise therefore of laborious virtue is painful in its progress, and only delightful as it approaches the goal. But there are mercenary ruffians, who, though endowed with little true courage, are ready, for their miserable hire, to throw away their lives, which are of still less value. Thus much concerning courage; of which we may delineate the nature, from the observations above made [a].

We

[a] Vid. Magna Moral. l. i. c. xiii.; and Eudem. l. iii. c. i.

BOOK III.

Chap. 10.

Of the definition and nature of temperance.

We now proceed to ſpeak of temperance, which, as well as courage, is employed in regulating the irrational, and merely animal part of our conſtitution. Temperance, we have ſaid, is the habit of mediocrity in our affections with reſpect to the objects which afford pleaſure; and alſo (though in a different manner, and an inferior degree) with reſpect to thoſe which give pain. Ungoverned voluptuouſneſs is the reverſe of temperance. We farther proceed to examine what kinds of pleaſure it is the office of temperance to regulate. Pleaſures are commonly diſtinguiſhed, as either corporeal or mental. Of the latter kind is the pleaſure which we derive from virtue or from knowledge; with both of which we are delighted, becauſe we love them; and that, without any bodily ſenſation, but merely through mental affection. Neither temperance nor voluptuouſneſs are converſant about ſuch pleaſures, nor about any others not originating in the body. Men fond of the marvellous, and who delight in relating idle ſtories from morning to night, are called prattlers, not profligates: nor are thoſe guilty of intemperance who indulge exceſſive grief for the loſs of their fortunes or of their friends. Temperance relates therefore to bodily pleaſures only, but not even to them univerſally. It reſtrains not the gratification which the eye receives from colours, figures, and pictures, nor that given to the ear by declamation or muſic. There is a propriety, doubtleſs, in the affection with which we deſire, and the degree in which we indulge, thoſe pleaſures; but they who act properly in ſuch particulars, are not denominated temperate; nor thoſe who act improperly, intemperate. Nor do temperance and intemperance apply to our reſtraint or indulgence with regard to the pleaſures derived from the ſenſe of ſmell, except by way of acceſſion,

ceſſion, that is, when grateful odours are conſidered as an acceſſory to agreeable ſenſations derived from the taſte or touch. To be delighted with the fragrancy of flowers and fruits, and of thoſe aromatics which perfume the altars of the Gods, is never regarded as ſenſuality; but a propenſity to vicious indulgence may appear in the pleaſures received from thoſe artificial ſcents which are employed for heightening perſonal allurements, and from the odour of thoſe delicacies which form the luxury of our tables; becauſe, in theſe caſes, the perceptions of one ſenſe naturally bring into our thoughts the perceptions of other ſenſes, which are too often indulged with groſs and beaſtly intemperance. The inferior animals, when hungry, are delighted with the ſmell of their food; but this delight in them happens alſo, as above explained, by way of acceſſion; dogs are pleaſed with the ſcent of the hare, becauſe they delight in eating that animal; and lions are pleaſed, not with the bellowing of the bull, but with devouring him; and the bellowing only pleaſes them, becauſe it is a proof that their prey is near to them. The ſight of the deer or wild goat alſo delights them, becauſe it affords the expectation of ſoon taſting their fleſh. Temperance, therefore, is converſant about thoſe pleaſures only, which are common to us with beaſts; and in which an exceſſive indulgence is therefore juſtly deemed the loweſt depravity. Thoſe pleaſures depend entirely on the touch and taſte, but far more on the former; the taſte being properly that ſenſe which diſcriminates different flavours, as is done by thoſe who critically examine wines and ſauces. But the beaſtly ſenſualiſt has little or no pleaſure in any thing except mere corporeal contact in eating and drinking, as well as in venery. Wherefore the voluptuary Philoxenus wiſhed his neck as long as a crane's, that his gratification in the act of ſwallowing might be the more durable.

BOOK III.

durable. Temperance, therefore, is chiefly converſant about regulating the pleaſures of that ſenſe, of which, as it is of all the moſt common, the improper indulgence is the moſt blameable and moſt debaſing; ſince it belongs to us, not as men, but as mere animals. To love and take delight in ſuch gratifications, is to diveſt ourſelves of the man, and to put on the wild beaſt: for the more liberal pleaſures of the touch, ſuch as the warmth produced by friction and exerciſe in the *gymnaſia*, fall not under this head; intemperate voluptuouſneſs in contact, not extending to the whole body, but centering in particular parts of it.

Chap. II.

Natural and adventitious deſires.

Of our deſires and appetites, ſome are common and natural; others, peculiar and adventitious. Every animal needs and deſires nouriſhment, either dry or moiſt; and ſometimes both; and in the vigour of life, every man, as Homer ſays, wiſhes for a mate. But all do not deſire either the ſame objects; nor is every particular object alike neceſſary to the happineſs of every individual; the deſire of particular objects, therefore, is often conſidered as peculiar and adventitious. This deſire may nevertheleſs be natural to him who feels it, ſince different men have different inclinations; and one perſon may receive much delight from that which cannot afford any gratification to another. In our natural deſires, there are few improprieties; the ſole error conſiſting in exceſſive indulgence. Gluttony, which, inſtead of ſatisfying, overloads the ſtomach, is the vice only of the moſt abject of the human kind. But in adventitious and unnatural pleaſures, there is ſcope for the wildeſt and moſt various errors; which reſult, not only from the exceſſive degree, but from the improper and even odious objects, of our deſires; as well as from the unbecoming manner and unſeaſonable occaſions on which they are indulged.

dulged. Intemperance, then, is an excefs with regard to pleafure; and juftly reprobated. With regard to pain, the office of temperance is different from that of fortitude. The intemperate man is grieved at miffing pleafure; which, by his perverfity and folly, is thus abfurdly converted into a perpetual fource of pain; fince he defires it with diftreffing anxiety, and both abufes it when prefent, and forrows after it when it is gone. But temperance, which is not to be feduced by pleafures within its power, cannot grieve at the lofs of thofe which are placed beyond its reach. Extreme infenfibility to pleafure is not the lot of human nature: even brute beafts prefer one kind of food to another. The fault therefore of being too little affected by pleafure, as it feldom or never occurs, is not diftinguifhed by a name. But temperance holds the middle place between this namelefs vice and the oppofite extreme. The man endowed with temperance is fo far from delighting in, or enjoying, the pleafures of the voluptuary, that he beholds them with deteftation and difguft. He indulges in none but lawful pleafures, and in them feafonably and foberly; and not being intoxicated by them when prefent, does not painfully long for them when abfent. His health, his fortune, and above all his honour and his duty, prefcribe laws to his appetites. The profligate prefers fenfual pleafures to all things befide: the man of temperance eftimates them at their true value, and that a low one [a].

Chap. 12.

Comparifon of intemperance and cowardice.

Intemperance is more voluntary than cowardice; the former proceeding from the defire of pleafure, the latter from the averfion to pain: and fuch is the nature of pain that it difturbs and deftroys the frame of mind of thofe who behold its approach, and

[a] Magna Moral. l. i. c. xxii. Eudem. l. iii. c. ii.

and anticipate its pangs. Pleasure not producing these effects, the intemperate indulgence in it is therefore more voluntary, and consequently more blameable; especially since there are innumerable opportunities in life for restraining our pursuit of unlawful or improper pleasures, and thereby acquiring a confirmed habit of temperance, the several acts of which are unattended with danger. The reverse of this happens as to cowardice; the opportunities for correcting it are much fewer in number, and the experiment is dangerous. But though particular instances of cowardice are in some measure involuntary, through the invincible terror which produces them, and which impels those affected with it to throw away their shields, and to commit other shameful actions, yet the frame and habit of mind from which such actions flow, seems to be more a matter of choice; whereas the frame and habit of mind from which intemperance flows, seems less voluntary than the particular instances of it; for no one can will or choose, that by his internal constitution he should be the sport of vicious propensities, and ungovernable appetites. The word denoting intemperance in Greek is applicable to the wanton and unchastised petulance of boys, which bears a near analogy to what is called intemperance in men. Which of the two was the primary meaning of the word, it is not material to inquire; for the transition is extremely natural from the one signification to the other, nothing standing more in need of chastisement than depravities which increase by indulgence; to which depravities, passions as well as boys are peculiarly liable. For boys are actuated almost solely by passion, pleasure being their ruling pursuit; the desire of which, unless it be restrained by higher principles and controlled by authority, will transgress all reasonable bounds; and, gaining strength by by repeated acts of indulgence, will finally destroy and extinguish the light of reason itself. Our desires therefore ought to be few and moderate, and as obedient to the dictates of reason, as boys to the commands of their master. By such habitual regulation, they will gradually harmonise with the higher powers of our nature, and at length terminate in the same excellent and honourable end; exhibiting the steady lustre of virtue; and exactly conforming, as to their object, degree, time, and all other circumstances, to the strict rules of propriety. So much concerning temperance.

ARISTOTLE's ETHICS.

BOOK IV.

INTRODUCTION.

HAVING treated of the virtues of courage and temperance, which, how different ſoever in many reſpects from each other, agree in this particular, that they both conſiſt in the proper government of the irrational or merely ſenſitive part of our nature, the author proceeds in the fourth book, to explain the nature of liberality, magnificence, magnanimity, meekneſs, courteſy, plain-dealing, and facetiouſneſs. As things are beſt underſtood by compariſon, he points out and defines the blameable extremes (for example, of niggardlineſs and profuſion) which ſtand in direct oppoſition to each other; and which are both of them contrary, though not always in a like degree, to the praiſeworthy habit which lies between them. He ſhows that there is an intermediate, but anonymous habit, highly deſerving of approbation, between the extremes of ambition and blameable inſenſibility to honour: obſerving on this and other occaſions, that many of the virtues, as well as of the vices, are not accurately diſtinguiſhed by names; and that from this imperfection of language, much confuſion reſults; for when the intermediate and praiſeworthy habit is nameleſs, each of BOOK IV.

the extremes will ſtrive to thruſt itſelf into the middle place, which is the poſt of honour; and that habit which is approved as virtue by one claſs of men, will be condemned as vice by another. He examines whether ſhame can be claſſed with the virtues, ſince it ſeems rather a paſſion than a habit. He explains what is meant by a conditional virtue, in oppoſition to virtue ſimply and abſolutely; and proves that ſhame is at beſt only a virtue of the conditional and imperfect kind.

BOOK IV.

ARGUMENT.

Liberality.—Vices opposite thereto.—Magnificence; its contraries.—Magnanimity.—Meekness; its contraries.—Courtesy; its contraries.—Plain-dealing; its contraries.—Facetiousness; its contraries.—Shame.

BOOK IV. Chap. 1.

Liberality, and the vices contrary to it.

WE proceed to speak of liberality, which seems to be that virtue which bears a peculiar relation to property. For the praise of liberality is not acquired by courage in war, moderation in pleasure, or justice in judgment, but by the propriety of our behaviour in receiving or bestowing money, or whatever things can be measured by money; and principally in bestowing them. Of the propriety of our conduct in relation to property, prodigality and niggardliness are the two contrary and blameable extremes. Niggardliness always refers to those who set more than a just value on money: but prodigality is sometimes employed to express extravagant profusion joined with inordinate intemperance; for those are called prodigals, who waste their fortunes in ruinous pleasures, and thus signally debase themselves by complicated worthlessness. Yet prodigality more properly signifies one simple vice, that of ruining ourselves by our own fault; for he ruins himself by his own fault, who wastefully consumes his property, that is, the means by which his life is ſupported; and in this acceptation we take the word. Property falls under the deſcription of things uſeful; which may either be uſed rightly or abuſed; and he only can uſe them rightly, who is adorned with the virtue appertaining to them; namely, liberality. The uſe of money conſiſts in expending or beſtowing it: for the taking or keeping of money relates to poſſeſſion rather than to uſe. The virtue of liberality therefore is more conſpicuous in beſtowing handſomely, than either in receiving what is our due, or in refuſing what we ought not to accept. For virtue conſiſts rather in acting our part well, than in avoiding what is amiſs. This active virtue alone is the proper object of praiſe and gratitude; for it is more meritorious to part with what is our own, than to abſtain from what belongs to another; which latter may be praiſed indeed as juſtice, but not as liberality; and to accept what is ſtrictly due to us, is not entitled to any degree of praiſe. None are more beloved than the liberal, becauſe their virtue is extenſively uſeful, diffuſing itſelf in benefits. But the motive from which their actions proceed, is what chiefly conſtitutes their excellence; for liberality, like every other virtue, muſt keep the beauty of propriety in view; ſelecting its objects, and proportioning its extent, according to thoſe rules which right-reaſon preſcribes. The critical moment for beſt conferring a favour muſt alſo be carefully ſtudied; and they muſt be conferred cheerfully, at leaſt not painfully: and when any one of theſe conditions is wanting, whatever acts of bounty a man may perform, he will not carry off the palm of virtuous and graceful liberality. If the gifts beſtowed on others occaſion pain to ourſelves, it is a proof that we prefer money to the beauty

beauty of generous actions; and if we are rapacious in acquiring money, we cannot be truly liberal in employing it. A man of real beneficence will not be importunate in solicitation. He will be delicate as to accepting favours; but will enrich himself by the diligent management of his own affairs, that he may acquire materials for his bounty, which will be distributed with caution, that it may never fail the deserving. It belongs to his character to be more provident for others than for himself; and to extend the measure of his beneficence far beyond those limits which the prudence of selfishness would prescribe. But our liberality is relative to our wealth; it consists, not in the value of our gifts, but in the temper and habit of the giver; and he who gives the least of all, may be the most liberal of all, if what he gives bears the highest proportion to his substance [r]. Men of hereditary estates are more inclined to liberality, than those whose fortunes are their own work; the former have never known the severities of want; and all men are disposed to love and cherish their own works, as parents and poets. It is not easy for a liberal man to be rich, since he is nice in receiving money, not retentive in keeping it; and always ready to give it away, on no other account than that of the proper or beneficent purposes to which it may be applied. Fortune, therefore, is continually accused of enriching those who are least worthy of her favours. But this happens naturally, without the interference of fortune; since wealth cannot well be possessed by those who employ not the ordinary means by which it is acquired and accumulated. Yet true

[r] Verily I say unto you, that this poor widow hath cast more in, than all they which have cast into the treasury. St. Mark, c. xii. v. 43.

BOOK IV.

true liberality avoids unnecessary and superfluous expence, lest the source should be dried up, from which only its salutary streams can plenteously flow. Whoever lives beyond his income, is strictly a prodigal, and he only; for kings, how great soever their expenditure may be, are never branded with this appellation; because it seems difficult for their munificence to exceed the measure of their resources. The liberal man, both in great and in small matters, and both in giving and receiving, behaves with cheerful serenity, because his behaviour is always proper, and always consistent with his character. As propriety in giving and receiving depends on the same principle of moderation in our desires with regard to money, he who gives properly, will not improperly receive; since contraries cannot result from the same principle, nor subsist in the same subject. Should it happen that a liberal man consumes more than he ought, and on an improper occasion, he will doubtless lament it, but with that calm and moderate composure which becomes his character; for it is the part of virtue not only to joy and grieve from fit motives, but to assign proper limits to those emotions. The liberal man is, in matters of interest, of an accommodating temper; he is open to imposition and injury, because he does not value money beyond its real worth, and is more uneasy at having omitted to do what he ought, than at doing too much; living in direct opposition to the avaricious rapacity of Simonides[*]. The prodigal, again, is directly the reverse;

[*] A poet of the Isle of Ceos, and the first on record who prostituted his mercenary muse for the vile purpose of gain. He was born 558 years before Christ, and lived ninety years; the companion and favourite of many of the princes and grandees of his time. As his avarice increased with his age, he apologized for it by saying that the pursuit of money was the only delight which time had left to him. Conf. Fragment. Callimac.

reverſe; both his joy and his grief ſpring from improper motives, and both ſhew themſelves in unſeemly and immoderate degrees; which will be more manifeſt in the ſequel. Prodigality and avarice are both of them exceſſes, and both of them defects. Prodigality is exceſſive in giving, and defective in receiving; avarice is defective in giving, and exceſſive in receiving, and ſcraping together the meaneſt and moſt ſordid gains. The qualities which compoſe and ſupport prodigality, are not eaſily united: it is difficult for him who is careleſs of receiving, to continue laviſh in beſtowing; for his funds, if he is a private man, will ſoon be exhauſted. The prodigal, therefore, is better than the miſer, becauſe his malady is more curable. Age, and the experience of want, will correct his extravagance; and, as he ſtill ſhows a generoſity of nature, though unwiſely and unſeaſonably, cuſtom and good example will convert his thoughtleſs profuſion into decent and graceful liberality; ſince his deviations from the right path proceed rather from folly than from depravity and turpitude. For this reaſon ſuch a prodigal is preferable to the miſer; and alſo becauſe the former benefits many, and the latter, no one; not even himſelf. But thoſe who are prodigal of their own, are for the moſt part rapacious of what belongs to others; and finding it impoſſible to ſupply their wild extravagance by honourable means, abſtain from no ſource of gain, however impure and polluted it may be; ſo that even their bounties have nothing liberal in them, being with-held from virtue in diſtreſs, and laviſhed on paraſites, flatterers, and on the idle retinue of vice and folly. For the greater part of prodigals unite profligacy with

Callimac. apud Spanheim. v. i. p. 264 and 337. Plutarch. An ſeni capiend. Reſpublica, V. ii. p. 786. Athen. xiv. c. xxi. Fabric. Bibliot. Græc. V. i. p. 591.

with prodigality; and insensible to the beauty of virtue, fall victims to the allurement of pleasure. But though this happens to the undisciplined prodigal, yet, under proper management, he may be brought into the middle and right path; whereas avarice is incorrigible; for it is increased by old age and every kind of infirmity; and it seems more congenial to human nature than the contrary vice, there being in every country more hoarders than spendthrifts. It also extends to extraordinary lengths, and assumes a variety of forms; the immoderate love of money leading some men to daring rapacity, and others to sordid parsimony; for there are niggardly misers, and tenacious scrape-pennies, who either through a sense of justice, or through fear, are careful in abstaining from shameful gains, and meanly sparing of their property, lest they should be forced, as they say, on dishonest expedients for subsistence. Their maxim is, neither to borrow nor to lend, neither to give nor to receive; because, should they accept any thing from others, they think it will be difficult always to avoid giving to others something in return. But rapacious avarice sticks at no expedient by which money may be acquired; submits to the basest drudgery, practises pimping or usury, and thinks no profit too infamous or too minute, which, by frequent repetitions, may accumulate into a great gain. Both kinds are alike disgraced by their false estimate, and inordinate love of money; since, for the sake of profit, and that a small one, they encounter and endure a burdensome load of infamy; which is an evil that even the greatest profits cannot possibly compensate. Those who aspire to great and sudden acquisitions of wealth, such as tyrants who storm cities and plunder temples, are not branded with the reproach

of.

BOOK IV.

of avarice, but of impiety and villany. The pirate, the pickpocket, and the gamester, are guilty of illiberal rapacity; since the two first encounter, for the sake of gain, not only danger but disgrace; and the last plunders and ruins his friends and acquaintances, whom a man of liberal principles wishes always to benefit. They are all equally debased by a shameless preference of wealth to worth; and by bartering things incomparably more valuable, for unjust and illiberal gains. Illiberality, therefore, is the vice most properly opposed to the virtue of liberality; for it is a greater, more extensive, and more universal evil, than the vice of prodigality, which holds the contrary extreme. So much concerning mediocrity in our passions and actions with regard to money, and whatever money can purchase, as well as concerning the vicious extremes which are inconsistent with this praiseworthy and meritorious habit[t].

Chap. 2.

Magnificence, and its contraries.

We naturally proceed to treat next of magnificence; for that likewise seems to be a virtue respecting money; but differs from liberality in this, that it relates to money in one view only, namely, the spending of it; and in this, it exceeds the measure which mere liberality would prescribe. The very name of magnificence indicates a certain magnitude, joined with propriety, in expence; and the magnitude or splendour of our expence is estimated by the occasion on which it is employed; for that might be great in a trierarch[u], which would be small in an ambassador to the public solemnities of Greece; and the propriety depends both on the object of the expence, and on the

[t] Vid. Magna Moral. l. i. c. xxiv.; et Eudem. l. iii. c. iv.

[u] The rich citizens of Athens were liable to the burden of equipping gallies for the public service; in which they often vied with each other in displaying their patriotism to the ruin of their fortunes. Lys. Orat. passim.

BOOK IV.

the character and ſituation of the perſon who incurs it. He is not called magnificent who ſpends his money with propriety on ſmall or ordinary occaſions, like him

"Who often gave the hungry beggar bread:"

For magnificence is not ſimply liberality, but ſomething more; the former implying the latter, though the latter does not imply the former. Magnificence holds the middle place between two blameable extremes, of which the one, in matters of expence, falls ſhort of what is ſuitable to our circumſtances or to the occaſion, and the other oſtentatiouſly exceeds them. To be truly magnificent requires no ſmall degree of judgment; ſince it infers a graceful theory of moral propriety, and a ſkilful harmony in great expenditure; for as we ſaid in the beginning, habits are characteriſed by the acts and energies from which they ſpring, and which in a man of real magnificence muſt be great and decorous; the work worthy the expence, and the expence ſuiting and rather exceeding the work. A man truly magnificent, is actuated by the love of moral beauty, which is the principle of all the virtues. His generoſity is large and liberal, without ſtrictneſs of accounts; his conſideration being, not how much any thing will coſt him, but how it may be done moſt handſomely. For the magnificence is not in the expence, but in the manner of employing it; which muſt be ſuch, not merely as propriety would dictate, for this belongs to liberality, but ſuch as will ſtrike the ſpectators with wonder. It is moſt conſpicuous in temples, dedications, ſacrifices, and whatever concerns the Gods: and in thoſe honourable benefactions which generous patriots confer on the community; the equipment of gallies, public entertainments, and dramatic exhibitions. As magnificence muſt be conſiſtent with propriety, it can never be the

the virtue of a poor man, in whom every attempt towards exercising it must be egregious folly. It becomes those only who possess great hereditary wealth, or who have enriched themselves by great and splendid exploits; and it is most honourably displayed on the public occasions above mentioned. It may be shown also in matters of private concern, when they are such as occur but once in our lives, as a marriage; or such as interest the whole community, or at least the members of the government; as the reception and entertainment of strangers, and the honours and presents bestowed on them at their departure: for the expences of a magnificent man are public, not personal; and presents to strangers somewhat resemble dedications to the Gods. To build a house suitable to a great fortune, is a work of magnificence, for it is a public ornament; and works are magnificent in proportion to their durability, provided propriety always be observed, for the same monuments will not suit Gods and men, nor the same ornaments become tombs and temples. Magnificence, we have said, is not measured simply by the expence, but by the expence in reference to the object on which it is bestowed. The magnificence, doubtless, rises in proportion to the magnitude of that object; but a beautiful bauble, of little or no value, may be a magnificent present to a child; because, though trifling in itself, yet being considerable with respect to the occasion, it attests the noble liberalitty of the donor. True magnificance is far remote from unseasonable ostentation, which makes a parade of wealth on ordinary and mean occasions; the ostentatious man receives his guest at a friendly dinner, as if he were celebrating a marriage festival; and when he exhibits dramatic entertainments, decks, after the awkward fashion of the Magareans, his comic actors in the purple trappings of tragedy;

BOOK IV.

gedy; catching popular admiration by unſeaſonable and abſurd extravagance; while, on the other hand, he is meanly parſimonious at times when true magnificence might properly be diſplayed. The vice oppoſite to magnificence betrays niggardlineſs throughout, even in the midſt of the moſt profuſe expence; for, in ſome minute particular, an attention to a pitiful ſaving will be diſcovered, which ruins the beauty and gracefulneſs of the whole, as it proves that whatever has been done, was done ſparingly and painfully; and that the performance, if great, far ſurpaſſed the mind of the performer. Theſe two contrary habits are both of them vices, but not very reproachful ones, ſince they neither do harm to others, nor evince groſs turpitude in the mind which harbours them [x].

Chap. 3.

Magnanimity.

Magnanimity, as the name imports, is converſant about great things; what theſe are let us firſt conſider; contemplating not the habit itſelf, but the perſon actuated by it, which will bring us to preciſely the ſame concluſions. A magnanimous man is he, whoſe character being of great worth, is eſtimated by himſelf at its full value. He who forms a groſsly falſe eſtimate of himſelf is a fool; and none of the virtues are conſiſtent with folly: while the man who, conſcious of his defects, appreciates his ſmall merits by a fair and juſt ſtandard, may be praiſed for his good ſenſe and modeſty, but cannot paſs for magnanimous; which epithet always implies dignity and excellence; this beauty of the mind requiring, like that of the body, elevation and magnitude; for perſons of a diminutive ſtature, are not called beautiful, but neat and elegant. A mean-ſpirited [y] man under-rates his own merits; and the vain-glorious boaſter arrogates

[x] Eudem. l. iii. c. vi.

[y] Ariſtotle ſays "little-minded."

rogates to himſelf merits, of which he is by no means poſſeſſed; but the more ſolid merit he poſſeſſes, his vain-glory is the leſs; whereas mean-ſpiritedneſs is the greater, in proportion to the excellence of the worth which is ſo improperly appreciated by its poſſeſſor; for how contemptible would he be, even to himſelf, were his real character of little or no value! The magnanimous man eſtimates himſelf at the higheſt rate, yet no higher than he ought; and conſcious of his inward worth, thinks himſelf entitled to whatever is held moſt precious; to what the moſt exalted of men claim as the higheſt of all rewards; and to what all men confer on the Gods as their acknowledged due; in a word, to honour, the greateſt and moſt invaluable of external goods. Magnanimity, therefore, is peculiarly converſant about honour, and its contrary, ignominy; holding the middle place between vain-glory that unfairly courts undue honours, and mean-ſpiritedneſs that improperly rejects even thoſe that are due. But though, in point of propriety, magnanimity holds the middle place, yet, in excellence and dignity, it riſes to the ſummit; for it heightens and enlarges every virtue; and the moſt boaſtful vain-glory never proudly arrogated more than true magnanimity has fairly claimed. This illuſtrious habit of the mind cannot bear an alliance with any kind of vice. It is moſt oppoſite to cowardice or injuſtice; for, from what motive can he, who thinks of nothing ſo highly as of his own character, exhibit himſelf under ſuch deformities? And if we apply to particular inſtances, or ſurvey individual characters, we ſhall find that thoſe who affect magnanimity without real worth, infallibly expoſe themſelves to ridicule. For, honour, which is the meed of virtue, cannot belong to the worthleſs; and magnanimity forms, as it were, the ornament

BOOK IV.

ment of the virtues, ſince it cannot ſubſiſt without them, yet heightens, extends, and magnifies them, wherever they are found. True magnanimity then is a thing moſt difficult, ſince it implies the perfection of moral rectitude. It delights, moderately, in great honours beſtowed by the deſerving, as meeting with its due, or leſs: for with perfect virtue no honour can be fully commenſurate. It accepts however ſuch honours, becauſe nothing better can be beſtowed; but of vulgar honours, or from vulgar men, it is altogether diſdainful; and is as inſenſible to their reproach, as careleſs of their applauſe. Wealth, power, good or bad fortune, it will meet and ſuſtain with the ſame dignified compoſure, neither elated with proſperity nor dejected by adverſity; for to a magnanimous man thoſe things are deſirable chiefly as the ſigns of honour; and, if he bears honour itſelf with moderation, much more muſt he thus bear thoſe things which are only its ſigns, and deſired merely on its account; ſince to him who thinks not too highly of honour, nothing beſides can poſſibly appear great. Magnanimity, therefore, ſometimes paſſes for ſuperciliouſneſs; eſpecially ſince great external proſperity ſeems to heighten and increaſe it; for nobility is honoured; and men of wealth or power, being diſtinguiſhed by great ſuperiority of advantages, will always find perſons ready to do them honour; and though honour belongs properly to virtue alone, yet virtue, adorned with great external proſperity, will ſeem doubly entitled to pre-eminence. But, in reality, the moſt proſperous fortune, when deſtitute of virtue, affords not any juſt ground for ſelf-applauſe; it gives to us neither a high opinion of ourſelves, nor a fair claim to be highly thought of by others; and as it is incapable of inſpiring true magnanimity, it too frequently begets inſolence and fuperciliousnefs; fince worthlefs men cannot bear gracefully the gifts of fortune, but abufe their fancied fuperiority by treating others contemptuoufly and unjuftly; whereas the contempt fhown by the truly magnanimous, is juft; their opinions being formed on reflection, as thofe of the multitude are taken up at random. A man of magnanimity neither courts dangers, nor willingly encounters them on flight occafions. But when a worthy occafion requires it, he is unfparing of his life, thinking that to live is not, under all conditions, eligible. He is eager to confer favours, and afhamed of receiving them; becaufe the former is a mark of fuperiority, the latter the reverfe; he therefore repays every kindnefs with intereft, that the perfon who firft obliged him, may become his debtor. He hears with more pleafure a recital of the good offices he has performed, than that of the favours which he has received. Wherefore Thetis does not expatiate on her benefits to Jupiter[y], nor the Lacedæmonians on thofe which they had conferred on the Athenians[z]; but rather on the kindnefs they themfelves had received at their hands; for magnanimity having few wants, feldom needs that affiftance which it is always difpofed to afford; it is lofty towards the great and profperous, but behaves modeftly towards men in moderate circumftances; to rife above the former, has difficulty and dignity; but to magnify ourfelves in company with the latter, betrays a lownefs and littlenefs of mind, not lefs ungenerous and vulgar, than making a parade of our ftrength or courage amidft weaknefs and cowardice. Magnanimity contemns trivial honours; and difdains, even in great things, to act a fecond part. It is flow in action, and averfe to exertion, except when great honour may be obtained, or great actions are to

[y] Homer. Ilias. l. i. v. 503. & feq.

[z] Xenoph. Hellen. l. vi. p. 609—613. Edit. Leunclav.

BOOK IV.

to be performed: not busied about many things, but confined to those which are great and splendid. A magnanimous man is as open in his hatred as in his friendship; for concealment is the part of fear; he regards truth more than opinion, and shows himself manifestly in his words and actions, declaring his mind with full freedom; which indicates both his own love of truth and his contempt for the opinions of others; but this openness of character is liable to one exception, for he is much given to *irony*, dissembling his merits before the vulgar, who are unworthy to appreciate them. He can show undue complaisance for no one's humours, except those of his friends; for flattery is a low and servile vice. He is not prone to admire, for he deems nothing great. He is not mindful of injuries, which his magnanimity teaches him to despise. He is no man's panegyrist or slanderer; he talks not of himself, nor does he blame others; not speaking ill even of his enemies, except when their insolence excites his indignation. As to things of small import, or even daily use, he is no petitioner or complainer; for that would shew too much concern about them. His possessions are distinguished for their beauty and elegance rather than for their fruitfulness and utility; because the former qualities are more nearly allied to that independence and all-sufficiency to which he aspires. The gait of a magnanimous man is slow; his tone of voice grave, his pronunciation firm. Haste and rapidity betoken too much solicitude. *He* therefore is seldom in haste, who deems few things worthy of his pursuit; nor is he often eager who thinks few things of importance: quickness and sharpness of voice proceeding from earnestness and eagerness. Such then are the characteristics of magnanimity, of which mean-spiritedness is the defect, and vain-glory the excess; qualities which, though not

not very hurtful to others, yet ſhow much imperfection in the minds which harbour them. The little-minded man deprives himſelf of thoſe advantages to which he is entitled. He is ignorant of himſelf and of his own worth, otherwiſe he would aſpire to thoſe advantages which he really deſerves. His fault however conſiſts rather in ſluggiſhneſs than folly; he draws back from noble actions and illuſtrious enterpriſes, as things much above him; and even excludes himſelf from that external proſperity which fortune throws in his way. But the vain-glorious man is ignorant of himſelf ſtill more conſpicuouſly; and even to folly. He engages in undertakings the moſt honourable, but far above his abilities; and in which his ſignal failure manifeſtly convicts him of unworthineſs. He delights in the ornaments of dreſs, and all other ſhowy externals. He makes a parade of his proſperity, and boaſts of it in the vain hope of being honoured on its account. Yet mean-ſpiritedneſs is more contrary than vain-glory to true magnanimity; becauſe the former vice is more frequently met with, and is alſo attended with worſe conſequences. Such then is the nature of magnanimity, or that virtue which is converſant about great and extraordinary honours *.

Chap. 4. Of the propriety of affection and conduct with regard to honour.

There ſeems to be another virtue alſo converſant about honour, and bearing the ſame proportion to magnanimity, which liberality bears to magnificence. This virtue, as well as liberality, relates, not to what is great and extraordinary, but to what is ordinary and moderate: and as liberality teaches us to behave with propriety in the purſuit of ordinary and moderate profits, ſo this nameleſs virtue teaches us to behave with propriety in the purſuit of ordinary and moderate honours. A man

* Vid. Magna Moral. l. i. c. xxvi.; Eudem. l. iii. c. v.

BOOK IV.

man may either be more or leſs deſirous than he ought, of glory as well as of gain; he may ſeek both thoſe objects on improper occaſions, and by undue means. An ambitious man is more fond of honour than he ought; an unambitious man, leſs than he ought; not caring to reap the natural reward even of praiſeworthy exploits: the former recommends himſelf by his ſpirited manlineſs and emulation of excellence; the latter, by his moderation and modeſty; and from the imperfection of language in not aſſigning diſtinct names to the different degrees of our affections, the ſame word excites either praiſe or blame, according to the ſenſe in which it is taken: ambition is a ſubject of commendation, when it denotes a more than vulgar love of honour; it is a term of reproach, when it denotes the ſame affection in an immoderate and unwarrantable degree; and as a term is wanting to denote that middle ſtate of the affection, which is alone conſiſtent with propriety, the contrary extremes contend with each other for the vacant place of pre-eminence. Whatever things admit of exceſs or defect, admit alſo of this middle ſtate, which is alone praiſeworthy. This is the caſe with the deſire of honour, which may be too ſtrong, too weak, or in a moderate and proper degree; a degree not marked by any diſtinct term, and which, by the ambitious, is called low-mindedneſs; and by the low-minded, ambition; thus appearing to either extreme the vice oppoſite to itſelf. This happens with regard to ſome other virtues; each of the extremes uſurping the middle place, becauſe the middle itſelf is not diſtinguiſhed by a name.

Chap. 5.

Meekneſs, with its contraries.

Meekneſs is propriety of affection with regard to the cauſes and circumſtances which naturally provoke anger; or rather, as names are wanting to denote either a mediocrity or the

 oppoſite

oppofite extremes of this affection; meeknefs, though verging towards the anonymous extreme, confifting in defect, is thruft into the middle place. The extreme confifting in excefs, may be called irafcibility; and anger being a paffion excited by a variety of different caufes, and under a variety of different circumftances, it can only be commendable when it refults from a proper caufe, is directed towards proper objects, is feafonable in its commencement, moderate in its degree, and limited in its duration. If meeknefs be a praifeworthy quality, even the meek man muft be affected with anger under the conditions above fpecified. For meeknefs denotes freedom from unreafonable perturbation, and a due refiftance to paffion, in compliance with the higher powers of our nature; inclining, indeed, to the defective extreme; fince a meek man is not refentful of injuries, but always prone to pardon them. The incapacity of feeling juft provocation is certainly a fault; which, when it proceeds beyond a certain pitch, borders on folly; it denotes a ftupid infenfibility of character; and he who does not feel wrongs as he ought, cannot be well qualified to repel them; he will fubmit, with the meannefs of a flave, to infults offered either to himfelf or to his friends. An exceffive propenfity to anger difplays itfelf in a great variety of ways; it is excited by improper caufes, and is determined towards improper objects; it appears in immoderate or exceffive degrees; in fome men it burfts forth fuddenly into intemperate rage; in others, it fettles into unjuftifiable and permanent refentment. All thofe extravagancies of paffion do not take place at once; for multiplied exceffes of vice are deftructive of each other; and fhould they fall with their full weight on one individual, their burden would be intolerable. Irafcible men, though moved to paffion too ſuddenly, in immoderate degrees, and on improper occaſions, are yet eaſily pacified; if they be ſoon angry, they are alſo ſoon pleaſed, which is the beſt circumſtance attending them; and which happens from this, that they do not reſtrain their paſſion, but give free vent to it; their quickneſs of temper plainly ſhewing their affections and intentions, which they have no ſooner made manifeſt, than they are ready to be appeaſed. The exceſs of this diſpoſition, which takes offence againſt every perſon, and on every the ſlighteſt occaſion, receives its name, in Greek, from two words denoting the ſharpeſt aſperity of choler. The reſentful and implacable temper retains anger long, becauſe it does not give free vent to it; for, to vent anger in vengeance naturally appeaſes it, by ſubſtituting pleaſure in the ſtead of pain; but paſſion reſtrained, gathers ſtrength by compreſſion; and as it remains hid within the breaſt, the gentle power of perſuaſion cannot be applied for its alleviation; it muſt be digeſted by the internal vigour of the conſtitution, which is a work of time. A fell and ſavage temper directs its immediate anger againſt improper objects, and is implacable in its reſentment, until it is fully ſatiated with vengeance. The exceſſes of anger are more oppoſite than its defects to the virtue of meekneſs; becauſe they occur more frequently; becauſe human nature is too prone to be immoderate in its reſentment; and becauſe perſons of iraſcible and querulous tempers are the moſt troubleſome to live with. From what was above obſerved, it is plain that words cannot accurately expreſs all the conditions, as to time, place, perſon, cauſe, and degree, which render anger praiſeworthy or blameable. He who deviates a little on either ſide from the exact point of propriety, eſcapes blame, becauſe his ſlight error eſcapes obſervation.

tion. The incapacity of feeling or resenting an injury, is sometimes praised as meekness; too strong a propensity to anger, is sometimes extolled as manhood, and regarded as indicating a disposition fit for command. The precise middle point, in which alone propriety consists, cannot be accurately ascertained in words, because it is determined only by a perception of sense; and the senses do not perceive minute variations. This however is plain, that the middle habit is laudable, and the extremes blameable, more or less, in exact proportion to their greater or lesser deviations, in point of all, or any, of the conditions above specified. This laudable mediocrity, therefore, ought to be our constant aim; and let this much suffice concerning the dispositions and habits that have a reference to the causes and circumstances that naturally provoke anger [b].

Chap. 6.

Courtesy, with its contraries.

In the intercourse of life and society, there are men of a fawning disposition, ever prone to praise, totally averse to contention, and who think it incumbent on them to give pleasure to all with whom they converse. There are others of so peevish a temper, that they are continually contradicting and crossing all those with whom they have to do; and who feel not the smallest concern for the pain occasioned to others by their churlish asperity. That both these habits are blameable, is manifest; and also that there is an intermediate habit between fawning flattery and savage severity, which is truly laudable, because it distributes its approbation and disapprobation in due measure, according to the circumstances of the case. This intermediate habit is not distinguished by a name; it most resembles friendship, for should affection be added to the companionable qualities of a man endowed with this habit, he would

[b] Vid. Eudem. l. iii. c. iii.

BOOK IV.

would be a most delightful friend: but it differs from friendship in this, that it does not include any peculiar affection towards those with whom we converse; and the person adorned with this laudable habit, does not approve from love, nor disapprove from hatred, but because it is his nature and character to bestow his approbation and disapprobation agreeably to those rules which moral propriety prescribes; whether he has to do with acquaintances or strangers; with familiar friends, or with persons altogether unknown to him; except, that his behaviour to each of those classes of persons will be marked with such distinctions as circumstances require; for we ought not to testify as much pleasure at the merit of mere strangers as at that of our friends; nor to be equally complaisant to the follies of the latter, as to those of the former. The man of courtesy and civility (for these are the words by which the habit in question may most nearly be expressed) will, in the intercourse of society, behave himself universally as he ought: his aim will be, never needlessly to offend; but to gratify and please those with whom he lives, on all occasions on which it possibly can be done consistently with utility and propriety. But the courteous man will not betray his own interest or honour, or even those of the persons with whom he converses, for the sake of affording a small and unseasonable pleasure. He will resist their opinions, when to resist them gives small pain; whereas to approve them would be injurious or disgraceful either to others or to himself. His behaviour will vary with the rank and dignity, with the degree of his familiarity or connexion, and with a variety of other circumstances belonging to the persons with whom he converses, but will be always regulated by propriety. Pleasure, we have said, will be his aim; but without sacrificing

ſacrificing intereſt or honour to pleaſure, or a greater pleaſure to a leſſer. Such then is this intermediate habit, which is nameleſs in Greek; and of which the extremes are, on one hand, univerſal and indiſcriminate complaiſance, which, when it proceeds from motives of intereſt, is called flattery; and, on the other, churliſh aſperity and contentious peeviſhneſs. As there is no term to expreſs the intermediate and laudable habit, the extremes only ſeem to ſtand in oppoſition to each other, and alternately arrogate the praiſe of virtue, though in fact they are both vices; and as ſuch, in direct oppoſition to the praiſeworthy habit above deſcribed.

Chap. 7.

Plain dealing, and its contraries.

The virtue which lies between the extremes of diſſembling concealment and arrogant oſtentation is converſant about nearly the ſame objects with courteſy; except that this has a reference to the pleaſure of thoſe with whom we live, whereas that has a reference to truth in our words and actions. It is worth while to conſider alſo this praiſeworthy, though anonymous, habit; becauſe by thus ſhewing that each particular virtue conſiſts in mediocrity, we ſhall beſt explain the nature of virtue in general, and moſt clearly eſtabliſh the truth of our moral theory. The characteriſtics of thoſe who give pleaſure or pain in the intercourſe of ſociety, have already been deſcribed; we proceed to ſpeak of thoſe who are adorned by truth and frankneſs, or degraded by falſehood and diſſimulation. There are men who arrogate to themſelves good qualities, of which they are entirely deſtitute, and who amplify the good qualities of which they are poſſeſſed, far beyond their real meaſure and natural worth. The ironical diſſembler, on the other hand, either conceals his advantages; or if he cannot conceal, endeavours to depreciate their value; whereas the man of frankneſs and plain-dealing ſhews his character in its natural ſize: truth appears in all his words and actions; which repreſent him exactly as he is, without addition and without diminution. Each of theſe three habits diſplay themſelves either from the ſpontaneous impulſe of our character, or from motives of intereſt; and when men have not any reaſon for acting otherwiſe, they indulge the bent of their characters, either to plain-dealing on the one hand, or to the oppoſite kinds of deceit above ſpecified. There is a deformity in falſehood, which renders it odious in itſelf; whereas truth is beautiful and praiſeworthy: and plain-dealing is the intermediate habit or virtue between the oppoſite extremes or vices of him who would paſs himſelf for more than he is worth, and of him who conceals, or diſſembles, his advantages. Of thoſe two kinds of deceit the former is the moſt blameable; we ſhall treat of both, after having firſt ſpoken of plain-dealing. By this word we do not mean the faithful performance of contracts or engagements, nor any of thoſe things which have a reference to juſtice or injuſtice in our tranſactions; for ſuch matters as theſe belong to another branch of virtue: but we mean the undiſguiſed truth and downright honeſty which are apparent in ſome men's behaviour, when no intereſt whatever is at ſtake, merely becauſe ſuch plain-dealing is moſt agreeable to their character. Such men will naturally be juſt in their tranſactions, ſince they who avoid deceit which is harmleſs, will ſtill more avoid fraud which is injurious to others and diſgraceful to themſelves. This habit is praiſeworthy, even when it inclines to the defective extreme of diſavowing or concealing advantages that really belong to us; it derives a comelineſs from avoiding to make a parade of invidious diſtinctions, and of our own ſuperiority, which

which is always mortifying to others. The vice of oftentatious vanity, and falfe arrogation of merit, when it proceeds not from any interefted motive, fhews great weaknefs and levity; but its folly is more confpicuous than its turpitude; when it fprings from a love of honour or praife, which we muft be confcious that we do not deferve, it is indeed highly contemptible, but is in that cafe lefs odious than when it has its fource in the love of money, or of any thing by which money may be gained. The virtues and vices juft mentioned depend like all others not on our natural powers or propenfities, but on election and habit: it is from habit that fome delight in plain-dealing, others in deceit; and that fome take a pleafure in practifing deceit for the purpofes of glory, and others for thofe of gain. The former affume the femblance of qualities, of which the reality would entitle them to congratulation and praife; the latter arrogate to themfelves qualities, which, if they really poffeffed them, might be fuccefsfully employed in promoting the pleafure or alleviating the pain of others; and to which qualities it is not eafy to prove that they are only vain pretenders: to this clafs of deceivers belong phyficians, fophifts, and foothfayers. The ironical diffembler has more of the grace of propriety, becaufe he conceals or depreciates his real advantages, in order to avoid the fwelling pomp of oftentatious arrogance. Such men cannot appear to be actuated by motives of intereft: they are fometimes inclined to diffemble even the moft honourable advantages; as happened in the cafe of Socrates. But there is a littlenefs and affectation in diffembling advantages inconfiderable in themfelves, and too manifeft to be concealed; fuch diffemblers are contemptible, and that fometimes in point of vanity and oftentation; witnefs the Lacedæmonians with their fhort beggarly

BOOK IV.

dreſs; for an aſſumed poverty is frequently as oſtentatious as the parade of riches. Diſſimulation, therefore, to be graceful, muſt be uſed with reſpect to things not too open and viſible: but the arrogation of advantages which do not belong to us is the vice commonly oppoſed to the virtue of plain-dealing; becauſe it is the worſt of the two extremes.

Chap. 8.

Facetiouſneſs, and its contraries.

As life requires repoſe from ſerious employment, and this repoſe may be enlivened by amuſement, there ſeems to be a virtue relative to the intercourſe of men in their hours of relaxation and merriment, regulating both the matter and the manner of their converſation. The ſtrain of this converſation may be more auſtere or more ludicrous than it ought, or may flow in that happy medium which is alone conſiſtent with propriety. He who ſeeks to raiſe laughter on all occaſions indiſcriminately, without regard to decency, or to the pain inflicted on the object of his ridicule, is a low and contemptible buffoon: he who is himſelf totally incapable of exciting mirth, and who is ſo far from reliſhing, that he is highly offended with the innocent jeſts of others, indicates a roughneſs and ſavageneſs of character, unbending hardneſs, and unſocial auſterity; whereas true facetiouſneſs conſiſts in graceful flexibility of mind and manners, which can aſſume all ſhapes, and which becomes all; for as the habits of the body are known by its motions, ſo are thoſe of the mind. An immoderate propenſity to ridicule being a more prominent and more conſpicuous quality than the contrary extreme of ſullen and ruſtic gravity, and the greater part of mankind being inclined to delight in merriment, without anxiouſly examining whether it originates in a pure and proper ſource; buffoonery often paſſes for facetiouſneſs, although there be the greateſt difference between the coarſeneſs of the one, and the

the elegance of the other; for in facetiousness, which is the middle and proper habit, an easy pliancy of humour is adorned with a graceful dexterity which skilfully avoids whatever is indecent and illiberal; never debasing the delicate gaiety congenial to the character of well educated citizens, by the smallest approximation to the vile raillery of profligates and slaves. The progress of letters and civility has a powerful influence on the refinement of wit and humour; witness the difference between the ancient and modern comedy. In the former, the most shameful reproaches, expressed in the coarsest language, formed a principal source of the public entertainment; in the latter, the audience are taught chiefly to relish the faint insinuation, and the delicate hint: with respect to beauty and gracefulness, the two styles of writing are marked by the strongest differences. But by what circumstance is true facetiousness characterised? Whether does it consist in saying that only which becomes a well educated citizen? or, may it be characterized by the avoiding of offence? or, thirdly, by the communication of pleasure? Or rather is not such a habit in its nature indefinite, since things pleasing to one audience, may be highly offensive to another: for things which we are pleased to do, we will not be much offended to hear; and those which we are pleased to hear, we in some measure seem to do; but persons well educated prescribe just limits both to their words and actions. The laws prohibit certain reproaches, when made seriously; they should perhaps also prohibit malicious raillery. A man endowed with urbanity and facetiousness is a law unto himself. Such then is this intermediate habit; whereas the extreme of buffoonery renders the mind in which it subsists a slave to low humour; for the buffoon neither spares others nor

 himself;

BOOK IV.

himſelf; and provided he can excite laughter, condeſcends to ſay what no man of an elegant turn of mind would venture to repeat, or even endure to hear. But the auſtere and ſolemn character is, on the other hand, totally unfit for the intercourſe of ſociety in hours of relaxation; to the entertainment of which he not only does not contribute any thing himſelf, but glooms by his unſeaſonable ſeverity the merriment of others. There are then three laudable habits which have a reference to our behaviour in ſociety; the firſt conſiſts in a fair exhibition of our own characters; the other two relate to the pleaſure of thoſe with whom we live; and of theſe two, the one conſiſts in heightening that pleaſure in hours of relaxation; the other, in promoting it amidſt the ordinary employments of life [*].

Chap. 9.

Of ſhame.

Shame can ſcarcely be numbered among the virtues; for it ſeems to be rather a paſſion than a habit. It is defined, the fear of diſgrace; and, like another kind of fear, it appears on the countenance; for men, when aſhamed, bluſh, and when afraid of death, grow pale: both ſeem to be affections of the body, and therefore more properly to be claſſed with paſſions than with habits. Shame is not graceful in every period of life; it only becomes youth. Young perſons, we think, ought to be extremely ſenſible to ſhame; becauſe, as they are chiefly actuated by paſſion, they would be thereby ſeduced into many diſgraceful exceſſes, were they not reſtrained by a ſenſe of ſhame. We praiſe the bluſhing modeſty of youth, but nobody would think ſhamefacedneſs in old age a fit ſubject of commendation: for perſons of mature years ought to be incapable of any action, on account of which ſhame can be felt; for as ſhame can

[*] Magna Moral. l. i. c. xxviii.; Eudem. l. iii. c. vii.

can be felt only for things base or blameable, it cannot belong to men of confirmed virtue, who will avoid all such actions, whether they be really blameable in themselves, or only of evil report. Bad men alone can be guilty of bad actions; and it is the wildest absurdity to flatter ourselves, that though we do what is wrong, yet we may escape the guilt thereof by being heartily ashamed of our conduct. Shame is caused only by such actions as are voluntary; and base actions a good man will never voluntarily commit. Shame then can at best be considered only as a conditional virtue; that is, it may belong to a good man particularly circumstanced; for on the supposition, that he should have performed a bad action, he certainly would be ashamed of it. But the virtues, properly so called, are things desirable and graceful on their own account, simply and absolutely, independently of any suppositions or conditions whatever. Impudence indeed is a vice; but it does not therefore follow, that its contrary is a virtue; for there is not any room for shame, where nothing shameful is either done or intended. For a similar reason, self-command, which is often so highly commended, is only a conditional virtue, as shall be proved hereafter. We now proceed to speak of justice.

ARISTOTLE's ETHICS.

BOOK V.

INTRODUCTION.

THIS Fifth Book is entirely dedicated to the important ſubject of juſtice. Ariſtotle explains the different acceptations of the word, and diſtinguiſhes the different kinds of juſtice ſtrictly ſo called. Political juſtice, again, is either diſtributive or commutative; which laſt our author, for a reaſon given in the text, calls corrective. He ſhews wherein thoſe kinds of juſtice differ; the one being regulated by proportion, and the other by equality. The difference is pointed out between what our lawyers call the *mala in ſe*, and the *mala prohibita*; and the diſtinction clearly explained between *doing harm* and *committing injury*. Ariſtotle concludes with examining the nature of equity in contradiſtinction to that of juſtice; and illuſtrates his doctrine concerning the latter, by conſidering the queſtion whether a man can be guilty of injury towards himſelf. As the author introduces not any thing ſuperfluous, (for his account of the origin and uſe of money is eſſentially connected with the ſubject,) he comprizes within a narrow compaſs a ſolid and ſatisfactory explanation of thoſe great commanding principles which uphold civil ſociety; an explanation exempt from thoſe ambiguities and contradictions, which too often occur in the innumerable

BOOK V.

volumes in which his opinions have been unfaithfully reported, or unſkilfully commented. Yet had ſucceeding writers improved and enriched his obſervations, the preſent Book would have the faireſt claim to attention, as containing the firſt attempt to treat fully and ſcientifically the moſt important ſubject on which the pen of any author can poſſibly be employed.

BOOK V.

ARGUMENT.

Difference between intellectual and moral habits.—Different acceptations of the word injustice.—Justice strictly so called.—Distributive justice.—Corrective justice.—Retaliation.—Natural justice, independent of positive institution.—Misfortunes.—Errors.—Crimes.—Equity.

BOOK V. Chap. I.

Justice.

IN examining justice and injustice, we must explain to what kind of actions they relate; what kind of virtue justice is, and what are the extremes or vices between which this virtue may be found. We shall thus follow the same method which has been pursued in the preceding parts of this discourse. All describe justice as that habit which qualifies men to practise just actions with inclination and pleasure; injustice is the reverse; and this general description may suffice for our present purpose. Justice, we have said, is the habit which qualifies men to practise just actions with pleasure; because the moral habits differ essentially from the intellectual in this, that the latter, as well as mere powers and capacities, may be subservient to quite contrary purposes; and those endowed with the intellectual habits, or sciences, may exercise them spontaneously and agreeably in producing directly contrary effects. But the moral virtues, like the different habits of the body, are determined by their nature to

Difference between intellectual and moral habits.

BOOK V.

to one ſpecific operation: thus a man in health acts and moves in a manner conformable to his healthy ſtate of body, and never otherwiſe, when his motions are natural and voluntary; and in the ſame manner the habits of juſtice or temperance uniformly determine thoſe adorned by them, to act juſtly and temperately. Yet habits of all kinds are often known by their contraries; thus, if a good habit of body conſiſts in denſity and firmneſs of fleſh, a bad habit muſt conſiſt in its ſoftneſs and rarity. When the word denoting any habit is taken in different ſenſes, the word denoting its contrary is likewiſe, for the moſt part, employed with equal latitude: thus the different meanings of injuſtice correſpond with thoſe of juſtice; both thoſe words having reſpectively various ſignifications, which, on account of their near affinity to each other, are ſeldom accurately diſtinguiſhed; for when a word denotes two things totally unlike, its ſeparate meanings are manifeſt; as, for inſtance, in the Greek word which is applied equally to denote the collar-bone, and the key of a door. Let us examine then in how many acceptations the word injuſtice is uſed. A man who violates law is called unjuſt, as well as he who aſpires to any undue advantage, and is not contented with equality: ſince what is unlawful or unequal is unjuſt, and juſtice muſt be conformable to the principles of law and of equality. Injuſtice conſiſts in deſiring more than our ſhare, not of all things indiſcriminately which fall under the denomination of good, but of thoſe only which it is ſuppoſed to be good fortune to obtain; and which, though univerſally deemed good in themſelves, are often evils to thoſe who obtain them. Such goods mankind in general wiſh for and purſue; though, in fact, they ought

In how many acceptations the word injuſtice is taken.

ought rather to pray that things abſolutely good, may be good in relation to themſelves; and always to prefer and chooſe thoſe only which are likely to be ſo. An unjuſt man does not neceſſarily chooſe the greater ſhare; ſometimes he prefers the leſſer; and that always, when the things in his option are evils. But as the leſſer of two evils is in ſome meaſure a good, he ſeems always to deſire the greater ſhare, and is thence called in Greek an uſurper of more than his due; though, in reality, according to circumſtances, he chooſes ſometimes the greater, and ſometimes the leſſer ſhare, but always an unequal one; ſo that his real turpitude conſiſts in acting contrary to equality or to law; an oppoſition to both of which, is common to every ſpecies of injuſtice. Since, then, whatever is unlawful is unjuſt, juſtice may be ſaid to conſiſt in acting agreeably to the laws of our country. But laws regulate the tranſactions of life, either with a view to the benefit of the public at large, or with a view to the benefit of that portion of the ſtate which is inveſted with ſovereignty, whether that has been acquired by pre-eminence in virtue, or attained by any of thoſe other means through which ſovereign authority is eſtabliſhed. In one ſenſe, therefore, juſtice comprehends every thing that has a tendency either to produce or to maintain the happineſs of men in political ſociety. The law preſcribes to citizens who are ſoldiers, not to leave their ranks, not to fly, not to throw down their arms; that is, it commands them to behave themſelves with bravery. The law alſo prohibits all thoſe ſubject to its authority from adultery, and every ſpecies of debauchery which is injurious to others; which is nothing elſe than to command its ſubjects to be temperate. It alſo preſcribes meekneſs, in the injunctions, "thou ſhalt not ſtrike," "thou ſhalt not revile:" and in the ſame manner, partly by precepts, and partly by prohibitions, the law more or leſs accurately defines the rules and practice of the other virtues; ſo that juſtice, taken in the ſenſe of conformity to law, comprehends the whole of virtue, not indeed ſimply and abſolutely, but in reference to thoſe with whom we are connected; being another name for the ſtrict performance of all thoſe relative duties which are eſſential to the happineſs of ſocial life. Viewed in this light, juſtice is the firſt and brighteſt of all the virtues; more worthy of admiration than either Heſperus or Lucifer; ſince according to the proverb,

"Juſtice alone compriſes every virtue."

It is indeed the perfection of virtue, ſince it is not only the beſt conſtitution of our internal frame, but the external exerciſe of whatever is praiſeworthy in behaviour towards others; and even the whole community, however extenſive, of which we are members[d]. There are many capable of acting uprightly within a limited domeſtic ſphere, whoſe imperfections become manifeſt

[d] This paſſage is expanded and adorned by Cicero in language the moſt glowing and impreſſive, "Eſt quidem vera lex, recta ratio, naturæ congruens, diffuſa in omnes, conſtans, ſempiterna quæ vocet ad officium jubendo, vetando a fraude deterreat; quæ tamen neque probos fruſtra jubet, neque improbos jubendo aut vetando movet. Huic legi nec abrogari fas eſt, neque derogari ex hac aliquid licet, neque tota abrogari poteſt. Nec vero aut per Senatum, aut per populum ſolvi hac lege poſſumus. Neque eſt quærendus explanator, aut interpres ejus alius: nec erit aliud lex Romæ, alia Athenis, alia nunc, alia poſthac: ſed et omnes gentes, et omni tempore una lex et ſempiterna et immortalis continebit; unuſque erit communis quaſi magiſter et imperator omnium Deus ille, legis hujus inventor, diſceptator, lator; cui qui non parebit, ipſe ſe fugiet, ac naturam hominis aſpernabitur; ac hoc ipſo luet maximas pœnas, etiamſi cætera ſupplicia, quæ putantur, effugerit." Fragment. de Republic. l. iii.

manifeſt on a wider and more exalted theatre. Wherefore Bias well obſerved, "that government ſhows the man;" for he who is entruſted with the exerciſe of power, is placed in multiplied relations with reſpect to others, and the whole commonwealth. Juſtice, therefore, ſeems to contribute to the benefit rather of thoſe towards whom it is exerciſed, than of thoſe who are endowed with this virtuous habit; becauſe it is the nature of this habit always to bear a reference to our tranſactions with the world. The worſt of men are thoſe whoſe vices injure themſelves and their friends; the beſt are thoſe, whoſe virtues benefit not only themſelves and their friends, but the community at large, and the whole ſociety of mankind. This, indeed, is a noble, becauſe a difficult taſk. Juſtice, then, conſidered in this view, is not a part, but the whole of virtue; and its contrary, injuſtice, is not a part, but the whole of vice. Wherein virtue and juſtice differ, is evident from the obſervations above made. They are preciſely the ſame thing viewed under two different aſpects; and denominated virtue when conſidered in relation to the mind adorned by this praiſeworthy habit; but called juſtice when conſidered in relation to thoſe towards whom it is exerciſed.

Chap. 2.

Juſtice properly ſo called.

But our preſent inquiry is concerning juſtice taken in a more limited ſenſe, and denoting one virtue in particular; and alſo concerning injuſtice as ſignifying one particular vice, diſtinct from every other. That ſuch a ſpecific injuſtice, as well as juſtice, exiſts, appears from the following conſideration; that he who commits any other baſeneſs, is indeed guilty of wrong, but does not thereby benefit his fortune; which is plain, from the examples of him who throws away his ſhield through cowardice,

BOOK V. cowardice, who reviles his neighbour through ungovernable asperity of temper, or who refuses, through illiberality, any pecuniary aid to those who have claims on his bounty. But a man may benefit his fortune by usurping more than his due share of worldly goods, without incurring the blame of all, or any, of these vices. His conduct, however, is culpable, and we arraign his injustice. There is then a particular kind of injustice differing from that above mentioned, and bearing the relation to it, of a part to the whole: in the first sense, unjust is synonymous with unlawful; in the second, it implies the breach of a particular class of laws, namely, that which prohibits any man from benefiting himself at the expence of his neighbour. One man commits adultery for the sake of gain, another pays dearly for his criminal pleasure; the vice of the former, is aggravated injustice; that of the latter, is profligate intemperance. All other wrongs may always be referred to some particular species of vice; the commission of adultery, to intemperance; the desertion of our companions in war, to cowardice; an assault, to unbridled violence of anger: but that wrong which is committed for the sake merely of gain, is referred to no other vice than that of injustice; not that injustice above described, which is synonymous with wrong in general, but a specific vice, bearing the same relation to the former, which the species does to the class under which it is included; for injustice, both in its large and in its limited sense, has always a reference to our transactions with others; its very essence consists in our behaving amiss in those transactions: but injustice, strictly so called, implies that our misconduct results from the desire of promoting our own profit or honour,

or

or whatever we think gainful to ourſelves[e]; whereas injuſtice, largely taken, comprehends all thoſe improprieties in our behaviour towards others, which are inconſiſtent with the character of a virtuous man. We proceed then to explain the nature and properties of juſtice and injuſtice, ſtrictly ſo called. This ſpecies of injuſtice was ſaid to conſiſt, not in what is unlawful merely, but in what is alſo unequal; for whatever is unequal is unlawful; ſince laws, properly made, aſſure to each individual his equal ſhare, that is his due, in his tranſactions with his fellow-citizens; but many things are unlawful which are not unequal, becauſe laws relate to many other objects beſides the diſtribution and adjuſtment of intereſts and honours; enforcing, by authority, the practice of every virtue, and upholding a ſyſtem of education by which this practice may, through diſcipline and cuſtom, be rendered eaſy and agreeable. Whether ſuch an education properly falls under the ſcience of politics, will afterwards be examined[f]; for under all forms of government indiſcriminately, perhaps the character of the good man will not be found compatible with that of a good citizen. The particular kind of juſtice now under conſideration, is employed either in diſtributing to each citizen his due ſhare of honour, wealth, and all other advantages, in the political partnerſhip, or commonwealth, of which he is a member; or in regulating, by the rules of right, thoſe tranſactions, whether voluntary or involuntary, which happen between fellow-citizens; and where wrong has on either ſide been committed, in correcting this wrong,

[e] Ariſtotle ſays, "for the ſake of honour, money, ſafety, or for that which would include all theſe in one word."

[f] Ariſtotle examines this queſtion in his Politics, which work is merely a continuation of his Ethics to Nicomachus.

BOOK V.

wrong, by again ſetting the parties, as far as may be, on a foot of equality with each other. Voluntary tranſactions are thoſe in which both parties voluntarily concur; ſuch as buying, ſelling, borrowing, lending, letting, hiring, pledging, depoſiting. Involuntary tranſactions are either ſecret or open; the ſecret are, theft, adultery, poiſoning, ſeduction of other men's ſlaves, proſtitution for hire of other men's wives, premeditated murder, and the bearing of falſe witneſs. The open but involuntary tranſactions include all violent and manifeſt aggreſſions on the perſons, property, or reputation of others; ſuch as aſſault, maiming, impriſonment, death, robbery, ſlander, inſult.

Chap. 3.

Diſtributive juſtice.

Juſtice implies equality; and this equality lies in the middle between two extremes, the greater and the leſſer: for whatever admits of diviſion into two unequal parts, may alſo be equally divided. But equality, being a relative term, always ſuppoſes the compariſon of two things at leaſt. Diſtributive juſtice, therefore, always implies two things, and alſo two perſons between whom thoſe things are divided. If the perſons are exactly equal, ſo ought to be their ſhares; but if the perſons are unequal, the ſhares ought alſo to be unequal in the ſame proportion: for complaints and ſtrife always will ariſe, when either perſons of unequal worth meet with preciſely the ſame treatment; or when perſons of nearly equal worth are diſtinguiſhed from each other by too conſiderable differences. This is univerſally acknowledged; but men's notions of worth vary with their political principles. In democracies it is meaſured by liberty; in oligarchies, by wealth or birth; in ariſtocracies, by virtue. Juſtice, however, plainly conſiſts in proportion, which is the equality of ratios; and proportion, whether diſcrete or continuous,

continuous, always implies four terms; ſince when continuous, one of the terms muſt be taken twice. Diſtributive juſtice always requiring four terms at leaſt, implies that the ſhares bear the ſame proportion to each other as do the perſons among whom theſe ſhares are diſtributed; for proportion is applicable to all quantities, and not merely to numbers. If the firſt ſhare therefore be to the firſt man, as the ſecond ſhare to the ſecond; then alternately, the firſt ſhare will be to the ſecond ſhare, as the firſt man to the ſecond man; and as each of the antecedents is to its conſequent, ſo will both the antecedents be to both the conſequents. This is what is called by mathematicians geometrical proportion, conſiſting, as we have ſaid, in equality of ratios; which equality is in the middle between exceſs and defect; for if one of the ratios were greater or leſſer than the other, the proportion, or, in other words, the juſtice of the diſtribution, would be deſtroyed. In diſtributive juſtice, the four terms are all of them diſtinct, the one from the other; conſiſting of two perſons, and two ſhares, at leaſt; none of which can be taken twice in the ſeries. The proportion therefore is not continuous, but diſcrete; and when proportion is violated, injuſtice immediately follows. This evidently appears in actions: for the injurious perſon has more, the perſon injured has leſs, than their reſpective ſhares of good; of evil, the reverſe; for the leſſer evil is conſidered as a good [e].

Chap. 4.

Commutative and corrective juſtice.

The remaining ſpecies of juſtice is properly diſtinguiſhed by the epithet of corrective: it applies to the mutual tranſactions between men, whether voluntary or involuntary. It differs from

[e] I thought it unneceſſary to ſubjoin with Ariſtotle, that the leſſer evil is conſidered as a good becauſe it is to be preferred to the greater; that good is always deſirable, and, of two goods, the more deſirable is the greater.

BOOK V.

from distributive justice in this, that the latter consists in geometrical proportion, and requires that the shares should have the same ratio to each other as the persons among whom they are divided; so that each citizen may find himself treated according to his deserts, and those who contribute most to the public benefit may meet with proportionally higher remunerations. Corrective justice also implies equality, but an equality of a different kind, founded not on geometrical, but on arithmetical, proportion; for the law does not make any difference in its correction or punishment, whether a good man has injured a bad one, or a bad man a good. It contemplates merely the hurt done or the injury sustained; and endeavours to set the two parties, the one of whom is wronged by the other, on the same foot of equality on which they formerly stood. The words gain and loss are not indeed applicable in all cases where one man is injured by another; they can be properly used only when the injuries done may be estimated in money; but in all cases whatever, he who has committed an injury should be compelled, as far as may be, to make reparation, which, when complete, reduces the parties to that condition of equality from which they set out, by giving back to the loser what had been taken from him by the gainer. Corrective justice, then, holds the middle place between gain and loss. In their disputes with each other, men have recourse to a judge, as to a living fountain of justice; who, as it is his business to adjust differences, and mediate between contending parties, is often styled a mediator. This office he performs by finding the middle term between the unequal extremes of gain and loss; in the same manner as if, a line being divided into two unequal parts, he cut from the greater part its excess above half the line, and added

added it to the leſſer. When the whole is divided equally, each party has his due, becauſe the ſhares are alike; and this equality is the middle arithmetical term between the greater and the leſſer extreme. It is the duty of a judge to find this middle term; from which function, he appears in Greek to have derived his appellation; for juſtice in this language means an equal diviſion; and a judge, an equal divider. When, from two equal quantities, a part is taken from the one and added to the other, the latter will exceed by two parts: for were the part taken away deſtroyed, it would exceed by one; it exceeds the middle term therefore by one; and this term exceeds the quantity from which the part was taken away by one. By this means we may learn, that in order to correct inequality, and thereby to do juſtice, we muſt take from the greater extreme that by which it exceeds the middle, and add this exceſs to the leſſer. This plainly appears in geometry by means of a diagram; but the ſame thing holds in all other arts, which would ſpeedily be ſubverted, and all human ſociety overturned, unleſs equality and juſtice were tolerably well maintained in the actions and intercourſe of life; and proper correctives applied where theſe bonds of ſociety are materially violated. The words gain and loſs are introduced by the voluntary tranſactions of men; in which, he who got more than he gave in exchange, was ſaid to gain by the bargain; and he who got leſs, to loſe; as in buying and ſelling, and all other legal contracts.. But when the bargain was equal, each party was ſaid to have his due. Juſtice, then, even in ſuch tranſactions as are involuntary, conſiſts in a middle term between a certain kind of gain and loſs, and requires that the parties ſhould be reduced, as nearly as may be, to that condition of equality in which they

 ſtood

BOOK V. Chap. 5.

ſtood with regard to each other, before any ſuch tranſaction took place.

Retaliation does not apply to juſtice, either diſtributive or corrective.

Retaliation ſeems to ſome to be the whole of juſtice. This opinion was held by the Pythagoreans; who defined juſtice to be "reciprocity of doing and ſuffering." But retaliation will not apply either to diſtributive or to corrective juſtice; although the law of Rhadamanthus ſays, "The completeſt juſtice conſiſts in making a man ſuffer the ſame ills that he has committed." This rule, however, is liable to innumerable exceptions. Thus, if a general ſhould ſtrike a ſoldier, the blow muſt not be retorted; but to ſtrike a general, or any other perſon inveſted with authority, requires that the offender ſhould be puniſhed more ſeverely than by mere retaliation. The difference alſo is very great between voluntary and involuntary injuries; to the latter of which Rhadamanthus' rule is totally inapplicable. Yet the commercial intercourſe of nations, and of individuals in the ſame nation, is maintained by a reciprocation, not indeed of the ſame, or ſimilar, but of proportional benefits and injuries. When injuries are offered by one ſet of perſons, and cannot be retorted by another, the latter claſs look on themſelves as nothing better than ſlaves: when benefits, on the other hand, are conferred, but without any proſpect of being returned, there is an end to that interchange of good offices, which is the main pillar of civil ſociety; a truth acknowledged by thoſe commonwealths who have erected temples to the Graces on the moſt conſpicuous ſituations; that man might continually be reminded of the duty of gratitude, the favourite virtue of thoſe divinities; and that thoſe who had received and returned favours, might always be ready to renew the laudable contention among themſelves, by mutually provoking each other to works of kindneſs.

 The

BOOK V.

The nature and uſe of money.

The comfort of life requires an interchange of different works and exertions. The bricklayer, for example, muſt exchange the production of his labour with the ſhoemaker; and the bargain will be juſt, when the works exchanged bear the ſame proportion to each other, as do the exertions of the artiſans by whom they were produced. If the exertions of the bricklayer be more valuable for their duration, or their difficulty, than thoſe of the ſhoemaker, the works produced by the latter muſt, to render the bargain equal, bear the ſame proportion numerically to thoſe produced by the former: thus, if the bricklayer has conſumed a thouſand times as much labour in making a houſe, as the ſhoemaker has done in making a pair of ſhoes, a thouſand pair of ſhoes muſt be given for one houſe. The ſame thing happens with reſpect to all other arts, which derive their whole utility from the mutual exchange of different ſorts of labour, and which could not long be maintained unleſs the exertions of one artiſan in one way were nearly balanced and compenſated by thoſe of another artiſan in another. A community could not ſubſiſt, compoſed wholly of phyſicians, or wholly of huſbandmen; it muſt conſiſt of phyſicians and huſbandmen, and other claſſes of individuals employed in different trades and different profeſſions. But that operations and works of ſuch different kinds ſhould be fairly exchanged for each other, it is neceſſary that they ſhould be nearly commenſurate; that is, that all of them ſhould be capable of being eſtimated with tolerable accuracy by compariſon with one common meaſure. Hence the introduction of money; by means of which all thoſe operations and works are compared in value with each other, and their relative exceſſes or deficiencies aſcertained with ſufficient correctneſs for all practical

BOOK V.

tical purpofes. In reality, value depends on the mutual wants of men, which form the great bond of fociety; for unlefs their wants were mutual, exchange could not be effected: but money is ufed by convention as the reprefentative of all things wanted; fince it ferves as a pledge and furety, that whenever thofe wants occur, they will be fpeedily gratified; and its name is derived from the word fignifying law, which indicates that it is founded, not on nature, but on convention; and that human laws, which have thought fit to employ it as a meafure of value, may, at pleafure, fet this ufe of it afide, and employ fome other meafure in its ftead. Money, which reprefents the value of all other things, varies in its own; but its variations are lefs confiderable than thofe of moft other fubftances. It ferves therefore to fix their price, and to render them commenfurate with each other, thus performing a function effential to the exiftence of civil fociety; for communities could not fubfift without exchange; nor exchange, without equality; nor equality, without a common meafure. The various kinds of labour, and the works thereby effected, cannot indeed be accurately compared, and exactly meafured, either by each other or even by money; but they may, by means of the latter, be eftimated with fufficient correctnefs for maintaining that commercial intercourfe which is effential to the fupply of our numerous exigencies [h].

From

[h] Ariftotle illuftrates this fubject by fhewing how the exchangeable value of a houfe and a bed are compared with each other, by reducing both to the common meafure of a certain number of minas. The text is corrupt, and the example fuperfluous; but it is of importance to obferve how well our author explains the nature of traffic, money, labour, exchangeable value or price, on juft notions of which all theories of political economy ought to be founded. In various parts of his works he makes the important diftinction between labour confumed in ufe, and labour employed in production. That

of

BOOK V. Chap. 6.

In what sense justice consists in mediocrity.

From the explanation given of justice and injustice, it is manifest that a just action holds the intermediate place between doing and suffering an injury. The doer has more, the sufferer less, than he ought; and justice is mediocrity, not indeed in the same sense with the other virtues, which lie between two contrary and vicious extremes, but because it is productive of equality in our dealings, and gives to each individual that share which truly belongs to him; whereas injustice contains in it two opposite faults, giving to the one party more than his due, and robbing

of a servant or domestic slave is of the first kind; that of a manufacturer or artisan, of the second. The labour of the artisan or manufacturer is concentrated and fixed in his work; the labour of a builder in a house built, of a weaver in the web. (ἡ ενεργεια εν τῳ ποιουμενῳ οιον ἡ οικοδομησις εν τῳ οικοδομουμενῳ, και ἡ ὑφανσις εν τῳ ὑφαινομενῳ, &c. Metaph. l. ix. c. viii. p. 939.) Having distinguished between productive and unproductive labour, he observes that every work or production may be employed in two different ways, either in the way of use or that of exchange. Thus a pair of shoes may either be worn or they may be sold (οιον ὑποδηματος, ἡ τε ὑποδεσις, και ἡ μεταβλητικη, Politic. l. i. c. ix. p. 305.). Every production or commodity has, therefore, in reference to the wants of human life, two different values, a value in use and a value in exchange. These different values ought to be distinguished, because things that have the greatest value in use, have often very little value in exchange, and things that have a great value in exchange have often very little value in use. The exchangeable value of commodities, according to Aristotle, is always relative to the labour requisite for procuring them; and the quantity of productive labour is exactly measured by the work or production in which this labour is fixed and embodied (Metaph. l. ix. c. viii. p. 939.). But commodities or productions are so complex in their nature, that they cannot be compared with each other without some common measure. The metals, in consequence of their usefulness and beauty, their facility of division without injury, and of transportation without much labour, above all, their extreme durability, have been adopted by very general consent as the fittest measures of the exchangeable value of all other commodities. But neither the metals in general, nor any one metal in particular, is an exact measure. At different times and places, their own values are found to vary; and therefore they cannot be an exact, that is, an invariable measure of the value of other things. But though the exchangeable value of the metals varies, Aristotle maintains that it is less variable than that of any other commodity (πασχει μεν ουν και τουτο το αυτο, ου γαρ αει ισον δυναται· ὁμως δε βουλεται μενειν μαλλον. De Moribus, l. v. c. viii. p. 65.).

BOOK V.

robbing the other of his right. The virtue of juſtice, then, is that by which a man practiſes by preference and with pleaſure fairneſs in his dealings, not arrogating to himſelf more than his due proportion of good, nor declining to bear his equal ſhare of evil. He treats other men as he would wiſh to be treated by them, aſſigning to each his fair proportion, and following the ſame invariable rule, when his own intereſt is at ſtake, and when he is only adjuſting the differences of others. Injuſtice is directly the reverſe; it leads men in all their tranſactions to give an undue preference to themſelves; and when they are entruſted with ſettling the concerns of others, always to do this unequally, by giving an undue advantage to one of the parties. This much may ſuffice concerning the nature of juſtice and injuſtice.

Chap. 7.

Juſtice applied to actions in a ſenſe different from that in which it is applicable to perſons.

Since the commiſſion of every unjuſt action does not neceſſarily make an unjuſt man, it may be inquired whether, in this reſpect, there be any diſtinction between particular acts of injuſtice, bearing the ſame name, ſuch as theft, adultery, and robbery; or whether the difference of the external acts is altogether immaterial as to conſtituting the vice of injuſtice, even when thoſe acts are performed knowingly; for a man may know that the object of his paſſion is his neighbour's wife; and yet, if he acts merely from the blind impetuoſity of appetite or deſire, without deliberate intention, he is not an adulterer. The ſame holds in all other caſes in which wrong is done; the mere perpetration of the act does not infer the vicious ſtate of mind from which ſuch acts naturally flow. The difference between retaliation and juſtice was formerly mentioned; but, in our inquiries reſpecting the latter, it muſt be remembered, that we have in view chiefly

chiefly that kind of juſtice which may be called political, ſince it is eſtabliſhed for the comfort and all-ſufficiency of ſociety among freemen and equals; whether the government, being democratical, require that each citizen ſhould be dealt by alike; or whether it admit of thoſe diſtinctions of birth, wealth, and abilities, which are allowed their due weight under other forms of government. Where ſuch equality does not prevail, there is not any room for what is ſtrictly called juſtice, but only for that virtue which, on account of its reſemblance, receives the ſame name. Juſtice takes place among thoſe who being capable of injuring each other, are reſtrained by law from mutual encroachments; and thoſe encroachments muſt be made, before injuſtice can be committed; though, as we formerly obſerved, the converſe of the propoſition does not hold, that injuſtice always is committed, when ſuch encroachments are made, becauſe injuſtice implies the deliberate purpoſe of wronging others for the ſake of benefit to ourſelves; a propenſity ſo ſtrong in human nature, that few men are capable of being entruſted with power, without uſing it tyrannically: wherefore law and reaſon ought to bear ſway, and rulers to be the guardians of equal juſtice; contented with thoſe rewards and honours which have been aſſigned to them for upholding the public good by their impartial adminiſtration. Their power is of a different kind from that of fathers and deſpots, in the exerciſe of which there is not any room for the virtue of juſtice ſtrictly ſo called, ſince no one can, in propriety of language, be ſaid to commit injuſtice againſt himſelf, or what entirely belongs to himſelf; becauſe no one ever deliberately propoſed to do real harm to either, and could not poſſibly do

 ſuch

BOOK V.

ſuch harm for the ſake of benefiting himſelf: but ſlaves, who are a kind of property, and alſo children, until they have attained a certain age, are ſo intimately connected with their maſters and parents, that no ſuch relations as thoſe of political juſtice can ſubſiſt between them; for political juſtice implies laws; and laws ſuppoſe an equality, not indeed of ranks and perſons, but of rights and obligations. Wherefore ſomething more nearly reſembling political juſtice takes place between huſbands and wives; but this, which is called œconomical juſtice, is alſo different from the former.

Natural juſtice independent of poſitive inſtitution.

Political juſtice is founded either on nature or on law. The natural, is that which has every where the ſame force and authority; the legal, is that which depends on human inſtitution, rendering actions juſt or unjuſt, which are in themſelves indifferent; as that no more than one mina ſhould be required for the ranſom of a priſoner; that a goat ſhould be ſacrificed rather than two ſheep; regulations reſpecting individuals, as that Braſidas ſhould be honoured with heroic worſhip; and thoſe that come in the ſhape of decrees or reſolutions. Some are of opinion that all juſtice whatever depends on poſitive inſtitution; which they endeavour to prove by obſerving that the laws of nature remain every where unalterably the ſame: fire, for example, which burns and warms in Greece, has preciſely the ſame powers in Perſia; whereas the rules of juſtice are liable to perpetual variations. This, however, is true only in a certain ſenſe; for though among the gods in heaven, what is natural is, perhaps, unalterable, yet, in this lower world, many inſtitutions of nature are capable of being changed and modified by circumſtances. Yet the diſtinction between what is natural

and

and conventional, is not thereby destroyed; unless we should infer that, because some men are capable of using both hands with equal dexterity, it is not natural for mankind in general to use one hand more dexterously than the other[1]. Men's notions of justice are often warped by their interests; and this great measure of human actions varies like the measures of wine and corn, which the dealers in those articles have of different sizes; using the larger when they buy, and the smaller when they sell. Great variations result also from the different forms of government; although, as we shall shew hereafter, there is one form of government naturally the best. Justice is a general term; and differs from an act of injustice, as an universal does from a particular. That is unjust which is contrary to nature or to law; and the same thing, when done, is an unjust action. An unjust action is a wrong; and when we rectify a wrong, we are said to do justice. But the force of those terms will be afterwards more fully explained.

Chap. 8.

Distinction of misfortunes, errors, and crimes.

Injustice, as applicable to actions, consists in what we have now said; but it does not belong to persons, unless it be committed voluntarily; for when a man acts without intention, the quality of his action, as good or bad, just or unjust, is, in reference to the agent, merely an accessory, not springing essentially from himself, and neither entitling him to praise, nor subjecting him to blame. That, therefore, which is unjust, is

[1] He gives the reason more generally in Magna Moral. l. i. c. xxxiv. p. 167. το γαρ ως επι το πολυ διαμενον, τουτο φυσει δικαιον προφανως. "That which is invariable and constant is manifestly natural justice." Political justice, on the other hand, varies with the arrangements and exigencies of men in society. He therefore concludes βελτιον αν δικαιον το κατα φυσιν, "That natural injustice is the better of the two;" a conclusion agreeable to his observations in the first Philosophy. See Analysis, p. 92, & passim.

is not injustice in the agent, unless it be committed voluntarily; that is, as formerly explained, unless the action, with all its circumstances, depend entirely on our own power, and be performed knowingly, with intention, and without constraint. Thus, to make the act of striking parricide, we must know the person whom we strike, the nature of the instrument with which the stroke is inflicted, and the motive through which we are impelled to such a horrid crime. The action must also depend entirely on our own power; for in many natural events, we are both agents and patients knowingly, though not voluntarily; witness old age and death[k]. The same happens as to justice and injustice. When a man restores a deposit involuntarily through fear, he cannot be said to act justly, since the justice of the action is not caused by himself: it is a mere accessary or appendage, quite foreign to his design or purpose. In the same manner, he cannot be accused of injustice, who is constrained involuntarily not to restore a deposit. Voluntary actions are performed with, or without election; deliberate actions are performed with election; and those that are without deliberation are without election. In the intercourse of life, one person may hurt another in three ways; either ignorantly, in which case the hurt done is called an error; as when we are mistaken either in the person or the instrument; or when the action turns out to be of quite a different nature from that which we intended: a man may be hurt by a blow meant merely for rousing him; a wound may be given casually; and one person may receive a blow which was intended for another. When the harm is not only done unintentionally, but happens altogether unexpectedly, it is called a misfortune; when the consequences

[k] See Analysis, p. 109.

quences of the action might have been foreseen and expected, the harm done, without any mischievous purpose, is properly termed a fault; for a fault is that evil which originates in ourselves; and a misfortune, that of which the cause is external. Harm done knowingly, but not deliberately, is an injustice; as those injuries which proceed from anger and other passions, that are either necessary, or at least natural. Yet the persons who have committed such injuries, are not branded with the reproach of injustice or wickedness; which falls only on wrong proceeding from wilful pravity. The law, therefore, well distinguishes between premeditated crimes, and those committed through passion; for the source of the latter may be traced up rather to him who provoked the passion, than to him who yielded to its violence. In all such cases, the question is, not whether the deed was done, but whether it was done justly; for anger always proceeds from some real or supposed injury. But in all other disputes, the question turns on some fact, which one party affirms, and the other denies; and as to which, either the one or the other, unless his memory deceives him, must plainly be guilty; for every deliberate wrong is manifest injustice, whether it consist, as above explained, in violating the law of equality, or in violating that of proportion. The virtue of justice, on the other hand, is exercised only in such acts as are done voluntarily and deliberately. Involuntary acts are, or are not, entitled to pardon, according to circumstances. Those are pardonable, which proceed from complete and habitual ignorance; those are not, which proceed from a temporary ignorance, occasioned by the blind impetuosity of passion, either extravagantly excessive in its degree, or highly improper in its object.

BOOK V. Chap. 9.

Solution of doubts respecting justice.

Doubts may arise, whether the doing and the suffering of injustice, have been defined with sufficient precision. First, shall we hearken to Euripides? One of his characters reasons thus:

> I slew my mother; the defence is plain,
> She *with her* will, or *'gainst my* will, was slain.

Can any person be injured willingly? or must every injury be unwillingly suffered as it is willingly inflicted? A man, it is said, may be injured willingly; since an intemperate man willingly hurts himself. But this argument is not conclusive, for the intemperate man does, what he thinks he ought not to do; his passion makes him act against his deliberate will; for no one can deliberately will what he thinks mischievous to himself. To injure then, is not only to hurt knowingly, but to hurt against the will of the sufferer; for when his will consents, he may indeed be hurt, but is not injured. Glaucus was not injured by his disadvantageous exchange of armour with Diomed, because it was voluntary.

> "Brave Glaucus then, each narrow thought resign'd
> (Jove warm'd his bosom, and enlarg'd his mind),
> For Diomed's brass arms of mean device,
> For which nine oxen paid (a vulgar price)
> He gave his own of gold divinely wrought,
> A hundred beeves the shining purchase bought."
>
> Iliad VI. v. 290. et seq.

Secondly, Whether is the injustice in him who makes an unfair distribution, or in him who receives more than his due? If the former is asserted, those persons distinguished by liberality and equity, who are inclined rather to refuse their full propor-

 tion,

tion, than to arrogate more than their juſt ſhare, will ſometimes injure themſelves. It may be anſwered, that theſe perſons, liberal and equitable as they are as to things of a particular nature, will not decline their full ſhare of goods in general; and of ſome kinds, ſuch as praiſe, glory, and whatever is honourable and laudable, will be inclined to arrogate more than fairly belongs to them. But the difficulty is ſolved by the obſervation above made, that no one can be the willing victim of injuſtice; ſo that men cannot injure, although they may hurt, themſelves. Beſides, the injuſtice is plainly in him who makes the unfair diſtribution; for by him the unjuſt action is begun and completed; whereas he who holds more than his due ſhare, may often do it ignorantly and innocently. The word action is taken in different ſenſes. It is applied to inanimate things. The ſword, or any other warlike inſtrument, is ſaid to ſtrike or kill, as well as the hand of one man moved by that of another; or a ſlave, by the command of his maſter. None of thoſe injure, although they are the inſtruments of injuſtice. Unjuſt judgments may proceed merely from ignorance; but that judge only is unjuſt, who paſſes unjuſt decrees, knowingly, from partiality to one party, or ill-will to the other. Between ſuch a judge and one of the parties, the iniquity, as well as its fruits, are ſometimes divided; the latter gets more land than he ought, and the other gets money to which he is not entitled. Injuſtice, however, in judgment, as well as every other ſpecies of injuſtice, always conſiſts in arrogating to ourſelves more than our due proportion of advantage, whether this conſiſts in benefiting our fortune, indulging our partiality, or gratifying our reſentment. Men think, becauſe injuſtice ſeems to be

always

BOOK V.

Juſtice, a matter of more difficulty than commonly imagined.

always in their power, that therefore juſtice is eaſy. The thing, however, is far otherwiſe. To commit vicious actions is indeed always in our power, but to acquire either virtuous or vicious habits is the work of time and cuſtom; and the vice is not in the act, but in the frame of mind and habit of the actor. They think alſo, that to diſtinguiſh between juſt and unjuſt tranſactions requires but ſmall diſcernment; becauſe it is eaſy to underſtand the laws promulgated on this ſubject. But the juſtice or injuſtice is not in thoſe tranſactions themſelves, except by way of appendage or acceſſion, when, together with the ſimple performance of the act, certain diſpoſitions and affections, and thoſe uniform and habitual, concur in the agent. To know, therefore, what conſtitutes or contributes to juſtice, is ſtill more difficult than to know what conſtitutes and contributes to health. The medicines of hellebore, honey, and wine, as well as the operations of cutting and burning, are indeed eaſily known; but to underſtand when, how, and to whom, we ought to adminiſter the one and to apply the other, is a thing of no leſs difficulty than to be a ſkilful phyſician. It is alſo a falſe opinion, that a good man is capable of acts of wickedneſs; becauſe, were he inclined to indulge guilty paſſions, he is more likely to do it with impunity than any other. But, as we above obſerved, the vice or wickedneſs is not in the act itſelf, but in the frame or habit of mind of him by whom that act is performed. The art of healing does not conſiſt in performing operations and in adminiſtering medicines; it conſiſts in doing theſe things properly, that is, in the intellectual habit or ſkill of the phyſician. Juſtice takes place only among thoſe who are ſharers in that kind of goods, of which a certain proportion contributes to their

BOOK V.

their happineſs; but of which either the exceſs or the defect has a tendency to deſtroy it. The Gods, perhaps, cannot have too much power and proſperity; and beings incurably wicked, cannot have too little of either; ſince, by them, the means of good will always be converted into ſources of evil. But men are benefited by a due proportion, and by that only.

Chap. 10.

Of the nature of equity in contradiſtinction to juſtice.

We proceed to ſpeak of equity, and to conſider what relation it bears to juſtice. It is not the ſame thing, nor yet is it different in kind; for it is a praiſeworthy quality as well as juſtice, but is ſpoken of as ſomething better than mere juſtice, and really is ſo, for it is the correction of ſtrict, that is, of legal juſtice; which often needs to be modified by equity, becauſe laws being in their nature general, cannot decide rightly in the indefinite variety of particular caſes. The lawgiver is contented with making a rule, which fairly applies to the greater part of caſes; well knowing that it will not include the whole, and the fault is neither in the law nor the lawgiver, but in the nature of things. When an exception to the rule occurs, which the lawgiver did not foreſee, this exception is admitted in equity, which thus ſupplies the defect of law, as the lawgiver himſelf would do, were he preſent in court, and as he would have done by amending his law, had he been aware of the exception. Equity, then, is better than legal juſtice, being its amendment; and ſupplying that defect of laws, which ariſes from their univerſality. The variety of human tranſactions cannot be compriſed within general rules. Occaſional decrees therefore become requiſite; which vary with each variation of circumſtances, for the meaſure of what is indefinite muſt be indefinite itſelf, like the leaden ruler in the Leſbian architecture, which changes its own ſhape according to that of the ſtones to which

 it

BOOK V.

it is applied. It is manifeſt, therefore, that equity is a ſpecies of juſtice, and contraſted with another ſpecies to which it is preferable. A man of equity is he who deliberately and habitually exerciſes this virtue; who prefers it in all his dealings to the rigour of juſtice; and who, even when the law is on his ſide, will not avail himſelf of this advantage to treat others injuriouſly or unhandſomely.

Chap. 11.

That a man may hurt, but cannot be guilty of injury towards himſelf.

Whether juſtice be taken in its larger ſenſe, of diſobeying the laws; or in its ſtricter acceptation, of depriving others of their property, it is plain, from the obſervations already made, that no one can be guilty of injuſtice towards himſelf. A man may ſpontaneouſly and knowingly commit an unprovoked injury; he may even deſtroy his own life, in direct oppoſition both to the laws and to right reaſon[k]. He thereby certainly does an injury; but to whom? Not to himſelf, becauſe he ſuffers voluntarily. The injury is therefore done to the ſtate; which, on this account, puniſhes ſelf-murder with infamy. As to the other kind of injuſtice, which does not comprehend wickedneſs in general, but which conſiſts, like cowardice, in one ſpecific vice, we cannot, without a total confuſion of thought, ſuppoſe that a man is guilty of it towards himſelf; for in that caſe, the ſame thing

[k] The Oxford edition very properly ſupplies the word λογου of which ορθου is the ordinary epithet, and of which it muſt here be the adjunct, to render the paſſage intelligible. Suicide is always ſpoken of by Ariſtotle as a baſe and cowardly crime, as a mean dereliction of all perſonal dignity, and a groſs violation of all ſocial duty. Cicero ſometimes (for on this ſubject he is not conſiſtent) ſpeaks otherwiſe. "Atque hæc differentia naturarum tantum habet vim, uti nonnumquam mortem ſibi ipſe conſciſcere alius debeat, alius in eadem cauſſa non debeat." De Officiis, l. i. c. xxxi. Here he ſpeaks of ſuicide as a duty; probably out of deference for his admired Cato. But his language is very different elſewhere. Confer. Tuſc. Diſp. l. i. c. xxx. Somn. Scip. c. iii. Had Ariſtotle's Ethics been equally well known, Cicero's Offices would not have been ſo long regarded as the pureſt and moſt ſolid production of heathen morality.

thing would be both added to and taken from the ſame perſon, at the ſame time. Injuſtice, therefore, always implies two perſons at leaſt; and if it did not, the diſtinctions formerly made concerning ſpontaneity, deliberation, retaliation, and aggreſſion, would be totally deſtroyed. Retaliation cannot deſerve the epithet of injurious; but could a man injure himſelf, injury would be conſiſtent with the moſt complete retaliation, namely, the doing and ſuffering preciſely the ſame thing, under preciſely the ſame circumſtances; beſides a man might ſuffer injury voluntarily, which was formerly proved to be impoſſible. Still further, the commiſſion of wrong always implies ſome ſpecific act; but by no ſuch act can a man do wrong to himſelf. He cannot commit adultery with his own wife, he cannot be guilty of houſebreaking with regard to his own houſe, he cannot ſteal his own property: univerſally, therefore, he cannot do an injury to himſelf. It is an evil to ſuffer, as well as to do, wrong, but the latter is by far the worſt evil of the two, becauſe it is blameable and baſe. The former, however, may ſometimes, by concurring with other circumſtances not eſſentially connected with it, be attended with far more deplorable conſequences; in the ſame manner as a fall, by ſtumbling, may ſometimes have worſe effects than a pleuriſy, becauſe it may occaſion a man's capture by the enemy, and, in conſequence thereof, his ignominious death. But the ſcience of Ethics, no more than that of Phyſics, pays attention to conſequences not eſſentially inherent in the ſubject, and connected with it merely by way of appendage or acceſſion. It is ſaid metaphorically, not indeed that a man can exerciſe juſtice towards himſelf, but that one part of him may exerciſe juſtice towards another. This juſtice, however, reſembles, not the political juſtice above examined, but the juſ-

 tice

BOOK V.

tice of fathers and masters towards children and slaves; whose relation to each other bears a near similitude to that of the rational and irrational parts in the human constitution. The passions often rebel against reason, as slaves do against their masters; and as the latter seem guilty of injustice, so do the former. Let thus much suffice concerning justice, and the other moral virtues[1].

[1] The doctrine of justice is explained on the same principles delivered in this Book, Magna Moral. l. i. c. xxxiv.; & Eudem. l. iv.

ARISTOTLE's ETHICS.

BOOK VI.

INTRODUCTION.

IF philosophy consist in explaining phænomena, seemingly indefinite in number, by a few distinct principles of action, this Sixth Book affords one of the finest specimens of it ever exhibited. According to Aristotle, moral virtue is appetite or affection disciplined by reason and custom; which, enabling us to make a fair estimate of excellence, teaches us to prefer and pursue it[a]. To explain, therefore, the different acceptations of the word reason; or, in Aristotle's language, to describe the different powers of the understanding, must form an essential part of every complete treatise of Ethics. By modern philosophers those powers are not accurately distinguished; although, according to our author, the powers of intellection differ as widely from each other as those of sensation. Colours, flavours, sounds, and odours, and other objects about which the senses are conversant, are not more distinguishable from each other, than the different classes of speculative and practical truths, which are perceptible by what our author calls the demonstrative and deliberative faculties of the understanding[b]. Reasoning

BOOK VI.

[a] Magna Moral. l. i. c. xxii, p. 161.

[b] Magna Moral. l. i. c. xxxv. p. 169.

Reaſoning on this principle, that powers muſt differ from each other, which exert themſelves in different actions and effectuate different ends, he treats ſeparately of art, ſcience, prudence, intellect, and wiſdom; he explains the nature and functions of each of thoſe habits; examines the difference between what are called natural virtues, and thoſe which are acquired by exerciſe and cuſtom; and proves that none of the acquired virtues can ſubſiſt without that intellectual habit which he calls prudence.

BOOK VI.

ARGUMENT.

Senſation, intellect, and appetite.—Their different offices.—The five intellectual habits—Science—Art—Prudence—Common ſenſe—Wiſdom.—Quickneſs of apprehenſion.—Juſtneſs of ſentiment.—Importance of the intellectual habits.—Virtue, natural and acquired.—Their difference.

BOOK VI. Chap. I.

Tranſition to the intellectual virtues.

HAVING formerly ſaid that, in moral matters, mediocrity only ought to be the object of our preference, as being alone conſiſtent with right reaſon, it is proper that this ſubject ſhould be more diſtinctly explained. Whoever exerciſes reaſon has, in all his habitual actions, a certain aim, according to which he regulates his behaviour; moderating his paſſions when too ſtrong, invigorating them when too weak, and always bending them to propriety, as a bow is rendered more or leſs tenſe in order to hit the mark. This obſervation is indeed true, but not ſufficiently explicit to be practically uſeful; for, in all other matters in which ſcience is concerned, we ought certainly to do what right reaſon preſcribes, that is, neither too much nor too little. Thus the phyſician ought to act with regard to his patient; but by knowing that this is his duty, he will not be rendered much the wiſer as to what operations ought to be performed, or what medicines ought to be adminiſtered. It is neceſſary, therefore, to ſpeak more definitely concerning the habits

BOOK VI.

bits of the mind, to explain what right reaſon is, and to point out what are the boundaries which it aſſigns to our paſſions and actions. The habits or virtues of the mind were formerly divided into the moral and intellectual; concerning the moral we have already treated; it remains to examine the intellectual, having previouſly ſpoken of the ſoul itſelf. In this, we formerly diſtinguiſhed two parts, the rational and irrational; and the former may alſo be divided into two, namely, that faculty by which we underſtand thoſe ſciences whoſe principles are certain and neceſſary, and which cannot poſſibly be otherwiſe than they are, and that by which we comprehend other branches of knowledge; for if there be any reſemblance or affinity between the truths recogniſed, and the powers which recogniſe them, it is natural to think that things, ſo extremely different as are the neceſſary and contingent, ſhould be perceived and known by different faculties [e]. Knowledge, then, may be divided into that which is demonſtrative and ſcientific, and that which is deliberative and probable; for no one deliberates about things which neceſſarily exiſt after one certain manner, and which cannot poſſibly exiſt after any other. Let us examine, then, what is the beſt habit of each of theſe faculties: the beſt habit of any thing is, in other words, its virtue; and the virtue of each object is aſcertained by its fitneſs for performing its peculiar function.

Chap. 2.

Senſation, intellect, and appetite, their different offices.

There are three principles in man, which, either ſingle or combined, are the ſovereign judges of truth and conduct. Theſe are, ſentation, intellect, and appetite. Of theſe three, mere ſenſation cannot alone be the foundation of any judgment reſpecting conduct, that is, the propriety of action; for wild beaſts have

[e] See alſo Magna Moralia, l. i. c. xxxv. p. 169.

have perception by ſenſe, but are totally unacquainted with propriety. Affirming and denying are the operations of intellect, deſire and averſion are thoſe of appetite; and ſince moral virtue implies the habit of juſt election, and election or preference reſolves itſelf into deliberation and appetite, every act of virtuous preference requires, that there ſhould be accuracy and truth in the compariſon, as well as correctneſs and propriety in the deſire. Of that intellectual faculty which bears not any relation to life and practice, and which is employed, not in deliberation, but in demonſtration, the ſimplicity of abſtract truth is the proper and only object; but deliberative moral wiſdom bears in all its operations a reference to human happineſs; and terminates, not in the diſcoveries of ſpeculation, but in the exertions of action[d]. This latter faculty, then, only attains its end, when well-ordered appetite harmoniſes with ſound practical reaſon; from the combination of which elements, reſults that moral election or preferenee, peculiar to man; which may be called either impaſſioned intelligence, or reflecting appetite; and which is the ſole fountain of whatever is laudable and graceful in behaviour and manners[e]. This practical reaſon is ſuperior to that converſant about production: for production, as we above obſerved, is imperfect in itſelf, and continually remains ſo, until the work, for the ſake of which it operated, be produced. But the operation of practical reaſon terminates in nothing better than the pleaſure of its own energies. It is not given to us for the gratification of appetite: but appetite itſelf is

[d] In conformity with what is here ſaid, Ariſtotle in his Topics, b. v. c. i. p. 226. diſtinguiſhes ſcience from virtue, by ſaying that the former is in one part of the ſoul, and the latter in more than one.

[e] ἡ δε προαιρεσις, κοινον διανοιας και ορεξεως. De Animal. Motu. c. vi. p. 706.

BOOK VI.

is implanted in us for the ſake of that virtuous moral action, which conſtitutes an eſſential part of human happineſs. Such, then, is man, an intellectual but impaſſioned being, exerciſing his faculties concerning things contingent and future. The paſt cannot be an object of deliberation or preference. No one chooſes, that Troy ſhould not be taken; and Agathon ſays rightly,

"All things to God are poſſible, ſave one;
"That to undo, which is already done."

As truth, then, is the object of both our rational faculties, (the ſpeculative and practical,) their excellencies muſt conſiſt in thoſe habits by which truth is moſt clearly diſcerned.

Chap. 3.

The five intellectual habits. Firſt, ſcience.

Let theſe habits be the five following; art, ſcience, prudence, wiſdom, intellect. In matters of opinion we are liable to be deceived; not ſo in matters of ſcience. The former relates to things variable in their nature, of whoſe very exiſtence we may doubt, unleſs when they are actually perceived; the latter is converſant about things unalterable, neceſſary, and eternal, incapable of being generated, exempt from corruption; the knowledge of which admits not of degrees between total ignorance and abſolute certainty. All ſcience may be taught, and all teaching implies principles, namely, thoſe truths which are previouſly known by experience or reaſon. The firſt principles are acquired by induction, that is, by intellect operating on experience[e]. Science, then, may be defined a demonſtrative habit, diſtinguiſhed by thoſe properties which we have aſcribed to it in our Analytics[f]. The principles of ſcience muſt be perceived with the cleareſt evidence; for unleſs they be more evident than the concluſions drawn from them, thoſe concluſions will not form

[e] See Analyſis, p. 57. Comp. p. 161.

[f] See Analyſis, p. 77.

form ſcience ſtrictly ſo called; becauſe their truth does not neceſſarily proceed from the truth of their premiſes; with which they are connected, not eſſentially, but only by way of acceſſion or appendage [a].

Chap. 4. Art.

Things in their nature variable, and which might either have never been, which may ceaſe to exiſt, or whoſe mode of exiſtence is liable to perpetual alterations, are of two kinds; productions or actions. Theſe things are ſufficiently diſtinguiſhed from each other even in popular diſcourſe; ſo that a rational habit of action muſt be different from a rational habit of production. Since building, which is a rational habit of production, is an art, and every other ſuch habit is alſo an art, and every art is alſo the habit juſt mentioned, art may be defined the habit of making or producing a certain work agreeably to the rules of right reaſon. All art is employed in examining and contriving how it may beſt form and faſhion thoſe productions or works of which the efficient cauſe is in the maker, not in the materials. Things which exiſt neceſſarily, are not the ſubjects of art; nor thoſe which are produced naturally; for the latter have their efficient cauſe in themſelves [b]. Art, then, is converſant after a certain manner about the ſame things as fortune. Wherefore Agathon ſays,

"In friendly ties are art and fortune bound."

Artleſſneſs is the contrary of art; it is the producing of ſuch works awkwardly; according to erroneous principles of reaſon.

Chap. 5. Prudence.

In explaining the nature of prudence, let us conſider firſt, who they are that deſerve this appellation. It ſeems to be the part of a prudent man to deliberate wiſely about his good or advantage; not in particular points merely, as health or ſtrength, but

[a] See above, p. 65. Conf. p. 115. [b] See above, p. 109.

BOOK VI.

but as to the general happineſs of life. This is indicated by our calling thoſe men prudent in their affairs, who take proper means for attaining valuable purpoſes, which are not the proper objects of particular arts. Prudence then implies deliberation; and no one deliberates about things invariable in their nature, and which cannot be otherwiſe than they are; nor about things which are not in their own power. Prudence then is not ſcience, becauſe the objects of ſcience are things invariable; it is not art, becauſe the object of prudence is action, not production. It remains then, that prudence ſhould be a rational and practical habit, bearing a reference to the happineſs and miſery of human life. The end of production conſiſts always in the work produced; but action is often its own end; for happineſs, which is a kind of action, is perfect in itſelf. Pericles, and other great ſtateſmen, are called prudent on account of their ſingular ability in effecting the good of human kind; the great buſineſs of œconomy, both political and domeſtic. The word, in Greek, denoting the moral virtue of temperance, is compounded of two other words, which may be literally tranſlated, "the preſervative of prudence;" for temperance tends to preſerve this intellectual excellence. Pleaſure and pain do not deſtroy every exerciſe of the underſtanding, for inſtance, that which relates to mathematical truth; but that exerciſe only which relates to the practcial concerns of life. For the exceſſive love of pleaſure, or the exceſſive abhorrence of pain, ſubſtitutes new principles of action quite different from thoſe by which wiſe and good men are actuated. Prudence, then, is a rational and practical habit, effective of human happineſs. We ſpeak of excellence in art, but prudence is itſelf excellence. In the arts, voluntary errors are the beſt; but, in matters

matters of prudence, they are the worſt; as in all the moral virtues. Prudence, then, is not an art but a virtue; and the virtue of that faculty of the mind which is converſant about opinion and probability, diſcerning in ſuch things truth from falſehood. As it relates to the practice of life, which, with all men, is a conſtant object of thought, prudence, when once acquired, is not, like other habits of the underſtanding, liable to be forgotten or loſt.

Chap. 6. Intellect.

Since the object of ſcience, as above obſerved, is univerſal and demonſtrable truth, and whatever is demonſtrable muſt be founded on principles, it is manifeſt that there muſt be primary principles[i], which are not ſcience, any more than they are art or prudence. They are not ſcience, becauſe all ſcience is demonſtrable; they are not art or prudence, becauſe theſe have for their ſubject things contingent and variable: neither are they wiſdom, becauſe, as we ſhall ſee hereafter, wiſdom, and the higheſt wiſdom, is converſant about truths ſuſceptible of demonſtration. Since then none of the four habits juſt mentioned; neither ſcience, nor art, nor prudence, nor wiſdom, can afford thoſe primary principles; and ſince all the habits of the underſtanding are reducible to five, it follows that intellect, operating on experience[k], is the only ſource from which thoſe great and primary truths can be ſuppoſed to flow.

Chap. 7. Wiſdom.

Wiſdom is ſometimes taken for ſkill in the arts; and applied, for inſtance, to Phidias, who was a ſkilful ſculptor; or Polycleitus, the ſkilful ſtatuary. But there is a wiſdom of a far ſuperior kind, which does not denote excellence in any of thoſe operations or arts to which Homer alludes in ſpeaking of Margites: "The Gods had not formed him for digging or ploughing,

[i] See Analyſis, p. 92. & ſeq. [k] See Analyſis, p. 57. Comp. p. 161.

BOOK VI.

ing, nor made him ſkilful in any other work;" but a wiſdom abſolute and univerſal, ſince it relates to the univerſe and its principles; contemplating, not merely, like other ſciences, the qualities or properties of things, but the things themſelves, or ſubſtances[k]; and, therefore, of all ſciences the moſt accurate as well as the moſt ſublime; comprehending both the higheſt demonſtrations, and the vindication of thoſe primary truths on which all demonſtration is built[l]. To ſay that prudence is more valuable than wiſdom, is to prefer man to all other beings in the univerſe. One thing may be ſalutary and good for human kind; and another for fiſhes: but abſtract qualities remain perpetually the ſame; and in like manner wiſdom is permanent and ſtable, but prudence muſt vary its maxims with each alteration of the ſubject about which it is employed. The buſineſs of prudence conſiſts in providing for the good of thoſe peculiarly recommended to its care; and whoever beſt underſtands how to promote the good of each tribe or of each individual, to him we ſhould be moſt inclined to commit their direction and management. Wherefore ſome of the inferior animals ſeem to be endowed with a kind of prudence, in foreſeeing and providing what is neceſſary for the preſervation of their own lives. The unalterable ſtability of wiſdom clearly diſtinguiſhes it from civil policy, which, if it would attain its end, the public good, muſt be guided by circumſtances; and the different tribes of animals require, in health as well as in diſeaſe, different kinds of management, which are reſpectively moſt conducive to their well-being. It will not avail to ſay, that as man is the nobleſt of animals, therefore the virtue of prudence,

[k] Theſe are God and Intellect—the beſt ſubſtances, ἐν οὐσίᾳ μὲν, ὁ θεὸς καὶ ὁ νοῦς, &c. Moral. Eudem. l. i. c. viii. p. 201.

[l] See above, Analyſis, p. 86. & ſeq.

prudence, which is converſant about human happineſs, merits the preference to every other[m]; for that there are many natures more divine than man, is atteſted by thoſe glorious luminaries, and that beautiful arrangement which adorns the univerſe. Wiſdom, then, comprehends both intellect and ſcience, applied to the higheſt purpoſes, the diſcovery of the moſt valuable truths. Wherefore we call Thales, Anaxagoras, and others of their character, wiſe, indeed, but ſurely not prudent, ſince they manifeſtly neglect their private concerns and perſonal advantage, and apply their thoughts to the inveſtigation of ſubjects as lofty and difficult as they are completely uſeleſs for the ordinary purpoſes of human life. But the virtue of prudence is directed ſolely to thoſe purpoſes; and he is juſtly deemed the moſt prudent, whoſe advice is moſt conducive to public proſperity. This great object is not to be attained by abſtract ſpeculations. Prudence muſt be converſant about particulars; for all practice relates to particulars only; wherefore many men, ignorant of theory, are more uſeful than thoſe acquainted with it; for inſtance, empirics, than phyſicians. What avails it to know that light food is ſalutary, unleſs we alſo know, for inſtance,

[m] According to Ariſtotle, prudence is, as it were, wiſdom's ſteward, holding a delegated authority in leſſer concerns; that the maſter may have leiſure for more important purſuits, ἡ φρονησις ὡσπερ επιτροπος τις εςι της σοφιας, και παρασκευαζει ταυτῃ σχολην, και το ποιειν της αυτης εργον. Magn. Moral. l. i. c. xxxv. p. 172. Theſe more important purſuits conſiſt in ſpeculations concerning God; in meditating on, and worſhipping him: ει τις δε η δι' ενδειαν, η δι' ὑπερβολην κωλυει τον θεον θεραπευειν και θεωρειν, αυτη δε φαυλη. Moral. Eudem. c. xv. p. 291. This employment is the chief end of man; the natural exerciſe of his nobleſt faculties, ὑτος της ψυχης ὁ ορος αριςος, τα ἡκιςα αισθανεσθαι τυ αλλυ μερυς της ψυχης, ἡ τοιυτον. The leſs we are diſturbed by bodily paſſions, or haraſſed by worldly cares, the more likely we are to approach to this ultimate term of mental enjoyment. Idem ibid. Religion cannot be eradicated from the mind, unleſs the underſtanding be deſtroyed: μηδε τυς θευς φοβεισθαι υκ ανδρειος, αλλα μαινομενος. Magna Moral. c. v. p. 151.

BOOK VI.

ſtance, that the fleſh of birds is light? Prudence being a practical virtue, eſſentially includes the knowledge of particulars. Yet even here general and ſuperintending principles are not without their uſe.

Chap. 8.

Policy, general and particular.

Prudence and policy are the ſame habits, but applied to different ſubjects. Policy is general or particular: the general conſiſts in legiſlation; the particular, in deliberations and decrees; for as decrees apply general principles to particular caſes, they immediately precede execution; and therefore thoſe who buſy themſelves about decrees, in propoſing or procuring them, are peculiarly conſidered as workmen in the trade of politics. Prudence chiefly relates to the management of our private affairs, and while directed to this purpoſe preſerves its proper name; but when our prudence extends to the affairs of others, it is called œconomics, legiſlation, politics; which laſt is either deliberative or judicial. Yet politics is ſometimes contraſted with prudence; too much concern about other people's affairs ſeeming unfavourable to our own happineſs. Wherefore Euripides ſays, in the perſon of Philoctetes,

> "How can the name of wiſe to me belong
> Who might have mingled in the martial throng,
> Unvex'd with buſineſs and exempt from care,
> Taking of ſpoils my honourable ſhare;
> Yet choſe by over-anxious thoughts to move
> The direful hate of all-commanding Jove?"

But a prudential regard to our own intereſt requires, perhaps, that we ſhould not be regardleſs of politics, ſince our own good is involved in that of the Public; and many are extremely ill-fitted to provide even for their own. Young perſons may become good geometers, and render themſelves ſkilful in the

arts

arts depending on the mathematical ſciences. But it is ſcarcely poſſible for a youth to have the virtue of prudence, becauſe this virtue is converſant about particulars, the accurate knowledge of which requires obſervation and experience, which muſt be the work of time. The mathematics are converſant merely about abſtractions formed by ourſelves; the notions of which are clear and preciſe. But the knowledge of nature, and of thoſe cauſes by which nature ſubſiſts, is far more complicated, requiring continually the aſſiſtance of that experience in which it originates. As to practical truths, reſulting from long experience, young men may indeed repeat them, but they ſeldom feel their full force. In applying theory to practice, errors may ariſe from miſtaking either the general or the particular propoſition; for example, that all heavy waters are bad, or that this water is heavy. Prudence is manifeſtly different from ſcience; being the perception of thoſe particular and practical truths which admit not of demonſtration; whereas intellect is employed about thoſe general and primary principles which require not any proof. In the chain of mental faculties, intellect and prudence then form the two extreme links; prudence holding the extreme of individuality, and intellect that of generalization. Prudence then may be called common ſenſe, ſince it is converſant about objects of ſenſe; but in a manner ſpecifically different from that in which the other ſenſes are reſpectively converſant about their particular objects.

BOOK VI.

Prudence implies deliberation, which word has a leſs extenſive meaning than inveſtigation, becauſe deliberation is that ſpecies of inveſtigation which relates to the practical concerns of life. It is not ſcience, nor opinion, nor conjecture; not ſcience, Chap. 9.

BOOK VI.

becauſe no one deliberates about that which admits of demonſtrable proof: not conjecture or gueſſing, becauſe theſe are quick and rapid, but deliberation is a work of time; and it is a common maxim, that we ought to be prompt in execution, but ſlow in deliberation. Deliberation is not preſence of mind, any more than happineſs of conjecture; it is not ſcience, which cannot err; nor opinion, the rectitude of which conſiſts in truth, whereas that of deliberation conſiſts in utility; ſince wrong deliberations are hurtful. Beſides, every opinion is a propoſition either affirmative or negative; whereas deliberation neither affirms nor denies, but inveſtigates and inquires. Good deliberation is rectitude of counſel; but, as rectitude is taken in different ſenſes, it is not every kind of rectitude, particularly it is not that by which an intemperate or bad man may contrive right means for attaining his wicked ends. His right deliberations terminate in much miſchief; whereas good deliberation naturally terminates in advantage. This, however, may ſometimes be attained without good deliberation, ſince a right concluſion is ſometimes inferred from wrong premiſes. Good deliberation alſo muſt be ſeaſonable: its reſult muſt be drawn at a right time, muſt proceed from right premiſes, and muſt terminate in ſome valuable purpoſe, whether that be happineſs in general, or ſomething thereto conducive. *Good counſel*, then, conſiſts in diſcovering proper means for attaining thoſe ends which prudence approves as worthy objects of purſuit.

Chap. 10.

Quickneſs of apprehenſion.

There is a readineſs of apprehenſion in ſome men, which makes them be diſtinguiſhed as intelligent; while others are equally remarkable for their ſlowneſs and ſtupidity. This quickneſs of thought, or acuteneſs in deciſion, is ſomething quite different from ſcience or opinion, ſince all men are capable of learning

learning ſciences and forming opinions; nor does it belong to any ſcience in particular, as phyſic, which is converſant about health, or geometry, which is converſant about magnitude; nor does its proper ſubject conſiſt in things which happen caſually, or in thoſe which are unalterable and eternal; but it is moſt conſpicuous in thoſe things which are matters of deliberation and doubt. It is converſant, then, about the ſame ſubject with prudence, though not preciſely in the ſame manner; for prudence ſpeaks with a voice of authority, commanding one action and prohibiting another; but the intellectual excellence, now under conſideration, is rather critical than commanding; it does not govern and regulate our actions, but enables us to underſtand the regulations which prudence preſcribes; and follows the dictates of this ſovereign virtue, as an intelligent youth goes along with the leſſons of his teacher.

Chap. II.

Juſtneſs of ſentiment.

That juſtneſs of ſentiment by which ſome men render themſelves ſo commendable, is nothing more than a nice diſcernment of the virtue which we called equity; in proof of which it may be obſerved, that thoſe who are moſt equitable in their tranſactions, are alſo the moſt diſtinguiſhed by their fellow-feeling with others, and the moſt inclinable to excuſe their pardonable errors. Pardon is nothing more than an equitable deciſion; that is, indulgence flowing from right reaſon. The intellectual habits above deſcribed, readineſs of apprehenſion, juſtneſs of ſentiment, prudence, intelligence, or common ſenſe, are all of them converſant about the ſame objects, and all of them conſpire to the ſame great end of making men behave well in the practical concerns of life. Theſe concerns are all of them particular, depending on time and circumſtances; and the habits that have reference to them, muſt therefore be different

BOOK VI.

from thoſe which are converſant about general and abſtract truth. In practical matters, prudence regulates and commands, ſentiment criticiſes and approves, and intelligence, or common ſenſe, operating on obſervation and experience, furniſhes thoſe firſt principles, which are equally eſſential to the due ſelection of ends, and the proper adjuſtment of means. As theſe firſt principles ſpring up in the mind, without teaching or reaſoning, merely from obſervation and experience, they ſeem to be the gift of nature; and juſtneſs of ſentiment, as well as the other virtues depending on them, ſeem alſo to be natural, and to belong to men at a certain period of life, who ſeem then naturally to attain underſtanding and ſentiment; whereas art, ſcience, or wiſdom, (as above explained,) never ſeem to grow up naturally, but always to be the work of application and ſtudy. Common ſenſe, then, that is, intellect operating on experience, being the ultimate judge of whatever is practically good, we ought to reſpect the opinions of old and prudent men, not leſs than demonſtration itſelf; becauſe they ſee with the eye of experience, which alone can diſcern right principles of conduct. Such, then, is the nature of prudence in contradiſtinction to that of wiſdom; virtues which are converſant about different objects, and which reſpectively belong to different faculties of the ſoul.

Chap. 12.

The value of the intellectual virtues, how to be eſtimated,

Doubts may ariſe in what reſpect theſe intellectual virtues are uſeful; for wiſdom, as above explained, has not any reference to mutable and material things, and therefore ſeems not to have any tendency to promote human happineſs. Prudence, indeed, is converſant about worldly affairs; but wherein conſiſts its utility, ſince it only deliberates concerning honourable, juſt, and other actions conducive to happineſs, which a virtuous man has learned to practiſe? If virtue be a habit, how

is

is it to be improved by the reflections of prudence? Persons possessed of health or strength would not be more strong or more healthy, though endowed with the skill of physicians and masters of exercises. But prudence, it will be said, though not necessary for the practice, is useful to the acquisition of virtue. Is skill in physic necessary or useful to the acquisition of health? If this were the case, we ought, when sick, to study physic, instead of calling a physician. Besides these doubts, it is not easy to determine the relative value of wisdom and prudence; and why the latter, which is inferior in dignity, should prescribe rules for the exercise of the former. Having proposed these difficulties, it is our duty, if possible, to solve them. First of all, wisdom and prudence, though they terminated not in any distinct and separate end, would be things highly desirable in themselves, since they are respectively the virtues of two mental faculties. But they are productive causes of human happiness, not indeed as physic is the cause of health, but as health itself is the cause of a healthy habit. The great business of human life is performed by the co-operation of prudence with moral virtue. The latter makes us pursue right ends; and the former makes us employ fit means for attaining them. To that power of the soul, which discovers itself in the growth and nutrition of the body, no such spontaneous function belongs; since its operations are carried on altogether independently of our own wills; and it is entirely beside our power to accelerate or retard them. As to the doubt whether prudence contributes to the practice of just and honourable actions, it will be best solved by tracing those actions to their real souree. Acts of virtue, in general, may be performed by those who are

Their utility in practice.

BOOK VI.

are not virtuous men, involuntarily, ignorantly, through fear of the law, or through any other motive which does not imply the habitual love of virtue, and the deliberate preference of it merely for its own ſake. This habit, then, makes our ends right and good; but how to attain thoſe ends, is the work, not of moral virtue, but of another principle. There is a power of the mind, call it cleverneſs, keenneſs, or ſagacity, of which the nature conſiſts in enabling us to accompliſh our purpoſes; and which, when the purpoſes are good, is praiſeworthy; when they are bad, this cleverneſs changes its name, being juſtly reproached as villany. Prudence, though not the ſame thing, (ſince a villain cannot be called prudent,) yet requires for its foundation this natural dexterity, which is determined to the ſide of honour and propriety by habitual acts of virtue. For reaſonings alone cannot ſupply correct principles of conduct. The ends beſt to be purſued, appear ſuch to good men only. Vice diſtorts the judgment; and even in men of naturally keen minds, produces the greateſt practical errors: wherefore it is impoſſible to be prudent without being morally virtuous.

Chap. 13.

Natural virtue different from virtue properly ſo called.

It is neceſſary to ſpeak farther of virtue; for, as natural ſagacity, though ſimilar, is not the ſame with prudence, ſo natural virtue, though ſimilar, is not the ſame with virtue properly ſo called. Our capacities and diſpoſitions are the work of nature; and therefore, in ſome ſort, our morals are ſo likewiſe; men being born with propenſities to juſtice, temperance, and fortitude. But this natural aptitude is not the virtue of which we are in queſt. Strong natural propenſities, and ſtriking differences of manners, appear in children, and even in wild beaſts; and this native vigour being unenlightened by reaſon, has a tendency to do much mifchief, like the irregular motions of giants when deprived of their eye-fight. But when the intellectual eye opens, and affection is difciplined by reafon, then that moral virtue difplays itfelf; which bears the fame relation to the natural, which prudence bears to that doubtful quality above mentioned, which, though fomewhat refembling it, is yet fpecifically different. As virtue properly fo called implies prudence, fome have refolved all the virtues into modifications of this intellectual excellence. Socrates did this; faying, rightly, that none of the virtues could fubfift without prudence; which is nothing elfe than right reafon, (which all philofophers now add to the definition of virtue,) applied to the fubject of morals; but he erred in thinking that the whole of moral rectitude depended folely on the underftanding, and in calling the virtues fciences. Virtuous men, indeed, muft act, not only according to right reafon, but with right reafon; that is, the right reafon which regulates their conduct, muft be a principle in themfelves. The virtues then, though not fciences, cannot fubfift without that principle of reafon from which all the fciences fpring; in other words, prudence is requifite for conftituting the character of the truly good man. The queftion therefore may be anfwered, whether the virtues can exift feparately. It fhould feem that they may; becaufe the fame perfon not being born with equal aptitude to them all, he may poffefs fome of them, though ftill deficient in others. This indeed is true with regard to the natural virtues; but with regard to thofe which conftitute the character of the truly good man, it is impoffible; for none fuch can be exercifed without prudence, and with this fingle intellectual excellence, all the moral virtues neceffarily co-exift; fince prudence not only fhews us

how

BOOK VI.

how best to obtain our ends, but always implies that the ends themselves are good. Yet prudence, extensive and dignified as its function is, ought not to be preferred to wisdom, which is conversant about still higher subjects, and is the virtue of a nobler faculty[x]. Physic is not better than health; though it prescribes rules by which health may be attained[y]. To set prudence above wisdom, is the same absurdity as to set policy above the Gods; because policy regulates the national religion, as well as all other public concerns[z].

[x] See above, p. 285.

[y] The art of physic does not make use of health, it only contrives how health may be preserved or restored. It is for the sake of health, and therefore less valuable. See above, p. 149. & seq.

[z] The intellectual virtues are treated of more briefly in the last chapters of the first, and first chapters of the second Book of the work intitled Magna Moralia; and in the fifth Book of the Ethics to Eudemus.

ARISTOTLE's ETHICS.

BOOK VII.

INTRODUCTION.

HAVING examined the virtues and vices, ſtrictly ſo called, the author proceeds to habits which, though often confounded with them, are yet eſſentially different; namely, ſelf-command, and its oppoſite, incontinency; heroic virtue, and its oppoſite, beaſtly depravity; which ſometimes ſhews itſelf in ſavageneſs and ferocity, and ſometimes in unnatural perverſions of the concupiſcible appetites. There is not any ſyſtem of Ethics that accounts ſo fully and ſo clearly for the important diſtinction between weakneſs and wickedneſs, as is done in this Seventh Book.

BOOK VII.

ARGUMENT.

Vice.—Weakness.—Ferocity.—Self-command, and its contrary.—Unnatural depravities, different from vices.—Voluptuousness more detestable than irascibility—Reasons of this.—Intemperance and incontinency.—Their difference.

BOOK VII. Chap. I.

In morals three things to be avoided.

We now proceed, making a new division, to observe, that in morals three things ought to be avoided; vice, weakness, and ferocity: the opposites to the two first are manifest, namely, virtue and self-command; and to the third, we may set in opposition a virtue more than human, something heroic and divine, such as Homer makes Priam ascribe to Hector;

> " And last great Hector, more than man divine,
> For sure he seemed not of terrestrial line*."

Ferocity, and its opposites.

So that should we believe what is said of the deification of illustrious men, their pre-eminent worth might be properly opposed to savageness and ferocity: for virtue belongs not to gods, any more than vice to beasts; the excellencies of gods are above virtue, and the depravities of beasts are specifically different from vice. The Lacedæmonians, when they admire any one exceedingly, say, " you are a divine man;" but as such men are seldom to be met with, so beastly depravities are seldom to be found in the human race; they occur rarely, and chiefly

* Iliad, b. xxiv. v. 223. & seq.

BOOK VII.

chiefly among barbarians. They are sometimes produced by diseases or wounds; and the excesses of human vice are reproached as beastly. But concerning such enormous depravities, we shall afterwards have occasion to speak; and we have already considered vice properly so called. It remains therefore that we now treat of incontinency and self-command; which seem not to be entirely the same with the habits of vice and virtue, nor yet altogether different from them. We shall first mention the prevailing opinions on this subject, and next state our own doubts: when difficulties are removed, and probabilities established, the theory will be sufficiently correct for all practical purposes. Firmness and self-command appear then to be respectable and praiseworthy habits; and their contraries, weakness and yielding softness, appear to be, in the same proportion, both blameable and contemptible. The man of self-command is steady to the decisions of his reason; the weak man is easily moved from them. The latter, knowing that his actions are bad, yet commits them through passion; the former, knowing that his appetites are bad, yet restrains them through reason. Some confound self-command with temperance, and the want of it with intemperance; others think that those habits are widely different from each other. Prudence appears to some to be totally incompatible with the want of self-command; others think, that men, highly distinguished by their prudence and abilities, are often extremely deficient in this particular. A man is said to lose the command of himself, and to be mastered, not only by pleasure, but by anger, honour, and gain. Such are the prevailing opinions on this subject[b].

It

[b] The subjects treated in this Book are explained nearly in the same words in the sixth book of the Ethics to Eudemus.

Concerning ſelf-command, and its contrary.

It ſeems difficult to explain how a man, who entertains juſt conceptions of things, ſhould voluntarily reſign his independence; and how he who, as Socrates obſerved, has ſcience to direct him, ſhould allow himſelf to be domineered over by inferior principles, and dragged in captivity like a ſlave. Socrates, indeed, maintained, that this could not happen to him who poſſeſſed real ſcience, and that none acted amiſs but through ignorance only. But this opinion is manifeſtly at variance with the phænomena; for if paſſion were cauſed by ignorance, the ignorance ought to precede the paſſion, which is plainly not the caſe; for the man who errs through want of ſelf-command, only does ſo when ſtimulated by paſſion; well knowing, before his paſſion is excited, that the actions to which it moves him are wrong. Some philoſophers maintain that none can err againſt demonſtrative knowledge, but that many daily err againſt that which is only probable; and that the love of pleaſure, though it cannot prevail over ſcience ſtrictly ſo called, may yet be too ſtrong for opinion. But if opinion merely, that is a faint and wavering impreſſion of truth, is the only power that makes reſiſtance to the ſtrength of appetite, it is not wonderful that the latter ſhould obtain the victory; nor ought thoſe to be blamed, in whom the ſtronger principle prevails. But this we find is not true; for men are highly blamed for indulging their corrupt appetites. If neither ſcience nor opinion can take part in this mental conflict, prudence remains as the only antagoniſt. But this is abſurd; for the want of ſelf-command cannot ſubſiſt in the ſame mind with prudence; a prudent man will not voluntarily commit bad actions; and prudence, as we have above ſhewn, is a practical principle, implying the exiſtence of all other virtues[c]. Self-command ſuppoſes

Difficulties concerning this quality.

[c] See p. 303.

poses the presence of strong passions, and those blameable either in their nature or in their degree: if they were not blameable, they ought not to be resisted; and if they were not strong, there would be little praise in resisting them. Temperance, as above explained, is inconsistent with the presence of any such passions. Temperance and self-command cannot therefore belong to the same character. If self-command implied an immoveable adherence to every conclusion of the understanding, it would, when this conclusion happened to be false, be nothing better than obstinacy; and if the imperfection opposite to self-command consisted in easily departing from certain opinions or resolutions, it would sometimes be a very respectable quality; as in the case of Neoptolemus, who is represented in Sophocles' tragedy as easily departing from the resolution which he had taken, by the advice of Ulysses, because he could not bear to tell a lie; and those who' having once yielded to the seductions of sophistry, continue pertinaciously to adhere to them, are surely not commendable on that account. Great weakness of resolution, when accompanied with great stupidity, might sometimes be a virtue; because through extreme irresolution, a man might be tempted to do directly the reverse of what he foolishly intended. Besides, he who led a life of voluptuousness through deliberate choice, and on conviction of its being the best kind of life that he could pursue, would not be in a condition so totally hopeless, as he who followed the same plan through want of self-command, in direct opposition to the dictates of his own reason. The former having been corrupted by argument, might also, by argument, be reformed; but the latter, resisting the persuasion of his own mind, would be totally incurable; and obnoxious to the proverb,

"Of drinking still, e'en when the water chok'd."

BOOK VII.

Besides, wherein does self-command, and the weakness opposite to it, properly consist; are the objects about which these habits are conversant, limited to a certain class? Such are the doubts of which we must endeavour to find the probable solution.

Chap. 3.

Whether persons deficient in self-command err knowingly.

We proceed first to examine whether a man gives up the command of himself knowingly; and, if so, how that can happen: we shall also inquire, whether self-command, and the inability to restrain our appetites, have a reference to all pleasures and pains indiscriminately, or to certain definite kinds of them; and whether it belongs to the same habit of mind to resist pleasure, and to encounter pain; with several other questions naturally connected with the present speculation. Does inability to restrain our appetites appear in the improper pleasures that we pursue, or in the improper manner in which we pursue them, or in both these united? Self-command, and its opposite, incontinency, when taken in the strictest acceptation, have a reference to the same things about which temperance and intemperance were formerly proved to be conversant[d]; but the kind of relation which they bear to these things is exceedingly different. The intemperate man obeys his appetites knowingly and deliberately, thinking that he ought always to follow the impulse of present pleasure; the man, merely weak and incontinent, also obeys his appetites, but without thinking that he is thereby acting the part which becomes him. Whether the perceived impropriety of his conduct be the result of certain or only probable knowledge, makes not any material alteration; since some opinions, as Heraclitus proves, hold as firm possession of the mind, as if they were conclusions of science.

[d] See above, p. 218. & seq.

BOOK VII.

ſcience. But a man is ſaid to underſtand, either when he actually exerciſes this faculty, or when he is barely poſſeſſed of it. It is exceedingly difficult to conceive how he ſhould act againſt his underſtanding in the former caſe, though not at all extraordinary that he ſhould do ſo in the latter. He may underſtand both the general precept, and the particular caſe to which it is applicable; but if he does not actually make the application, his knowledge will not avail him. In practical matters, there are general propoſitions which relate to the agent, and others which relate to the object of his action; and each of theſe have particular propoſitions which naturally fall under them. A man may be poſſeſſed of the knowledge of all the general propoſitions, and alſo of the knowledge of all the particular ones; and yet, if there be any one of the latter, concerning which his underſtanding does not, in the moment of action, exert its operation or energy, it is not wonderful that he ſhould fall into the greateſt practical errors. This operation or energy is manifeſtly ſuſpended in the caſe of perſons aſleep, drunk, or mad; whoſe condition nearly reſembles that of men under the influence of paſſion. Anger and luſt plainly alter the bodily frame, and ſometimes produce madneſs. Such is the ſtate of thoſe unable to reſtrain their appetites. It is no proof of the contrary, that ſuch perſons talk reaſonably; for ſome madmen will repeat the verſes and reaſonings of Empedocles; and boys may be taught to ſtring together demonſtrations, although they know not what they ſay; for to appropriate truth to ourſelves, it muſt be rendered congenial to the mind; which is the work of time. Such perſons no more underſtand the concluſions which they pronounce, than comedians feel the paſſions which they fictitiouſly exhibit. There is alſo a philoſophical

phical cauſe reſulting from the phyſical nature of man, which may explain why he often through paſſion acts contrary to the dictates of his underſtanding. In all practical morality, there is to be conſidered, beſides the general precept or propoſition, alſo the particular one, which reſults from a perception of ſenſe. When theſe two propoſitions coaleſce, there is not merely an aſſent of the mind, but in practical matters, action muſt immediately and neceſſarily enſue. Thus, if the general propoſition be, "ſweet things ought to be taſted;" and the particular, "this before me is ſweet;" it is neceſſary that, unleſs reſtrained by ſome obſtacle or argument, I ſhould immediately taſte what is before me. Although the mind, therefore, may have the knowledge of ſome general propoſition which ought to prevent taſting, yet, if appetite conſpires with the two propoſitions above mentioned, appetite will, in thoſe deſtitute of ſelf-command, be indulged, in oppoſition to right reaſon; and theſe propoſitions will be alleged by them in excuſe for their infirmity. They will appear therefore to act licentiouſly on argument; but, in fact, argument is not in itſelf contrary to right reaſon, but only by way of acceſſion or appendage to appetite, which has the power of moving and changing the whole frame of the body, and thereby diſtorting the intellects. Beaſts, therefore, cannot be blamed for this want of ſelf-command, becauſe they have not any perception of general precepts, their higheſt powers conſiſting in imagination and memory. How men enſlaved by their appetites reſume the exerciſe of their underſtandings, needs not here be explained; this change has nothing in it peculiar; ſince it entirely reſembles what happens to all mankind when they awake from ſleep, or to drunkards when they recover from a fit of intoxication; ſubjects which belong to the pro-

BOOK VII.

vince of the phyſiologiſt. Socrates then ſaid true, that ſcience, properly ſo called, could not be overcome by appetite, which only diſturbs our perception of particular and practical truths.

Whether incontinency be a ſpecific imperfection, denoting, without any addition to it, infirmities of a peculiar kind, comes next to be inquired. It is manifeſtly converſant about pleaſures and pains; and as pleaſures are either neceſſary, namely, ſuch as are eſſential to the health of the body and the preſervation of the ſpecies; or though not neceſſary, yet in themſelves eligible, ſuch as victory, honour, wealth, and ſuch other external advantages, it is to be remarked that we do not call thoſe incontinent who are too eaſily maſtered by the latter pleaſures, and who are inclined to indulge them in a degree not warranted by right reaſon, without adding the particular cauſe or object which overſets them, ſuch as gain, honour, anger. They are incontinent, that is wanting in ſelf-command, not ſimply and abſolutely, but as to gain, honour, anger; and the definition of incontinency in general no more applies to them, than the general definition of a man to an Olympic victor. It is doubtleſs an imperfection in a man's character that he is actuated by too eager a deſire of honour or of wealth; but incontinency, taken abſolutely, is blamed, not merely as an imperfection, but either as general depravity, or at leaſt as a particular vice; which conſiſts in purſuing with too much eagerneſs the pleaſures of the taſte and touch; or in avoiding, ſoftly and weakly, the pains originating in thoſe ſenſes, cold and heat, hunger and thirſt. Continency and incontinency, taken ſimply and ſtrictly, are converſant therefore about preciſely the ſame objects with temperance and intemperance; though the relation which they bear to thoſe objects be extremely different. The intemperate man purſues pleaſure willfully and deliberately, thinking it always the proper object of his preference; wherefore his intemperance is more odious in proportion to the debility of his deſires; for what exceſſes might he be expected to commit, were he ſtimulated by the warmth of youthful paſſions? Deſires and pleaſures, as we have already explained, are either natural, (of which ſome are even highly reſpectable and honourable,) or unnatural; or thirdly, they hold an intermediate rank, being natural under certain conditions, and unnatural under others; in which laſt claſs we may place the deſires of gain, glory, or victory. Deſires of the firſt and laſt kind do not ſubject thoſe who gratify them to blame, provided they do not indulge them to exceſs; ſo that thoſe who delight in their own honours and advantage, or in the honour and advantage of their parents or children, and take proper means to promote objects naturally ſo dear to them, are juſtly reſpected on this account; although even here, extremes are dangerous; as was exemplified in the caſe of Niobé, whoſe pride in her children made her contend with the gods; and in that of Satyrus, ſurnamed Philopater, whoſe zeal for the honour of his father proceeded to the extravagance of folly. But ſuch deſires, being highly natural in themſelves, have nothing in them of wickedneſs or turpitude, only their exceſſes being hurtful or uſeleſs, ought to be carefully avoided. In indulging ſuch deſires beyond the limits preſcribed by right reaſon, we are indeed guilty of an error which ought to be ſhunned, but which is not culpable, like that want of ſelf-command, properly called incontinence. Theſe errors bearing ſome analogy to each other, fall under the common denomination of weakneſs; but that word, when applied to the one, does not mean the ſame thing, as when it is applied

BOOK VII.

to the other, any more than the epithet bad, applied to a player or a phyſician, means the ſame thing, as when it is applied to a man. Self-command then, and its oppoſite weakneſſes, are converſant about the ſame ſubjects with temperance and intemperance. When the words are applied to other ſubjects, they are extended by way of ſimile beyond their ſtrict acceptation, and therefore other words muſt be added to them in order clearly to expreſs our meaning. To ſay ſimply that a man is wanting in ſelf-command, denotes that he is liable to be overcome by the ſeductions of ſenſual pleaſure, but does not immediately ſuggeſt to us that he is liable to be overcome by anger, honour, or gain.

Chap. 5.

Unnatural depravities, their difference from vices.

Some things naturally pleaſe all animals; others are naturally pleaſant only to certain tribes; and a third claſs, though not congenial to any ſpecies of animals in their ſound and natural ſtate, are yet agreeable to ſome individuals of the ſpecies, either through certain bodily defects, through perverſe habits, or through pravity of nature. From this laſt kind reſult the fierce and beaſtly propenſities incident to ſome individuals of the human ſpecies; witneſs that ſavage female who delighted in tearing to pieces women with child, and in devouring their young; and thoſe barbarians around Pontus, who feaſt, ſome of them on raw, others on human fleſh, and who make mutual preſents of their children to eke out their horrid entertainments; witneſs alſo the ſhocking ſtories told of the tyrant Phalaris. Theſe are beaſtly depravities, and others, not leſs abominable, are ſometimes produced through diſeaſes and madneſs, as was exemplified in that wretch who ſacrificed and eat his mother; and in the ſlave who killed his companion that he might devour his liver. Some perſons, through diſeaſe or

cuſtom,

custom, delight in plucking out their hair, biting off their nails, or in eating coals or earth. In nearly the same class we may place pæderasty. Such depravities, whether originating in natural corruption, custom, or malady, exceed the limits of vice, and cannot be reproached with epithets characteristic of merely human pravity, except by way of metaphor or similitude. Thus he who should fear even the buzzing of a fly, would be degraded by cowardice more than human, and brutish. A man was afflicted with a malady which made him tremble at the sight of a cat; and there are some nations of distant barbarians who have so little use of their reason, and who are so completely guided by their sensations, that they are scarcely distinguishable from brutes. Madness, epilepsy, and other diseases also subject those afflicted by them to strange perversities of desire; and from the same source of rational nature vitiated and changed, either by malady or custom, we see spring those excesses of folly, cowardice, intemperance, and savageness, which transcend the boundaries of merely human wickedness. We may suppose a man stimulated by brutal appetites, and yet restraining them; Phalaris for instance, restraining his desire to eat a boy, or to abuse him as the instrument of an absurd venereal pleasure; and it may happen on the other hand, that a monster in a human shape may not only feel such propensities, but want self-command to restrain them. In speaking of men, such abominations cannot be called vices simply and properly; they are something worse: depravities originating in disease or brutishness, not springing from the improper indulgence of natural appetite. It is manifest then, that self-command and weakness, continency and incontinency, are conversant about the same subjects with temperance and intemperance, and that there is another species

BOOK VII.

of continency, so called metaphorically, though conversant about different objects.

Chap. 6.

Reasons why voluptuousness is more detestable than irascibility.

Incontinency of anger appears a lesser deformity than incontinency as to pleasure. The reasons of this are, that anger seems to listen to reason, though it does not hear it distinctly; like officious servants, who before they have received their orders fully are in too great a hurry to execute them, and therefore often do it amiss; and dogs which bark at the least noise, before they know whether it proceeds from a friend or an enemy. In the same manner anger, without waiting for reason's last commands, is precipitated through the warmth and quickness of its nature, into over-hasty acts of inconsiderate vengeance; concluding, at every real or supposed insult, that the author of it is worthy of indignation and punishment. The conclusions of anger are indeed often erroneous; but sensuality, without stopping to draw any conclusions at all, at the first prospect of pleasure, rushes to enjoyment; it is therefore the more degrading imperfection of the two, since the sensualist yields to mere appetite, whereas the angry man is led astray by the appearance, at least, of reason. Besides this, it is to be observed, that all our faults seem to be more or less entitled to indulgence and pardon, in proportion as they are more or less natural, or more or less common. But transports of anger are far more natural than excesses in criminal pleasure: the former seem to be congenial to some races of men; as in the family of him who apologized for beating his father by saying, that *he* beat my grandfather, and my grandfather, the father before him; and this little boy, pointing to his son, will beat me when he is able; the fault runs in our blood. Another, when dragged by his son to the door, desired him to stop there, because he had only

only dragged his own father thither. Anger besides is open and undesigning; but the passion of voluptuousness is artful, and therefore unjust. The cestus of Venus is pregnant with wiles.

> "In this was every art and every charm
> To win the wisest and the coldest warm;
> Fond love, the gentle vow, the gay desire,
> The kind deceit, the still reviving fire,
> Persuasive speech and more persuasive sighs,
> Silence that spoke, and eloquence of eyes*."

The incontinency of voluptuousness is therefore worse than that of anger; since it more nearly approaches to deliberate wickedness. It may be observed to the same purpose, that no person afflicted with pain is addicted to insolence; for insults are committed with pleasure, but anger is always accompanied with pain; wherefore insolence, which is of all things the most provoking, is incompatible with anger. The different kinds of incontinency have now been sufficiently explained, the human, the brutish, and that originating in diseases; the first kind only is conversant about the same objects with the vice of intemperance; a thing never ascribed to brutes, except metaphorically, or comparatively; when any class of animals is remarked as peculiarly obnoxious for its lust, voracity, or mischief. For brutes, being incapable of deliberation and election, cannot be deformed by vice, strictly so called; their ferocity, how formidable soever it may be, is a less evil than human vice; since they are destitute of that best principle of man, which, by corruption, becomes the worst; and bad effects flowing from a principle, are thereby rendered more dangerous.

A bad

* Iliad, XIV. v. 247. & seq.

BOOK VII. Chap. 7.

A bad man is capable of doing ten thousand times more mischief than a beast.

With respect to the pleasures and pains of the touch and taste, which it falls within the province of temperance to regulate, we may be so constituted as either to conquer those by which the greater part of mankind are subdued, or to be conquered by those over which the greater part are victorious. The terms, self-command, or continency, and its opposite, incontinency, are most properly applied in speaking of pleasures; the terms, firmness and softness are respectively most applicable to those who shew more than an ordinary strength of mind in resisting pain, or more than an ordinary weakness in yielding to this adversary. The greater proportion of mankind float between the opposite extremes of firmness and softness, continency and incontinency; verging, however, for the most part, rather to the imperfections of incontinency and softness. Since some pleasures are altogether unnecessary, and of these which are necessary, the excesses are carefully to be shunned, he who pursues unnecessary or immoderate pleasures, with deliberate election, and merely for their own sake, is guilty of intemperance; a vice the more incurable, because those who harbour it are not liable to repentance. The vice opposite to intemperance consists in rejecting, through insensibility, even necessary or commendable pleasures: the virtue of temperance lies in the middle between these blameable extremes. With regard to bodily pains, a man may fly from and avoid, even those which ought to be encountered, either through deliberate election, or through mere weakness and infirmity of nature; and as one person is led captive by pleasure, another may be overcome by the painful irritation of desire.

desire. Bad actions are aggravated, when they are committed without impulse from any violent passion. To strike in anger, is an extenuation of the assault; and, in like manner, base actions, done without temptation, are rendered still baser; for, in what shameful excesses would he who commits them be likely to indulge, were he stimulated by fierce desires and headstrong appetites? Intemperance, then, properly so called, is more odious than that weakness which we have called incontinency; and continency, which enables us to conquer pleasures is preferable to that resisting firmness, which merely prevents us from being subdued by pain. Softness, or effeminacy, consists in yielding to slight pains; and is illustrated in him who trails his flowing garments on the ground, rather than submit to the uneasiness of tucking them up; thus exhibiting, without necessity, a picture of disease and infirmity, and thinking that there is no misery in resembling the miserable. That a man should be overcome by great pleasures or great pains, is not a matter of wonder; and his defeat is entitled to pardon, provided his resistance has been vigorous; as is exemplified in the Philoctetes of Theodectes, when bit by the snake, and in the character of Cercyon in Cercinus' play of Alopè. The bursts of agonising pain are as natural on such occasions as those of laughter, when long and earnestly suppressed; an instance of which was seen in Zenophantus. But a man is truly contemptible, when he softly yields to slight and inconsiderable sufferings, unless this happens through disease, or through some natural infirmity in his race. In the kings of Persia, effeminacy is hereditary; and manly firmness is not expected in women. A playful character is more allied to softness than to intemperance; for playfulness is the repose and relax-

BOOK VII.

ation of the mind. The want of self-command originates, either in rashness or in debility. Weak men deliberate, but want strength of mind to persevere in their resolutions; rash men are hurried away by passion, without deliberating at all. Our own preparations and exertions have great power even over our bodily feelings; a man may accustom himself to bear tickling without suffering the uneasy sensation which it excites; and, in the same manner, by calling up pains and pleasures to the mind, by rendering them objects of perception and examination, and moderating by reason the affections which they naturally stir up in us, we may acquire the power of resisting and conquering those formidable enemies, whenever we are obliged actually to contend with them in real life. Men of quick tempers, and those disordered by melancholy, are peculiarly deficient in self-command; the former, through their mobility; and the latter, through that vehemence and impetuosity which renders them slaves to their fancies, how wild soever they may be.

Chap. 8.

He that is properly intemperate, is not given to repentance; because, acting with deliberate election, he remains firm in his perverse purposes. He, on the other hand, who sees the right path, but, through weakness of character, does not pursue it, is liable to repent of his misconduct. His faults therefore are curable[f]; and the mental malady under which he labours, resembles rather the epilepsy, which comes by fits, than the consumption or dropsy, which are unremitting and continual. His weakness, indeed, is specifically different from vice; for the latter can conceal itself, and even assume the mask of virtue; but

[f] Aristotle says, "contrary to what was stated in our doubts;" he doubted how a man who knowingly erred, could ever be cured of his errors. See above, p. 311.

but the former is always undisguised and open. This infirmity of nature is the less inexcusable in proportion to the strength of passion, and the total absence of reflection; and the persons disgraced by it resemble those who are speedily intoxicated and overcome by such a small quantity of wine, as would produce no perceptible effects on ordinary constitutions. Yet mere weakness of character is attended with as bad consequences as vice itself; and is chargeable with the reproach which Demodocus made to the Milesians, that though they were not a stupid people, yet they acted stupidly. In like manner, the weak man acts viciously; but does not, like the intemperate man, give a deliberate preference to vice. His mind, therefore, is still open to persuasion, and his life capable of reformation, since his character is not so totally depraved as to make vice his end and aim. In the affairs of life, this end and aim forms a practical principle, which cannot be taught any more than the axioms and postulates of geometry; and the perception of which results entirely from virtue, either natural or acquired. The temperate man pursues right ends, from which he feels no inclination to deviate; the character of the intemperate man is directly the reverse. Between these two, an intermediate place is held by him, who is hurried into bad actions by the impetuous strength of passion; but whose mind is not so totally vitiated as to make the gratification of sensual appetites the deliberate object of his pursuit. Persons of this description do bad actions; but as the principle of action itself, which is the main thing, still remains sound, their condition is not hopeless. They are indeed better than those who are intemperate on principle; but still they are the objects of great disapprobation; whereas those who, though liable

liable to be moved by corrupt desires, have yet sufficient strength of mind to restrain and curb them, are held praiseworthy; notwithstanding their characters fall far short of that perfect temperance, with which no improper desire is compatible.

Chap. 9.

Difference between incontinency and intemperance is that between weakness and wickedness.

That firmness of mind called continency, implies a resolute adherence to right opinions in opposition to the seductions of appetite: it is totally different from obstinacy, which often yields to passion, but perversely resists the dictates of reason. Obstinacy bears the same analogy to true firmness, that prodigality bears to liberality; and rashness to courage. It is inseparably connected with self-conceit, ignorance, and clownishness. An obstinate man takes pleasure in resisting conviction; victory, not truth, is his aim; and, as if his opinions were laws, he is mortified and provoked by their rejection or reversal. His character, therefore, so far from implying firmness and self-command, is rather a-kin to incontinency; since he is diverted from propriety of thought and action, by the allurements of false pleasure. A man may want stedfastness in his purposes, without being chargeable with incontinency or weakness. Of this we have an example in the character of Neoptolemus in Sophocles' Philoctetes. Pleasure made that young hero change his resolution; but an honourable pleasure, the love of truth, after he had been persuaded by Ulysses to consent to be made an accomplice in falsehood; for incontinency and intemperance do not originate in pleasure simply and absolutely, but in that kind of sensual pleasure which is blameable and base. Men, as we have said before, may be diverted from propriety of conduct by being too little, as well as by being too much affected by bodily pleasures. Both extremes are bad; but as the former is observed in few persons,

and

and on few occaſions, it is not diſtinguiſhed by a name; and the praiſeworthy habit of continency is contraſted with that blameable diſpoſition which conſiſts in being too ſtrongly affected with the deſire of ſenſual gratifications. Temperance and ſelf-command are in common diſcourſe often confounded, from the reſemblance which they bear to each other; but the man deſerving the praiſe of true temperance is above ſelf-command, becauſe his character is ſuch, that he could not derive any enjoyment from baſe or blameable pleaſures. The man endowed with continency or ſelf-command, reſiſts, indeed, and overcomes ſuch pleaſures; but ſtill to him they ſeem to be pleaſures, and he occaſionally feels an inclination to enjoy them. In like manner, intemperance and incontinency are often confounded, for both lead to the ſame voluptuous kind of life; but the former prefers pleaſure on principle; the latter purſues it againſt principle.

Chap. 10.

Additional proofs thereof.

Men deficient in ſelf-command may have cleverneſs but cannot have prudence; which latter is a practical principle, implying not only that we know, but that we do, what is right. In reference to the underſtanding, wit or cleverneſs are nearly the ſame with prudence; but in reference to the will they are very different from it, becauſe prudence always implies a rectitude of moral election; it is therefore abſolutely incompatible with the dominion of vicious paſſions. How ſuch paſſions ſhould be indulged knowingly, has been explained by ſhewing that the knowledge of thoſe who indulge in them, is confined to mere ſpeculations which are not applied; that it is knowledge not rouſed to energy, but lying in a ſluggiſh ſtate of mere capacity, like the knowledge of perſons aſleep or intoxicated. The incontinent man is only wicked by halves,

becauſe

BOOK VII.

becauſe he is not wicked on principle; as he acts without deſign, he is not chargeable with injuſtice. He either does not deliberate at all; or if he deliberates, is like a ſtate which has good laws, but does not obey them; as Anaxandrides reproached the Athenians,

"The ſtate conſults how to make void the law."

The real profligate, on the other hand, obeys laws, and thoſe bad ones. A man is praiſed for ſelf-command, when he excels moſt others in that habit; he is blamed for incontinency, when he yields to temptations, to which moſt men are ſuperior. The incontinency of thoſe who deliberate rightly, but have not firmneſs to perſiſt in their reſolutions, is more curable than that originating in melancholy; which, through its quickneſs and vehemence, impels thoſe affected by it to act without deliberation; and an incontinency depending on cuſtom, is more curable than that which ſprings from nature. For cuſtom is more moveable than nature, ſince the difficulty of changing the former, depends on its reſemblance to the latter.—As the Poet Euenus ſays,

"Habits by long continued care impreſt,
Are ſtrong as nature in the human breaſt."

Let this much ſuffice for a deſcription of the habits of continency and firmneſs on the one hand; of incontinency and ſoftneſs on the other; and on the relations which thoſe habits bear to each other[*].

[*] The four chapters which follow in the original of this work, are mere tranſcripts from the Sixth Book of the Ethics to Eudemus; they treat of pleaſure; a ſubject more fully and more philoſophically explained in the Tenth Book of the Ethics to Nicomachus; of which the reader will find the tranſlation in its proper place.

ARISTOTLE's ETHICS.

BOOK VIII.

INTRODUCTION TO BOOKS VIII. AND IX.

BOOK VIII.

In these Books Aristotle treats of friendship, a subject, he observes, intimately connected with morals; " since friendship, if not a particular virtue, at least shines most conspicuously in the virtuous." He explains the nature of friendship, and resolves the doubts concerning it. He divides it into different kinds, according to the principles in which it originates, and shews how the best kind of friendship may be acquired, maintained, and uninterruptedly enjoyed. Friendships differ, not only according to the sources from which they spring, but according to the condition of the persons by whom they are cultivated. Our author examines the friendships between equals, and the friendships of inferiors with the great; he explains the relations which friendship bears to justice, and how both are modified by political institutions. The rules of friendship are far less precise than those of justice, because the subject to which they apply is far less definite; scarcely any two cases being exactly alike. The author explains what is meant by loving our friends as ourselves, and wherein true self-love consists, in opposition to blameable selfishness. He expatiates on the exquisite delight of virtuous friendship, like a man who (as appears from the history of his life) had warmly felt its charms. The whole treatise, indeed, comprised in the following two Books, is distinguished by just sentiment as much as by solid argument; it is equally full and perspicuous, rejecting paradox, disdaining declamation, and shewing, by an illustrious example, how an important moral subject may be unfolded with scientific accuracy, and impressed with practical energy.

BOOK VIII.

ARGUMENT.

Utility and beauty of friendship.—Qualities by which it is generated.—Three kinds of friendship.—These kinds compared.—Characters most susceptible of friendship.—Unequal friendships.—Their limits.—Friendships founded on propinquity.

BOOK VIII. Chap. 1.

Utility and beauty of friendship.

WE proceed next to treat of friendship, which is either a particular virtue, or which at least shines most conspicuously in the virtuous. It is also most essential to the enjoyment of life, for without friends no one would choose to live, though possessed of all other advantages [a]. The rich and powerful stand most in need of friends, without whom their prosperity could neither be preserved nor enjoyed; for wherein consists the pre-eminence of power and wealth, but in the pleasures of beneficence, which is most laudably exercised towards friends? And how could this precarious pre-eminence be maintained without the steady assistance of friendly adherents? In poverty and other distresses, friendship seems our best, or rather our sole, refuge. It is necessary in youth as the preservative against irreparable

[a] Si quis in coelum adscendisset, naturamque mundi, et pulchritudinem siderum perspexisset, insuavem illam admirationem, &c. "To ascend to heaven, and behold the nature of the universe, and the beauty of the stars, would afford an admiration barren of delight, unless we had some one with whom we might talk of those wonders." Cicero de Amicitia, c. 23. Cicero's Treatise on Friendship abounds with sparkling passages: he has often expanded and embellished Aristotle's remarks; but considered as a philosophical work, it neither shews that deep insight into human nature, nor takes that comprehensive view of the subject, which form the principal merit of the Greek original.

BOOK VIII.

reparable errors; it is neceſſary in old age, as the conſolation amidſt unavoidable infirmities; it is neceſſary in the vigour of manhood, as the beſt auxiliary in the execution of illuſtrious enterpriſes, both ſharpening our thoughts and animating our exertions.

> "By mutual confidence and mutual aid,
> Great deeds are done and great diſcoveries made:
> The wiſe new prudence from the wiſe acquire,
> And one brave hero fans another's fire[b]."

Friendſhip is implanted by nature in parents towards their children, as appears manifeſtly, not only in the human race, but in the various tribes of birds, and in moſt animals; it prevails alſo among thoſe of the ſame claſs or family, but chiefly among men; whence philanthropy is ſo often the juſt ſubject of praiſe. During long and dreary journies, in every man the traveller meets, he beholds the face of a friend; ſuch congenial ſympathy ſubſiſts among the human race! Friendſhip holds mankind together in communities and cities; and lawgivers ſtudy more earneſtly how to promote friendſhip than how to maintain even juſtice itſelf; for concord, which is a-kin to friendſhip, is the perpetual aim of all wiſe legiſlation, which unceaſingly ſtrives to extirpate the ſeeds of diſſenſion and ſedition, as of all things the moſt hoſtile to its views. When concord ripens into friendſhip, the rules of juſtice are ſuperfluous, but juſtice without friendſhip is inſufficient for happineſs; and the moſt perfect and moſt comprehenſive juſtice is that which moſt reſembles friendſhip in its operations and effects. Friendſhip unites beauty with utility, it is not only neceſſary but ornamental; we praiſe it as a virtue; we deſire it as adding luſtre to our characters;

[b] Iliad, X. v. 265. & ſeq.

BOOK VIII.

Doubts concerning the nature of friendship.

characters; and to be a good friend seems to many synonymous with being a good man. Yet various doubts may be started concerning the nature of friendship. Some think that it results from similarity of character and pursuits, and cite the vulgar proverb, "that fowls of a feather flock together." Others maintain that this similarity more naturally begets emulation and hatred; quoting from Hesiod,

> "Potters hate potters; bards quarrel with bards."

They seek the principles of friendship in the high philosophy of nature, saying either with Euripides,

> "The parched earth longs for refreshing showers;
> The skies, heavy with rain, seek to unload
> Their weight of waters on the solid earth."

or with Heraclitus, "that each nature requires and seeks its counterpart:" thus the best harmony results from differences, and thus all things proceed from contrary elements. Other philosophers, particularly Empedocles, assert directly the reverse, "that like draws to like." The consideration of these physical difficulties we at present omit, because they are beside the purpose of this discourse, which is confined to the examination of such questions only as have a reference to life and manners; as whether friendship can subsist among all sorts of persons, or only among the virtuous; whether there are various kinds of friendship specifically different; for those who think there is but one kind, because friendship admits of different degrees of warmth and intensity, trust to a fallacious proof, since other general terms as well as friendship comprehend divisions of things specifically different from each other, and yet partaking more or less, in a stronger or weaker degree, of the characteristic quality

 which

BOOK VIII.

which the general term denotes. But of this subject we have formerly treated [c].

Chap. 2.

The proper objects of friendship, or the qualities by which it is produced.

To illustrate the nature of friendship, we must examine what are the qualities by which it is excited or produced. Whatever is an object of our friendship, must promote either our good, our pleasure, or our utility; and as utility is desirable merely as the cause of what is either good or pleasant, the causes of friendship ultimately resolve themselves into goodness and pleasure; considered, not absolutely in themselves, but in reference to the person in whom the friendship is generated; whether that person has just notions of what is good and pleasant, or takesth ose for *real* goods, which are only *apparent*. The qualities by which friendship is excited are not, when abstractedly considered, able to produce this amiable disposition; for that which is an object of friendship is loved on its own account; and it is necessary that between friends there should subsist a reciprocity of affection. Things inanimate therefore cannot be the object of friendship. A drunkard indeed loves wine; but it would be ridiculous to say that he desires its good, although he indeed wishes for its safety, that he himself may drink it. Mere good-will may subsist on one side, without meeting a return; and persons who have not any opportunity of being acquainted, may mutually bear to each other much good-will; but friendship not only implies a reciprocity of affection, but requires that this reciprocity should be known to both parties.

Chap. 3.

Three kinds of friendship.

Friendship may be distinguished into three kinds, according to the three qualities by which it is produced; and in each of the three there must be a known reciprocity of affection depending on the cause in which the friendship originates. When this cause is utility, men love each other as long as mutual advantage

[c] See Analysis, p. 65. & seq.

vantage results from their friendship: a similar observation is applicable when their affection is founded on pleasure. Neither the utility nor the pleasure which any man affords, constitute an essential and unalterable part of his character; and when on account of those circumstances he himself becomes an object of friendship, he is so, merely by way of accession or appendage to qualities not inseparably connected with him, and which being actually removed, he himself ceases to be an object of friendship. Friendships founded on utility prevail most among persons advanced in years; for interest, not pleasure, is their aim. Manhood, and even youth, often imitate too faithfully the selfish manners of age; choosing their friends according to views of interest. Persons of this character delight but little in each other's society. Even their convivial hospitality has personal advantage for its object. Youthful friendships however, for the most part, are founded on pleasure; for youth is the age of passion, which pursues and prefers present and immediate gratification. But as our pleasures change with our years, youthful friendships are as easily dissolved as they were speedily contracted. Besides, youth is much addicted to love, which is full of mutability, its principal ingredients being pleasure and passion, so that it varies many times in a day. Youthful attachments, while they last, produce close and habitual intimacy, because such friendships have no other foundation than the delight resulting from mutual intercourse. The only perfect friendship subsists among those who resemble each other in virtue, because those who love their friends for their virtue, love them for what is not a temporary appendage, but a permanent essential in their characters. The worth of a virtuous friend is not relative to circumstances, but universal and absolute, comprehending

BOOK VIII.

ing both pleaſure and utility, and uniting all thoſe qualities which either produce friendſhip or render it unalterable; but his ineſtimable value cannot be fairly appreciated, except by thoſe who are his rivals in moral or intellectual excellence; for men delight chiefly in thoſe qualities which reſemble their own. Such friendſhips are rare, becauſe virtuous men are rare; and even *they* cannot perfectly know each other, until, according to the proverb, they have conſumed many buſhels of ſalt together. Time and familiarity are requiſite for proving mutual affection, and for creating that ſteady confidence which cements friendſhip. Friendly acts produce rather an inclination to friendſhip than the thing itſelf, which muſt be the effect of time and habit operating on excellencies reciprocally exerted, and mutually experienced, in thoſe who are reſpectively conſcious of being the objects of love and affection the one to the other.

Chap. 4.

The different kinds of friendſhip compared with reſpect to their durability.

Friendſhips founded on utility and on pleaſure bear a reſemblance to that founded on virtue; for virtuous men afford both pleaſure and utility to their friends. But friendſhips of the former kind are the more durable in proportion as they originate on both ſides in nearly the ſame principle, that is in nearly the ſame kind of pleaſure or utility. Thus, they naturally laſt long between men recommended to each other by their companionable qualities, their wit and pleaſantry; they are leſs durable among lovers, when, as for the moſt part happens, the love on the one ſide ariſes from an admiration of beauty, and on the other from the attentions beſtowed by the lover. When beauty is impaired by years, the admiration ceaſes, the attentions are withheld, and the friendſhip founded on this kind of love is ſometimes at an end; but many times alſo it laſts, when cemented by congenial manners, ſtrengthened and

and confirmed by long habits of familiar intercourſe. Friendſhips founded on the love of gain are of all the moſt unſtable; for perſons governed by this principle are not friends to each other, but both to their reſpective intereſts. All perſons promiſcuouſly, the good, the bad, and thoſe of an intermediate character, may feel towards each other that kind of friendſhip which originates in pleaſure or utility; but good men only can be the objects of friendſhip properly ſo called, independent of circumſtances and reſulting from what is moſt eſſential and moſt unalterable in the character itſelf. The friendſhips of the virtuous are not to be deſtroyed by fortune, nor ſhaken by calumny. What accident or event can change or diſturb confirmed habits of virtue? What calumny can prevail againſt known and approved worth? The friendſhip formed from intereſt therefore, like alliances between ſtates, and thoſe formed from pleaſure, like the friendſhips of our boyiſh years, are called friendſhips only by way of ſimilitude or metaphor; and thoſe metaphorical friendſhips reſemble other metaphors in this, that they do not naturally mingle, or eaſily blend and unite; for how ſeldom do we ſee the ſame perſons friends to each other on the combined principles of profit and of pleaſure? Such then are the different kinds of friendſhip. That formed by the virtuous alone deſerves the name, the others are ſo called merely by a figure of ſpeech.

Chap. 5.

The characters moſt ſuſceptible of friendſhip.

Men procure the denomination of friendly as they do that of virtuous, either from their actions or from their habits. Friendly actions can take place only among thoſe who are members of the ſame ſociety; but the habit of friendſhip may ſubſiſt among perſons widely ſeparated from each other, though, when their

BOOK VIII. their ſeparation continues long, their friendſhip is apt to be forgotten; whence it is ſaid,

"Long abſence often is the bane of friendſhip."

Old perſons, and thoſe of auſtere characters, are, from this principle, but little diſpoſed to friendſhip; becauſe in them both the love of pleaſure, and the power of communicating it, is commonly ſo much weakened, that they have not any great inducement to keep company with each other; for as pleaſure is the great aim of nature, the ſociety of thoſe who are capable neither of affording nor reliſhing it, cannot poſſibly be deſired; and if they occaſion real and poſitive uneaſineſs, will not long be endured. Thoſe who, without delighting in each other's ſociety, are however reſpectively the objects of mutual approbation, may have great good-will towards each other with very little friendſhip; for nothing is ſo productive of friendſhip as the habitual intercourſe of life. The wretched ſeek ſuccour in ſociety, but the happy ſeek ſociety for itſelf, and can leaſt of all men bear ſolitude; but the love of ſociety itſelf is founded on the pleaſure afforded by thoſe with whom we live; which pleaſure implies that their characters be agreeable, and much of the ſame ſtamp with our own. Friendſhip, therefore, as has been often ſaid, prevails chiefly among the virtuous, to whom only that is good and pleaſant, which is good and pleaſant abſolutely and eſſentially, independently of any circumſtances that may concur, or of any conſequences that may follow; and to whom the mutual enjoyment of their correſpondent excellencies is of all things the moſt delightful.

Chap. 6. Friendſhip cannot at

Aged perſons and thoſe of auſtere characters are unfit for friendſhip in proportion to their auſterity, and to their averſion to society. Young people therefore sooner form friendships than the old and austere; who, though they may often bear great good-will to each other, and shew much readiness in mutually conferring the most essential services, are yet slow and cold in sentimental attachment, because they are averse to that social intercourse in which chiefly it originates. Friendship in its highest perfection cannot extend to many; and for a similar reason that it is impossible for us to feel the passion of love for many persons at once. There is an intensity in friendship as well as in love, which naturally confines it to one object. Men have different tastes, each of which has something in it too peculiar to be alike pleased with many; and it is right that it should be so. Friendship, besides, requires long and intimate knowledge, which is not easily obtained of many characters by one person, who cannot live in equal and close familiarity with them all. Friendships of interest or pleasure are indeed speedily contracted, because their offices may be speedily performed, and many are able to fulfil them. Of the two, those of pleasure most resemble true friendship, especially when the pleasure is mutual, and resulting from the same objects and pursuits. Such are the friendships of youth, which are of a warmer and more liberal kind than those formed among money-getting men on the cold principle of interest. Men prosperous in their circumstances prefer pleasure to utility; they choose the society of agreeable friends, since worth itself, joined with harshness and austerity, soon becomes offensive and irksome; but if they loved and preferred, as right reason would direct, agreeable qualities only when ennobled by virtue, they would find in their friends all advantages united. Men invested with power have two distinct classes of friends; the one chosen from taste, the other

once comprehend many objects.

The great have two distinct classes of friends.

BOOK VIII.

other from intereſt. The friends calculated to pleaſe are not qualified to benefit them; for as they ſeek pleaſure diſtinct from virtue, and purſue intereſt diſtinct from honour, merry buffoons are beſt qualified for the firſt purpoſe, and dexterous knaves beſt adapted to the ſecond; the man of virtue alone anſwering the double end of pleaſure and utility. But a virtuous man cannot live in friendſhip with the great unleſs *they* be as much diſpoſed to reſpect his ſuperiority of virtue, as he is diſpoſed to honour their ſuperiority of fortune, becauſe the law of equality, which is the ſoul of friendſhip, would otherwiſe be violated; and as men in power are generally too much intoxicated with their proſperity [e] to make this juſt ſacrifice, they ſeldom enjoy the ineſtimable benefit of virtuous friendſhip. Such then are thoſe kinds of friendſhip in which men interchange either pleaſures or utilities on both ſides, or exchange pleaſure on the one ſide for utility on the other. They reſemble true friendſhip in this, that they are productive of pleaſure or profit; but they differ from it in many other reſpects, and particularly in being eaſily ſhaken by calumny, and eaſily ſubverted by a change in the external circumſtances of thoſe between whom they prevailed.

Chap. 7. Unequal friendſhips: their limits.

Friendſhip, ſtrictly ſo called, requires, as we obſerved, equality; but there is alſo a ſpecies of friendſhip which ſubſiſts between perſons of extremely unequal conditions; namely, that between fathers (or thoſe who hold the place of fathers) and children; huſbands and wives; rulers and thoſe ſubject to their authority. This ſpecies of friendſhip admits of many ſubdiviſions: the friendſhip of a father towards his ſon, differs from that

[e] Non enim ſolum ipſa fortuna cæca eſt, ſed eos etiam plerumque efficit cæcos, quos complexa eſt. "Fortune is not only herſelf blind, but ſhe, for the moſt part, renders thoſe alſo blind whom ſhe embraces." Cicero de Amicitia, c. xv.

that of a husband towards his wife, and that of a king towards his people; it differs also from that of a son towards his father; for the parties standing in this and other relations, have each of them their respective offices and their respective duties; the habitual performance of which can alone give stability to their friendship. When the pre-eminence is greatly on one side, whether in the power of bestowing profit or pleasure, the friendship ought to be greater on the other, in nearly the same proportion, that the rules of equal justice may thus be maintained. But equality in point of justice consists primarily in this, that each man should have his due: tha the shares should be nearly equal in quantity, is only a consequence that sometimes follows from this rule; for when the persons are equal in worth, then only their shares should be equal in value. But in point of friendship, equality in quantity or worth is a primary consideration; for between persons extremely unequal as to virtue, power, wealth, and other causes productive of distinction, friendship cannot easily subsist. The gods are the great benefactors of mankind, but they are far too exalted for our friendship. Kings do not choose their friends among the lowest classes of their people: nor do men eminently distinguished by virtue and wisdom, associate with persons of no consideration or merit. It is impossible accurately to ascertain the precise limits beyond which the elevation of the one party becomes too great to admit of friendship with his inferior. The friendship may still subsist, after many advantages are taken from the one and accumulated on the other. But with the exaltation of the latter to divinity, the relation of friendship would unquestionably cease [d]; wherefore it is doubted, whether a man can wish for the

[d] Does this bear any reference to the friendship between Aristotle and his pupil Alexander?

BOOK VIII.

the deification of his friend, since this would be to wish for the destruction of their friendship. Perhaps he does not even wish for him all human advantages; for a man desires that every good thing may happen to his friend, provided only what is a good to his friend be not an evil to himself; and it would be a great evil to himself to lose a good friend.

Chap. 8.

The ordinary foundations of unequal friendships.

Most people, through vanity, wish rather to be beloved than to love. They are therefore fond of flatterers; who are, or rather pretend to be, a kind of unequal friends, that love more than they are loved. Love is near akin to honour, which most men desire, not indeed for its own sake, but for the advantages which accrue from it. They delight in marks of distinction from the great, which they regard as pledges of future and more solid bounties. Those who are ambitious of honour from persons well acquainted with them, and whose characters are esteemed for equity, wish thereby to confirm their good opinion of themselves. They delight in thinking favourably of their own characters, in consequence of this impartial verdict in their favour; and the pleasure which they take in being the objects of love and approbation, is the cause for which they desire external marks of honour and respect. To be loved, therefore, is better than to be honoured, and friendship is still more than honour ultimately desirable. The former however consists more in loving than in being loved; in proof of which we may allege the behaviour of mothers who give out their children to nurse, pleased with loving them and knowing that they are well, without expecting or desiring any return of affection. To love one's friends is a common topic of praise; and the *virtue* of friendship depends on the strength and propriety of our affection, which can alone render it permanent, levelling all those inequalities, and removing all those obstacles which

BOOK VIII.

which might interrupt its duration. Such is the friendſhip of virtuous men, who being ſtable in themſelves, remain ſtable in their relations to each other; neither requiring nor admitting any aſſociation with the worthleſs. Theſe laſt are inconſtant in all their ways, and there can be no ſtability in their relations to each other, ſince none of them acts uniformly or conſiſtently, nor remains long like unto himſelf. Their friendſhip is but a league in villainy, which, for the moſt part, ends when it ceaſes to be profitable: when pleaſure conſpires with profit it is naturally more durable. The friendſhips reſulting from contraries reſolve themſelves into the principle of utility; as thoſe between the poor and rich, the learned and ignorant; for a man is always ready to give ſomething in exchange for that of which he ſtands in need. In the ſame claſs we may place, without much violence, the handſome and the ugly, the lover and the object of his affection. Wherefore ſome lovers juſtly incur ridicule when they expect to meet with a return of love ſimilar to their own. Were their perſons calculated to inſpire a mutual paſſion, their expectation would be reaſonable; but when they are the reverſe, their pretenſions are ridiculous. Perhaps contraries do not primarily affect each other, but both of them are fond of that intermediate condition which is preferable to either. Thus what is dry loves moiſture, only that it may attain an intermediate ſtate; and that which is warm affects cold, only that it may be reduced to a due temperature[e]. But ſuch queſtions may be omitted, as beſide the purpoſe of the preſent diſcourſe.

Chap. 9.

Of the relation which friendſhip bears to juſtice.

Juſtice and friendſhip, as we already obſerved, ſeem to belong to the ſame perſons, and to be converſant about the ſame objects. They are both found in every partnerſhip or community,

[e] See Analyſis, p. 111. & ſeq.

munity, even among those who sail in the same vessel, and those who fight under the same standard; and in proportion to the closeness of the partnership or community, the more closely and intimately is the friendship cemented. The proverb says rightly, "that all things are common among friends;" for friendship results from the community of goods, advantages, and pleasures; it is most perfect among brothers and companions; and in the same proportion as the ties of the partnership or connexion are loosened, and fewer things are common, the friendship becomes less intimate, and even the rules of justice seem less binding. It is a more heinous crime to rob our friends than our fellow-citizens, and our fellow-citizens than strangers. Not to succour a brother in distress is more odious than to refuse similar assistance to a stranger; and to strike a father is the most atrocious of crimes. Friendship and justice thus march hand in hand, and the vigour of the one is followed by equal intensity in the other. But all other connexions and partnerships are but parts of the great partnership of political society, which utility first collected and still holds together. Public utility therefore is that chief and ultimate aim of which wise legislators never lose sight. To promote particular branches of this utility, all inferior associations are formed; fleets sail, armies march; their aim is wealth or victory; to invade, conquer, and plunder; to subdue provinces, and storm cities. Even the peaceful communities of tribes and wards, and those mirthful assemblies which meet to feast, to drink, and to dance, depend on the same principle; for legislators have not merely present and temporary advantage in view, they look farther, to the permanent comfort and sure enjoyment of life, and therefore establish solemnities during which human industry may

repose

repose from past labours, and prepare for future exertions, by which the gods are honoured, and the heart of man is gladdened. The ancient solemnities of this kind were held towards the end of autumn, the season of greatest leisure, when men having gathered in the earth's productions, might offer the first fruits to the gods. Political society, then, comprehends all other partnerships or associations; from the varieties of which the different kinds of friendship result.

BOOK VIII.

Chap. 10.

Of the different forms of government.

There are three just forms of government, each of which is liable to deviate into a corrupt form, which is a counterfeit resemblance of the former. The just forms are royalty, aristocracy, and what may be called timocracy, because all men enjoying a certain income are entitled to a share in the government. This last, most writers distinguish by the general name of polity, or a republic. It is the worst of all legal governments, as royalty is the best. Tyranny is the corrupt resemblance of royalty, for both forms are monarchical; but they differ most widely, a tyrant consulting only his own advantage, a king only that of his people; for the latter does not deserve the name, if he be not in all things pre-eminent, independent, and all-sufficient in himself; so that with him personal considerations being superfluous, he can have no other reasonable pursuit but that of the public good. If kings are not of this description, they might as well be chosen by lot. Tyrants, on the other hand, pursue only their own interest, and their government is the worst of all, since it stands in direct opposition to royalty, which is of all the best. As kings may be corrupted into tyrants, so aristocracies degenerate into oligarchies, through the corruption of the magistrates, who make an unjust distribution of honours and emoluments, of which they usurp and retain the greater

greater part for themselves, accumulating enormous wealth as the instrument of exorbitant power, and continually narrowing, through selfishness, the basis of the government. Timocracy naturally degenerates into democracy, which is nearly akin to it; since whenever men of limited fortunes are entitled to share the government, power will have a natural tendency to fall into the hands of the people. Democracy therefore is a less deviation from what is called a republic, than tyranny is from royalty, or oligarchy from aristocracy; and in this particular circumstance, it is less depraved and odious than the other two vicious forms of government. Of political revolutions we find the resemblances, and, as it were, the patterns in what passes in families. The paternal authority is the model for that of kings, for children are their fathers' dearest concern. Whence Homer addresses Jupiter by the appellation of father, denoting the near affinity between royal and paternal power. But in Persia fathers are tyrants, treating their sons as slaves; and slaves are treated merely as best suits the interest of their masters. This may be agreeable to the nature and principles of servitude, but the Persian system, in extending these principles to children, is vitious in the extreme; for different descriptions of persons require different modes of governance. Domestic authority is the best model for aristocracy, for the authority of a husband is founded on the superiority of his abilities and his virtues. He exercises those functions which this superiority enables him best to perform, leaving to female care those offices which women are best qualified to fulfil; since if he usurped all management to himself, his equitable aristocracy would degenerate into an unlawful and rigid oligarchy. When women, being rich heiresses, acquire thereby more than their due share of power, their authority alſo originates in an unjuſt oligarchical principle, ſince, in their prepoſterous pre-eminence, wealth is preferred to worth: the gifts of fortune, to the diſtinctions of nature. Timocracy reſembles the equal commonwealth of brothers, among whom there is no other diſtinction than that made by a ſlight difference of age; for when this difference is very great, brotherly friendſhip cannot eaſily ſubſiſt. Democracy reſembles thoſe families which are without a head; or in which all avail themſelves of the maſter's weakneſs, to aſſert equality, and to defy controul.

Chap. 11.

Of the variations thereby occaſioned in the nature and intenſity of friendſhip.

Friendſhip, as well as juſtice, varies with the different forms of polity; ſince both ultimately depend on the different relations in which men ſtand to each other in ſociety. The relation of a king to his ſubjects, is that of a benefactor to thoſe benefited by his care. He provides for the welfare of his people, as a ſhepherd does for that of his flock: whence Homer calls Agamemnon the ſhepherd of the people. Of a ſimilar kind is the relation of a father to his children, but pre-eminent in the magnitude of benefits, ſince he is the cauſe of their exiſtence itſelf, which ſeems of the utmoſt moment, as well as of their education and nurture. A father is naturally a king in his own family; and the ſame holds with regard to more remote anceſtors and their deſcendants, the former of whom are entitled to honour from the latter, and therefore the friendſhip between them is not that of equals, but is modified by the natural and indelible ſuperiority of the one party to the other. The relation of huſband to wife is ſimilar to that which prevails in ariſtocracies between the magiſtrates and citizens. The honours and advantages belonging to the former, reſult from the ſuperiority of their abilities and virtues. The huſband's honour is

BOOK VIII.

pre-eminent not abſolute, he has his duties as well as his rights; both parties have their allotted functions, namely, thoſe which are beſt adapted to their reſpective characters. The relation of brothers is that of equal companions, reſulting from the near ſimilitude of their ſtrength and ſtature, their common education, and ſimilar manners. They reſemble a republic, ſtrictly ſo called, in which the citizens are treated juſtly, when they are all treated alike; and as they cannot all rule at once, the government is managed by rotation. Their juſtice conſiſts in equality, and their friendſhip is that of equals. In corrupt governments there is little juſtice, and therefore but little friendſhip. Tyranny, which is the greateſt corruption of all, ſcarcely admits of any friendſhip at all. Since there is nothing common between the ſovereign and ſubject, there is not any room for juſtice, nor therefore for friendſhip. The relation of a tyrant to his ſubjects is that of an artiſt to an inſtrument, of the ſoul to the body, of a maſter to a ſlave. The intereſt and ſafety of all theſe ſubſervient things are conſulted by thoſe who make uſe of them; but there cannot be any friendſhip nor any juſtice between living and inanimate objects, becauſe they cannot enjoy any thing in common. Neither can men have friendſhips with horſes, cattle, or ſlaves, conſidered merely as ſuch; for a ſlave is a living inſtrument, and an inſtrument a lifeleſs ſlave. Yet conſidered as a man, a ſlave may be an object of friendſhip; for certain rights ſeem to belong to all thoſe capable of participating in law and engagement. A ſlave then, conſidered as a man, may be treated juſtly or unjuſtly, and therefore may be a friend or an enemy. There is little friendſhip and little juſtice in tyrannies; but moſt of both in republics, becauſe, among equals there are moſt common rights, and moſt common enjoyments.

Friendſhip,

BOOK VIII. Chap. 12.

Of friendships founded on propinquity of blood.

Friendſhip, then, reſults from the community of rights and enjoyments among perſons living in the ſame commonwealth, belonging to the ſame tribe or diſtrict, ſailing in the ſame veſſel; in which, and all ſimilar caſes, the parties ſeem mutually engaged to each other to maintain and uphold their reciprocal advantages. The friendſhip ariſing from hoſpitality is of the ſame nature; but that depending on propinquity in blood, or congeniality of character, may perhaps be referred to a different principle. Friendſhips between relations, though they branch out into many kinds, may be all traced to one ſource, namely, the affection between parents and children. Parents love their children as parts of themſelves, and children love their parents as the ſource from which they ſpring. The love of the former is the ſtrongeſt, becauſe they better know their children for their own, than the children can know them for their parents; becauſe the production more belongs to its author, than the author to his work; and becauſe parents know and love their children for a longer time, that is, immediately from their birth, whereas children cannot begin to love their parents till they become capable of perception and intelligence. The love of parents for their children is merely an expanſion of ſelf-love, for they ſtill regard their children as parts of themſelves; but children have, in their own minds, a ſeparate and independent perſonality, diſtinct from that of their parents, which they are inclined, however, to revere as the fountain of their blood. From the common relationſhip of brothers to the ſame father, they become mutually related to each other; wherefore they are ſaid to come from the ſame blood, which flows in different ſtreams, or from the ſame ſtock, which ſpreads into different branches. Their friendſhip is confirmed by nearneſs of age, ſameneſs of

BOOK VIII.

education, and ſimilarity of purſuits. They are companions as well as brothers, and therefore warmed with all that affection for each other, which conſort and ſociety is calculated to inſpire. The connexion between other relations originates in the ſame principle, and is more or leſs intimate in proportion to their proximity to the common ſource. Children ſhould love their parents as men do the gods, ſince they are to them the authors of the greateſt benefits; their life, nurture, and education; and the friendſhip between them, from their continual intercourſe of life, contains far more than any other, whatever is ſweeteſt and moſt uſeful. Brothers, we have ſaid, are companions, whoſe fellowſhip will be the more intimate, in proportion to the ſimilarity of their virtuous characters and honourable purſuits, and to the confirmation which the affection of their early years derives from confidence approved by time and experience. The friendſhip between more diſtant kinſmen depends on the ſame circumſtances, according to which it will either invigorate or decay. That between huſband and wife is moſt ſtrongly prompted and enforced by nature itſelf; for domeſtic ſociety is more natural than even the political; ſince it is prior and more neceſſary, being eſſential to the preſervation of the ſpecies, and common to all kinds of animals. But with the inferior tribes, this ſociety is limited by the ſole end of reproduction; in man it extends to all the offices of life, which naturally divide themſelves between huſband and wife, each ſupplying what their reſpective qualities beſt enable them to furniſh for the accommodation and comfort of the other. The induſtry and excellencies of each are thus brought into the common ſtock of domeſtic happineſs, which their diſtinctive virtues are calculated wonderfully to augment, ſo that this kind of

Between huſband and wife.

friendſhip

friendſhip is recommended and ſtrengthened by every circumſtance of pleaſure as well as of utility. Their children too form a new and powerful tie, being a common good, in which they mutually ſhare; and which has the ſtrongeſt effect in binding them indiſſolubly together. The varieties of friendſhip thus depend on the various kinds of juſtice, which themſelves reſult from the multiplied relations of men in civil ſociety. For very different rights and very different duties have place between friends, ſtrictly ſo called, and thoſe who are partners in the ſame concern, companions in the ſame ſtudies, or who are mere ſtrangers the one to the other.

Chap. 13.

Diſputes between friends, how they ought to be adjuſted.

There are then three kinds of friendſhip; each of which depends on a different principle, and in each of which the friendſhip may ſubſiſt either between equals, or between perſons extremely unequal, not only as to their reſpective worth and dignity, but as to the relative importance of their friendſhip to each other. When the friendſhip ſubſiſts between equals, equal attentions and an equal degree of affection ought, as much as poſſible, to be aimed at; but when the pre-eminence is greatly on one ſide, the affection and attentions of the inferior ought to riſe in the ſame proportion. The friendſhip founded on utility is that which is by far the moſt likely to produce between the parties mutual altercation, and often mutual reproach. When the connecting principle is virtue, friends are eager to benefit each other; the only rivalſhip between them is, who ſhall do to the other moſt good, and he who gains the victory in this amicable conteſt, is ſo far from creating ill-will in his friend, that he only provokes him to new works of kindneſs. Nor are mutual accuſations frequent where the ſole end of the friendſhip is pleaſure. While this purpoſe is attained, the parties keep com-

pany

BOOK VIII.

pany with each other; and when it is not, a mutual ſeparation is ſo eaſy, that complaint would be ridiculous. But when utility is the principle, refuſals on one ſide muſt be as frequent as exactions on the other, and both parties will think they are ill treated, becauſe each expects more than his due. As law is either written or unwritten, ſo friendſhip founded on utility is either legal or moral; the firſt is where exact returns are ſpecified, as if you give to me that, I will give to you this; or where the agreement is more liberal than merely from hand to hand, and allowing a ſpace of time to be interpoſed before the ſervice performed on the one ſide is requited by an equal ſervice on the other. When friendly confidence is repoſed by one party in the other, an action at law is not granted by ſome nations, for the fulfilling even of conditions, the reality of which admits not of any uncertainty; for to them it ſeems equitable, that he who has imprudently truſted to the good faith of another, ſhould not be entitled to correct by law the error of his own credulity. The moral friendſhip founded on utility takes place, where ſomething is given, or ſome ſervice is rendered, without the ſpecification of any thing, or any ſervice to be given or done in return. Yet by the party who has conferred the benefit, an equal, or even more than equal return is on many occaſions expected; and when this is not made, he complains of ill treatment. His complaint is occaſioned by what occaſions almoſt all other complaints of breach of friendſhip, his unſteadineſs of principle, giving liberally, but craving like a niggard: affecting the praiſe of generoſity in the firſt part of the tranſaction, but ſhewing in the laſt that he is guided merely by intereſt; for moſt men, though they love what is honourable, prefer what is uſeful. It is honourable to do good without expecting a return; it is useful to have every good action requited with interest. Yet those who have received favours ought to requite them according to their ability, when such requital is desired by their benefactors, for no man's friendship can be obtained against his will; so that when we have met with an act of generous friendship, from one who afterwards appears not to entertain for us any friendly disposition, we ought doubtless, when able, to make a suitable return; when this return is not in our power, even the interested benefactor himself would not be so unreasonable as either to require or expect it. When favours are conferred, we must consider therefore, both the man and his motives, in order to determine whether they ought to be returned, and in what manner the return should be made. It is sometimes a matter of doubt by what standard this return should be measured, whether by the benefactor's good will, or by the advantage therefrom resulting to the person benefited. The latter is often inclined to extenuate his obligations, and to think the favours which he has received both slight in themselves, and such as many others would have been ready to bestow on him. The benefactor on the other hand, represents them as the greatest favours that he could possibly have done, such as none other would have conferred, and enhanced too by being bestowed in a moment of danger, or some other exigency. Since utility is the sole basis of such friendships, and of the actions proceeding from them, ought not the advantage accruing to the person obliged, to be regarded as the just standard of the obligation incurred, and of the return to be made? For *his* exigency required relief; a relief afforded to him in expectation of an equal return; and the assistance bestowed on the one hand is exactly measured by the benefit

BOOK VIII.

benefit received on the other. His return therefore ought to be equal to this benefit, or greater, which will make his conduct laudable and honourable. In virtuous friendships there is not any room for such complaints. In them intentions, not consequences, form the standard of obligation; for, as we have often observed, the deliberate election of the will is the principle by which all questions concerning virtue and morals must be determined.

Chap. 14.

The same subject continued.

Unequal friendships are extremely productive of altercations and differences, each party desiring to have more than his due, which has a tendency to disturb, and finally dissolve concord. He who is pre-eminent in virtue and ability, claims a proportional share of regard and affection; thinking that men should always be considered suitably to their characters. In the same manner, he who is most useful, expects to be loved and regarded in proportion to his utility; saying, that friendship would be a burden if it were not returned on the one side proportionally to the benefits conferred on the other. They think that the same rule is applicable to friendship which holds in a partnership in trade, where he who employs most stock also receives most profit. The needy man holds a very different language, saying, that it is the duty of a friend to assist his friend in distress; and asking what benefit could otherwise result from the so much envied friendship of the good and great. Both parties are partly in the right, since both ought to have the advantage; the good and great in point of honour, the inferior and indigent in point of gain; for honour is the meed of beneficent virtue, and gain is the cure of distressing poverty. This rule obtains in states. Those who benefit the public, are honoured by the public, for honour is a public reward; but to expect

expect from the public, both great honours and great gains is highly unreasonable; since the public would thereby submit to an inferiority of advantage in both points at once; a disgraceful inferiority which every individual would spurn. For reciprocal and proportional favours equalise and preserve friendship, the good and great benefiting their friends as to their characters or their fortunes, the needy inferior giving in return the only thing he can give, honour, and even of this not always a full proportion; since it is impossible sufficiently to honour the gods and our parents: but those are commended who do it to the best of their power; for the returns of friendship must be limited by possibility. Wherefore it is not allowable for a son to renounce his father, though the latter may renounce the former. For the son has to pay obligations, which are too great for him ever to discharge; he must always therefore remain a debtor. But the father, on the other hand, to whom the debt is due, may discard and abandon a worthless son, though he will seldom do it, but for excess of wickedness; since both paternal affection and natural humanity strongly oppose so cruel a measure[e].

[e] The subject of this and the following Book is less fully treated in the seven last chapters of the second book of the Magna Moralia; and in the thirteen first chapters of the seventh book of the Ethics to Eudemus.

ARISTOTLE's ETHICS.

BOOK IX.

ARGUMENT.

Friendſhip does not admit of preciſe rules.—Diſſolution of friendſhip when juſtifiable.—Analogy between our duties to ourſelves, and thoſe to our friends.—Happineſs of virtue.—Wretchedneſs of vice.—Good-will.—Concord.—Exquiſite delight of virtuous friendſhip.

BOOK IX. Chap. 1.

According to what rules the returns of friendſhip may be beſt eſtimated.

WHERE friends poſſeſs qualities totally diſſimilar, and extremely different in value, their friendſhip, as we have ſaid, muſt be equaliſed and maintained by a due obſervance of thoſe rules of proportion which obtain in the commercial intercourſe of ſociety; where the ſhoemaker and weaver, and other artizans, exchange the productions of their ſeveral manufactures according to their reſpective values. That this might be done conveniently, the uſe of money was eſtabliſhed, which ſerved as a common meaſure, with which all other things were compared, and by which their relative worth was eſtimated. Lovers often accuſe the objects of their affection, that they do not meet their warmth of love with equal ardour, when perhaps there is nothing in themſelves that is at all lovely. The perſons beloved, on the other hand, often accuſe their admirers, that

BOOK IX.

that they once made to them the moſt magnificent promiſes, but now totally deceive them. The origin of theſe complaints is, that the friendſhip of the one party is founded on pleaſure; that of the other on utility: on delight which the one has no longer the power to excite, and benefit which the other has no longer the means to confer; ſo that as the cauſes of ſuch friendſhips are variable and inconſtant, the friendſhips themſelves muſt be deſtitute of ſtability; which is the caſe with all others, except thoſe ſubſiſting between virtuous men in conſequence of their congeniality of characters. Thoſe who are friends through intereſt, not only are likely to diſagree, when either of them ceaſes to meet with a return, but when the return is not ſuch as he either wiſhed or expected; for an improper return is conſidered as none at all. We have an example of this in *him* who promiſed a muſician that he ſhould be paid according to his performance, and being aſked next day for the reward which he had promiſed, ſaid that it had already been beſtowed, ſince he had given one pleaſure in return for another. But profit, not pleaſure, was the return which the muſician expected; for in order to obtain what they want, men willingly part with that which is either ſuperfluous, or which they can moſt eaſily ſpare; which is the baſis of all commercial intercourſe. It is aſked, who ought to aſcertain the meaſure of the return, he who has performed the ſervice, or he who has received it? The former ſeems to commit his intereſt to the diſcretion of the latter: as Protagoras is ſaid to have done, for he deſired his diſciples to eſtimate the value of what they had learned, and to pay him accordingly. In ſuch caſes, ſome approve the rule, "clear bargains make ſure friends." Thoſe who receive payment in advance, and then perform nothing worthy

worthy of the magnificence of their promiſes, are liable to the reproach of injuſtice; a reproach which perhaps the ſophiſts neceſſarily incur, ſince unleſs they received their payment in advance, nobody would think their labours worthy of any pecuniary remuneration. In virtuous friendſhips, there is not any room for complaint, becauſe each party deſires only the heart and affections of his friend; and the only contention between them is, which ſhall be productive of moſt good to the other. Such is the friendſhip that ought to ſubſiſt between thoſe who teach and thoſe who ſtudy philoſophy, the value of which cannot be appreciated in money; and to the teachers of which no adequate honours can be aſſigned. Their ſcholars muſt honour them as they do their parents and the gods; not ſufficiently, for that is impoſſible; but in proportion to the extent of their ability; ſhewing to them all the reſpect they can, ſince they never can ſhew to them enough. In thoſe friendſhips where certain and full returns are expected, it is deſirable that they ſhould prove ſatisfactory to both parties; but when this cannot take place, it ſeems juſt as well as neceſſary, that he who has received the favour ſhould determine the return moſt proper to be made; becauſe he is the beſt judge of the value of the advantage which he has received, and of the value of the pleaſure which he has enjoyed. It is thus in thoſe bargains where confidence is repoſed by the one party in the other; for the fulfilment of which, the party diſappointed is not entitled in ſome countries to any legal redreſs; his cauſe muſt ſtand or fall according to the good faith or diſhoneſty of him in whom he voluntarily confided. This rule is founded on the principle, that he who has received a favour is better qualified to aſcertain its value, than he who conferred it: for men eſtimate too highly the

BOOK IX.

the favours which they beſtow, as they are apt to do all good things which proceed from themſelves. The perſon firſt benefited decides therefore what return he ſhould make, becauſe he beſt knows the value of the benefit which he has received; but this benefit is perhaps more juſtly eſtimated by the value which he ſet on it, while it was ſtill an object of his deſire, than by that which he continues to ſet on it after it has been put into his poſſeſſion.

Chap. 2.

That it is impoſſible to aſſign preciſe rules for the proper exerciſe of friendſhip.

A doubt may be ſtarted as to filial friendſhip, whether fathers ought in all things to be obeyed? In matters reſpecting health, ought a ſon to follow the advice of his father or his phyſician? In electing a general, ought he to prefer to him a perſon ſkilled in war? In the ſame manner it may be doubted, whether favours are beſt beſtowed on friends, or on men of merit; and whether we ought to be grateful to our benefactors or liberal to our friends, when we have not the means of exerciſing both gratitude and liberality. All theſe queſtions are too indefinite to admit of ſuch general ſolutions as may be practically uſeful; becauſe there is not any one caſe exactly ſimilar to another, but each is marked by circumſtances peculiar to itſelf, and diſtinguiſhable in their degrees of magnitude, as well as of propriety or neceſſity. It is manifeſt in general, that all advantages ought not to be accumulated on any one individual, and that before we are liberal to our friends, our debts of gratitude ought to be diſcharged towards our benefactors. Yet this rule will not always hold, as in the caſe of a man ranſomed from robbers, and whoſe ranſomer, perhaps a perſon of no value, ſhould afterwards ſtand in need of the ſame favour, or, at leaſt, ſhould demand back his money. In both caſes, the man ranſomed, if his own father happens alſo to be in captivity, will prefer ranſoming his father, if his fortune does not enable him to acquit both obligations at once. Though it is ſaid in general, therefore, that every kindneſs ought to meet with its due return, yet caſes may be propoſed in which generoſity is, in point of propriety or neceſſity, a paramount duty even to gratitude itſelf. Sometimes the ſame favours, done by different perſons, are of very different values; and the benefactor therefore has not always a right to expect a preciſely ſimilar return. When a bad man obliges a good one, or a knave lends money to a man of property and probity, the perſons obliged may, with propriety, decline to return exactly ſimilar favours; ſince thoſe favours are, in different circumſtances, of very different values. The knave by lending runs no riſk of loſing his money, but the honeſt man would run this riſk by lending to a knave; nay, ſhould he only ſuſpect him of being either a knave or a ſpendthrift, he will not act abſurdly in refuſing to return his favour in kind. It is evident therefore, as we have often obſerved, that all rules concerning the paſſions and actions of men are preciſe, only in proportion as the ſubjects to which they relate are definite. We ought not (to anſwer the queſtion firſt ſtarted) to have deference, in all particulars, even to our fathers, ſince all kinds of ſacrifices are not offered to Jupiter. Our parents, brethren, companions, and benefactors, are ſeverally entitled to their reſpective marks of kindneſs and regard. This is ſufficiently indicated by general practice; for relations, principally, are invited to aſſiſt at marriages and funerals, as things eſſentially intereſting to the whole family, and all its branches. To provide for the ſubſiſtence of our parents, who are the cauſes of our being, is a duty as indiſpenſable, and ſtill more honourable, than even that of providing for our own. We ought to honour

BOOK IX.

honour them too as we honour the gods; but each parent is entitled to diſtinctive marks of our reſpect, a reſpect different in kind from that beſtowed on perſons unrelated to us, but eminently conſpicuous for their abilities or virtues. Our ſeniors, in proportion to their years, ought to be treated with more or leſs deference. With companions, familiarity and full freedom of ſpeech is allowable; with kinſmen, neighbours, fellow-citizens, in a word, with every deſcription of perſons with whom we are connected, it is incumbent on us to behave ſuitably to the relations of affinity or utility in which thoſe perſons ſtand to ourſelves, as well as to their own perſonal merit and inherent virtues. When the relations between others and ourſelves are ſtrong and intimate, the rules of our behaviour towards them are more eaſily defined; the ſtrict limits of our duty are with more difficulty aſcertained towards perſons remotely and faintly connected with us. Yet we muſt not be deterred by this difficulty from inveſtigating thoſe rules of conduct which will enable us to behave towards all men with propriety.

Chap. 3.

Juſtifiable grounds for the diſſolution of friendſhips.

Doubts are ſtarted concerning the diſſolution of friendſhip between perſons whoſe characters no longer remain the ſame, or at leaſt no longer continue to bear the ſame relation to each other. Where friendſhips are contracted for the ſake of pleaſure or utility, it is not wonderful that when neither utility accrues to the one party, nor pleaſure to the other, ſuch friendſhips ſhould of courſe be ſubverted; for the foundations are deſtroyed on which only they ſtood. But a man may juſtly complain of bad faith in him who affected to cheriſh his character and his virtues, while intereſt or pleaſure were at bottom the ſole grounds of his regard; for differences between friends chiefly proceed from this, that they think their friendſhip founded

founded on one principle, when it is really founded on another. When therefore a man is deceived, and thinks without reaſon that he is loved for his character and his virtues, he has himſelf only to complain of; but he may complain of the duplicity of his pretended friend, when the hypocriſy of the latter is the ſource of his own miſtake; and he may complain of him more juſtly than men do of coiners and clippers, ſince he is defrauded by him in an object more valuable than money. But when our friend changes his manners, and contracts by evil communication a depravity of character, ought we ſtill to regard him with affection? Or, is it impoſſible to love that which ceaſes to be amiable? "Like," we have ſaid, "draws to like;" and a good man neither can nor ought to love a bad one. Are we then inſtantly to renounce and forſake him? Not unleſs he has unalterably renounced and forſaken his character; for while he is not totally incorrigible, it is our duty to endeavour to reform his morals, a thing incomparably more important than alleviating his pecuniary diſtreſs, and alſo more peculiarly the work of friendſhip. To detach ourſelves entirely from a friend who becomes worthleſs, has nothing in it unreaſonable; ſince he is not in fact the ſame man with whom we contracted the friendſhip; and when we find that there is not any hope of his ever again becoming ſuch, we naturally wiſh to have done with him. But what ſhall we ſay when one of the friends remains what he was, and the other changes for the better. Can their friendſhip continue to ſubſiſt? Or is this alſo impoſſible? The queſtion will be beſt anſwered by propoſing a caſe where the difference is great in the extreme. Of two perſons who are friends in their early years, the one may remain a child in underſtanding through life, and the other may become a man of the moſt diſtin-

BOOK IX.

diſtinguiſhed abilities. What friendſhip can ſubſiſt between ſuch different characters, who can neither take any pleaſure in each other's ſociety, nor have any occupations and purſuits in common? As all congeniality of mind is at end between them, their friendſhip, it ſhould ſeem, muſt ceaſe. Yet will the ſuperior, if he is a man of humanity, treat the friend of his youth very differently from what he would do an abſolute ſtranger. The remembrance of his early affection will ſtill cling to his heart; and he will never entirely abandon an ancient attachment, unleſs on account of extreme worthleſſneſs in him who was its object.

Chap. 4.

The analogy between the duties which we owe to ourſelves, and thoſe which we owe to our friends.

The duties which we owe to our friends, ſeem analogous to thoſe which each individual willingly pays to himſelf. We ought, it is ſaid, to wiſh their good, or what appears to us to be ſuch, and to promote it to our beſt ability, merely on their own account. With this kind of diſintereſted affection, mothers are animated towards their children, and thoſe friends towards each other, between whom ſome diſguſt has ariſen which, though it interrupts their intercourſe, does not deſtroy their mutual kindneſs. Others ſay that friends muſt ſpend much of their time together, have the ſame inclinations and purſuits, and ſympathiſe with each other in their joy as well as in their ſorrow. On whichever or how many ſoever of thoſe conditions friendſhip principally depends, we ſhall find that all of them belong to the affections by which a good man is animated towards himſelf; and by which all men are animated in proportion as they either approximate, or only think they approximate, to an honourable and praiſeworthy character; which, in queſtions concerning human nature, is juſtly conſidered as the ſole unerring ſtandard.

The happineſs of virtue.

The virtuous man only is at peace within himſelf,

himſelf, ſince all the powers of his mind are actuated by the ſame motives, and conſpire to the ſame end: always aiming at good, real and intrinſic, the good of his intellectual part. To him exiſtence is a benefit, which he earneſtly wiſhes may be preſerved, eſpecially the exiſtence of the thinking principle within him, which is peculiarly himſelf; for every individual ſtrives after its own good, real or apparent; which in the virtuous man only coincide: but could an individual love its change into ſomething quite different from itſelf, the good of the latter would be to the former a matter of ſlight concern. In Deity all goods are accumulated, becauſe he is ever and invariably that which he is; and in man the thinking principle is the part that is properly and permanently himſelf. He who purſues the good of his mind, is pleaſed in his own company, being delighted with the recollection of the paſt, as well as animated with the proſpect of the future; and having ever at command innumerable ſpeculations, in which he exerciſes himſelf with the moſt exquiſite pleaſure. Both his joys and his ſorrows are reſpectively conſiſtent with themſelves, ſince they invariably proceed from fixed and regular cauſes; for he does not delight at one time in what will excite his repentance at another; and thus harmonized within his own breaſt, he is ſimilarly affected towards his friend, whom he conſiders as a ſecond ſelf; and his ſympathy for whom, when it reaches the higheſt perfection, reſembles that internal concord which is experienced in his own mind, when the various principles of his nature coaleſce into one movement, and flow in the ſame homogeneous ſtream of virtuous energy. Yet many men of very irregular lives ſeem to be highly ſatisfied with themſelves. Is this becauſe they miſtake their own characters? It ſhould ſeem ſo, ſince

The wretchedneſs of vice.

 the

BOOK IX.

the complete villa in is always viſibly at variance with himſelf; and all others are ſimilarly affected in proportion to their progreſs in wickedneſs; willing one thing, yet deſiring and preferring another; as thoſe who allow themſelves to be ſubdued by vicious pleaſure, and who may be ſaid, with their eyes open, to ruſh into voluntary deſtruction. In the ſame manner others, through lazineſs or cowardice, avoid that conduct which they know moſt likely to promote their happineſs. When men proceed to the laſt ſtage of depravity, they become as odious to themſelves as they are deteſtable to others, and therefore often deſtroy their own lives; and even before they arrive at this deplorable condition, they fly from, and avoid themſelves; preferring any kind of ſociety to that of their own reflections; the paſt crimes which haunt their memory, and the meditated guilt which is continually occurring to their fancy. As they have nothing in them that is amiable, they cannot be the objects of their own love. Neither their joys nor their ſorrows are conſiſtent. Their whole ſoul is in ſedition, diſtracted between contending principles, the pleaſure of one giving pain to another; and when the worſt principle prevails, a foundation is laid for the bittereſt remorſe. If ſuch be the wretchedneſs of wickedneſs, how ſtrenuouſly ought we to exert ourſelves to become good men, that we may live in friendſhip with ourſelves, and be worthy of the friendſhip of others.

Chap. 5.

Of good-will.

Good-will reſembles friendſhip, but is not the ſame thing. Good-will we may entertain for thoſe not perſonally known to us, and without being ourſelves conſcious of it. This cannot happen with regard to friendſhip, as we formerly obſerved. Beſides every act of friendſhip implies an affection and expanſion of the ſoul, it is alſo much connected with cuſtom; whereas

whereas mere good-will arises suddenly, as towards the combatants in the public games, to one or other of whom we immediately wish well, though we would not make any great exertion in order to promote his victory. Good-will, then, is but a sudden and superficial emotion; and at best but an element of friendship, as the first element or beginning of love is the pleasure received by the eye; without which, though the passion of love cannot commence, yet that pleasure does not by any means constitute this passion, to which it is necessary that we should not only delight in the object when present, but exceedingly long for it when absent. Speaking metaphorically, we may call good-will an incipient and indolent friendship; which, through time and custom, naturally improves into friendship strictly so called; not that founded on pleasure or utility, which have but little to do with good-will, since he who has received a favour ought in justice to return it; and he who does a kindness in expectation of meeting with a greater, has good-will only to himself. Good-will, in one word, is always excited by some laudable quality, such as generosity, or courage: witness the manner in which we are affected by the prize-fighters, abovementioned.

Chap. 6.

Of that kind of concord which friendship implies.

Friendship implies concord, which is not merely agreement in opinion. This latter may prevail among persons totally unknown to each other; and what connection has friendship with sameness of opinion concerning the heavenly motions, and other such subjects? Concord prevails among cities and commonwealths, when they conceive the same designs to be conducive to the common interest, and agree in the same measures for promoting them. It relates therefore to practical subjects only, and those of a certain magnitude in themselves, and bear-

ing

BOOK IX.

ing an important relation to the parties concerned; for example, that the magistracies should be elective; that an alliance should be made with the Lacedæmonians; that Pittacus should be archon, when he himself is willing to discharge that honourable office [a]. When each party wishes the same thing for himself, then dissension ensues, because the factions in the state, though they agree in the object, yet differ as to the person. But genuine concord requires that each party and each individual should obtain his wish; as when both the people and the better sort agree in choosing virtuous men for their magistrates. This concord is, as we have said, the basis of political friendship. It is conversant about matters essentially useful to the comfortable subsistence of men in society; and can only be found among men of virtue, who being firm in their purposes, and not variable like the Euripus, are alone qualified to maintain the relations of concord and amity with themselves and others. As justice and utility have long regulated their private behaviour, they carry the same principles along with them into their public administration. But neither concord nor friendship can durably subsist among dishonest men, who will be continually striving to engross every advantage, and to shift off every burden; and who must soon fall into sedition by their endeavours to compel others to comply with those rules of justice which they themselves disdain to practice.

Chap. 7.

Why there is more love in those who confer bene-

How comes it that men love those to whom they have done good, better than these love their benefactors? Most are of opinion that this happens because debtors are more concerned about the safety of their creditors, than the creditors are about theirs,

[a] Diogenes Laertius, l. i. seq. 75. tells us, that Pittacus laid down the archonship after he had held it ten years; to which transaction Aristotle seems here to allude.

fits than in those who receive them.

theirs, and that merely from motives of intereſt; which Epicharmus[a], perhaps, would ſay, is judging of mankind by the worſt examples among them. The accuſation, however, is certainly too juſt, for with regard to the ſervices which they have received, the greater part are of weak memories, and more willing to receive benefits than inclined either to confer or to return them. Yet the queſtion juſt ſtarted muſt be ſolved on deeper principles than thoſe of debtor and creditor, which imply nothing of love or friendſhip, but depend entirely on dull conſiderations of intereſt. Thoſe to whom we have done good, are objects of our love and affection, though they neither return, nor ſhould ever be expected to return, the obligation: for we are naturally diſpoſed towards them as artiſts are towards their works; and particularly poets towards their poems; which they love as parents do their children; that is, much more than their productions, were they endowed with life and perception, would love them. For each individual loves every excellence proceeding from himſelf in proportion as he deſires and loves his own exiſtence, the energies of which are concentrated and preſerved in his works. Beſides, our own good actions are more pleaſing ſubjects of reflection, than any paſt benefits that we may have received: for the firſt are honourable, and the ſecond only uſeful; and utility, however delightful in proſpect, is often forgotten with the occaſion which required it; whereas honour is permanent and unalterable; and every praiſe-worthy deed is not only pleaſing in proſpect, but delightful on remembrance, above all moſt tranſporting when actually exerciſed; giving

[a] A diſciple of Pythagoras, who ſeems to have had better principles of morality, than he is ſaid to have entertained of religion. Vid. Cicer. de Natur. Deorum, l. i. and Menag. ad Diogen. Laert. l. iii. ſect. 9. & ſeq.

BOOK IX.

giving to us a consciousness of that kind of existence which is most peculiarly agreeable to our nature, the happiness of which results not from passive sensations, but from active exertions. Besides, whatever is obtained with much labour, is naturally regarded with much affection. Those who have acquired their fortunes, delight in them far more than those who succeed to hereditary wealth; and for a similar reason, maternal tenderness often rises to the highest pitch. On such principles we may explain why the affection of those who confer benefits, which is commonly a work of some exertion, should be stronger than that of those who receive them, which requires no exertion at all.

Chap. 8.

Of the different senses in which a man is said to love himself.

It is doubted which we ought to love most, ourselves or our friends. Selfishness is branded as a vice of the blackest die, and thought to sink deeper into each individual, in exact proportion to the worthlessness of his character. A bad man has nothing but himself in view; while a good one loses sight of himself, and aims chiefly at friendly or honourable actions; and this the more in proportion to his progress in virtue. Yet these observations ill accord with what is commonly said, that a friend wishes to promote our good for our own sakes, and though we should ever remain ignorant of his good offices; which is surely the disposition of each individual towards himself, and comformable to this disposition are all the other circumstances, and all the proverbial expressions by which friendship is indicated and ascertained; as that friends have but one soul, that all things are common between them, that friendship is equality, and that the knee is nearer than the foot. But a man stands in all those relations to himself, and being most his own friend, ought most to love himself. These contradictions cannot

cannot be reconciled but by diſtinguiſhing the different ſenſes in which a man is ſaid to love himſelf. Thoſe who reproach ſelf-love as a vice, conſider it only as it appears in worldlings and voluptuaries, who arrogate to themſelves more than their due ſhare of wealth, power, or pleaſure. Such things are to the multitude, the objects of earneſt concern and eager contention, becauſe the multitude regards them as prizes of the higheſt value; and in endeavouring to attain them, ſtrives to gratify its paſſion at the expence of its reaſon. This kind of ſelf-love, which belongs to the contemptible multitude, is doubtleſs obnoxious to blame; and in this acceptation, the word is uſually taken. But ſhould a man aſſume a pre-eminence in exerciſing juſtice, temperance, and other virtues, though ſuch a man has really more true ſelf-love than the multitude, yet nobody would impute this affection to him for a crime. Yet he takes to himſelf the faireſt and greateſt of all goods, and thoſe the moſt acceptable to the ruling principle in his nature, which is properly himſelf, in the ſame manner as the ſovereignty in every community is that which moſt properly conſtitutes the ſtate. He is ſaid, alſo, to have, or not to have, the command of himſelf, juſt as this principle bears ſway, or as it is ſubject to control; and thoſe acts are conſidered as moſt voluntary which proceed from this legiſlative and ſovereign power. Whoever cheriſhes and gratifies this ruling part of his nature, is ſtrictly and peculiarly a lover of himſelf, but in a quite different ſenſe from that in which ſelf-love is regarded as a matter of reproach; for all men approve and praiſe an affection calculated to produce the greateſt private and the greateſt public happineſs; whereas they diſapprove and blame the vulgar kind of ſelf-love as often hurtful to others, and always ruinous to thoſe who indulge it. A

Self-love, well underſtood, wherein it conſiſts.

BOOK IX.

bad man, we have ſaid, is really at variance with himſelf; purſuing a conduct directly oppoſite to what his own duty and his own intereſt moſt powerfully recommend. But the man of morals obeys and follows the dictates of his intellect; and every intellect, when free and uncircumſcribed, neceſſarily prefers and purſues its own individual good. The virtuous man indeed ſtrenuouſly exerts himſelf in the cauſe of his friends and his country; and readily lays down his life for their ſake. He willingly reſigns honours and emoluments; but firmly defends the firſt ſhare of generoſity and probity. The tranſports of one glorious day, he would not exchange for a whole life of liſtleſs inſignificance; one year ſpent in honourable exertion, he prefers to ages vulgarly and caſually conſumed; nay, a ſingle effort of ſplendid virtue is more valuable in his eyes than an indefinite ſeries of ſmall and ordinary actions; and, on ſuch principles, he is ready to lay down his life in the cauſe of his friends or country. He is ready alſo to employ his fortune in their ſervice; ſo that, while they are enriched at his expence, he may acquire an unrivalled ſhare of well-merited applauſe. As to offices and honours he is ſimilarly affected, eaſily relinquiſhing them all; nay, even the fame of illuſtrious actions, when it appears to him more praiſe-worthy, to give an opportunity to others of performing them, than to effect them by his own agency. Thus, amidſt all his liberalities, he is ſtill moſt ſelfiſh, ſince he ſtill claims for himſelf what is incomparably moſt valuable, that internal delight ariſing from the conſciouſneſs of merit.

Chap. 9.

Whether friendſhip be the greateſt good in proſperity or in adverſity.

It is diſputed whether or not happy men need friends. Happineſs ſeems all-ſufficient in itſelf without ſuch auxiliaries; whence they ſay,

"When Fortune's goods abound, what boots a friend?"

Yet

Yet on the other hand, it appears abſurd, if happineſs includes all good things, to deprive it of friendſhip, which of external goods is the greateſt. Beſides, if friendſhip, as we above proved, conſiſts rather in conferring favours, than in receiving them, and it is honourable to do good to thoſe who are peculiarly recommended to our love in preference to all others, proſperous and happy men muſt ſtand in need of fit objects, towards whom they may exerciſe their beneficence. It is diſputed, therefore, in which of the two ſtates men require friends the moſt, the ſtate of proſperity, or that of adverſity; the former needing favourites as much as the latter does benefactors. It is alſo abſurd to think that happineſs can be enjoyed in ſolitude; man being a ſocial and political animal by the conſtitution of his nature itſelf; without conforming to which, human happineſs cannot be attained; nor ſo completely attained in caſual or indifferent ſociety, as in that of amiable and virtuous friends. What is the meaning then of the obſervation firſt made, or by what arguments can it be juſtified? The people regard only thoſe as their friends who promote their utility, and friends of this kind a proſperous man does not need; nor does he ſeem greatly to need thoſe who may adminiſter to his pleaſure, ſince his life being delightful in itſelf, he has not much occaſion for adventitious enjoyment. Thoſe two claſſes of friends being excluded as unneceſſary, it is too haſtily inferred that he needs not any friends at all. For we ſaid in the beginning, that happineſs is energy, that is, a thing conſiſting in our own exertions, not reſulting from our acquirements or poſſeſſions; and the life of a good man conſiſts in a ſeries of virtuous and delightful energies, which will be far more unbroken and uninterrupted, if he contemplates them not only in

The exquiſite pleaſure of virtuous friendſhip.

 himſelf,

BOOK IX.

himſelf, but in thoſe who are around him, whoſe behaviour he is able to view more attentively and more ſteadily than he can poſſibly do his own[i]. Friends of this deſcription, therefore, he requires, that he may ſympathize with their ſentiments, and participate in their actions; for a good man is charmed with good actions more than a ſkilful muſician with the fineſt melody; and as the latter is provoked by diſſonance, ſo is the former grieved by depravity. Beſides, as Theognis[k] ſays, virtuous friends exerciſe, improve, and perfect each other. But if we examine the matter more deeply, we ſhall find that one good man is naturally an object ultimately deſirable to another; for a good man delights in what is naturally delightful, and values what is really and abſolutely valuable; and as the life of animals conſiſts barely in ſenſation, but that of man both in ſenſation and intellection, and that not merely in the capacities but principally in the exerciſe of thoſe powers, for the ſake of which the capacities are given to us, it is plain that the more widely we extend the ſphere of our energies, our happineſs will be the more complete; provided thoſe energies be, like every thing that is good, definite in their nature, not variable and undetermined, like the lives of bad men, which appear under innumerable forms of wretchedneſs. But neither ſuch lives, nor thoſe overwhelmed by an accumulation of pains and ſorrows, (of which we ſhall ſpeak hereafter,) are calculated to make us rightly

[i] ωσπερ ουν όταν θελωμεν αυτοι αυτων τον προσωπον ιδειν, εις τον κατοπτρον εμβλεψαντες ιδωμεν, όμοιως και όταν αυτοι αυτους βουληθωμεν γνωναι εις τον φιλον ιδοντες γνωρισαιμεν αν, &c. "As when we wiſh to ſee our own countenances, we muſt view it in a looking-glaſs; in the ſame manner when we wiſh to know our own characters and virtues, we muſt contemplate thoſe of our friend; for a friend, as we ſay, is another ſelf." Magn. Moral. l. ii. c. xv. p. 194.

[k] The gnomic poet of Megara, ſome of whoſe ſententious verſes are ſtill preſerved.

15

BOOK IX.

rightly appreciate the value of exiſtence, which to wiſe and good men is an object ſo truly deſirable. For when we ſee or hear, we are conſcious of thoſe perceptions; and when we think and theorize, we are conſcious of thoſe intellections; and the higher and nobler our thoughts are, the more pleaſure we derive from the conſciouſneſs of entertaining them. This conſciouſneſs makes us feel the pleaſure of exiſtence; for the energy of life itſelf, which is of all things moſt delightful, conſiſts in nothing elſe but perceiving and thinking. But a good man, being affected towards his friend nearly as towards himſelf, derives therefore the higheſt gratification from communicating his thoughts and reflections with others like himſelf, and living with them in a perpetual participation of intellectual and moral enjoyments; ſince he thereby attains nearly as clear a perception of their pleaſurable exiſtence as he has of his own. This indeed is human ſociety properly ſo called, in contradiſtinction to that of cattle, which conſiſts in feeding at the ſame ſtall. Since then his own life is, to a good man, a thing naturally ſweet and ultimately deſirable, for a ſimilar reaſon is the life of his friend agreeable to him, and delightful merely on its own account, and without reference to any object beyond it; and to live without friends is to be deſtitute of a good, unconditional, abſolute, and ultimately deſirable; and therefore to be deprived of one of the moſt ſolid and moſt ſubſtantial of all human enjoyments.

Chap. 10.

Different kinds of friendſhip require different limitations as to number.

Ought this reaſoning to make us deſirous of multiplying the number of our friends? Or ought we to adopt as to friendſhip what ſeems to be well ſaid with regard to hoſpitality,

"For many gueſts are often worſe than none."

In

In the ſame manner ought the number of our friends to be limited? Of friends choſen from motives of utility or convevience, it undoubtedly ought; for more than ſerve our purpoſe, are only obſtacles and hindrances; and it is impoſſible for us to return the ſervices or civilities of too numerous a liſt. Neither need thoſe choſen from motives of pleaſure to be many; for too much ſeaſoning is pernicious in diet. But as to friendſhips ſtrictly ſo called, originating in ſympathy of minds and congeniality of characters, ought there to be defined limits, beyond which that number ought not to extend; any more than the populouſneſs of a city, which, for the ſupply of mutual wants, requires more than ten, but, for the ſake of wiſe regulation and good morals, ought not perhaps to exceed ten myriads of inhabitants? The number of friends, even virtuous friends, muſt be limited by the extent of human activity, which is incapable of cultivating beyond a certain proportion, who muſt all likewiſe be friends to each other, on the ſuppoſition, which is neceſſary, that they ſhould ſpend their time together in amicable concord. This cannot eaſily happen to a great multitude, eſpecially ſince ſuch is the inſtability of human affairs, that we cannot cordially ſympathize with many perſons at once, for if we ought to rejoice with one, it will too often happen that we ought to grieve with another. Many friends, therefore, are neither to be deſired nor expected, and their number will be the ſmaller in proportion to the cloſeneſs of the intimacy; for intimate friendſhip is almoſt as excluſive as love, which admits but one only object. Experience juſtifies this obſervation, for the friendſhips moſt celebrated have ſubſiſted between two only. In political life we ſee popular men, who ſeem to have innu-

innumerable friends. They are often flatterers of the multitude. But a public character without flattery may, by his real worth, recommend himself to the gratitude of many who are his friends politically. But friends, strictly so called, cannot be numerous. Happy is the man who finds only a few such!

Chap. II.

Whether the company of our friends is most desirable in our prosperity or in our adversity.

Whether are friends most desirable in prosperity or in adversity? Both conditions of life peculiarly require them; the prosperous, that they may have objects towards whom to exercise their beneficence; the unfortunate, that they may have sources from which they may derive relief. The necessity for friends is greatest in the latter, who therefore seek persons who may be useful to them; but the lustre of friendship shines most conspicuous in the former, who seek persons with whom they may spend their time agreeably, and whom it is a real pleasure to benefit. The company of friends is delightful both in prosperity and adversity. In the latter, our grief is alleviated by their sympathy; whether it be that they disburden us of part of our sufferings, or that their sympathy is itself delightful. Both causes seem to concur, for in misfortune the presence of a friend affords a mixed pleasure. The very sight of him cheers our minds; and if he has any dexterity, he knows how to administer to us that kind of comfort of which our tempers and characters are most susceptible. Besides, we ourselves, in his presence, endeavour to moderate our sorrow, that we may not be the cause of suffering to our friend; and persons of firm minds are careful how they impart their secret misfortunes, and reject all excess of commiseration as unsuitable to the dignity of their characters; whereas women, and womanish men, delight in echoing groans and sympathetic lamentations. In all things the

best

BOOK IX.

best characters are the fit models for imitation; and as amidst prosperity the best men delight in the presence and congratulation of their friends, which is agreeable to the benevolence of their nature, we ought therefore to be forward in calling those who love us to participate in our joy, but very backward in calling them to participate in our sorrow; remembering

"Their own misfortunes are enough to bear."

Above all, we must summon their presence when, without giving much trouble to ourselves, we may greatly benefit *them*. But, on the other hand, to act with laudable propriety, we must go readily and uninvited to the house of mourning; for it is as honourable as delightful to assist our friends in distress, especially without any solicitation on their part, which might lessen them in our esteem. It is our duty strenuously to co-operate with fortune in promoting the prosperity of our friend; but to be slow and modest in craving his assistance; yet without too fastidiously rejecting his beneficence; which has sometimes made a breach in very solid friendships.

Chap. 12. — Conclusion.

As love enters first by the eye, so friendship is produced by the habitual intercourse of life; and as the sense of sight is that which lovers would be most unwilling to lose, so habitual intercourse is the advantage which friends would be most unwilling to resign. Friendship is a community of enjoyments; and as a man delights in the energies of his own existence, so he also does in those of his friend; wherefore, in whatever those energies principally consist, their chief enjoyment results from exerting them in company; some drinking and playing dice together, while others make parties of hunting, practise their exercises, or cultivate philosophy. The friendship of bad men

is

is as corrupt and unſtable as themſelves; and is ſo far from being advantageous to either party, that it tends only to plunge them both ſtill deeper in depravity and wretchedneſs: whereas virtuous friendſhips grow continually more firm and more intimate, the example and admonitions of good men mutually improving and perfecting each other[1]. Thus much concerning friendſhip. It remains that we ſhould next treat of pleaſure.

[1] Ariſtotle quotes a few words from Theognis which have this meaning.

ARISTOTLE's ETHICS.

BOOK X.

INTRODUCTION.

THIS Book treats of pleaſure and happineſs. It is too conciſe to admit of abridgment, and ſufficiently perſpicuous not to require elucidation. In the concluding chapter, Ariſtotle ſhews the inſeparable connection between Ethics and Politics; and prepares the reader for an eaſy tranſition from the former to the latter. By way of concluſion to theſe ſhort introductions, I ſhall obſerve, that Ariſtotle's Moral Philoſophy is, perhaps, of all others the leaſt liable to the following objection, which has been often made by thinking men to the too faſhionable philoſophy of the times: "A profeſſed ſceptic can be guided by nothing but his preſent paſſions; and to be maſters of his philoſophy, we need not his books or advice, for every child is capable of the ſame thing without any ſtudy at all."—GRAY. BOOK X.

BOOK X.

ARGUMENT.

Pleaſure—Its ambiguous nature—Defined.—Happineſs—Intellectual—Moral—Compared.—Education.—Laws.—Tranſition to the ſubject of Politics.

BOOK X. Chap. 1. The love of pleaſure.

WE proceed to treat of pleaſure, a thing moſt congenial to our nature; and by which, therefore, and its oppoſite, pain, the motions of the minds of children are guided as by a rudder. In morals the main point is attained, when our love and hatred, our grief and joy, are reſpectively excited by natural and worthy cauſes; ſince theſe affections are as extenſive as the multiplied affairs of life itſelf, and their proper regulation is of the utmoſt importance to virtue and happineſs. For we are all prompted by nature to purſue pleaſure, and to avoid pain; the conſideration of which ought not to be omitted in a treatiſe of this kind, eſpecially as the opinions concerning them are perplexed by much contradiction; ſome regarding pleaſure as the higheſt good, others calling it a thing contemptible in the extreme, whether from the real conviction of their minds, (which perhaps may be the caſe with ſome,) or becauſe they think it beſt to ſpeak of pleaſure in terms of reproach, ſince moſt men are tempted to diſgrace themſelves by indulging in it immoderately. Severe moraliſts, therefore, think that they cannot too much ſtigmatiſe pleaſure, that thoſe whom they wiſh to benefit

BOOK X.

Not to be too feverely condemned.

benefit by their difcourfes may be deterred from excefs, and confined within the bounds of propriety. They fhould take care however, left this proceeding be not attended with effects contrary to their expectation; for in practical matters, men pay lefs attention to what is faid than to what is done; and when opinions, juft and reafonable within certain limits, are carried to a length manifeftly inconfiftent with experience, they are rejected difdainfully and completely; even the truth which they contain being overwhelmed and loft in the furrounding falfehood. Thus thofe detractors of pleafure, when they are obferved on any occafion to purfue it with much eagernefs, appear to the bulk of mankind no better than hypocritical voluptuaries; for the people at large are not capable of making diftinctions; they confider things in the grofs, and therefore continually confound them. The truth, therefore, beft ferves not only to enlighten our underftandings, but to improve our morals. For when our doctrines are true, our lives will more naturally be conformable to them; and our precepts being confirmed by examples, will produce conviction, and excite emulation of our virtues, in thofe with whom we live. But enough on this fubject: we proceed to enumerate the opinions held concerning pleafure.

Chap. 2.

Different opinions concerning it.

Eudoxus[a] thought pleafure the chief good, becaufe he perceived it to be univerfally defired by all animals, rational and irrational; that every thing is good in the fame proportion as it is defirable: that animals find out, each tribe, what is beft for themfelves, as they do their proper food; and that therefore the

[a] Eudoxus of Cnidus τουτον αντι Ευδοξου Ενδοξον εκαλουν δια την λαμπροτητα της φημης. See his life in Laertius, B. viii. fect. 86, &c. By a pun on his name, he was called "Illuftrious."

the ſupreme good muſt conſiſt in that which is univerſally and moſt eagerly deſired by them all. The regularity of his life added great weight to his arguments, for he was a man of ſingular temperance; ſo that his commendation of pleaſure did not appear to proceed from any prejudice in its favour, but rather to be extorted from him by the force of truth. His argument he confirmed by conſidering pain; which, being the contrary to pleaſure, all animals endeavoured to ſhun and eſcape. That is chiefly deſirable, he remarked, which is deſirable ultimately and on its own account. This deſcription peculiarly applies to pleaſure, which no one deſires for the ſake of any thing beyond itſelf, nor finds the neceſſity of aſſigning any reaſon why he ſhould enjoy it; pleaſure always carrying its own recommendation along with it, and rendering every object, however valuable, to which it is joined, ſtill more deſirable, not excepting virtue itſelf. As pleaſure improves every other good with which it is combined, it is manifeſtly a good in itſelf; a good not inferior to that which it heightens. Yet Plato employed a ſimilar argument to prove that pleaſure was not the ſupreme good; ſince pleaſure, joined with virtue, is better than alone and ſeparate; which cannot happen to the ſupreme good, a thing incapable of augmentation, and diſdaining admixture. But what is that good or happineſs which mankind, by the conſtitution of their nature, are beſt qualified for enjoying? This only is the queſtion with which we are concerned in the preſent treatiſe. Thoſe who deny that which all deſire, to be a part of this happineſs, ſhould take care leſt they fall into an abſurdity. For *that* we ſay is truth, which to all appears ſuch; and he who is diſſatisfied with this kind of proof will not eaſily meet with a better. If only creatures

BOOK X.

void of underſtanding purſued pleaſure, much might be plauſibly urged againſt it: but what ſhall we ſay, when we find it an object of deſire with the beſt and wiſeſt of the human race? Nay even irrational animals may afford perhaps a ſtrong argument in favour of it, ſince in purſuit of what is beſt for their nature, they are actuated by a wiſdom far ſuperior to their own[b]. The argument drawn from pain, which is the oppoſite to pleaſure, ſeems not liable to the objection made to it. The objectors ſay, that though pain be an evil, this is not any proof that pleaſure, its contrary, is a good; becauſe both contraries are often bad, and the good is often ſomething intermediate between them. But this obſervation, though true in many caſes, is not applicable to the preſent. For if both were evils, both would be objects of averſion; but the one, we ſee, is univerſally purſued as a good, and the other univerſally ſhunned as an evil.

Chap. 3.

The ambiguous nature of pleaſure.

It forms not any objection to pleaſure, that it is not one of thoſe indelible qualities by which things are characteriſed and diſtinguiſhed; for neither to the claſs of qualities can the energies and operations of virtue itſelf, which are ſo highly and ſo juſtly praiſed, in ſtrict philoſophical language, be aſcribed: no, nor happineſs itſelf, which is of all things moſt valuable. It is farther objected, that pleaſure is of a vague indefinite nature, admitting of various degrees of intenſity; whereas whatever is truly good, ought to be uniformly perceived, and accurately defined[c]. But juſtice, fortitude, and the other virtues admit of various degrees, when conſidered as attributes of the perſons in whom thoſe habits exiſt; the ſame is true of health; yet the health of the mind, as well as that of the body, conſidered abſtractedly

[b] See Analyſis, p. 114. and Conf. p. 334. & ſeq.

[c] See Analyſis, p. 112.

abſtractedly in themſelves, are things ſufficiently definite, though they do not, in each individual, reach that ſtate of perfection which properly conſtitutes their nature [b]. The ſame thing may poſſibly hold with regard to pleaſure. It is further objected, that pleaſure is motion; and that all motions are imperfect, ſince they are only tendencies to certain ends [c]; whereas whatever is abſolutely good, ought to be complete and perfect in itſelf, independently of any ſeparate purpoſe for which it may ſerve. But, that pleaſure is motion, is not likely to be true; for all motion admits of ſlowneſs and celerity; ſince the motion of the univerſe itſelf, though it cannot be called ſwift or ſlow, abſtractedly conſidered, yet deſerves the former of thoſe epithets when compared with the peculiar motions which belong reſpectively to its parts [d]. But pleaſure is not characteriſed by either of theſe qualities. We may indeed be ſpeedily pleaſed, as we are ſpeedily made angry; and as walking, growing, or any other motion, is performed with celerity, in the ſame manner, we may rapidly change from a ſtate of indifference or pain, to a ſtate of pleaſure; but to the energy of pleaſure itſelf, that is, to pleaſure actually enjoyed, the epithets of ſwift or ſlow do not apply. This energy is complete in itſelf in every inſtant; and is not perfected by the accompliſhment of any diſtinct and ſeparate end, in which it terminates. It is therefore a thing totally different from generation or production, or motion of any kind; ſince all of theſe are mere changes of material ſubſtances, paſſing from one place, or one ſtate, to another; not indeed at random, but according to certain and fixed laws of motion and reſt, generation and corruption; ſo that from the ſame

[b] See Analyſis, p. 117. [c] Ibid. p. 119. [d] Ibid. p. 120. & ſeq.

BOOK X.

ſame materials out of which any compound is generated, into the ſame, that compound is, by corruption, diſſolved [e]. If pleaſure then be generation, pain muſt be corruption; and that which is generated by pleaſure, muſt by pain be diſſolved into the ſame materials from which it was produced. But to ſpeak thus of pleaſure and pain, is to talk unintelligibly; and to confound immaterial with material things. It is ſaid alſo, that pain conſiſts in natural deficiencies or wants, and that pleaſure is nothing elſe but the ſupplying of theſe wants. But deficiency and fulneſs are plainly affections of body; and if pleaſure is the ſupply of corporeal deficiencies, that which receives the ſupply ought to feel the pleaſure, which therefore reſides in the body; a concluſion reſulting from the premiſes, but highly unreaſonable. Pleaſure, therefore, is not the ſupply of bodily wants, though it accompanies this ſupply; as pain, on the contrary, accompanies the laceration or maiming of the body. The opinion ſeems to have ariſen from conſidering the pain of hunger, and the pleaſure of feeding; the latter of which muſt always be preceded by the former. But all pleaſures are not preceded by pain; thoſe, for inſtance, of the intellectual kind; and even thoſe of the ſenſes of ſmelling, hearing, and ſeeing; beſides innumerable enjoyments, reſulting from pleaſing recollections, as well as from agreeable and animating hopes. Of what deficiencies can ſuch pleaſures be the ſupply, ſince previouſly to their exiſtence in us, there was not any thing defective? With regard to groſs and reproachable pleaſures, which our adverſaries may cite in proof of their erroneous theory, the very name of pleaſures may, with propriety, be denied to them; ſince they are acknowledged as ſuch only by men of corrupt minds

[e] Analyſis, p. 107. & ſeq.

minds and perverse sentiments. Persons diseased are not fit judges of the relish of wholesome food; nor is that white, which appears such to those afflicted with an ophthalmy. It may be observed also, that pleasure is not desirable, unless it proceed from an honourable, at least an innocent source; any more than wealth is a good, when too dearly purchased by dishonesty. Different pleasures are adapted to different characters. Just men only know the pleasure of justice; as those only who have an ear for music, enjoy the pleasure of melody; the same differences are observable in other particulars. The very dissimilar gratifications which we derive from friends and flatterers show, that either pleasure is not in itself desirable, or that there must be pleasures specifically different from each other. A friend aims at promoting our good, a flatterer aims only at giving us pleasure; and the behaviour of the one is as universally and as justly praised, as that of the other is universally and justly condemned. None worthy of the name of a man, would choose to have the understanding of a child, that he might spend his life happily in childish amusements; nor would he submit to do base actions, whatever pleasure he might derive from them, and though assured that they should never afterwards be followed by pain or punishment. But, on the other hand, he would desire most earnestly to have the use of his eye-sight, of his memory, and of his understanding, as well as to be endowed and adorned with virtuous habits, although no pleasure whatever resulted from the exercise of those capacities or powers. That this exercise is necessarily accompanied with pleasure makes not any difference, since it is an object of desire on its own account, and independently of the delight which necessarily attends it. It seems plain, therefore, that

BOOK X.

pleaſure is not the ſupreme good, nor that all kinds of pleaſures are deſirable; and that whether or no pleaſures are deſirable ultimately, and on their own account, depends on the ſource from whence they ſpring. Such are the opinions held concerning pleaſure and pain.

Chap. 4.

Pleaſure conſiſts in exerciſing the proper energies of our nature, which it improves and perfects.

But what pleaſure is in reality, and under what claſs of things it ought to be arranged, will more fully appear from the following induction. The act of ſeeing is perfect in every inſtant of time, needing nothing to give to it the ſpecific completion and fulneſs of which its nature is ſuſceptible. Such alſo is pleaſure, a whole, perfect in each inſtant, and not more perfect than at the firſt inſtant, how long ſoever it may be enjoyed. Pleaſure therefore is not motion, becauſe all motion co-exiſts with a certain portion of time; and tends to a certain end, in which it terminates, being, from its very nature, imperfect; becauſe, as ſoon as the end is effected, the motion by which it was attained ceaſes to exiſt[a]. Thus of the art of building, the end is a houſe; and until the houſe is made, the building is imperfect; but when the houſe is built, the action or motion by which it was produced ceaſes to exiſt: and the parts of that action or motion are, until the whole is finiſhed, each different from another, and each imperfect in itſelf; as rearing the walls, chamfering the pillars, building the dome; all of which, as well as laying the foundation and adding the ornaments, are but parts of one action, which, taken together, conſtitute a whole, when the work is completed. The ſame holds, with regard to that kind of motion which conſiſts in change of place, and its various modes, namely, walking, jumping, flying, and others of that ſort; each of which conſiſts of imperfect parts, ſpecifically

[a] Analyſis, p. 117. & ſeq.

fically different from each other, and from the whole collectively. Thus, in the Olympic race, a different part of the stadium is run over in each particle of time, till the goal is attained; and as each part is different from another, so must the motions performed in them be all different; nay, though the same part be run over, yet if the racer proceed, in the one case, from the starting-post to the goal, and in the other, from the goal to the starting-post, a difference in the motions must arise from the difference in their directions. But concerning motion, we have treated accurately in another work[a]. Pleasure is manifestly a thing quite different; since it is complete in each *indivisible now*, that is, in each instant; not requiring for its perfection any the smallest portion of time: but motion, as we have elsewhere proved, cannot exist without time or succession. In the same manner, the act of vision, a point, and an unit, are things which have not any connection with generation, nor any kind of motion; every modification of which must belong to things not essentially wholes, but partible; and to them only. Of this kind is pleasure, essentially a whole, since essentially perfect; accompanying the operation of each percipient with regard to the perceptible object, when both the perceiving power is properly constituted, and the perceptible object the fairest and the best on which that specific act of perception can possibly be exercised[b]. To say that the perceiving power exercises its energies, or the substance in which that power resides, makes not any difference as to the present subject. Pleasure accompanies every act of perception by sense in a higher or lower degree, in proportion to the prevalence of the conditions above stated; and also every act of reasoning or intelligence.

But

[a] Analysis, p. 119 & seq. [b] Ibid. p. 51, & seq.

BOOK X.

But as the phyſician and the medicines which he preſcribes, are in different ſenſes the cauſes of health, ſo our percipient powers are enlivened and perfected in a different manner by the proper objects of thoſe powers, and by the pleaſure attending our perception of them. Each ſenſe has its appropriate pleaſure: the eye is delighted by ſights; the ear by ſounds; and in proportion to the ſoundneſs and vigour of the ſenſe itſelf, as well as the beauty and excellence of the object on which it is exerciſed, the pleaſure will be the greater; but pleaſure there always muſt be, wherever the agent and the object are naturally adapted to each other. Pleaſure does not perfect our energiſing powers as a pre-acquired habit, but rather as a ſupervenient end; in the ſame manner as beauty accompanies the flower of youth. The powers of man are not capable of unceaſing activity, and therefore our pleaſures cannot be continuous, for they are inſeparably connected with our energies. Things which delight when new, often ceaſe to give pleaſure, and that becauſe our attention is no longer rouſed by their preſence, nor the energies of our mind called forth in contemplating them. They are diſregarded as an old and familiar ſhow; and in proportion to the weakneſs of our exertions, our pleaſure is blunted. It may be ſuſpected that all love pleaſure, becauſe all are fond of life, which conſiſts in exerciſing the energies of our nature. Life then is energy, which each individual exerciſes on thoſe ſubjects in which he moſt delights; the muſician, on melodies; the mathematician, on theorems; and others, on other ſubjects. Pleaſure therefore is naturally deſirable, becauſe it perfects our energies, that is our life, in the continuance of which all delight. But whether life is deſired for the ſake of pleaſure, or pleaſure for the ſake of life, needs not at preſent be examined;

ſince

ſince theſe two ſeem ſo intimately combined as not to admit of ſeparation. Pleaſure, then, cannot exiſt without energy; and our energies are ſtrengthened and perfected by the pleaſures accompanying them.

Chap. 5. It ſeems to follow from theſe obſervations, that as energies or actions widely differ from each other, ſo muſt alſo the pleaſures by which they are perfected. This holds in the ſeveral operations both of nature and of art, the different kinds of which reſpectively terminate in different and appropriate ends; namely, animals, plants, pictures, ſtatues, houſes, and furniture. The action of the ſenſes, or what is called perception by ſenſe, manifeſtly differs from the action of the underſtanding; and the pleaſures reſpectively accompanying thoſe operations, bear a near affinity to the operations which they reſpectively accompany; for each operation or energy is encreaſed, improved, and perfected by a pleaſure that is a-kin to it. Thus the exertions of the geometer, the muſician, and the architect, are enlivened and invigorated by the delight which they take in their reſpective purſuits; and the cultivators of thoſe ſciences thereby improve themſelves gradually, until they attain the moſt conſummate ſkill, and moſt decided pre-eminence. But pleaſures, on the other hand, which are not a-kin to the operations which they accompany, are ſo far from improving and perfecting them, that, on the contrary, they weaken and obſtruct them. Thus, thoſe who are agreeably employed in reading or ſtudy, cannot, if they are lovers of muſic, perſevere in applying to their books and meditations, ſhould they happen to hear at a diſtance an agreeable melody; for the two pleaſures not being a-kin, the ſtronger overpowers the weaker. Wherefore, when we are much delighted with one thing, we cannot attend to

any

BOOK X.

any other. At a well acted play the mind is fixed in delightful transport, but when the stage players are bad, many spectators amuse themselves with sweetmeats[1]. Pleasures not a-kin to the operations which they accompany, have the same effect (though they produce it differently) with congenial pains; for these also have a tendency to weaken and destroy our energies. Thus, those to whom it is painful to write or to reason, have little inclination to do either, and commonly do them incorrectly. Of operations and the pleasures accompanying them, some are laudable and respectable; others are blameable and contemptible. The former are to be pursued, and the latter to be avoided. Pleasures are more a-kin to energies, than even the desires which precede them; for these desires are easily distinguishable from the energies which they prompt, both in their own nature and in point of time; whereas pleasures and energies are so difficultly separated even in thought, that many suppose them to be one and the same thing. They are indeed intimately connected; but as energies both of sense and intellect are often not only unpleasant but painful, it is absurd to think that pleasure and energy are the same, though the former cannot subsist without the latter. But it is of more importance to observe that the nature and qualities of our pleasures depend entirely on the nature and qualities of our energies. In this manner the pleasures of the sight differ in purity from those of the touch; and the pleasures of the ear from those of the palate; while the intellect affords pleasures totally dissimilar to any resulting from the senses. As each animal is endowed with peculiar energies, each having his appropriate work to effect, and his assigned task to perform, so each species is destined for the enjoyment of congenial and kindred pleasures; those of a man

[1] Aristotle says, "they do so most when the players are bad."

man differing ſpecifically from the pleaſures of the horſe or the dog, the animals with which he is moſt familiar. As Heraclitus ſays, an aſs would prefer ſtraw to gold, loving food more than money. But among individuals of the ſame ſpecies it might be expected that the ſame effects ſhould follow from the ſame cauſes; and that there ſhould be a complete community of pleaſures as well as of pains. Yet in the human race we find the thing far otherwiſe; one loving what another moſt deteſts, and that giving pain to one, which affords the moſt exquiſite pleaſure to another. This however need not appear extraordinary, if we conſider that the ſame food has a very different reliſh to a man in health, and to another in diſeaſe; and that the warmth agreeable to perſons of weak conſtitutions, is unpleaſant to thoſe of a firmer temperament. Innumerable other examples to the ſame purpoſe will occur; with regard to all which, we affirm *that* only to be right, which appears ſo to perſons rightly formed and properly conſtituted. Virtue therefore, and the man of virtue as ſuch, is the only natural and correct ſtandard; and thoſe only are true enjoyments, with which he is delighted. That the purſuits which *he* rejects and ſpurns, ſhould to others afford gratification, is not to be wondered at, ſince human nature is liable to corruptions and depravities of many kinds; and each corrupt individual will delight in pleaſures akin to the ſpecific depravity under which he labours[1]; which are pleaſures indeed to him, but to none beſides. But the queſtion is, what are the pleaſures of a man in his natural and moſt perfect ſtate? That they are inſeparably connected with his energies, we have above proved; ſo that if

[1] —— Mala mentis
Gaudia. VIRG. vi. 78.

BOOK X.

if there be peculiar works to be performed by a man, and peculiar tasks assigned to him, his proper and natural pleasures must consist in the operations by which his work is done, and his task accomplished. Other pleasures are only secondary, and separated by a wide interval.

Chap. 6.

Of happiness;

Having examined the nature of virtue, friendship, and pleasure, it remains to speak of happiness, the end, as we observed, of all human pursuits. Our discourse will be rendered more concise by resuming some conclusions already stated. Happiness, we said, consists, not in mere capacity unroused, or in mere habit unexercised; for were that the case, it might belong to a man who should remain for ever asleep, living the life of a plant, or involved in the greatest calamities; since a man thus circumstanced might be endowed with the noblest capacities, and most excellent and most honourable habits. Happiness, then, must be classed with operations or energies, some of which, as we already remarked, are necessary for the attainment of farther and distinct ends, and others are desirable merely on their own account; with which last, happiness is, manifestly, to be numbered. Energies terminating in themselves, and desirable merely on their own account, include all the amiable and laudable actions which proceed from confirmed habits of virtue; they appear also to include those innocent amusements which are sought so entirely for their own sake, that men often pursue them to the prejudice of their health or fortune. In such amusements it is common for the wealthy and powerful to place the principal enjoyment of life, and persons most dexterous in promoting them are not unfrequently the highest in esteem with princes; since they are the best qualified for supplying them with those gratifications, of which they have the strongest relish.

BOOK X.

reliſh. In ſuch amuſements the vulgar, too, are apt to place happineſs, becauſe they ſee them purſued as ſuch by thoſe who, in the gifts of fortune, are greatly their ſuperiors. But neither the vulgar nor the great ought to ſerve for models. Virtue, intellect, ardent feelings of the heart, and exalted energies of the mind, are not appendages of greatneſs; and though men inveſted with power, but incapable of taſting genuine and liberal pleaſure, often ſeek delight in groſs gratifications of ſenſe, this affords not any proof that ſuch deluſive purſuits are entitled to a juſt preference. Children think all things inferior in value to their own childiſh amuſements; and as different objects pleaſe men and children, ſo good and bad men might be expected to have very different delights; but, as we have often ſaid, thoſe things only are truly valuable and truly delightful, which are recognized as ſuch by men of virtuous habits; for, as our habits are, ſuch will be our pleaſures and our purſuits. Happineſs, then, cannot conſiſt in mere recreative paſtime; for it is abſurd to think that all our ſerious exertions and ſtrenuous labours ſhould terminate in ſo frivolous an end [k]. We do not labour that we may be idle; but, as Anacharſis juſtly ſaid, we are idle that we may labour with more effect; that is, we have recourſe to ſports and amuſements as refreſhing cordials after contentious exertions, that having repoſed in ſuch diverſions for a while, we may recommence our labours with encreaſed vigour [l]. The weakneſs of human nature requires frequent remiſſions of energy; but theſe reſts and pauſes are only the better to prepare us for enjoying the pleaſures of activity. The amuſements of life

[k] Neque enim ita generati à natura ſumus, ut ad ludum et jocum facti eſſe videamur. Cicero de Offic. l. i. c. 29.

[l] Ludo autem et joco, uti illo quidem licet; ſed ſicut ſomno et quietibus cæteris. Ibid.

BOOK X.

life therefore are but preludes to its buſineſs, the place of which they cannot poſſibly ſupply; and its happineſs, becauſe its buſineſs, conſiſts in the exerciſe of thoſe virtuous energies, which conſtitute the worth and dignity of our nature. Inferior pleaſures may be enjoyed by the fool and the ſlave, as completely as by the hero or the ſage. But who will aſcribe the happineſs of a man to him, who, by his character and condition, is diſqualified for manly purſuits?

Chap. 7.

intellectual;

If happineſs conſiſts in virtuous energies, the greateſt human happineſs muſt conſiſt in the exerciſe of the greateſt virtue in man; which muſt be the virtue or perfection of his beſt part, whether this be intellect, or whatever principle it be, that is deſtined to command and bear ſway; having knowledge of things beautiful and divine, as being either divine itſelf, or at leaſt that principle in us which moſt approximates to divinity. The greateſt human happineſs, then, is theoretic and intellectual; which well accords with the properties which we formerly found, by inveſtigation, to be eſſentially inherent in that moſt coveted object. The intellect is the beſt principle in man; its energies are the ſtrongeſt, and the objects about which it is converſant are far the moſt ſublime. The energies of intellect are alſo the longeſt and moſt continuous, ſince we can perſevere in theoriſing and thinking much longer than in performing any action whatever. Pleaſure, it was obſerved, muſt be an ingredient in happineſs; but contemplative wiſdom offers pleaſures the moſt admirable in purity and ſtability, and the pleaſures of knowledge continually encreaſe in proportion to our improvement in it; certainty concerning the ſublimeſt truths affording ſtill higher delight in proportion to the intenſe efforts of intellect by which they were diſcovered. That all-ſufficiency, which we remarked as a property of happineſs, belongs to intellectual energies

energies more than to any other; for though the ſage, as well as the moraliſt or the patriot, ſtands in need of bodily accommodations, yet in exerting his higheſt excellencies, he is not like them dependant on fortune, both for his objects and his inſtruments; for objects towards whom he may exerciſe his virtues, and inſtruments which may enable him to effectuate his ends. Even unaſſiſted and alone, though perhaps better with aſſiſtants, he can ſtill think and theorize; poſſeſſing in the energies of his own mind, the pureſt and moſt independant enjoyments. Theſe enjoyments are valuable peculiarly on their own account, ſince they terminate completely in themſelves; whereas all practical virtue has, beſide the practice itſelf, ſome diſtinct and ſeparate end in view. The tranquillity of leiſure is naturally more agreeable than the buſtle of buſineſs; we toil for the ſake of quiet, and make war for the ſake of peace. But the practical virtues are moſt conſpicuouſly exerciſed in political and military functions, the latter of which none but the moſt ſavage and ſanguinary minds would ſubmit to from choice, converting friends into enemies for the mere pleaſure of fighting with them. Politics, too, forms an operoſe and troubleſome occupation, which would not be undertaken from the ſole love of exerciſing political functions, independently of diſtinct and ſeparate ends; power, wealth, and honour; in one word, proſperity to ourſelves, friends, or fellow-citizens. But intellectual energies are complete and perfect in themſelves, ſupplying an exhauſtleſs ſtream of pure and perennial pleaſure, which in its turn invigorates and enlivens the energies, and thus encreaſes and refines the ſource from which it unceaſingly ſprings; all-ſufficient, peaceful, and permanent, as far as is compatible with the condition of humanity. Were unalterable permanency

BOOK X.

added to ſuch a life, its happineſs would be more than human; but even within a limited term, its ineſtimable delights may be enjoyed by thoſe who attain the perfection of their age and faculties; living not merely as partners with a frail and compound nature, but according to the ſimple and divine principle within them, whoſe energies and virtues as far tranſcend all others, as the intellectual ſubſtance in which they reſide excels all other ſubſtances of which our frame is compoſed [m]. We ought not, therefore, according to the vulgar exhortation, though mortal, to regard only mortal things; but as far as poſſible, to put on immortality, exerting ourſelves to taſte the joys of the intellectual life. This is living according to the beſt part of what we call ourſelves, which, though ſeemingly ſmall in bulk, is incomparably greater in power and in value than all things beſides [n]. The intellect indeed is the beſt and ſovereign part of our conſtitution, and therefore ſtrictly and properly ourſelves. It is abſurd therefore to prefer any other life to our own. What was above obſerved will apply here. The pleaſure and good of each individual muſt conſiſt in that which is moſt congenial to his nature [o]. The intellectual life, therefore, muſt be the beſt and happieſt for man; ſince the intellect is that which is peculiarly himſelf.

Chap. 8.

and moral.

The moral life follows next, both in fitneſs and in dignity; for the practice of juſtice, fortitude, and other virtues, are highly

[m] Analyſis, p. 50. & ſeq. [n] Ibid.

[o] In the third chapter of the third book of the Topics, p. 209, there is an excellent practical rule for diſtinguiſhing real goods from thoſe merely of opinion, και η το μεν δι' ἑαυτο, το δε, δια την δοξαν αἱρετον· οιον ὑγιεια καλλους, ὁρος δε τω, προς δοξαν, το, μηδενος συνειδοτος, μη αν σπουδασαι ὑπαρχειν. Things deſirable in themſelves are to be preferred to thoſe which are deſired merely on account of the opinion entertained of them, as health to beauty; but we may know what thoſe things are that are good merely in opinion, by the following teſt, "they are thoſe about which we would not give ourſelves much trouble, if no perſon were to know that we poſſeſſed them."

highly ſuitable to the nature of man, and eſſentially requiſite in ſocial intercourſe, that mutual wants may be ſupplied, and mutual duties may be performed; that individual paſſions may be regulated with propriety, and rendered as ornamental to thoſe affected by them, as beneficial to the public. Moral virtue, then, is intimately connected with the paſſions and affections, many of which have their origin in the body; and, on the other hand, it is equally connected with the intellectual virtue of prudence; ſince the firſt principles of this practical wiſdom originate in good moral habits; and thoſe habits only are good which prudence juſtifies and approves. The moral virtues, therefore, are eſſential to the well-being of our compound nature; but the virtues and happineſs of the intellect are, like the intellect itſelf, ſeparate and independent: thus much only I ſhall ſay concerning it, for to treat more accurately of our intellectual part, belongs not to the ſubject of the preſent diſcourſe. The happineſs reſulting from its energies, requires but few external advantages; fewer by far than are requiſite for the exerciſe of political or moral virtues. The ſage indeed, as well as the patriot, muſt be furniſhed with the neceſſaries of life; and although the labours of the latter have more connection with the body and its wants, yet this circumſtance need not make any great difference in their perſonal accommodations; but it will make a difference of the greateſt magnitude as to the exerciſe of their reſpective energies. For the man of liberality muſt be furniſhed with the means of beneficence; and the man of probity or equity, with the means of making, for received favours, fair and reaſonable returns; mere intentions are obſcure and doubtful; and being often pretended, can only be clearly aſcertained when carried into effect. In the ſame

Pre-eminence of the former proved.

manner, fortitude shines most conspicuously when armed with power to repel dangers; and temperance displays its brightest charms, amidst temptations to voluptuousness. The vulgar controversy, whether virtue consists principally in action or intention, proves that both are requisite to its completion. But actions are dependent on external circumstances; and the greater and more illustrious they are, they require, for their performance, the greater number of instruments and auxiliaries. Speculation, on the other hand, is far less operose; it would be rather obstructed than benefited by a cumbersome apparatus of externals; which, how useful soever they may be for the display of practical virtue, are not at all essential to the exercise of intellectual energy. That the latter composes the best and firmest portion of human felicity may appear also from this, that it is difficult to conceive in what operation or energy besides, the felicity of the gods, whom universal consent acknowledges most happy, can possibly consist. In the exercise of justice? It would be ridiculous to suppose those celestial beings employed in making bargains, restoring deposits, or in performing any other actions about which the virtue of justice is conversant. There is, if possible, still less room among them for courage. Can it redound to their glory, that they encounter dangers manfully? Liberality cannot be ascribed to them, unless we suppose, absurdly, that they make use of money, or something equivalent. The praise of temperance is beneath those who have not any unruly appetites to restrain. Were we to go through the whole catalogue of the moral virtues, we should find that they are conversant about actions totally unworthy of the grandeur and sublimity of the gods. Yet we all believe those glorious beings to live exercising the energies

The exercise of intellectual energy the best and firmest portion of human happiness.

energies of their nature, not ſleeping like Endymion. After what manner, then, can they be employed? Not in practical virtue, far leſs in productive induſtry. It remains therefore that they live an intellectual life; which, as eſſentially belonging to the gods, muſt be pre-eminent in happineſs; a happineſs pure and permanent, to which the life of man, in proportion as it is intellectual, will more nearly approximate; and of which inferior animals, as they are deſtitute of the divine principle of intellect, can never in any degree partake. Happineſs is not an acceſſory to the energy of thought. It is connected with it ſubſtantially and indiviſibly; a rich ſtream, unalterably flowing from an inexhauſtible ſpring. The ſage indeed requires bodily health and bodily accommodations; but the meaſure of his external advantages needs not be large; for ſuperfluity will neither aſſiſt his own exertions, nor ſharpen his judgment concerning the performances of others. To diſplay the beauty and gracefulneſs even of moral virtue, it is not neceſſary for him to be maſter of the ſea and of the land. A mediocrity of circumſtances is ſufficient for the exhibition of moral excellencies; which is evident from this, that they appear more frequently in private perſons than in thoſe inveſted with power. This mediocrity, therefore, as it contributes moſt to virtue, is moſt conducive to happineſs. Solon well delineated the condition of thoſe whoſe happineſs he admired, ſaying, "that they had enjoyed a moderate proportion of the goods of fortune, performed moſt illuſtrious actions, and lived correctly and ſoberly[o]." Anaxagoras ſeems not to have thought happineſs an attribute of wealth or power, when he ſaid[p], that it would not ſurpriſe him,

[o] See Hiſtory of Ancient Greece, v. i. c. vii. p. 305 and 306.

[p] In the Ethics to Eudemus, l. i. c. iv. p. 197. the circumſtance here alluded to is more

BOOK X.

him, ſhould he be deemed a very abſurd perſonage by the multitude; who judge, and who are capable of judging, only by externals. The opinions of wiſe men are likely to be conformable to reaſon; but in practical matters, experience alone can afford conviction; and thoſe opinions only are to be approved, which the lives of thoſe who hold them, confirm. There is ſtill a farther reaſon why thoſe who moſt cultivate their intellectual powers ſhould alſo be moſt happy; for ſuch perſons not only attain the beſt temper of mind, and the higheſt perfection of their own nature, but they are alſo the moſt pleaſing in the ſight of the Divinity. If the gods (as they appear to do) concern themſelves about human affairs, it is reaſonable to conclude that they ſhould moſt delight in the energies of intellect, which are the beſt, and higheſt, and moſt congenial to their own; and that they ſhould remunerate and reward thoſe who love and honour thoſe exereiſes and occupations which they themſelves hold dear; and who, in preferring and adorning the intellectual part, act rightly and honourably[q].

Having

more fully explained. "Anaxagoras of Clazomené, being aſked who moſt deſerved the epithet of happy? anſwered, not ſuch men as you would imagine, but, on the contrary, ſuch perſons as to you would appear egregious fools. He probably anſwered thus, becauſe he perceived him with whom he was converſing incapable of appreciating happineſs by any other ſtandard than that of mere externals, power, wealth, beauty, &c. whereas he himſelf thought *that* man the happieſt who lived exempt from pain or perturbation, practiſing juſtice, and cultivating his underſtanding."

[q] The higheſt energy of intellect conſiſts in contemplating the Divinity; and when any inferior principle in man, through its rebellion and irregularity, reſtrains him from thus meditating on and worſhipping God, that principle is deſtructive of human happineſs. Eudem. l. vii. c. ult.

BOOK X. Chap. 9. The efficacy of education.

Having thus delineated virtue, friendſhip, and pleaſure, ought we to conſider our undertaking as now finiſhed? Or ought we rather to conſider, as has been already ſaid, that in practical matters, practice, and not theory, is the main object; and that, independently of good actions, the mere ſpeculative knowledge of virtue is not of any avail. The important queſtion then is, how men may be rendered virtuous? If moral diſcourſes ſufficed for this purpoſe, they could not be purchaſed, as Theognis ſays, at too high a price. But the influence of ſuch leſſons extends only over the liberal minds of ingenuous and well-diſciplined youths, who may thereby be retained within the paths of honour and duty: they are too feeble to controul the multitude, whoſe wickedneſs is to be reſtrained, not through the dread of ſhame, but through the fear of puniſhment; ſince the many, being enſlaved by their appetites, make it the buſineſs of their lives to purſue ſenſual pleaſures, and to avoid bodily pains; having no taſte nor perception of refined and laudable enjoyments. What eloquence can perſuade, what words can transform men thus brutified? It is impoſſible, at leaſt hardly poſſible, for reaſoning to extract the evils which cuſtom has riveted; and when all favourable circumſtances concur, the felicity of thoſe is ſtill worthy of envy, who, through the combined energy of conſpiring cauſes, are retained and confirmed in the practice of virtue. This ineſtimable poſſeſſion, ſome aſcribe to the bounty of nature; others think that that they have acquired it by cuſtom; and a third claſs acknowledge themſelves indebted for it to inſtruction. The virtue beſtowed by nature evidently depends not on our own exertions; it is given by a certain divine diſpoſal, to thoſe

BOOK X.

whose lot is surely beyond that of all other men most fortunate. Instruction and reasoning will not succeed, unless the mind is previously wrought on by custom, as a field is ploughed and prepared for receiving and nourishing the good seed: for those who are not habituated to love what is amiable, and to detest what is odious, would neither listen to, nor understand, exhortations to virtue; because their affections lead them not beyond the pursuit of course animal gratifications, the unrestrained appetite for which is of too stubborn a nature to yield to mere reason; and which, when no contrary passion intervenes, can be checked only by force. Before virtue therefore can be acquired, affections congenial to it must be implanted; the love of beauty and excellence, the hatred of baseness and deformity; which preparatory discipline cannot take place, except in those states which are governed by good laws; for a life of soberness and self-command is irksome to the multitude, and peculiarly unpleasing to the headstrong impetuosity of youthful passions, which must therefore be bridled by the authority of law; that what is painful by nature, may become pleasant through custom. The superintending aid of discipline ought not to be confined to children, but must extend to adolescence and manhood; the greater proportion of human kind remaining through life rather slaves to necessity, than subjects of reason; and more susceptible of the fear of punishment, than sensible to the charms of moral excellence. Legislators, therefore, it is said, ought to employ admonitions and chastisements, as well as punishments that are final; admonitions, for those whose character and morals render them open to conviction; chastisements, for those whose immoderate and beastly passion for

Of laws.

selfish

ſelfiſh pleaſures muſt be ſubdued and corrected by coarſe bodily pains; (the pains inflicted on them ſtanding as nearly as poſſible in direct oppoſition to the pleaſures which they unlawfully purſued;) and total extermination, or perpetual baniſhment, for the extrème evils of incurable profligacy and incorrigible villany. Since then the condition of the greater proportion of mankind is ſuch, that to be kept within the bounds of propriety and virtue, they require not only the benefits of early inſtitution, but the watchfulneſs of perpetual diſcipline through life, good laws become eſſentially neceſſary for upholding this diſcipline by their coercive authority. The influence of fathers over their children is too feeble for that purpoſe; or indeed the influence of any individuals not inveſted with public authority. Law has a compulſive and neceſſary force, ſince it is acknowledged as the commanding voice of prudence and reaſon; and its power is not invidious, like that of men, who are apt to offend us, when they oppoſe, even moſt juſtly, our favourite propenſities. In Lacedæmon, the legiſlator, with the aſſiſtance of a few friends, eſtabliſhed a regular plan of public education and moral diſcipline; things neglected in the greater part of ſtates, where men, in theſe particulars, live like the Cyclops:

> By whom no ſtatutes and no rights are known,
> No council held, no monarch fills the throne;
> Each rules his race, his neighbour not his care,
> Heedleſs of others, to his own ſevere.
>
> Iliad ix. v. 127, & ſeq.

A public education, when good, is doubtleſs preferable to a private one; but what is omitted by the public, individuals ought, as far as poſſible, to ſupply; inſtructing and benefiting their

BOOK X.

their children and friends; which task they will be the better qualified to perform, if they are acquainted with those principles of legislation from which public happiness flows; for the same principles that operate conspicuously on nations, will also have their due weight within a narrow domestic sphere, especially since the ties of blood, and the remembrance of benefits, will recommend paternal examples, and enforce paternal admonitions. Private education enjoys this peculiar advantage, that it may be adapted to the disposition and character of each individual. Besides this, physicians who have few patients, and masters of exercises who have few scholars, are most likely to be attentive to those intrusted to their care. But their power of being useful to them depends on their skill in their respective professions; and although some, from experience merely, without science, may learn to be good physicians to themselves, while they are incapable of curing any besides, yet it is always most desirable, whether it be our business to benefit one or many, to instruct one or many, that we should understand those general theorems from which the particular rules of practice flow. A teacher of morality therefore ought to be acquainted with the science of legislation, that he may apply to the improvement of individuals the same maxims which have been found beneficial to communities. But how is this science to be acquired? It seems to be a branch of politics, and ought therefore to be learned from statesmen. Yet do not statesmen differ from physicians, painters, and all those employed in other liberal arts, or other learned professions, in this important particular, that all the rest not only exercise but teach their respective vocations? whereas statesmen are

The science of legislation, how to be acquired.

never

never the teachers of politics, nor are the teachers of politics often employed in affairs of ſtate. The ſophiſts who profeſs politics, take not any ſhare in the public adminiſtration; and the ſtateſmen, who adminiſter public affairs, do not profeſs politics; they neither give lectures on the ſubject, nor write treatiſes concerning it; although this employment would be more uſeful and more dignified than that of poliſhing their pleadings and embelliſhing their ſpeeches. Neither do they tranſmit their political knowledge to their children and friends, which they certainly would, if they were able, ſince they could not bequeath to them a nobler preſent, nor one more beneficial to their country. It is plain, therefore, that the knowledge of ſtateſmen is a matter, not of ſcience, (which always may be taught,) but of experience merely; and this experience, which is ſufficient to form politicians, muſt be eſſentially neceſſary to thoſe who would underſtand politics as a ſcience. The ſophiſts who pretend to teach this ſcience, deviate widely from the mark. They neither know what is the nature of politics, nor what are its objects; otherwiſe they could not regard it as a ſubordinate branch of rhetoric, nor think it an eaſy matter to copy good laws from one ſtate, that may be ſafely adopted by another[r]; as if it were not a work of the utmoſt delicacy, and requiring much reach of thought, and much experience, to adapt laws and inſtitutions to occaſions and exigencies, and to change and vary them according to each variation of circumſtance. In muſic and painting, the vulgar of mankind are contented with perceiving the effect, which is the only thing of which

[r] How ſtrongly applicable is this remark to the ſophiſts of the preſent day

they

BOOK X.

they are judges; but perſons ſkilled in thoſe elegant arts muſt underſtand how this effect is produced, what colours kindly blend, and what ſounds ſweetly harmonize. Laws are productions or works of political art; an art which, being practical, cannot, any more than the art of phyſic, be learned merely from books; for though medical books not only contain recipes or preſcriptions, but accurately diſtinguiſhing different habits and different maladies, diſtinctly point out how each ſeparately is to be treated and cured, yet all theſe obſervations cannot be of the ſmalleſt uſe to men totally deſtitute of experience in the healing art. The ſame holds with regard to treatiſes on the ſubject of politics, which cannot be of much value to thoſe who have not learned by their own obſervation to appreciate and apply them. An aptitude and readineſs for acquiring knowledge, books, doubtleſs, may communicate and augment; but real practical knowledge cannot poſſibly be acquired without the aid of experience. As our predeceſſors, therefore, have left the ſcience of legiſlation unfiniſhed, it may be proper here to examine it, as well as to treat the ſubject of politics in general, that the philoſophy which bears a reference to the affairs of human life may be perfected to the beſt of our ability. We ſhall firſt collect what appears to us judiciouſly written by others on particular branches of the ſubject. We ſhall, then, from a wide ſurvey of commonwealths and governments, endeavour to explain the means through which thoſe political edifices in general, and the different kinds of them in particular, are preſerved or ſubverted; as well as to unfold the cauſes which render ſome conſtitutions worthy of applauſe, and others liable to cenſure. The reſult of our ſpeculations will enable us to determine which

Tranſition to the treatiſe on "Politics."

is the beſt form of government; and what are the different regulations reſpectively beſt adapted to each particular conſtitution [a].

[a] The method here laid down by Ariſtotle agrees not preciſely, either with that followed by the editors of his Politics in Greek, or with the arrangement which, for the ſake of perſpicuity, I thought fit to give to my tranſlation.

In the act of finiſhing this firſt volume, I was much pleaſed to read the following paſſage in an excellent diſcourſe lately delivered before the Univerſity of Cambridge: "Ariſtotle's Nicomachean Ethics afford not only the moſt perfect ſpecimen of ſcientific morality, but exhibit alſo the powers of the moſt compact and beſt conſtructed ſyſtem which the human intellect ever produced upon any ſubject; enlivening occaſionally great ſeverity of method, and ſtrict preciſion of terms, by the ſublimeſt, though ſobereſt, ſplendour of diction. If moral philoſophy, I mean ſpecifically and properly ſo called, is to be ſtudied as a ſcience, in ſuch ſources it is to be ſought. Thence will be formed a manly intellectual vigour, an ingenuous modeſty and dignity of habit, an energy of thought and diction, and a reach of comprehenſive knowledge, which diſtinguiſhes the true Engliſh ſcholar. On the contrary, it is to be feared that the feeble ſpeculation which almoſt all modern ſyſtems of morality encourage, and the ſuperficial information they afford, ſuperſeding the neceſſity of all active and real employment of the faculties, have operated more fatally upon the mental habits of the riſing generation than total ignorance could poſſibly have done." See "Benevolence excluſively an Evangelical Virtue," p. 19, & ſeq. by Thomas Rennell, D. D. late Fellow of King's College, Cambridge.

INDEX.

A

B

C

D

E

F

Divided

8

Kaimes,

K

L

M

N

O

P

Q

R

S

T

U

W

X

Y

Z

END OF THE FIRST VOLUME.

Published by

Facsimile Publisher
Ashok Vihar, Delhi-110052 (India)
Website: www.facsimilepublisher.com

Distributed by

Gyan Books Pvt. Ltd.
5, Ansari Road, Daryaganj, New Delhi-110002 (India)
E-mail: books@gyanbooks.com, Website: www.gyanbooks.com

4 444000 817675